The State Hermitage Museum, St. Petersburg

and

Fabergé Arts Foundation

in association with
Harry N. Abrams, Inc., Publishers

FABERGÉ:
IMPERIAL

Géza von Habsburg
Marina Lopato

JEWELER

Participating museums

State Hermitage Museum
St. Petersburg, Russia
18 June – 15 August 1993

Musée des Arts Décoratifs
Paris, France
24 September 1993 – 2 January 1994

Victoria and Albert Museum
London, England
26 January – 10 April 1994

This exhibition is co-organised by the Fabergé Arts Foundation,
Washington, D.C., and the State Hermitage Museum, St.
Petersburg, in collaboration with Art Services International,
Alexandria, Virginia.

This exhibition is sponsored by EGF-Parfums Fabergé Paris and
Elida Gibbs, U.K.
Additional funding has been provided by Ford Motor Company.

Library of Congress Cataloging-in-Publication Data

Habsburg-Lothringen, Géza von.
    Fabergé : imperial jeweler / Géza von Habsburg, Marina
Lopato.
        p. cm.
    "In collaboration with Art Services International, Alexandria,
Virginia."
    Exhibition catalog.
    Also issued in French and Russian.
    Includes bibliographical references and index.
    ISBN 0-8109-3320-9
    1. Faberzhe (Firm)—Exhibitions.   2. Fabergé, Peter Carl,
1846–1920—Exhibitions.   3. Art objects, Russian—
Exhibitions. 4. Goldwork—Russia (Federation)—
Exhibitions.   5. Silverwork—Russia (Federation)—
Exhibitions.   6. Enamel and enamelling—Russia
(Federation)—Exhibitions.   7. Nicholas II, Emperor of Russia,
1868–1918—Art patronage—Exhibitions.   I. Lopato, M. N.
(Marina Nikolaevna)   II. Gosudarstvennyi Ermitazh
(Russia)   III. Fabergé Arts Foundation.   IV. Art Services
International.   V. Title.
NK7398.F32A4   1993
739.2'092—dc20   93-4398
                                                         CIP

Published in 1994 by Harry N. Abrams, Incorporated,
New York. A Times Mirror Company
All rights reserved. No part of this publication may be reproduced
without written permission from the publishers

Translators: Alexander Kan, Nadia Pushkina
Editors: Nancy Eickel, Mark Markin
Editorial assistance: Sally Hoffmann
Designer: Derek Birdsall, Omnific Studios, London
Printed and bound by Amilcare Pizzi S.p.A., Milan

Head exhibition designer: Patrick Utermann, Munich

A Note on Transliteration

For the benefit of the general reader, Russian names that will be
familiar from previous publications have retained their Western
spellings, such as Carl Fabergé, Alexander III, Nicholas II, and
Bolshaya Morskaya Street. A modified Library of Congress
transliteration system was employed with names beyond the
immediate family circle of Tsar Nicholas II. Among the exceptions
are the names Alexei (in association with the Tsarevich), Xenia,
and Felix.

    Prefixes of Russian inventory numbers have also been
transliterated.

Contents

At the Rebirth of St. Petersburg

White nights of the northern city,
Blue eyes of one of its women.

Light brims up over the Pole, limning
With surfaces of serenity

Gold spires, green squares, grey river
Where today's dusk is tomorrow's dawn.
Sheets of light under the swansdown
Sky sweep through, around, over,

Unsilting every dulled sense,
Flexing every frozen mood
Of the stranger from a lower latitude.
Peeling from lulled waters, sky-silence,

How can such fineness run so rich?
—Laminations of light, ermine, almond,
Dissolved into the wholly transparent:
A fluid purity to leach

Out the crass, the quotidian,
Mind blanched to take stronger hues

And above all her eyes! That blue's
Even more confirmatory than

All those wide-winged whitenesses:
With an unstinting radiance
Of acceptance, of endurance
Inexhaustible as the rich skies.

Profound plenitude, then:
Not the thin blue of the shallows,
Of the village-girl gaze that goes
With blonde plaits; nor like the alien

Flat amethyst ovals of sprites with
Snake-fascinations, snake-fears
In the cold springs, white-birch-hidden meres,
Projected unfeeling from myth.

—And yet the inhuman has firmed
The depth and strength of that blue:

Here life's been indentured to
Troll, golem, the undead, the damned,

Mean fury has raved, ravenous,
Down these streets, with claws of torture,
War, famine, lies, slaughter.
Terror-hammer, falsehood-furnace

Crushed the selfish, or just weak, to mere
Clinker, to twisted scrap; but
The fine, the firm, with eyes half-shut
Was forged through years in that fire

To a gentle strength, to a charm
Against all that's false and cruel;
And that blue is the sheen of a steel
It took white heats to anneal.

But now the white night is cool,
The eyes upon mine are calm.

Robert Conquest

List of Lenders

Her Majesty Queen Elizabeth II
Her Majesty Queen Elizabeth The Queen Mother
Her Majesty Queen Margrethe of Denmark

Central Naval Museum, St. Petersburg
Elagin Palace Museum, St. Petersburg
Mrs Tatiana N. Gubareva, St. Petersburg
Kremlin Armoury Museum, Moscow
Pavlovsk Palace Museum, Pavlovsk
'Peterhof' State Museum-Reserve, Peterhof
State Hermitage Museum, St. Petersburg
State Historical Museum, Moscow

Lady Myra Butter and Lady Georgina Kennard
Ermitage Ltd., London
Kasteel Huis Doorn, Doorn, The Netherlands
Musée des Arts Décoratifs, Paris
Dmitri Martyniuk
Joan and Melissa Rivers
Mrs A. Kenneth Snowman, London
Gerald M. Sylvar
Baron Hans Heinrich Thyssen-Bornemisza, Lugano
Victoria and Albert Museum, London
Wartski, London
Madame Josiane Woolf, France
A La Vieille Russie
The Cleveland Museum of Art, Cleveland, Ohio
The FORBES Magazine Collection, New York
Hillwood Museum, Washington, D.C.
New Orleans Museum of Art, New Orleans, Louisiana
Walters Art Gallery, Baltimore, Maryland

Private collections

Several anonymous loans have been organized by courtesy of
Wartski, London; A. Tillander, Helsinki; and A La Vieille
Russie.

Director's Statement

The name Fabergé is world-renowned. Objects bearing his trade mark are the dream of collectors and museums. Fabergé exhibitions have flooded the world; his name resounds like a fairy tale of luxury and beauty.

Fabergé's beautiful objects not only bring us immeasurable pleasure but they also teach us a lot. They show us how jewellery, an applied art form, can become great art and enter the world's cultural heritage alongside masterpieces of painting and sculpture. Furthermore, they teach us that the crafts and other disparate art forms should be treated with equal respect. The Fabergé style is one of historicism, a combination of methods, techniques, and aesthetics of various epochs. This style was once condescendingly labelled eclecticism. Only recently has it been accorded the same rights as other traditionally respected art styles.

Fabergé's oeuvre is a marvellous merger of European and Russian artistic traditions, and not only because of the renowned Imperial Easter eggs. Fabergé workshops produced masterpieces equally eloquent in the stylistic languages of both Russia and western Europe.

Objects bearing the Fabergé name perfectly combine the personal tastes and talents of the founder of the jewellery firm and its many masters. Personal and group efforts were brought together without sacrificing individuality. The style rightfully bears the name of Fabergé, but proudly standing behind that name, unforgotten, are those masters who created it.

The Fabergé style is an amalgam of world achievements in art, but at the same time it embodies many of the characteristic features of the twentieth century. Fabergé's reputation swept across Europe at the dawn of this century, beginning with the 1900 *Exposition Universelle* in Paris. It continues to shine as brightly at the end of the century, as is evidenced by this exhibition, among the largest and most representative of those organised to date.

In enjoying the art of Fabergé we can see distinctly how labour and creativity combine to produce masterpieces, and how real art, which constitutes the pride of humankind, is born. The State Hermitage, the collections of which were a source of inspiration for Fabergé himself, is happy and proud to be a participant and a host of this exhibition, and to be able to share its treasures with thousands of art admirers.

Mikhail Piotrovski
Director
State Hermitage

Researchers of The State Hermitage who worked on the catalogue:
V. A. Chernyshev
M. Dobrovolskaia
O. G. Kostiuk
M. N. Lopato
K. A. Orlova
E. S. Shchukina
L. A. Yakovleva
L. A. Zavadskaia

Chiefs of restoration workshops:
A. I. Bantikov
V. V. Kashcheev
V. A. Kozyreva
N. S. Pinyagina

Chief designer:
V. A. Pavlov

Deputy Director:
V. Yu. Matveev

In Great Britain the name of Carl Fabergé is firmly linked with the Victoria and Albert Museum, thanks to the astonishingly popular appeal of the Fabergé exhibition held here in 1977. The British public was enchanted by the remote and exotic world revealed in miniature by Fabergé's jewelled objects.

The European tradition of royal and imperial goldsmiths creating works of art from hardstone can be enjoyed in the V&A's Medieval Treasury, Renaissance, and Jewellery galleries. Paradoxically, given the association between the name of the Victoria and Albert Museum and that of Fabergé, the Museum has but four examples of Fabergé in its permanent collection.

To be offered the chance, therefore, of participating in the international tour of *Fabergé: Imperial Jeweller* could not be resisted: it provides a dual opportunity to satisfy a public hunger for beauty, and to celebrate fine craftsmanship. The product of the Fabergé workshops has been admired and acquired by bourgeois, aristocratic, and royal collectors as far afield as Bangkok and Copenhagen. For a British audience the rarities belonging to our own Royal Family will have a particular and special appeal.

We are particularly pleased to show *Fabergé: Imperial Jeweller* at the V&A as one of the exhibition's organisers, the Fabergé Arts Foundation, shares the Museum's historic aims, namely, to increase public understanding and enjoyment of art, craft, and design. The Foundation's admirable objective of restoring the House of Fabergé in St. Petersburg, and its unrivalled success in this exhibition, of bringing together for the first time objects from numerous Russian as well as Western collections, underlines the international appeal of the art of Fabergé.

Elizabeth Esteve-Coll
Director
Victoria and Albert Museum

PARFUMS FABERGÉ
PARIS

It is with great pleasure that Parfums Fabergé have agreed to be the major sponsor of the *Fabergé: Imperial Jeweller* exhibition. This unprecedented event brings together a collection of the works of Carl Fabergé, remarkable both for its comprehensiveness and its outstanding artistic value.

Adding to the exceptional nature of this exhibition is the renown of the museums that host it: the State Hermitage in St. Petersburg, the Musée des Arts Décoratifs in Paris and the Victoria and Albert Museum in London.

The intent behind this exhibition – passionately brought to life by two authoritative experts in Fabergé's works, Dr. Géza von Habsburg and Dr. Marina Lopato – is to perpetuate the innovative spirit of Carl Fabergé, creative genius and Jeweller to the Court of the Tsars.

Carl Fabergé's constant desire to reach perfection in his works through innovation, his obsession with detail and his determination to use only the best materials is the same spirit which today represents the philosophy of Parfums Fabergé.

In staging this event, we are particularly pleased to be able to help revive the splendour, perfection and timeless genius that was Carl Fabergé.

We are also confident that this event will be an opportunity to further develop the historical ties between Russia and the rest of Europe – ties epitomised by the saga of the Fabergés, French Huguenots who settled in Germany and in Russia and whose descendants are currently living in Europe and other parts of the world. This event will hopefully form a small part of one of the most important chapters of contemporary history – a chapter being written before our very eyes.

Helmut Ganser
Chairman
Parfums Fabergé
London

Patrick J. Choël
Chairman
Parfums Fabergé
Paris

Introduction

The Fabergé Arts Foundation initiated plans for this exhibition and book in March 1991 at a conference of curators and Fabergé specialists held in New York City. The conferees – Géza von Habsburg, Marina Lopato, Anne Odom, Mary Ann Allin, and Joyce Lasky Reed – envisioned an exhibition that would do justice to the artistry of Carl Fabergé's work and his place in the exciting period of European culture from 1870 to 1917.

An unusual opportunity to organize this exhibition was presented by extraordinary developments in Russia. After more than seventy years of repression, Russia could begin to honour, freely, its cultural heritage. And as part of that reaffirmation of its past, Carl Fabergé's contribution to Russian art could again command the respect in his own country that it has earned abroad.

Glasnost – the opening of the Soviet system – presented an even more specific opportunity: the archives of the Hermitage harbouring the historical records of the House of Fabergé could now be explored. The archival material was ultimately translated, and it provides the historical framework for this exhibition.

Six months after that initial meeting in New York – just days after the new Russia was nearly swept away by the almost successful coup of August 1991 – a symposium took place in St. Petersburg, in the brilliantly restored Hermitage theatre. Gathered for the occasion to advance the exhibition plans was an eminent group of Russian and Western Fabergé specialists. (Joining the original conferees were A. Kenneth Snowman, Ulla Tillander-Godenhielm, Galina Smorodinova, and Tatiana Muntian, all of whom have contributed chapters to this catalogue, as well as Margaret Kelly of the FORBES Magazine Collection, Irina Polinina of the Kremlin Museum, and a number of private collectors.)

This meeting in the historical centre of the city was held a few steps from Fabergé's house, which once served as the workshop producing many of the objects of art that had inspired the establishment of the Fabergé Arts Foundation.

Founded by Americans and Russians in 1990, the Fabergé Arts Foundation has dedicated itself to restoring the master artist's house at 24 Bolshaya Morskaya and transforming it into a museum. It is our hope that his extraordinarily designed and crafted objects – some of which have been hidden in Russia for seven decades, while long ago others became treasures of the crowned heads of Europe and still other works found their way into museums and private collections – will one day be exhibited in their place of origin on a rotating basis.

Growing from this meeting in September 1991 and subsequent exchanges, the Fabergé conferees developed a plan for gathering these objects more immediately from the principal museums and private collections of the world and exhibiting them at three renowned museums: the Hermitage, the Musée des Arts Décoratifs, and the Victoria and Albert Museum.

This project has been nurtured by the Director and the curatorial staff of the State Hermitage Museum and supported by the donors, friends, and corporate sponsors of the Fabergé Arts Foundation. The Foundation greatly appreciates the enthusiastic endorsement of Patrick Choël, the visionary chairman of EGF-Parfums Fabergé in Paris. Major funding for *Fabergé: Imperial Jeweller* has come from this company and its London affiliate in an unprecedented European commitment to the renaissance of Russian culture. Special thanks are owed to Jean Riddell, without whose steadfast guidance from the very beginning, this project would have faltered. On the corporate level the Foundation wishes to acknowledge the early encouragement received from Haka Corporation of Helsinki and JV FILCO of St. Petersburg.

The supervision of this complex exhibition and its catalogue has primarily been the responsibility of Dr Géza von Habsburg. As Chief Curator of *Fabergé: Imperial Jeweller*, his vast knowledge, exhibition experience, and tireless efforts, seasoned with humour and diplomacy, have brought this presentation to life. Accolades also go to Dr Marina Lopato, Russian Curator of the exhibition, who spent long hours in neglected archives locating documents of historic importance to the world of Fabergé.

Special mention is due to Lynn Kahler Berg and Joseph W. Saunders of Art Services International for solving the complicated coordination and administration of this exhibition. Our thanks are also offered to Ludmila Bakayutova, who united Western zeal with Russian procedures.

This international exhibition opens a new chapter in the story of Fabergé, one that may again inspire and support the most talented designers and craftsmen of jewellery. In the process it may also revitalize the economic and cultural life of St. Petersburg.

Fabergé Arts Foundation
Washington, D.C., and St. Petersburg

Foreword

Scholars of Fabergé have been severed from their main source of information in Russia for over seventy years. It is only recently that Russian archives have begun to produce their long-awaited harvest of reports and records. A plethora of documents pertaining to the Imperial Cabinet and its commissions to the House of Fabergé have been unearthed in recent months. Valentin Skurlov has discovered Franz Birbaum's memoirs, which are published here for the first time in extenso. Further documents have provided new information on the Moscow Branch of Fabergé and on the last years of the firm's activities. In addition to the two design books from the Holmström workshop with Wartski in London, quantities of drawings from the Fabergé workshops – beginning with sketch-books of jewellery designs, the design books of Henrik Wigström, and detailed drawings for important silver commissions – have come to light. This sudden deluge needs to be presented in order to be digested.

What precedes justifies another scholarly showing of Fabergé's art and an accompanying art historical book. In keeping with the chosen leitmotiv of patronage, objects were largely selected to illustrate Fabergé's links with many of the ruling families of his time. Concurrently, Fabergé's omnipresence in the history of the Russian Imperial Family, beginning with Tsar Nicholas' coronation in 1896 and ending with the 1914–1918 War, will be demonstrated. Other themes include the firm's foreign clientele and the patronage of industrial leaders in Russia as well as the Church, Army, and Navy. Special attention is paid to the output of Fabergé's hitherto underrated Moscow branch and its rich local custom. In addition, all of the cities in which this exhibition is held have strong historical connections to the House of Fabergé, and the links that bind St. Petersburg to London and Paris are clearly established.

The curators, also on behalf of the Fabergé Arts Foundation and Art Services International, which have served as organizers and coordinators of *Fabergé: Imperial Jeweller*, would like to acknowledge and thank the following and many others for their generous contributions of time, talent, and treasures.

Lenders cannot be praised enough for their willingness to separate themselves from their prized possessions for several months. We are fortunate that H. M. Queen Elizabeth has graciously lent a fine array of objects collected by Queen Alexandra and Queen Mary. H. M. Queen Elizabeth The Queen Mother, with her habitual kindness, agreed to part temporarily with two of her treasures. H. M. Queen Margrethe of Denmark has generously lent selected pieces of Fabergé's monumental set of silver that was presented to her great-grandfather King Christian IX. Loans from Western institutions and private collectors account for about one half of the objects in the exhibition.

For the first time more than one hundred fifty objects and documents from the Fabergé workshops, the essential part of the holdings of most Russian museums, will travel abroad. These include large selections from the State Hermitage and the Moscow State Historical Museum, and the most representative pieces from the Pavlovsk and Peterhof Palaces. The Directors and Curators of these and other Russian museums have generously cooperated with this ambitious project. In this context the previous Director of the State Hermitage Museum, Vitali Suslov, must be thanked for readily accepting the additional burden of this exhibition and actively encouraging its completion. Simultaneously, the present Director, Mikhail B. Piotrovski, has seen the project through to its termination with proverbial generosity. Galina Komelova, Chief Curator of Western Art at the State Hermitage; Aleksandr Shkuko, Director of the Moscow State Historical Museum, and his predecessor, Konstantin Levykin; Vadim Znamenov, Director of the Peterhof Palace Collections; and Yuri Mudrov, Director of the Pavlovsk Palace Collections have all readily agreed to some of the choicest loans. Larisa Piterskaia of the Elagin Palace Museum has offered a recent acquisition from the relatives of a Fabergé designer, and Irina Rodimtseva, Director of the Kremlin Museums, has acquiesced to loan some of her institution's treasures.

In addition, those at the two prestigious museums that are hosting the exhibition in Europe must be thanked for their cooperation and enthusiasm. At the Musée des Arts Décoratifs in Paris we gratefully acknowledge Monsieur Thierry Bondoux, Director General; Madame Daniéle Giraudy, Director and Chief Curator; Madame Evelyne Possémé, Curator; and Dominique Pallut, *Service des Expositions*. Our appreciation extends to the Victoria and Albert Museum, where Mrs Elizabeth Esteve-Coll, Director, Mrs Linda Lloyd Jones, Head of Exhibitions, and Sally Mason, Philippa Glanville, and Richard Edgcumbe have worked to ensure the success of this exhibition in London.

Our thanks are also offered to those Russian Curators who have contributed specialist articles or descriptions of their works by Fabergé. At the State Hermitage Museum we send our respects to Karina Orlova and Larisa Zavadskaia, Assistant Curators of Western Art; Magdalena Dobrovolskaia and Evgenia Shchukina, Curators of the Numismatic Department; and Vladimir Chernyshev, Curator of the Carriage Repository. Galina Smorodinova of the Moscow State Historical Museum, Tatiana Muntian of the Moscow Kremlin Armoury, Nina Vernova of the Peterhof Palace Collections, and Nelly Nesterova of the Pavlovsk Palace Collections are to be thanked, as is Boris Ometov, Director of the Department of State Inspection of Monument Protection, who contributed a learned article about the Fabergé houses in St. Petersburg.

As always, special appreciation goes to The FORBES Magazine Collection in New York, the Forbes family, and in particular to Christopher Forbes, who has generously acceded to our many requests. The Collection's Director, Margaret Kelly, and her assistant, Mary Ellen Sinko, have patiently and kindly borne the brunt of our never-ending inquiries for loans and information. Margaret Kelly's support for this project was particularly invaluable.

Anne Odom, Chief Curator at Hillwood Museum in Washington, D.C., has put her deep erudition at our disposal, which is reflected in her enlightening essay on Fabergé's Moscow workshop. Directors and Curators of several American museums must be recognized for their support of this project and for their generous loans: E. John Bullard III, Director of the New Orleans Museum of Art in Louisiana; Frederick Fisher, Director of Hillwood Museum; Evan H. Turner, Director, and Henry Hawley, Curator, of The Cleveland Museum of Art in Ohio; and Robert P. Bergman, Director, and William R. Johnston, Associate Director/Curator, of the Walters Art Gallery in Baltimore, Maryland.

We would also like to thank our colleagues for their contributions of scholarship and professional expertise: A. Kenneth Snowman of Wartski, London, for his article, his time, and his support; Geoffrey Munn for his assistance in obtaining elusive loans; Paul Schaffer of A La Vieille Russie, New York, for his valuable time, description of objects, and his article; Peter Schaffer for his support;

Alexander von Solodkoff of the Ermitage Gallery, London, for his essay and choice objects from his gallery; Ulla Tillander-Godenhielm of A. Tillander in Helsinki for her article and her assistance in obtaining loans; and Carol Aiken for her technical analysis of select Fabergé pieces.

All those who actively collaborated in the production of this catalogue must also be thanked: editor Nancy Eickel, editorial assistant Sally Hoffmann, and translator Nadia Pushkina in Washington, D.C.; editor Mark Markin and translator Alexander Kan in St. Petersburg; catalogue designer Derek Birdsall of Omnific Studios in London; and the printing firm of Amilcare Pizzi s.p.a. in Milan.

Finally, our congratulations must be expressed to Dipl. Arch. Dr Patrick Utermann of Munich, who has designed an exhibition installation with both visual and emotional impact. His concepts have been further enhanced at each venue by the interpretations of the fine exhibition designers at the hosting museums in St. Petersburg, Paris, and London.

What began almost three years ago as a mere idea has blossomed into this ambitious project, with all the complications engendered by thirty-two lenders, including eight in Russia, exhibition venues at three prestigious institutions, and a catalogue translated into three distinct languages. This is quite an accomplishment, even when judged by the highest standards of international exhibition practice today!

Dr Géza von Habsburg, New York City
Dr Marina Lopato, St. Petersburg

Fabergé in Our Time

A. Kenneth Snowman

This event, the first to be inspired by the recently established Fabergé Arts Foundation, represents in a sense the *deuxième noces* of Carl Fabergé. The exhibition's effect upon the public of St. Petersburg, where these works are to be shown first, promises to be uniquely fascinating.

The notes which follow are, in the main, random thoughts prompted by this occasion and expressed against the confused background of what we are pleased to call our contemporary art world. There is an illuminating parallel to be drawn between the initial success with which Fabergé's products were greeted when they were first introduced to an astonished and delighted Russian aristocracy and the enthusiasm demonstrated by so many collectors today.

The gold, enamel and gem-set compositions designed by the Petersburg master and his artists were offered to Russians at a time when they were particularly susceptible to just such an injection of glamour and novelty, for they were a bored and disenchanted society. The more percipient among them were also apprehensive about the future of their country.

There are those who will find this parallel with our own time too striking to be entirely dismissed. The analogy, however, must not be unduly pressed since, after all, works of high technical proficiency have found a welcome in most communities and in most periods. From a technical point of view, they nevertheless represent an apogee reached by goldsmiths, lapidaries, jewellers and enamellers in the long history of a noble craft. We may not take every object from the Fabergé workshops to our hearts today, but neither can we reject any single item from his extravagantly varied repertoire on the grounds of careless or slovenly execution. There was no place for the slap-dash or sloppy, deficiencies which play such a prominent role in our own time.

Fabergé was not always guiltless when it came to occasional examples of what the present writer has called *edelkitsch*. Sometimes he went overboard in the matter of prettifying his confections and his taste is not invariably our taste. Fashion, however, as the wiser among us recognise, is not an absolute concept but is always on the move, open to differing interpretations which are themselves constantly subject to modification or even rejection.

The House of Fabergé devoted its energies towards the design, production and sale of attractive toys for the rich. In this they succeeded and continue, in absentia, to succeed long after the business was closed down by the Bolsheviks in 1918. Having once and for all rejected the Marxist philosophy which defined equality as the only true morality and acknowledged that, in the course of the world's history, works of considerable beauty have been created which have been entirely unavailable to the vast majority of the population, then perhaps one should revise one's view of the unique importance of equality for its own sake. Equality of opportunity, a noble ideal, is something quite other. Masterpieces of visual art could always and can always be seen and enjoyed by anyone interested enough to go and look at them provided they were or are not privately owned. Elitism has really been given a bad name in our time.

Although Fabergé's clientele was, in the main, found among the wealthy classes, it should be pointed out that his own personal revolution began in 1870 when, at the age of twenty-four, he took over the entire control of his father's rather conventional jewellery business. He transformed it by insisting that the value of an object should reside in the craftsmanship lavished upon it rather than the materials of which it was composed. Indeed it was to become, under his personal dictate, a vulgarity to flaunt large precious stones, often of questionable quality, in rather shoddy settings as had formerly been the custom in Russia. It was therefore more a question of taste and inclination and perhaps a love of novelty rather than a simple lust for expensive things that directed the solid citizens of Petersburg to the front door of Fabergé's shop in such numbers.

Reaction in this field, as in others, is historically inevitable. Having been restricted in artistic experiment by our didactic forebears a century ago, we have since that time been conducting ourselves rather like a mob of unruly school-children let loose in a sweet-shop, grabbing and devouring without criticism everything within reach. This has led to an acceptance which is finally more tedious than the unnecessarily solemn and claustrophobic art sometimes imposed by the Victorians. The permissive society may have much to commend it, but a permissive aesthetic can only bring disaster.

One of the ugliest stains discolouring the fabric of our end of the twentieth century has been contributed by an alarming number of stuntmen masquerading as painters and sculptors with the connivance of a further number of near-illiterate critics and gallery directors, cynical dealers and ignorant patrons. The common factor which unites these pretentious individuals (the present tense is sadly mandatory since the situation largely persists) is a total lack of respect for, or knowledge of, their more cultivated forebears.

Why, indeed, should these people attempt to fulfil the demanding requirements of true artistic endeavour when they can so easily and profitably get away with fraudulent jumbles of brushstrokes and meaningless heaps of rubbish left on the gallery floor to be admired by the simple-minded?

How many times, one cannot help wondering, have normally responsible auction houses and galleries put on display non-figurative panels, painted by overpraised contemporary masters, the wrong way up? We know it happens, but not exactly how often. On how many occasions has one found examples of these pointless trivialities portentously labelled *Untitled*, as though the profound creativity of the artist were quite beyond the understanding of a mere member of the public? Of course, the possibility that the perpetrator could not be bothered to think up a title for his or her masterpiece cannot be entirely dismissed.

Fortunately, a stable element which is not so easily taken in is preserved in every society, and there are encouraging signs today that more and more art lovers are indeed becoming less naive. The pendulum of fashion is again on the swing, and our present attitude in the matter of realism is reflected in our renewed and welcome respect for anything that shows evidence of work well done. Art schools are now being allowed to invite back the live models, some of whom had been peremptorily banished from the studio dais, with the happy result that students are again able to draw an elbow correctly having been vouchsafed the privilege of actually seeing for themselves what an elbow looks like.

Thus, it follows that in the domain of the goldsmith and jeweller, work by craftsmen working for firms of the calibre of Fabergé, Tillander and Hahn in Russia, and Lalique, Giuliano, Cartier, Tiffany and Boucheron elsewhere, dismissed with scorn a generation ago by the more way-out progressives, are all the more appreciated in this changed climate. Well-designed and diligently made objects are increasingly sought by collectors all over the world.

The Tsar Alexander III had encouraged young Carl in his new enterprise and even collaborated to some extent with him in the plan to design a very special Easter egg to be presented to his Tsarina, Maria Feodorovna.

The custom of giving these eggs on Easter morning and exchanging three kisses was deeply engrained in the Russian Orthodox way of life. This day was considered the most important of the calendar, and the egg, symbol of the Resurrection, was an essential part of it.

Some of these elaborate confections contain mechanical toys, such as a peacock which steps fastidiously across a table top, pauses, turns its plumed head, spreads its tail feathers, which coruscate with brilliantly coloured enamel, and automatically closes them again. Another contains an authentic working model of the Trans-Siberian Express in gold and platinum. Several of the Imperial eggs in rock crystal are reminiscent of the products of the sixteenth-century Saracchi workshops in Milan; others derive from South German or French goldsmiths and silversmiths. Many of the most original of the eggs, however, were clearly inspired by Fabergé's own lively imagination.

As we have seen, the examples ordered by Alexander III for Maria Feodorovna were to some extent the result of a joint conspiracy between the House of Fabergé and the Tsar himself, who took a personal interest in both the design and the nature of the surprise contained within the eggs. When his son ascended the throne, the picture changed for the worse politically as a result of the new Tsar's significantly weaker character. The Marquis of Halifax observed that Charles II 'would slide from an asking face', and in this respect Nicholas II was in much the same case. He would greet a member of his Court in the morning with his customary affability, without ever a hint or sign that the wretched man would, that very afternoon, receive his *congé* by letter from the Tsar. Thus, nearly incapable of making any decision himself, he characteristically left even the matter of the planning of the Imperial eggs to be given to Alexandra Feodorovna and the Dowager Empress entirely to Fabergé.

Among the firm's most attractive compositions were everyday objects of function – cigarette and cigar boxes, clocks, miniature frames, pencil-cases, scribbling blocks, letter-openers, bell-pushes – and a hundred other articles of domestic use. It remains a very special pleasure today for a smoker to bring out a beautifully made gold case by Fabergé and almost subconsciously enjoy again and again the elegance of its style and manufacture.

The art of the lapidary was in constant demand in the House, and the best of the carvings of animals, birds and fish, usually measuring between two and six centimetres in length or height, must be regarded as original works of sculpture, influenced though they undoubtedly were by the Japanese netsuke. They are a continuing source of delight and impart a lively sense of well-being. There is nothing here of the sterile quality so painfully evident in contemporary German copies.

The flower studies often combine the arts of the goldsmith, enameller, lapidary and jeweller. These carefully observed *objets de vitrine* were possibly intended to reassure the recipient, during a chilly winter, that the pleasures of a warmer season were to come. They usually consist of a single flower spray casually placed in a pot of rock crystal. The lapidary has carved the little pot with a special cunning in order to give the impression of its being partly filled with water, a favourite Fabergé stratagem. Other stones were occasionally used as vases to hold the plants with their coloured enamel petals and delicately veined nephrite leaves.

Fabergé worked in many different manners, and some of his most successful pieces are 'Russianised' pastiches in the style of Louis XV or Louis XVI. Medieval Russia and Renaissance Italy, among others, also provided occasional sources of inspiration. It is not always realised that he was also one of the leading protagonists of the Art Nouveau movement.

Edward VII's beautiful and generous-hearted Queen Alexandra was an early collector of these floral essays in addition to her well-known affection for the animal sculptures. Her sister the Tsarina Maria Feodorovna (both Danish princesses before they married) had introduced her to the enchanting world of Fabergé. The results of this enthusiastic Royal patronage may be seen today in the incomparable Sandringham collection in England, from which a number of outstanding objects have been generously lent to this exhibition by Her Majesty Queen Elizabeth II.

The firm was dedicated to the idea of giving pleasure, and under the watchful eye and with the lively imagination of Carl Fabergé, this aim seems to have been richly fulfilled. Whenever these twinkling delicacies are gathered in a group one catches one's breath. The English poet Thomas Traherne put it felicitously:

Rich Diamond and Pearl and Gold
  in evry Place was seen;
Rare splendors, Yellow, Blew, Red, White and Green,
Mine Eys did evry where behold.

History of the House of Fabergé

Géza von Habsburg

The first two monographs written about Fabergé some forty years ago are chiefly based either on the reminiscences of Henry Bainbridge's firsthand experiences with Carl Fabergé himself, or on A. Kenneth Snowman's talks with Eugène Fabergé, the jeweller's eldest son, in the early 1950s. Some of this information is corroborated in short notes made by Léon Grinberg after a long talk he had with Eugène Fabergé in Paris. Bainbridge was Fabergé's representative in London from 1908 to 1917, and he travelled yearly to St. Petersburg to meet the master himself. He published the first highly personal monograph on the subject in 1949.[1] Snowman, today the doyen of Fabergé scholars, published his pioneering findings in 1953.[2]

In the years that followed, scholarship was restricted, and only a few new sources were made available. These included Fabergé's London sales ledgers;[3] two design books depicting the output of the workshops of August and Albert Holmström between 1909 and 1915;[4] an auction of Fabergé designs;[5] and most recently, the design books of Henrik Wigström.[6]

Our eyes are now focused on Russia. Archives in St. Petersburg and Moscow have finally begun to produce their long-expected harvest of original documents.[7] A further primary source has been revealed in the memoirs of Franz Birbaum, dated 1919.[8] Large quantities of original drawings are emerging, thus permitting firsthand insight into the early jewellery production of the Fabergé workshops, as well as into the lesser known realm of the Moscow workshops. This new information allows us to fill in numerous gaps, as it helps to revise some erroneous assumptions and to confirm others.[9]

The Formative Years (1866–1885)

Carl Fabergé was born in 1846 in St. Petersburg. His father Gustav, of Huguenot extraction, was an unassuming jeweller who had been independently active since 1841.[10] In 1860, fourteen-year-old Carl Fabergé accompanied his parents on their move to Dresden. From there his father sent him on a tour of Europe, with stops in Frankfurt, Florence, and Paris. Back in St. Petersburg by 1866 as a full-fledged master, Carl joined Hiskias Pendin, August Holmström, and Wilhelm Reimer, all of whom had been employed by his father. In 1868 a Finnish goldsmith, Erik Kollin, was attached to the firm. Four years later Carl Fabergé took over his father's workshop, with Kollin as his first head workmaster.

From 1866 to 1885 is somewhat of a blank in Fabergé's oeuvre. Birbaum describes the earliest products of the house as *somewhat clumsy gold bracelets, which were fashionable at the time, brooches and medallions in the form of straps with clasps.... They were decorated with stones and enamels and samples can still be seen in the old drawings of the firm.*[11]

These must have been similar to what is known of the production of Gustav Fabergé, Carl's father. A newly discovered scrap-book with jewellery designs spanning the last three decades of the nineteenth century has surfaced, partially filling the existing gap (cat. 348–354). In it Fabergé appears to be totally linked to the mainstream of contemporary French jewellery. His designs for diamond-set sprays of flowers, some enamelled (figs. 9, 10), ears of wheat, and trailing ivy branches are all reminiscent of Masset Frères, I. Coulon, O. Massin, and the early production of Boucheron and Vever. Elaborate diamond-set pendant brooches suspended from tied ribbons (cat. 353), ribbon-knot necklaces, and bracelets painted mostly in white gouache on black paper would seem to indicate that Fabergé's genius was not yet at work. At times a lighter touch can be discerned, albeit it is still firmly anchored in the European mainstream. Here we find trelliswork bracelets made of diamonds and rubies, and Louis XV-style chatelaines and fringe necklaces (cat. 354). Some bolder designs, signed by Fabergé's younger brother Agathon, show largely diamond-and-emerald-set tiaras and a number of showy necklaces (cat. 348–350). *Favourite motifs were branches of blossoms, ears of wheat and artfully tied ribbons.... This was the best period for diamond work. The works of this period are characterised by a rich design, visible even at a distance. The fashion was for large diadems (figs. 11, 12), small egret plumes, necklaces in shapes of collars, breast-plates for the corsage, clasps and large ribbons.*

Virtually nothing of this style of jewellery confirming Fabergé's focus on traditional designs has survived from this period.[12] The account books of the Imperial Cabinet indicate that Fabergé vied with other better-known jewellers, Julius Butz, Edward Bolin, Friedrich Koechli, and Leopold Zeftingen, for Imperial commissions. Initially his share was modest, but it grew over the years, with Fabergé being mentioned only seven times in 1883 and seventeen times in 1888. In the nineteen years up to 1885, Fabergé had sold 47,249 roubles worth of items to the Imperial Cabinet. In the mid-1880s Fabergé's

1. Photograph of Carl Fabergé by Hugo Oeberg, *c.* 1905.

2. The Fabergé House at 24 Bolshaya
Morskaya Street, St. Petersburg, *c.* 1910.

annual orders still averaged 10,000 roubles while his competitor Bolin sold three times as much. Fabergé, however, rapidly insinuated himself into the good graces of the court officials by acting as an appraiser at the Hermitage and helping with repairs, free of charge.[13]

Amongst the earliest documented works by the Fabergé brothers and Erik Kollin are the copies made in 1885 after the Kerch gold jewels (p. 57, fig. 1), a magnificent hoard of gold jewellery dating from the fourth century B.C. that was exhibited at the Hermitage. *The execution of this work required not only considerable exactitude, but also the reintroduction of some long-forgotten methods of working. The brothers Fabergé overcame all the obstacles brilliantly and subsequently received orders for a whole series of copies of Kerch Antiquities.*[14]

Fabergé's designs during the tenure of Kollin hardly differ from what was being produced in other European centres during the 1870s. His antiquarian tastes are evident in the rare objects dating from this period, including gold cups and objects in the Renaissance style. *At that time settings of large engraved carnelians and other kinds of agate in the form of brooches, necklaces etc. was very popular. These settings were made of fine beads, or laces, interlaced with carved or filigree ornamentation.*

The Period of Agathon Fabergé (1882–1895)

In 1882, twenty-year-old Agathon Fabergé joined his brother Carl in St. Petersburg and worked with him for over ten years. This period was to be the richest and most creative in Fabergé's oeuvre, with the quality of objects produced remaining unsurpassed. It is generally assumed that the synergy between the two Fabergé brothers – Carl, with his interest in classical styles, and Agathon, the more lively and creative artist – combined with the advent of their brilliant second head workmaster, Mikhail Perkhin (1886–1903),[15] was the catalyst for the birth of the Fabergé *objet d'art*. Most of the Fabergé themes – the Imperial Easter eggs, animals, flowers, and objects of vertu in hardstones or precious metals – were first introduced during this decade. Birbaum's memoirs indicate that it was Agathon Fabergé who brought about the change in the House of Fabergé. *By nature more lively and impressionable, [he] sought his inspiration everywhere – in ancient works of art, in Eastern styles which had been little studied at that time, and in nature. His extant drawings are evidence of constant and*

*ceaseless questing. Ten or more variations of a theme can often be
found.*

Both of the Fabergé brothers had travelled. Carl, for
example, had acquired firsthand knowledge of Western styles
in Dresden, Frankfurt, Florence, and Paris. But at home both
had access to the richest source of inspiration available: the
Hermitage.[16] *The Hermitage and its jewellery gallery became
the school for the Fabergé jewellers. After the Kerch collection
they studied all the ages that are represented there, especially the
age of Elizabeth and Catherine II. Many of the gold and
jewellery exhibits were copied precisely and then used as models
for new compositions. Foreign antique dealers frequently
suggested making series of objects without hallmarks or the name
of the firm. This is one of the best proofs of the perfection of these
works, but the proposals were, of course, rejected. The compositions preserved the style of the past centuries, but the objects
were contemporary. There were cigarette cases and necessaires
instead of snuff-boxes and desk clocks, inkpots, ashtrays and
electric bell-pushes instead of objects of fantasy with no
particular purpose. . . . The 18th century works of art in the
Hermitage inspired the use of transparent enamel on engraved
and guilloched gold and silver.*

By the 1890s Fabergé had outstripped his competitors in the
field of objects and silver, while Bolin retained the edge in
jewellery. (The latter's turnover in 1896 in Moscow was
500,000 roubles.) Nevertheless, it was a pearl-and-diamond
necklace from Fabergé, worth 166,500 roubles, that was chosen
by Tsarevich Nikolai as his betrothal present to Princess Alix of
Hessen-Darmstadt in 1894.[17] In turn, Nikolai's parents paid the
highest price ever attained by Fabergé, 250,000 roubles, for
another necklace acquired for their daughter-in-law. By 1896
the turnover of Fabergé's Moscow branch, founded in 1887 to
cope with expanding production, had reached 400,000 roubles.[18] The firm's bread and butter were large and expensive
silver services and centre-pieces costing 50,000 roubles. Designs
for a Louis XVI-style service, commissioned in 1894 by
Alexander III for the Tsarevich, and projects for a monumental
service for the wedding of Grand Duchess Olga Aleksandrovna
in 1901, are preserved in the Hermitage (cat. 329–334) and are
well documented.[19]

Important commissions were undertaken for the Coronation
festivities of 1896 (cat. 105–112). Trips made by the Imperial

6. Fabergé's premises at Kuznetzki Most, Moscow, c. 1910.

Family to Denmark and to London were a source of excellent business for Fabergé, since many of their presents came from his workshops.[20] Further visible successes of the firm included distinctions at the Pan-Russian Exhibition in Nizhny Novgorod (1896) and at the Nordic Exhibition in Stockholm (1897), culminating in 1898–1900 with the building of new premises at 24 Bolshaya Morskaya Street[21] (figs. 2–5) and Fabergé's participation in the Paris *Exposition Universelle* in 1900.[22]

The Era of Franz Birbaum (1895–1917)

The Swiss jeweller Franz Petrovich Birbaum joined Fabergé in 1893, and after the death of Agathon Fabergé in 1895, became chief designer of the firm.[23] He was an eminent lapidary, a specialist in enamelling techniques, and a remarkable draughtsman. His advent coincides with the introduction of Fabergé's Art Nouveau idiom[24] and the fading out of the Louis XV, or 'cockerel' style, to be replaced by the more classical Louis XVI and Empire styles. Birbaum's role must have been considerable, as he claims to have designed most of the Imperial Easter eggs produced after 1900. *About 50 or 60 of these eggs were made and I composed more than half of them myself. It was not easy work as there could be no repetition of theme and the ovoid shape was compulsory.*

By the beginning of the new century, Fabergé's business had become the most important of its kind in Russia. *Production increased daily and it became necessary to assign goldwork to one workshop and subsequently silverwork to another. The brothers Fabergé had too much work and were unable to run the workshops properly, so they decided to establish autonomous workshops, whose owners would undertake to work only to their sketches and models of the firm and exclusively for it. . . . Each was allocated a specific form of production and their apprentices specialised in different forms of work. . . . The St. Petersburg workshops employed some 200 or 300 people before 1914. They were scattered all over the city until the firm built special premises in the Morskaya street. Afterwards the chief workshops were accommodated in the outbuildings in the courtyard but for reasons of lack of space some of them remained outside the main building.* After the Paris 1900 exhibition, and the international acclaim that came with it, all doors opened to Fabergé. His shop in London became the meeting place of Edwardian society. His St. Petersburg showrooms attracted Russian nobility by the score. *The Grand Dukes and Duchesses came with pleasure and spent a long time choosing their purchases. Every day from 4 to 5 all the St. Petersburg aristocracy could be seen there: the titled, the Civil Service and the commercial. In Holy Week these rendez-vous were particularly crowded as everyone hurried to buy the traditional Easter eggs and, at the same time, to glance at the egg made for the Emperor.*

In 1902, Fabergé was given the final accolade with a special charity exhibition held to benefit the Imperial Women's Patriotic Society Schools. Sponsored by Tsarina Alexandra Feodorovna, it was dedicated almost exclusively to Fabergé's works, most pieces were lent by members of the Imperial Family. Photographs of this exhibition (cat. 361–368) and descriptions in the press allow identification of a number of Fabergé's most important compositions.[25]

During the 1900s Fabergé was inundated with orders. In the decade between 1907 and 1917, over 10,000 objects were sold in London alone.[26] As of 1904, Fabergé also worked for the Siamese court.[27] American clients arrived, anchoring their yachts on the Neva.[28] The House of Fabergé became a family concern, with Carl's three sons, Eugène, Agathon, and Alexander, acting as designers alongside Birbaum. At its peak, some three hundred craftsmen worked in St. Petersburg and two hundred in Moscow (fig. 8), yet it still became necessary to pass orders to craftsmen outside the firm.[29] Approximately 150,000 items were sold worldwide.

The period of Henrik Wigström, Fabergé's last head workmaster (1903–1917), lacked the exciting inventiveness of his predecessor. After the disappearance of Art Nouveau's exuberance from Fabergé's designs, his style became drier and more classical. Although quality is still outstanding, the introduction of prefabricated parts documents the imprint of the industrial era on Fabergé. Typically for Fabergé, novelties continued to appear regularly each year. Some of Fabergé's strongly geometrical designs even seem to herald a nascent Art Deco style (figs. 13–14).

For Fabergé, the apotheosis of Romanov rule in 1913, with the lavish festivities for the Tercentenary celebrations, spelled out a last flurry of new orders. He designed and produced vast quantities of objects and jewels bearing the Romanov emblem and the date 1613–1913, such as the Kremlin's Romanov Tercentenary egg.[30] For example, the Imperial Cabinet files list

7. The Moscow sales room.

8. One of the Moscow workshops.

47 pins with the Romanov griffin attributed to Andreev's Grand Russian Orchestra, 135 tie-pins decorated with the Monomakh crown, and 43 similar brooches for the Moscow theatre's actors.[31]

With the declaration of war, Fabergé's era, that of Imperial munificence, soon came to a close. After the first euphoric victories, major losses occurred and hardship set in for all. Typically, the two eggs produced for Easter 1915 reflect the activities of the Empress and her daughters with the Red Cross (cat. 129).[32] As of September 1915, Fabergé's workshops began to suffer from a lack of skilled craftsmen due to conscription. Several letters addressed to the Office of the Imperial Court Ministry request exemption for twenty-three members of Fabergé's staff, including Kremlyev ('in case of his calling up the workshop has to be closed down') and Petuchov ('the only experienced master in enamel technique left who trained for such work for 8 years').[33]

Fabergé's list of unfinished commissions between 1 July 1914 and 1 October 1916 totalled 286,305 roubles: 80,000 roubles for the Imperial Cabinet, 53,000 for Grand Duke Mikhail Aleksandrovich, and 33,000 for the Emperor. In October 1915 he mentioned 'the commissions of His Imperial Majesty for the big egg of white quartz and nephrite demanding exquisite artistic work', and 2,200 badges for the Horse Artillery Life Guard 'given personally to me by H.I.H. the Grand Duke Andrei Vladimirovich'.[34] The Moscow silver factory was converted into making hand grenades and produced two million casings for artillery shells. Odessa was reduced from thirty-five masters to three specialists. One of the two eggs presented by the Tsar for Easter 1916 is the stark Military egg, formed of artillery shells containing a miniature of Nicholas and the Tsarevich at the front in Stavka.[35]

On 6 November 1916, Fabergé, as a precaution, formed a shareholder company (joint-stock association) with Averkiev, Bauer, Byiazov, and Marchetti as associates each holding twenty-one shares for a value of 90,000 roubles fully paid. Fabergé held 548 shares for himself, allotting forty shares to each of his sons and one share each to Antoni, Birbaum, Meier, and Jouves, corresponding to equity put in by Fabergé's house and estimated at 700,000 roubles.

The year 1917 witnessed the collapse of the old world order, with the March Revolution, the abdication of the Tsar on 15 March, the imprisonment of the Imperial Family, and the November Revolution. The firm was put in the hands of a 'Committee of the Employees of the K. Fabergé Company', which continued to operate until November 1918. At the end of 1917, Fabergé closed down his house, entrusting its contents to the Director of the Hermitage, left Russia via Riga and Germany, and settled in Lausanne, Switzerland. There he died on 24 September 1920.

Design and Style

Initially the idiom of the Fabergé firm was anchored in historicism. (A.K. Snowman dubbed Fabergé a 'cultural sponge'.) It took Carl and Agathon ten years to free the firm from the fetters of direct derivation and to acquire a style of its own.[36] With Erik Kollin, Fabergé had revelled in antiquarian styles; with his brother Agathon and his head workmaster Mikhail Perkhin, the firm's favourite style became Louis XV. But the inquisitive minds of the Fabergé brothers sought further inspiration in numerous other sources and styles, including Louis XVI, Empire, Gothic, Renaissance, Arabic, Persian, Indian, Chinese, and Japanese. Fabergé's 'house style' was based on a judicious assimilation of earlier styles, imbued with Russian feeling, given a touch of lightness and elegance, and executed with unique virtuosity. This was the *style Fabergé* – immensely popular and admired, slavishly copied, but never equalled – that accounted for Fabergé's success.

The niche filled by Fabergé's genius was the production of a never-ending stream of useful objects that rivalled each other in inventiveness. Each was of an exquisite artistic shape and perfection that was instantly recognizable, and therefore proved a perfect status symbol. One 'belonged' if one acquired such an expensive bauble or toy. Fabergé could rely on a uniquely gifted group of designers and on the superb craftsmanship of his chosen workmasters. He maintained an edge over any competition through constant innovation. This quest for novelty allowed him to claim that he melted down unsold objects at the end of each year. Proudly Fabergé could say of himself in an interview, 'If we were to compare my business to such firms as Tiffany, Boucheron or Cartier, they would probably find more precious objects. . . . They might have a single necklace of 1,500,000 roubles. But they are people of commerce rather that artist jewellers. I have little interest in

9. Fuchsia brooch. From a Fabergé album. Pencil on paper, 7.9 × 7.5 cm. Private collection, St. Petersburg.

10. Briar Rose brooch. From a Fabergé album. Signed and dated A. Fabergé 1885. Pencil and watercolour on paper, 6.1 × 10.1 cm. Private collection, St. Petersburg.

an expensive object if its price is only in the abundance of diamonds and pearls.' This credo set him aside from all his competitors. Fabergé furthermore maintained that any object not meeting his rigorous standard of perfection was destroyed.

Enamels

The most sought after objects from Fabergé have always been those crafted in gold or silver and covered with delicately coloured coats of enamel applied over cunningly engine-turned backgrounds. It was Fabergé's re-invention and perfection of the complicated technique of translucent enamel that brought him the highest praise from his competition. While others kept to 'safer' plain white, pale blue, or pink colours,[37] Fabergé adventured into inimitable and audacious primrose yellows, plum mauves, salmon pinks, lime greens, and Prussian blues. He offered more than one hundred colours from which his customers could choose. The most exquisite was undoubtedly Fabergé's 'oyster', a shimmering warm white reflecting the changing colours of a seashell (cat. 30).

Coats of enamel were applied over many variations of *guilloché* or engine-turning, another technique that Fabergé was the first to apply to art objects in Russia. The sunburst (cat. 195), wave (cat. 17), or *moiré* effects (cat. 102) engraved on the backgrounds enlivened otherwise plain surfaces. Further effects could be added in the form of painted swags of flowers, landscapes, or simulated agate inclusions applied under the penultimate coat of paint (cat. 253). A last coat of *fondant*, or transparent enamel, was lovingly polished for hours on a wooden wheel and buffed to give the object its unique gloss.

Precious Metals

Working in metal, Fabergé attained a technical prowess that was, and still is, the envy of many a goldsmith. His cigarette cases were celebrated for their elegance, their invisible hinges, and their closely fitting lids. In some of them he used a combination of burnished, varicoloured gold or silver surfaces invisibly welded together (cat. 281, 286, 292, 296). Others are in the *samorodok* technique, giving the surface an effect of natural nugget gold (cat. 284, 295). In still others, Fabergé employed eighteenth-century techniques such as *quatre couleur* gold. Flower swags pinned to frames or clocks often combine four colours of gold in one motif (cat. 1, 11). Commissions allowed

Fabergé to utilise his skills even in such simple objects as gold cigarette cases. For a series of cases made upon the request of M. Luzarche d'Azay, Arabic inscriptions were pierced and inset in silver in the burnished gold (cat. 283, 287, 288), or *samorodok* gold surfaces (cat. 295); in one case they were filled in *plique à jour* enamel (cat. 287).

Silver items were produced either in Moscow or in St. Petersburg. They were often modelled in wood or wax, then cast and chased. They range from silver services, christening sets, and ashtrays to tea sets with samovars, desk sets, and elaborate *surtout de table*. Some of the most original objects are animals shaped as electric table bells, cigar lighters, or decanters. Fabergé never skimped on the quality or quantity of silver: when working for his Imperial patrons, he used almost pure silver alloy of 88 or 91 *zolotniki*. When compared with that of his competitors, Fabergé's silver can be easily identified by weight alone.

Hardstones
In his quest for new themes, Fabergé soon struck upon the use of indigenous semiprecious stones for his objects of vertu, to be mounted in gold or silver. The accounts of the Imperial Cabinet for 1897–1898 include 'electric table bell, jade; another, nephrite; bonbonnière, nephrite, Gothic style; cup, heart-shaped, jade; idem porphyry with mouse and pearls; cup, nephrite, pink enamel handle; ashtray, jade, 4 griffons, topaz handle with red gold ring, Louis XVI style'.[38] Some models of Fabergé's most popular creations, his animals[39] and flowers,[40] can be traced to documents in the Imperial Cabinet as early as 1893. Since a hardstone-carving factory existed at Peterhof, near St. Petersburg, and in Ekaterinburg, Fabergé was able to order from these centres, as well as from the factory of Carl Woerffel in St. Petersburg. Many of the objects were reworked to comply with Fabergé's sense of perfection. *It is interesting to note that the cost of these improvements for the most part exceeded the original purchase price.*

Later, due to the shortcomings of his suppliers, Fabergé decided to acquire Carl Woerffel's factory and to open his own workshops, which he entrusted to P.M. Kremlyev, a stone carver from the Ekaterinburg Art School. Quality improved rapidly, and many of the finer works were carved by the master himself. He was assisted by twenty craftsmen. Another talented stone carver from Ekaterinburg was Derbyshev, who joined Fabergé in 1908. He was sent to Idar Oberstein and to Paris[41] before he returned to Russia in 1914.

Animals
It has been proved beyond any doubt that many of Fabergé's animal carvings are directly inspired by Japanese netsuke, of which he owned a large collection.[42] He was obviously attracted by the compact shapes of these ivory or wood toggles, as well as by the natural ease of their portrayals. They lose nothing of their charm in Fabergé's transposals into carefully chosen hardstone. His animals are lively, often humoristic, sometimes even caricatured, but never static and boring. They vary in style and quality depending on their origins.[43] The most celebrated assembly of this nature is the collection of Queen Alexandra, to which Queen Mary made later additions, and which now forms the British Royal Collection. Many of these charming creations originated in 1907 in a commission from King Edward VII to model the Queen's beloved animals in her zoo at Sandringham. Fabergé's London branch sold some 250 such animals, of which about 170 are in the collection of H.M. Queen Elizabeth II today.[44] Most of Fabergé's animals are one of a kind. (King Edward's dictum that 'We do not want any duplicates' comes to mind.) The most popular, the elephants, were nevertheless often repeated.[45]

Fabergé used many types of hardstones to characterise his animals. Some models, and in particular those from the Sandringham zoo, were realistically coloured: a seal of glistening obsidian sits on an ice floe of rock crystal;[46] pink aventurine quartz was used for pigs;[47] grey Kalgan jasper for the rhinoceros;[48] slimy green jade or bowenite for the frog or toad (cat. 164); smoky quartz for the mouse;[49] and brown-white chalcedony for 'Cesar', Edward VII's Norfolk terrier.[50] Fabergé also used the natural striations of a stone, mostly agate or jasper, to imitate the markings of animal fur. In rarer cases he chose 'unnatural' colours for his animals, producing such droll effects as a green cockerel, beaver, or sparrow, a pink rabbit, and a blue, red, or green elephant. A small group of Fabergé's animals are composed of several hardstones: a black obsidian cockerel with purpurine comb and jasper wattles, and a grey Kalgan jasper yawning hippo with pink rhodonite maw.

Animals with claws or beaks in gold or gilded silver are

sometimes hallmarked, which allows dating. A small number originates from the period of Mikhail Perkhin (before 1903), with the majority from that of Henrik Wigström (1903–1917).

Cartier's sales ledgers also list approximately two hundred hardstone animals, the descriptions of which are highly reminiscent of Fabergé's work. Since virtually no such early Cartier animal survives, it seems likely that these have been incorporated into Fabergé's oeuvre, especially since Cartier often used the same Russian sources that supplied Fabergé.[51]

Flowers

Fabergé's exquisite and rare floral compositions were derived from Oriental originals. *We first noticed this branch of Chinese art when a bouquet of chrysanthemums was brought in for repair. . . . The skilled range of tones and the translucence of some of the stones created a marvellous impression.*

Most of Fabergé's flowers stand in flawless, rock crystal vases carved to simulate water content. They have meticulously chased gold stems, finely carved nephrite leaves, and enamelled, diamond-set flowers or buds. Some, in the Japanese style, stand in bowenite pots. Very few repetitions appear in Fabergé's flora, which include lilies-of-the-valley (Alexandra

11. Diadem. From a Fabergé album. Signed and dated A. Fabergé 1885. Pencil on paper, 12.8 × 28.7 cm. Private collection, St. Petersburg.

Feodorovna's favourite flower), rowanberries, raspberries, and the dandelion seedclock. *The dandelions were particularly successful: their fluff was natural and fixed on a golden thread with a small uncut diamond. The shining points of the diamond among the white fluff were marvellously successful and prevented this artificial flower from being to close a reproduction of nature.*

Fabergé's designers often modelled their flowers on nature. An album of photographs from the Fabergé workshops[52] shows photographs of natural flowers, including a basket of lilies-of-the-valley almost identical to the celebrated 1896 basket in the Matilda Geddings Gray Foundation Collection in New Orleans.[53] Such visual documentation was used by Fabergé's designers as sources of their inventions.

Most flowers by Fabergé were unique. According to Birbaum, the cost of manufacturing them was considerable, in some cases as much as several thousand roubles. Alexander von Solodkoff[54] has identified only thirty-five flowers amongst 10,000 items sold in London in a ten-year period. Of these Queen Elizabeth II owns twenty.[55] All in all, about eighty flowers by Fabergé are recorded. They have been extensively

12. Diadem. From a Fabergé album. Pencil on paper, 12.7 × 21 cm. Private collection, St. Petersburg.

copied, with most variants bearing a full set of hallmarks. On the other hand, very few of the original flowers were hallmarked, since they were considered too fragile to be disfigured by a punch.

When Fabergé's flowers were exhibited in Paris, some experts criticised them, but they were an instant success with his competitors. *They were immediately copied by German and Austrian factories and appeared on the market in cheap versions. The enamel was replaced by varnish and the little vases of rock crystal by glass.*

It should be noted that Cartier's stock books between 1907 and 1917 list 169 flowers, including a forget-me-not acquired from Fabergé in 1909. The majority came from Cartier's chief supplier, Berquin-Varangoz, and must have resembled Fabergé's compositions. Like the animals, most likely they are irretrievably mixed up with Fabergé's oeuvre.

Figures

Approximately seventy hardstone statuettes from the Fabergé workshops have survived.[56] The origins of their technique hark back to Florentine *commessi* works of the seventeenth century. They are composed of colourful, semiprecious stones from Siberia, the Urals, and the Altai. The names of their modellers are recorded in Birbaum's memoirs as being Boris Froedman-Cluzel and Georgi Savitski.

These figures fit into four categories: a small number of them, possibly the earliest group, are genuine portrait figures, such as Fabergé's *dvornik*, Vara Panina (cat. 194), or Postnikov, the Dowager Empress' *kamerkazak*. The largest group is based on popular biscuit porcelain groups or 'concierge figures', such as the Russian national types from the Sir William Seed series.[57] These include several musicians, a policeman, a soldier, two peasants, and a cossack.[58] A small group represents special commissions, such as John Bull, Uncle Sam, a Chelsea pensioner, Queen Victoria, or Tweedledum and Tweedledee.[59] Finally, a late series of realistic caricatures of street vendors was produced for Emanuel Nobel, who was said to have ordered more than thirty figures from Fabergé.[60] With very few exceptions, each statuette is unique, with repetitions being carved from diversely coloured stones.

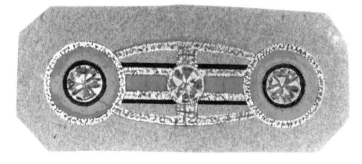

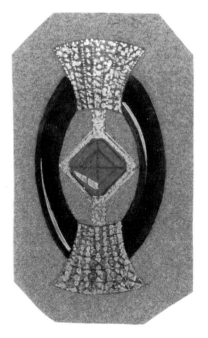

13. Two brooches in Art Deco style. From a Fabergé album. Pencil and gouache on paper, 5.7 × 9.5 cm.; 4.5 × 10.7 cm. Private collection, St. Petersburg.

These figures were cut, carved, polished, and assembled at Carl Woerffel's factory by P.M. Kremlyev, and later by Derbyshev, two of the firm's most gifted hardstone cutters. Silver or gold parts were added in Henrik Wigström's workshop. Some are signed 'Fabergé' under one foot, either in Latin script or Cyrillic, and sometimes with a date. Others, with silver mounts, are hallmarked.

Imperial Easter Eggs

Fabergé's first Imperial Easter egg was commissioned by Tsar Alexander III in 1885.[61] Due to its instant success, a permanent order was given to Fabergé, who crafted one egg after another for the Imperial Family. Ten were for Tsar Alexander III, who gave them to his wife Maria Feodorovna until his death in 1894. An additional forty-four were created for Tsar Nicholas II from 1895 until 1916 as presents for his mother, the Dowager Empress, and for his wife Alexandra Feodorovna, thus bringing this to a total of fifty-four eggs. It is also conceivable that some eggs were given to other members of the Imperial Family.[62] Forty-four Imperial Easter eggs are known to exist, of one we

have a photograph,[63] while a further five are known from descriptions.[64] One of the two half-finished Imperial eggs for 1917 has also survived.[65]

These eggs are now scattered over the world since their sale by Soviet commissars in the 1920s and 1930s. Ten have remained in the Kremlin Armoury, eleven are in the FORBES Magazine Collection, thirteen are in American museums, and the remaining ten are housed in private collections.

Problems concerning the chronology of these eggs is addressed in another chapter (see Lopato, 'A Few Remarks Concerning Imperial Easter Eggs'. Suffice it so say that earlier speculative datings of eggs have been somewhat thrown into disarray due to findings in the Imperial archives.

This series of Imperial Easter eggs is the most ambitious project ever entrusted to a goldsmith. The only conditions set appear to have been an oviform shape, a surprise of some form, and no repetitions. Surprises were frequently linked to some occurrence in the history of the Imperial Family – births, anniversaries, inaugurations. Some bear royal monograms and/ or dates, and many exhibit miniatures of the Imperial children,

14. Four parasol handles. From a Fabergé album. Pencil and watercolour on paper, 10.3 × 14.2 cm. Private collection, St. Petersburg.

or their abodes. Two contain models of Imperial vessels.

Fabergé took this commission extremely seriously, often planning eggs years ahead of time. Some did indeed require several years to finish.[66] Much secrecy surrounded the surprise in the eggs, which was never divulged in advance, not even to the Tsar himself. The solemn presentation of the egg was made by Fabergé or by his son Eugène, and the recipient was invariably delighted.

The first two eggs, each with a hen motif, appear to have been designed and produced under close supervision.[67] In the following years a certain dependence on earlier models can be detected.[68] By the mid-1890s, however, the designs of the eggs become increasingly audacious. Among the most felicitous examples are the 1897 Coronation Coach egg (cat. 110), the 1898 Lilies-of-the-Valley egg (cat. 23), the 1899 Pansy egg, the 1901 Gatchina Palace egg, the 1913 Romanov Tercentenary egg, and the 1914 Mosaic egg (cat. 29). The series ends on a subdued note with two plain Red Cross eggs for 1915 (cat. 129),[69] the simple Order of St. George egg,[70] and the stark Military egg for 1916.[71]

Some of Fabergé's clients dared to emulate the Imperial Family in their Easter customs, ordering their own eggs from Fabergé. A documented series was commissioned by Aleksandr Ferdinandovich Kelch, the Siberian gold magnate, for his wife Barbara, née Bazanova, between 1898 and 1904.[72] Single eggs were also made for the Yusupovs and the Nobels.[73]

1. Bainbridge 1966. Bainbridge first wrote about his experiences as Fabergé's representative in his autobiography *Twice Seven* (1933).

2. Snowman 1962.

3. Fabergé Archives, Geneva, cf. Habsburg/Solodkoff 1979, pp. 140–43; Solodkoff 1982, pp. 102–5.

4. Wartski, London. First published by A. K. Snowman, 'Two Books of Revelations', in Habsburg 1987, pp. 45–56; and in *Apollo* (September 1987), pp. 150–61. To be published in extenso in 1993.

5. Christie's, London, April 27, 1989: Designs from the House of Fabergé.

6. Published here for the first time by Ulla Tillander-Godenhielm in 'New Light on the Workshop of Henrik Wigström'.

7. The tireless sleuthing of Marina Lopato, Curator of Western Applied

Art at the Hermitage, St. Petersburg, and of Valentin Skurlov, an independent researcher, has borne rich fruit. Many of their discoveries are published here for the first time. Their exciting finds include the lists of sales made by Fabergé to the Cabinet of His Imperial Majesty, allowing a new dating of the first Easter eggs (Russian Central State Historical Archives f. 468 op. 13 del. 781 pp. 6ff.)
This author acknowledges a debt to both Ms Lopato and Mr Skurlov and thanks both of them for the use of their findings.

8. The memoirs of Franz Birbaum, Fabergé's chief designer between 1893 and 1917, were written in 1919 (CSHA f. 544 op. 5 del. 7) and are published in this catalogue.

9. A detailed chronology appears as a separate chapter (see Habsburg, 'Chronology of the House of Fabergé in Its Time'), thus allowing newcomers to the subject a complete picture of the firm's history.

10. For some of Gustav Fabergé's jewellery cf. Habsburg 1987, cat. 1–4.

11. All quotations in italics in this article derive from Birbaum's memoirs.

12. Solodkoff 1988, p. 51 (traditional, although of later date), and the overladen Bismarck box of 1884 (Habsburg 1987, cat. 404), surely Perkhin's earliest major work.

13. See correspondence dating from 1884 concerning Fabergé's application for the title of Court Supplier in Lopato, 'New Insights into Fabergé from Russian Documents'.

14. Chronology: 1885. Birbaum mistakenly states that the copies were commissioned by 'the German Emperor William II', instead of by Count Sergei Stroganov, President of the Imperial Archaeological Society. The lost technique to which Birbaum refers was granulation.

15. For a biography of Perkhin cf. Habsburg 1987, p. 324 and the Birbaum memoirs published here.

16. For a number of comparisons between originals and Fabergé copies at the Hermitage cf. Habsburg 1987, pp. 67ff. and cat. 648–54.

17. The account books of the Imperial Cabinet for 1894 give a total payment of 171,208 roubles to Fabergé, of which the necklace presented by the Tsarevich accounted for almost the total.

18. See Anne Odom's essay on the Moscow workshops, published here; a total of 238 workmasters, 30 boys, 31 tool machines. Turnover for gold and jewellery was only 30,000 roubles.

19. Both are documented in the Hermitage archives (CSHA f. 1 Inv. Year 1908 del. 46 p. 38; and CSHA f. 468 op. 8 del. 648 p. 1). The former cost 50,000 roubles. Another set for the same price was made in 1894 on the occasion of the wedding of Grand Duchess Xenia Aleksandrovna.

20. CSHA f. 468 op. 8 del. 13 p. 124, 'for making presents during their Imperial Majesties' travel to Copenhagen' (1893). Items from Fabergé totalled 4,464 roubles and included 3 elephants (smoky topaz, nephrite, and jade, total 780 rbls.), a mushroom, and 2 eagle cups (600 rbls). In 1894, on the Tsarevich's trip to London, there were a silver helmet for 700 rbls. (Equerry of the Prince of Wales), a bratina for 700 rbls (gentleman-in-waiting of the Prince of Wales), a matchbox for 75 rbls. (Mr Douglas, senior navigator of the *Victoria and Albert*), and a cup and glass for 175 rbls. (Chief of Police in London).

21. See Boris Ometov's essay on the Fabergé house, published here.

22. See Géza von Habsburg on the Paris 1900 *Exposition Universelle*, published here.

23. For Franz Birbaum cf. Birbaum Memoirs.

24. For Art Nouveau in the oeuvre of Fabergé cf. Solodkoff 1988, pp. 16–17.

25. CSHA f. 472 op. 43 del. 65 and *Novoye Vremya*, 9 March 1902, 'Exhibition of Artistic Items and Miniatures'; 10 March, 'The opening of the Jewellery Exhibition'; 17 March, 'New Items'. Recognizable items include the Twenty-fifth Anniversary chimney clock (1891) (cat. 4), Forbes' Lilies-of-the-Valley egg (1898) (cat. 23), Geddings Gray Lilies-of-the-Valley basket (1896), Kremlin Trans-Siberian egg (1900), Basket-of-Flowers egg (1901), the Hermitage Miniature Regalia (1900) (cat. 113), Forbes' Coronation Coach egg (1897) (cat. 110), Kremlin Pamiat Azova egg (1891), surprise of the Pansy egg (1899), Pratt's Pelican egg (1897), Baltimore's Gatchina Palace egg (1901), and Grand Duchess Xenia's *surtout de table* (1894).

26. See Géza von Habsburg's essay on the London Branch, published here.

27. The collection of the present King and Queen of Thailand, originally formed by King Chulalongkorn Rama V (published by Krairiksh 1984), consists largely of dark green nephrite objects. It also includes a figure of Buddha and a rosewater bowl, both of which have become objects of religious significance.

28. For Fabergé's American clientele, cf. Christopher Forbes, 'Fabergé Collecting in America', in Habsburg 1987, pp. 100–3, and Schaffer, 'Fabergé in America', published here.

29. *Cloisonné* objects were ordered from Feodor Rückert, Saltikov, and Maria Semenova in Moscow (cf. Odom, 'The Moscow Workshops'); hardstone objects were possibly acquired from Svietchnikov, Ovchinnikov, Dennisov-Uralski, Britzin, or Sumin, all Russian hardstone carvers. For Fabergé and the German hardstone-cutting centre Idar Oberstein cf. Habsburg 1987, p. 79 and cat. 291–292.

30. San Diego/Kremlin 1989/90, cat. 22.

31. CSHA f. 468 op. 44 del. 345 pp. 81–83.

32. Solodkoff 1984, pp. 104–5.

33. CSHA f. 472 op. 68 del. 120.

34. CSHA f. 472 op. 66 del. 120 pp. 34–40.

35. San Diego/Kremlin 1989/90, cat. 25.

36. Cf. Géza von Habsburg, 'Fabergé and Nineteenth-Century Historicism', in Habsburg 1987, pp. 66–72.

37. Habsburg 1987, cat. 593, 594, 600–8, 609, 610, for examples by Fabergé's competitors.

38. CSHA f. 468 op. 13 del. 2190 p. 15, 4 May 1898.

39. Bill to His Imperial Majesty's Cabinet, 17 May 1897 (CSHA f. 468 op. 13 del. 2190, 4 December: 'giraffe, carnelian, 2 rose-cut diamonds 57,942 $\frac{1}{2}$ roubles 80'; 11 January (CSHA f. 468 op. 13 del. 1843 p. 5); 24 January: 'frog, nephrite, brilliant eyes 53,867, roubles 115'.

40. Ibid., 28 April 1897: 'crystal glass with flower and 3 brilliants 55,503 $\frac{1}{2}$ roubles 67–50'.

41. Birbaum writes that he worked with Lalique, who was delighted by his work and wanted to make him his successor by marrying him to his daughter'.

42. The influence of Japanese netsuke on Fabergé's animals has been researched by Bandini (1980); Habsburg (1987), pp. 76–77 and cat. 352, 362–370, 636–647; and Munn (1987). Fabergé's collection of 500 netsukes

43. For the origins of Fabergé's animals cf. Habsburg 1987, pp. 76–79.

44. Many of the Queen's animals were exhibited for the first time at the Victoria and Albert Museum in 1977 (cat. A1–45; B1–31; C1–26).

45. For a typical group of elephants, all from one private collection dating back to pre-Revolutionary times, cf. Habsburg 1987, cat. 329–39.

46. Habsburg/Solodkoff 1979, p. 79.

47. Habsburg 1987, cat. 297, 298, 319.

48. Ibid., cat. 320.

49. Ibid., cat. 370.

50. Ibid., cat. 380.

51. Ibid., pp. 335–36.

52. Fersman Mineralogical Museum, Moscow.

53. Habsburg 1987, cat. 401.

54. Solodkoff 1988, p. 70.

55. V&A 1977, cat. E1–21.

56. Alexander von Solodkoff, 'Fabergé's Hardstone Figures', in Habsburg 1987, pp. 81–86.

57. Solodkoff 1988, pp. 82–89.

58. V&A 1977, cat. N1–10.

59. For John Bull and Tweedledum and Tweedledee cf. Krairiksh pp. 161, 163.

60. Solodkoff 1988, p. 83.

61. For a discussion of the origins of the Fabergé series cf. Lopato 1984, pp. 44–45, and Lopato, 'A Few Remarks Concerning Imperial Easter Eggs', in this book.

62. Habsburg 1987, p. 94 and n. 6.

63. Solodkoff 1984, p. 56.

64. Lopato 1984, pp. 44–45.

65. V&A 1977, cat. O 8.

66. As examples, the coach of the Forbes 1897 Coronation egg took George Stein fifteen months to complete; the peacock in the 1908 Sandoz Peacock egg was apparently developed over a period of three years.

67. CSHA f. 468 op. 7 del. 270 pp. 1–4, dated 15 February 1886, discusses in detail the production of a (lost) 'hen taking out of a basket the sapphire egg' costing 2,986 roubles.

68. Habsburg 1987, pp. 95–96.

69. Solodkoff 1984, pp. 104–5.

70. San Diego/Moscow 1989/90, cat. 26.

71. Ibid., cat. 25.

72. Habsburg/Solodkoff 1979, pp. 108, 118, and ill. 141.

73. Habsburg 1987, cat. 543; Habsburg/Solodkoff 1979, p. 166.

Chronology of the House of Fabergé in Its Time

Géza von Habsburg

1. Plaster bust of Carl Fabergé by Joseph Limburg, January 1903. Fabergé Archive, Geneva.

1685

Revocation of the Edict of Nantes. Together with other Huguenots, the Fabergé (or Faberger) family emigrates from France and settles in eastern Germany in Schwedt-an-der-Oder.

1800

Carpenter Peter Fabergé moves to Pernau (Livonia) and marries Marie Luise Elsner from Vaiha (Latvia).

1814

30 February, their son Gustav Fabergé is born.

c. **1830**

Gustav Fabergé moves to St. Petersburg and becomes apprenticed to goldsmiths Andreas Ferdinand Spiegel[1] and Johann Wilhelm Keibel.[2]

1841

Gustav Fabergé obtains the title of Master Goldsmith.
Birth of Edward VII of England.

1842

Gustav Fabergé opens a shop in Jacot's house at 12 Bolshaya Morskaya, marries Charlotte Jungstedt, and works as a jeweller with Johann Alexander Gunst[3] and Johann Eckhardt.[4] His address until the mid-1850s is no. 11 Bolshaya Morskaya Street, then no. 18, and in 1867, no. 16 Bolshaya Morskaya Street.

1845

Birth of Alexander III of Russia.

1846

Peter Carl Fabergé is born; baptized on 31 May at the Lutheran Church of St. Anne.

1848

Karl Marx and Friedrich Engels: *Communist Manifesto*.

1853–1856

Crimean War.

1855

Death of Nicholas I; Coronation of Alexander II.

1857

August Wilhelm Holmström joins Gustav Fabergé as chief jeweller.[5]

1858–1859
Carl Fabergé is educated at the German-speaking St. Anne's School, St. Petersburg.

1859
Birth of Wilhelm II. Ivan Goncharov: *Oblomov*.

1860
Gustav Fabergé moves to Dresden, leaving his shop in the hands of his friend and partner Hiskias Pendin[6] and the jeweller V. A. Zaiantkovski.[7]
Wilhelm I becomes King of Prussia.

1861
Carl Fabergé is confirmed in the Dresden Kreuzkirche. He also attends a commercial course.
The era of Great Reforms begins in Russia. 19 February, serfdom is abolished by the manifesto of Alexander II.

1861–1864
Fabergé travels throughout Europe as part of his apprenticeship, together with Julius Butz, son of the famous jeweller. They visit Frankfurt, where Fabergé is apprenticed to Joseph Friedman.[8]
They presumably visit Florence and Paris as well.

1862
Agathon Fabergé, Carl's brother, is born in Dresden.[9]
Otto von Bismarck becomes Prime Minister of Prussia. Ivan Turgenev: *Fathers and Sons*. Anton Rubinstein founds the St. Petersburg Conservatory.

1863
Christian IX is crowned King of Denmark. Marriage of his daughter Alexandra (1844–1925) to Edward, Prince of Wales.

1864–1866
Fabergé returns to St. Petersburg and enters his father's firm. Karl Marx founds the First International Workingmen's Association in London.

1866
9 December, Certificate of Temporary Merchant of the 2d Guild is issued to Fabergé. He begins selling jewellery to the Imperial Cabinet.[10]
Marriage of Tsar Alexander III to Princess Dagmar (1847–1928), daughter of Christian IX of Denmark (she then takes the name Maria Feodorovna).

1867
Fabergé, at age twenty-one, is registered as a member of the Merchant's Guild, no. 4321.
The United States acquires Alaska from Russia for $7.2 million.
Marx: *Das Kapital*, vol. I. Peter Tchaikovsky: *First Symphony*.
Discovery of the Kerch treasure in the Crimea.

1868
Birth of Nicholas II. Birth of Maxim Gorky.

1870
Birth of Vladimir Ilyich Ulianov, later known as Lenin. Founding of Partnership of Peredvizhnik Art Exhibitions (active until 1923).

1871
Birth of Rasputin. Wilhelm I becomes Emperor of Germany, with Bismarck as Chancellor. Feodor Dostoevsky: *The Possessed*.

1872
Fabergé pays merchant's duty in his own name and takes over his father's business. Erik Kollin becomes head workmaster.[11] Fabergé marries Augusta Jakobs, daughter of an overseer at the Imperial furniture workshop.
Birth of Princess Alix von Hessen-Darmstadt (later Tsarina Alexandra Feodorovna). Birth of Sergei Diaghilev. 28 November, opening of the first Peredvizhnik exhibition.

1873
Leo Tolstoy: *Anna Karenina*. Birth of Feodor Chaliapin. Birth of Sergei Rachmaninoff. Mikhail Bakunin: *State and Anarchy*.

1874
Birth of Eugène, Fabergé's first son (died in Paris 1960).
First mention of Fabergé in the lists of the Imperial Cabinet.[12]
Modest Moussorgsky: *Boris Godunov*.

1876
Birth of Agathon, Fabergé's second son (died in Helsinki 1951).
Balkan War. Tchaikovsky: *Swan Lake*.

1877
Birth of Alexander, Fabergé's third son (died in Paris 1952).

1879
Birth of Joseph Stalin. Tchaikovsky: *Eugene Onegin*. Tolstoy: *Confessions*.

2. Members of the Russian Imperial Family, *c.* 1880. Left to right (standing, back row): Grand Dukes Sergei Mikhailovich and Nikolai Nikolaievich the younger; (standing, second row): Grand Dukes Konstantin Konstantinovich (third), Nicholas Alexandrovich, future Tsar Nicholas II (fifth), Vladimir Aleksandrovich, Georgi Mikhailovich, Dmitri Konstantinovich, Prince Oldenburg, Piotr Nikolaievich; (seated, third row): Grand Duchesses Xenia Aleksandrovna, Maria Pavlovna, Elena Vladimirovna, Aleksandra Iosifovna, Tsarina Maria Feodorovna, Tsar Alexander III, Grand Dukes Mikhail Nikolaievich, Pavel Aleksandrovich; (seated at their feet, fourth row): Grand Dukes Kirill Vladimirovich, Mikhail Aleksandrovich, Boris, and Andrei.

1881
Death of Hiskias Pendin.
Assassination of Tsar Alexander II; Coronation of Tsar Alexander III. Founding of Russian Secret Police *Okhrana*. Anti-Jewish pogroms. Death of Moussorgsky.

1882
Agathon Fabergé joins his brother in St. Petersburg. The firm participates in the Pan-Russian Industrial Exhibition in Moscow.

1883
Fabergé is awarded a Gold Medal for his exhibits in the previous year and receives the right to wear it on a St. Stanislas ribbon. Death of Marx. Death of Turgenev.

1884
Birth of Nicholas, Fabergé's fourth son (died in Paris 1939).

1884–1885
Bismarck Box presented by Alexander III.[13]
Mikhail Perkhin joins the firm and later becomes head workmaster.[14] Production of *objets de fantasie* begins. Intensive Russianisation of Courland, Livland, and Estland.

1885
Traditional date of first documented Imperial Easter egg ('hen egg') made for Tsar Alexander III.[15]
Fabergé becomes Supplier by Special Appointment to the Imperial Court.[16] At the Nuremberg Fine Art Exhibition, Fabergé exhibits his gold copies of the Kerch Treasure and is awarded a Gold Medal.
Birth of Anna Pavlova. Private opera house of S. I. Mamontov established. Marx: *Das Kapital*, vol. II.

1887
Imperial Serpent Clock egg.[17]
The Moscow branch is founded, and Allan Bowe becomes Fabergé's partner.
Secret Treaty between Russia and Germany. Aleksandr Borodin: *Prince Igor*. Birth of Marc Chagall.

1888
At the Nordic Exhibition in Copenhagen, Fabergé participates *hors concours*; as a member of the jury he is awarded a Special Diploma.
Wilhelm II becomes Kaiser. Nikolai Rimsky-Korsakov: *Sheherazade*.

3. Tsar Alexander III with his family in St. Petersburg, *c.* 1888. Left to right: Tsarina Maria Feodorovna, with her arm around Grand Duke Mikhail, Tsarevich Nikolai, Tsar Alexander III (seated) with Grand Duchess Olga, Grand Duchess Xenia, and Grand Duke Georgi.

4. Tsarevich Nicholas Alexandrovich
with his bride Alix von Hessen, Coburg,
20 April 1894.

1889
Fabergé is awarded the Order of St. Stanislas, 3d Class, for his exhibition the previous year.
Tchaikovsky: *Sleeping Beauty*.

1890
29 August, Fabergé is named Appraiser of the Imperial Cabinet.
1 November, he is granted the Hereditary Honorary Citizenship.
The Imperial cruiser *Pamiat Azova* is launched. Tsarevich Nicholas Alexandrovich makes his trip to Greece, India, Ceylon, Singapore, Java, Japan, and China.
Bismarck retires. Tchaikovsky: *The Queen of Spades*.

1891
Imperial Pamiat Azova egg.[18]
The Tsarevich lays the first stone of the Trans-Siberian Railway terminus station. Birth of Sergei Prokofiev.

1892
Fabergé, in Copenhagen with Woerffel and Ovchinnikov for the Golden Wedding Anniversary of Christian IX and Louise of Denmark, is awarded the Order of St. Anne, 3d Class.
P. M. Tretyakov donates his gallery to the city of Moscow.
Tchaikovsky: *The Nutcracker*.

1893
Imperial Caucasus egg.[19]
Death of Gustav Fabergé. Franz Birbaum becomes designer.

1894
Imperial Renaissance egg.[20]
25 June, payment of 166,500 roubles to Fabergé for a pearl and diamond necklace as a betrothal present from the Tsarevich to his bride, Princess Alix of Hessen-Darmstadt.
Eugène Fabergé joins the firm.
20 October, death of Alexander III. 14 November, marriage of Nicholas II to Alix von Hessen, who takes the name of Alexandra Feodorovna at her Russian Orthodox baptism.
Death of A. G. Rubinstein.

5. Family gathering in Denmark, *c.* 1895.
Left to right: Edward VII as the Prince of
Wales, Dowager Empress Maria
Feodorovna, King Christian IX of
Denmark, Queen Louise of Denmark, and
Alexandra, Princess of Wales.

1895

Imperial Danish Palaces egg (cat. 5).

Death of Agathon Fabergé, Carl's brother. Carl's son Agathon enters the firm.

Birth of Grand Duchess Olga (first daughter of Nicholas II). Death of Engels. Marx: *Das Kapital*, vol. III. Rimsky-Korsakov: *Sadko*.

1896

Lilies-of-the Valley basket.[21] Imperial Revolving Frame egg.[22]

Nephrite 'Freedom' box (cat. 151). Renaissance Presentation dish (cat. 111).

Fabergé takes part in the Pan-Russian Exhibition in Nizhny Novgorod and is awarded the State Emblem. He also receives the Order of St. Stanislas, 2d Class.

Coronation of Nicholas II. Nicholas II and Alexandra Feodorovna visit France and England.

Thirty thousand workers strike in St. Petersburg. State assay-mark *kokoshnik* is introduced for gold and silver items.

1897

Imperial Coronation Coach egg (cat. 110). Imperial Pelican egg.[23]

Heart Surprise (cat. 22).

Nordic Exhibition is held in Stockholm with Eugène Fabergé as a member of the jury. Carl Fabergé is granted the Royal Warrant for the Courts of Sweden and Norway.

Birth of Grand Duchess Tatiana (second daughter of Nicholas II).

1898

Imperial Lilies-of-the-Valley egg (cat. 23). Kelch Hen egg.[24]

Fabergé buys premises at 24 Bolshaya Morskaya Street.

Death of Queen Louise of Denmark.

Russian Social Democratic Party is founded. Historical Costume Ball is held with participation of Nicholas II. First publication of *Mir Iskusstva* (World of Art) leads to an association of young painters and art lovers founded by Alexander Benois and Sergei Diaghilev. Exhibition of drawings by M. K. Tenisheva. First exhibition of watercolour painters and of works by Russian and Finnish painters, organized by Diaghilev. Opening of Alexander III Museum in St. Petersburg. Death of P. M. Tretyakov. Alexander Glazunov: *Raimonda*.

1899

Imperial Madonna Lily egg.[25] Imperial Pansy egg.[26]

Kelch Twelve-panel egg.

Birth of Grand Duchess Maria (third daughter of Nicholas II). Intensive Russianisation of Finland. First exhibition of paintings held by *Mir Iskusstva*. One hundredth anniversary of Alexander Pushkin's birthday widely celebrated. Tolstoy: *Resurrection*.

1900

Imperial Cuckoo egg.[27] Imperial Trans-Siberian Railway egg.[28]

Kelch Pine Cone egg.[29] Miniature Replica of the Imperial Regalia (cat. 113)

At the Paris *Exposition Universelle*, Fabergé, as a member of the jury, exhibits *hors concours* and is awarded a Gold Medal and the Cross of the *Legion d'Honneur*. Eugène Fabergé is awarded the rank and badge of an Officer of the Académie. Agathon Fabergé is granted a Government Gold Medal, and Mikhail Perkhin receives a Bronze Medal. New premises at 24 Bolshaya Morskaya are occupied. The Odessa branch is opened.

1901

Imperial Gatchina Palace egg.[30] Imperial Flower Basket egg.[31]

Kelch Apple Blossom egg.[32] Dutch Colony Presentation tray.[33]

Death of Erik Kollin. Fabergé's request to the Moscow City Authorities for permission to establish a trading house 'C. Fabergé. Moscow' with Allan Bowe is refused.

Birth of Grand Duchess Anastasia (fourth daughter of Nicholas II). Death of Queen Victoria; accession of Edward VII.

Posthumous exhibition of works by Isaak Levitan. Founding of 'Exhibition of 36', a new association of painters. First issue of *Artistic Treasures of Russia*. Chekhov: *Three Sisters*.

1902

Imperial Clover Leaf egg.[34] Kelch Rocaille egg.[35] Duchess of Marlborough egg.[36]

Exhibition *Artistic Objects and Miniatures by Fabergé* opens at the von Dervise House on the English Embankment. Fabergé is awarded the Bulgarian Commanders Cross for Civilian Services by Prince Ferdinand of Bulgaria. Eugène receives the Bulgarian Knight's Cross of St. Alexander.

Exhibition *150 Years of Russian Portrait Painting* is held at the St. Petersburg Academy of Sciences. Exhibition *Modern Style Architecture and Art* is held in Moscow. Gorky: *The Lower Depths*.

1903

Imperial Peter the Great egg.[37] Kelch Bonbonnière egg.[38]

Arthur Bowe opens a branch of the House of Fabergé at Berners Hotel in London. Henrik Wigström becomes new head workmaster after death of Mikhail Perkhin.[39] Death of August Holmström leads to the succession of his son Albert.

Two hundredth anniversary of founding of St. Petersburg. Foundation of Russian Socialist Revolutionary Party. Jewish pogroms in Russian provinces. Fifth and last *Mir Iskusstva* exhibition. New association of artists, 'Union of Russian Painters', is formed.

6. Left to right: Grand Duke Aleksandr
Mikhailovich with his wife Grand Duchess
Xenia Aleksandrovna; Grand Duchess Olga
Aleksandrovna (her sister); Tsar Nicholas
II (her brother) with his wife Tsarina
Alexandra Feodorovna, Gatchina, 1897.

7. The Grand Duchesses, 1902. Left to
right: Anastasia (in the arms of a nurse),
Maria, Olga, and Tatiana, all wearing
straw hats.

8. Tsar Nicholas II reading the manifesto
on the opening of the First State Duma in
the St. George's Room of the Winter
Palace, St. Petersburg, 27 April 1906.
Photograph K. E. Hahn.

1904

Imperial Alexander III Commemorative egg.[40] Kelch Chanticleer egg.[41] Imperial Pansy Flower frame.[42]

The London branch is moved to Portman House. Lady Paget's Fabergé exhibition opens in London.

Birth of Tsarevich Alexei (son of Nicholas II).

Russo-Japanese War; Japanese victory at Port Arthur. Vasilii Vereshchagin is killed on board the cruiser *Petropavlovsk*.

Exhibition of works by 'New Association of Painters'. Chekhov: *Cherry Orchard*.

1905

Imperial Colonnade egg (cat. 20).

Rasputin is introduced to the Imperial Family at Tsarskoe Selo. Disturbances begin in St. Petersburg. Between 100 and 1,000 workers are shot by troops during a demonstration before the Winter Palace. Grand Duke Sergei is assassinated by I. P. Kalayiev. Peace with Japan. Nicholas II grants concessions. Political parties become legal; founding of Octobrist Party; Leon Trotsky becomes leader of the workers' soviet in St. Petersburg; in December, armed uprising of workers in Moscow.

Exhibition of historical portraits organised by Diaghilev at the Tauride Palace, St. Petersburg. Rimsky-Korsakov is dismissed from St. Petersburg for his support of a student strike.

1906

Imperial Swan egg.[43]

London branch of the House of Fabergé is moved to 48 Dover Street, and Kiev branch is founded. Partnership with Allan Bowe is dissolved.

Death of Christian IX of Denmark. First Duma. Piotr Stolpyin becomes Prime Minister (until 1911).

1907

Imperial Rose Trellis egg.[44] Yusupov Twenty-Fifth Anniversary egg.[45] Yusupov Music box (cat. 190).

Otto Jarke replaces Allan Bowe as head of the Moscow workshop. Second Russian Duma is held in Moscow. Publication in Russia of the magazine *Golden Fleece* (until 1909) and the monthly periodical *Old Ages* for antique lovers. *Partnership of Painters* exhibition in Moscow features works by Natalia Goncharova and Mikhail Larionov. Death of critic V. V. Stasov. *Russian Art Exhibition* held at the Paris Salon. Gorky: *The Mother*.

1908

Imperial Peacock egg.[46] Imperial Alexander Palace egg.[47] Figure of 'John Bull'.[48]

Fabergé visits London; Agathon Fabergé assists in the reappraisal of the Crown's precious stones.

Ferdinand I becomes Tsar of Bulgaria. First issue of *Satiricon* magazine. *Russian Seasons* exhibition held in Paris. Exhibition of Russian art at the Vienna *Sezession*. Performance of Moussorgsky's *Boris Godunov* with Chaliapin.

1909

Imperial Standart egg.[49] Model of 'Chelsea Pensioner'.[50]

State Visit of Nicholas II to Italy.

Salon exhibition organised by K. Makovski in St. Petersburg. Maurice Denis visits Moscow. Monument to Gogol by N. Andreev erected in Moscow. Monument to Alexander III erected by Prince Paul Troubertzkoi in St. Petersburg. Founding of painters' association 'Young League' in St. Petersburg.

9. Tsarevich Alexei riding a pony, Tsarskoe Selo, 1909.
Photograph K. E. Hahn.

1910

Imperial Alexander III Equestrian egg.[51]
Fabergé is awarded the titles of 'Jeweller to the Court' and 'Manufacturing Councillor'. Kiev branch is closed. Lawsuit with Worshipful Company of Goldsmiths in London is decided. Death of Edward VII. Death of Tolstoy. Performance of Igor Stravinsky's ballet *The Firebird*, with scenography by Léon Bakst. Dostoevsky's *Brothers Karamazov* performed in the Moscow Art Theatre. First exhibition of 'Bubnovi Valet' association. Exhibition of Russian art in Brussels. Veskov: *Peter the Great* (film).

10. Grigory Rasputin surrounded by female admirers, *c.* 1910. Standing, fourth from left: Anna Vyrubova.

1911

Imperial Orange Tree egg.[52] Imperial Fifteenth Anniversary egg (cat. 30). Renaissance vase (cat. 168).
London branch of Fabergé is moved to 173 New Bond Street. Coronation of King George V. In Kiev, assassination of Prime Minister Stolypin, who is succeeded by V. N. Kokovtsev. Stravinsky: *Petrouchka*, with stage sets by Benois. Exhibition of theatre sets by Bakst in Paris. Henri Matisse visits Moscow. Death of Valentin Serov. Pan-Russian Congress of Artists held in St. Petersburg. Shakespeare's *Hamlet* produced in St. Petersburg by Gordon-Krey and Stanislavski. Literature and arts cabaret *Brodyashaya Sobaka* (Vagabond Dog) held.

1912

Imperial Napoleonic egg.[53] Imperial Tsarevich egg.[54] Carving of *kamerkazak* Kudinov, ordered by Nicholas II (cat. 43).
Fabergé and his son Alexander request authorisation for a Moscow partnership, 'Alexander Fabergé', with a capital of 60,000 roubles. Lenin takes over as editor of *Pravda*. First contacts of Lenin and Stalin. Exhibition *100 Years of French Painting* held in St. Petersburg. Count V. P. Zubov founds the Art Historical Institute, Museum of Fine Arts (now Pushkin Museum) in Moscow.

1913

Imperial Romanov Tercentenary egg.[55] Imperial Winter egg.[56] Romanov Tercentenary Presentation box (cat. 119). Tercentenary of the Romanov dynasty. Nicholas II visits Berlin. Seven hundred thousand workers go on strike.
Exhibition of works by Goncharova held in Moscow. Stravinsky: *The Rite of Spring*.

1914

Imperial Mosaic egg (cat. 29). Imperial Catherine the Great egg (cat. 9).
Agathon Fabergé catalogues the Russian Crown Jewels.
French Prime Minister Jules Poincaré visits Russia. One and a half million workers go on strike. Outbreak of First World War, with hostilities declared on 2 August. At the Battle of Tannenberg, 110,000 soldiers are killed and 96,000 Russian troops are taken prisoner.
Marinetti, leader of the Italian Futurists, visits Moscow. The *Salon des Independants* in Paris is joined by many Russian painters, including Malevich and Matyushin.

11. Tsarina Alexandra Feodorovna with the Tsarevich in a carriage on Red Square during the Romanov Tercentenary celebrations, 1913.

12. Tsar Nicholas II and Tsarina Alexandra Feodorovna on the balcony of the Winter Palace before announcing the entry of Russia into World War I, 2 August (20 July o.s.) 1914.

13. The Grand Duchesses, St. Petersburg, 1914. Left to right: Maria, Tatiana, Anastasia, and Olga.

1915
Imperial Red Cross egg with Imperial Portraits.[57] Imperial Red Cross egg with Icon (cat. 129).
The Bond Street shop of Fabergé is closed in London. Fabergé requests authorisation to open a sculpture factory in Petrograd at 44 Angliiski Prospekt. He also petitions to exempt his craftsmen from military service.
The Tsar visits the front at Stavka; 1.4 million Russians are killed and 970,000 are taken prisoner.

1916
Imperial Military egg.[58] St. George Cross egg.[59]
The firm of Fabergé is converted into a joint stock company with a capital of three million roubles and six hundred shares.
Nicholas II becomes commander-in-chief of the Army. Murder of Rasputin, 29 December.

1917
Imperial Twilight egg.[60]
Committee of the Employees of the Company C. Fabergé is formed (dissolves in November 1918).
February Revolution; abdication of Nicholas II; arrest of the Imperial Family at Tsarskoe Selo. Russia declared a Republic under Prime Minister Aleksandr Kerensky; Lenin and Trotsky return from exile.
October Revolution; Bolshevik Soviet Republic proclaimed.

1918
November, House of Fabergé closes in Petrograd. Fabergé emigrates with the help of the British Embassy.
16–17 July, Nicholas II and his family are executed at Ekaterinburg. All Grand Dukes and Grand Duchesses in territory held by the Bolsheviks are executed.

1920
24 September, death of Carl Fabergé at the Hotel Bellevue, La Rosiaz, Switzerland.

1925
Death of Augusta Fabergé.

1929
Carl and Augusta Fabergé are buried in Cannes.

14. Nursing the wounded, Tsarskoe Selo, 1915. Left to right: Grand Duchesses Maria and Olga, Tsarina Alexandra Feodorovna, Grand Duchesses Tatiana and Anastasia.

15. Aleksandr Feodorovich Kerensky, Chairman of the Council of Ministers of the Provisional Government, Petrograd, 21 August 1917.

16. Cataloguing and packing the contents
of the Catherine Palace, Tsarskoe Selo,
after the departure of the Imperial Family,
October 1917.

1. Andreas Ferdinand Spiegel (1797–1862), maker of gold boxes and jewellery; apprenticed 1817; master 1830 (Bäcksbacka, p. 56).

2. Johann Wilhelm Keibel (1788–1862), son of jeweller Otto-Samuel, maker of badges, orders, gold boxes, and jewellery; apprenticed 1808; master 1812; title of 'Court Goldsmith' in 1841; funeral crown for Nicholas I in 1855; Hereditary Honorary Citizen with Order of St. Stanislas (Bäcksbacka, p. 422).

3. Johann Alexander Gunst (active 1849–1872), master goldsmith, specialising in snuff-boxes and jewellery at St. Petersburg (Bäcksbacka, p. 64).

4. Johann Eckhardt (active c. 1820–1850), silversmith from Mitau (Bäcksbacka, p. 53).

5. August Wilhelm Holmström (1829–1903), journeyman 1850; master 1857; Carl Fabergé's workmaster and jeweller 1870–1903 (cf. Habsburg 1987, p. 326).

6. Hiskias Magnusson Pendin (Pondin or Pondinen) (1823–1881), goldsmith and jeweller; in St. Petersburg 1840; apprenticed 1846; master 1848 (Bäcksbacka, p. 203).

7. Zaiantkovski (active 1866–1870), master jeweller.

8. Joseph Friedman (born 1811), jeweller (Habsburg 1987, p. 38, n. 11).

9. Agathon Fabergé (1862–1895), Carl Fabergé's brother; educated in Dresden; brilliant designer and mainly responsible for the introduction of objects of fantasy at Fabergé's; Merchant of 2d Guild; resided at 79 Moika Embankment until 1893.

10. New information and dates in this chapter are based upon the research of Marina Lopato of the State Hermitage Museum and of Valentin Skurlov. I am much indebted to the former for sharing her information with me.

11. Erik August Kollin (1836–1901); apprenticed to August Holmström 1858; master 1868; head workmaster of Carl Fabergé 1870–1886 (cf. Habsburg 1987, p. 324).

12. Sale of eight rings set with brilliant and other precious stones, for a total of 1,657 roubles.

13. Habsburg 1987, cat. 404. This box is the first object by Fabergé that can be dated with certitude.

14. Mikhail Evamplievich Perkhin (1860–1903), self-taught jeweller; master and in Erik Kollin's workshop 1884; Fabergé's most brilliant head workmaster (1886–1903) (cf. Habsburg 1987, p. 324).

15. FORBES Magazine Collection, New York (Solodkoff 1984, p. 54). See also Lopato, 'A Few Remarks Concerning Imperial Easter Eggs'.

16. CSHA f. 472, op. 38, del. 38, pp. 1–5. Petition by State Secretary N. Petrov dated 25 April 1885 for Fabergé's obtaining of the title of Imperial Court Caterer and the right to use the State Emblem. According to Petrov, the Cabinet acquired jewellery for 47,249 roubles over a nineteen-year period.

17. Solodkoff 1984, p. 73. Collection of His Serene Highness Prince Rainier of Monaco.

18. Armoury Museum, Moscow (San Diego/Kremlin 1989/90, cat. 2).

19. Matilda Geddings Gray Foundation Collection, New Orleans (San Diego/Kremlin 1989/90, cat. 3).

20. FORBES Magazine Collection, New York (San Diego/Kremlin 1989/90, cat. 4).

21. Matilda Geddings Gray Foundation Collection, New Orleans (Habsburg 1987, cat. 401).

22. Lillian Thomas Pratt Collection, Richmond, Virginia (Solodkoff 1984, p. 72).

23. Lillian Thomas Pratt Collection, Richmond, Virginia (Solodkoff 1984, p. 75).

24. FORBES Magazine Collection, New York (Snowman 1962, pl. LXXXII).

25. Kremlin Armoury, Moscow (San Diego/Kremlin 1989/90, cat. 10).

26. Private collection, United States (San Diego/Kremlin 1989/90, cat. 11).

27. FORBES Magazine Collection (San Diego/Kremlin 1989/90, cat. 12).

28. Kremlin Armoury, Moscow (San Diego/Kremlin 1989/90, cat. 13).

29. Mrs Joanne Kroc, San Diego (Solodkoff 1984, p. 81).

30. Walters Art Gallery, Baltimore, Maryland (Habsburg 1987, cat. 541).

31. H. M. Queen Elizabeth II (Habsburg 1987, cat. 620).

32. Private collection, United States (Solodkoff 1984, p. 84).

33. Private collection, Argentina (Habsburg/Solodkoff 1979, p. 45).

34. Kremlin Armoury, Moscow (Solodkoff 1984, p. 85).

35. Private collection, United States (Snowman 1962, pl. LXXXIV).

36. FORBES Magazine Collection, New York (Solodkoff 1984, p. 11).

37. Lillian Thomas Pratt Collection, Richmond, Virginia (Solodkoff 1984, p. 87).

38. Snowman 1962, ill. 390.

39. For Wigström's biography cf. Habsburg 1987, pp. 324–25.

40. Kremlin Armoury, Moscow (Habsburg/Solodkoff 1979, p. 125).

41. FORBES Magazine Collection, New York (Solodkoff 1984, pp. 88–89).

42. Kremlin Armoury, Moscow (Habsburg 1987, cat. 400).

43. Heirs of the late Maurice Sandoz, Le Locle, Switzerland (Solodkoff 1984, p. 92).

44. Walters Art Gallery, Baltimore, Maryland (Solodkoff 1984, p. 92).

45. Heirs of the late Maurice Sandoz, Le Locle, Switzerland (Habsburg 1987, cat. 543).

46. Heirs of the late Maurice Sandoz, Le Locle, Switzerland (Solodkoff 1984, p. 94).

47. Kremlin Armoury, Moscow (San Diego/Kremlin 1989/90, cat. 16).

48. Private collection, London (Solodkoff 1988, p. 88).

49. Kremlin Armoury, Moscow (San Diego/Kremlin 1989/90, cat. 17).

50. H. M. Queen Elizabeth II (Habsburg 1987, cat. 385).

51. Kremlin Armoury, Moscow (San Diego/Kremlin 1989/90, cat. 18).

52. FORBES Magazine Collection, New York (San Diego/Kremlin 1989/90, cat. 20).

53. Matilda Geddings Gray Foundation Collection, New Orleans (San Diego/Kremlin 1989/90, cat. 21).

54. Lillian Thomas Pratt Collection, Richmond, Virginia (Solodkoff 1984, p. 98).

55. Kremlin Armoury, Moscow (San Diego/Kremlin 1989/90, cat. 22).

56. Private collection, London (Solodkoff 1984, p. 58).

57. Lillian Thomas Pratt Collection, Richmond, Virginia (Lesley 1976, cat. 50).

58. Kremlin Armoury, Moscow (San Diego/Kremlin 1989/90, cat. 25).

59. FORBES Magazine Collection, New York (San Diego/Kremlin 1989/90, cat. 26).

60. Private collection (V&A 1977, cat. 0 8).

New Insights into Fabergé from Russian Documents

Marina Lopato

Based exclusively on archival materials, this article will illuminate the history of Fabergé from the inside. We will look at him through the eyes of his contemporaries to show how he was accepted by the Imperial Court and by the press in the capital. Numerous orders and commissions that Fabergé received both from the Imperial Family personally and from the Court officially attest to the exclusive benevolence and trust he enjoyed. Fabergé, in turn, greatly valued the Court's high esteem and sought it in every way possible because his prestige was based on it.

Carl Fabergé's activities at the Imperial Hermitage and at the Court begin in 1866. This is confirmed by documents written eighteen years later in connection with the application for the title of 'Supplier to the Imperial Court'.

28 April 1884
To His Excellency
Imperial Court Minister
Director of the Hermitage

REPORT

For 15 years the well-known local jeweller Fabergé has been voluntarily repairing various antiques, gold- and silverware, and has never refused to be an appraiser with acquisitions. He was repeatedly invited both by me and my predecessor to estimate accurately the value, quality, and price of the stones and he has also helped me in placing and removing precious objects every day for several months in a row.

Wishing to encourage Mr Fabergé for his tireless activities and enormous assistance he rendered to the Imperial Hermitage with his selfless efforts, I am honoured humbly to ask Your Excellency to apply for the Supreme permission for the title of Supplier to the Imperial Court.

Director
of the Imperial Hermitage   Vasilchikov.

To His Excellency
Prince V. I. Druzkoi-Lubezkoi

Dear Sir,
Prince Vladislav Ignatievich,

In accordance to the wish expressed by His Excellency Imperial Court Minister to present a certificate of jeweller for Fabergé's 15-year long voluntary involvement in the work of the Imperial Hermitage, I am honoured to enclose such a certificate on behalf of the Antiquities Curator Stefani. I humbly ask You, dear Sir, to apply for Mr Fabergé's well-deserved award.

Allow me to assure You, dear Sir, of my humble devotion and dedication.

A. Vasilchikov.

Regrettably, the Hermitage archives has no documents of Fabergé's official service. He must have been invited first once, then again and again, until all the officers became acquainted with him and thought of him as one of them. All of the Hermitage was very much obliged to Fabergé.

To His Excellency
Imperial Hermitage Director
His Majesty's Court Hofmeister
Aleksandr Aleksandrovich Vasilchikov

From Imperial Hermitage
Antiquities Curator
Stefani

I am honoured to direct Your Excellency's attention to the useful activities of the jeweller Fabergé, who has been working at the Imperial Hermitage for 15 years now.

First invited in 1867, at the time of Your predecessor Hofmeister S. A. Gedeonov, Mr Fabergé has since permanently participated in all technical, at times quite laborious, researches relating to numerous objects of the Hermitage archaeological collection. Thanks to his conscientious work, he could always accurately determine the quality of old materials of which many of the Hermitage objects were made, and by doing this he significantly assisted their proper cataloguing. When we received findings from the annual diggings of the Imperial Hermitage Archaeological Commission, Fabergé, as a scholar and learned jeweller, always helped me in reassembling an ever historically true item out of a multitude of broken fragments. He would spend days and days at this painstaking work, repairing broken objects, bringing them back to their original shape. Now this magnificent Ancient Greek jewellery is the glory of our Hermitage. None of this work, though, has ever been properly awarded. Never has Fabergé, in spite of the many days he gave to the Hermitage, presented a bill, and as far as I know, even now he is not listed as serving for the State.

I make bold to direct Your Excellency's attention to the extremely useful activities of Mr Fabergé, who for 15 years – to which I am a personal witness – has conscientiously served the Hermitage and make bold to apply for an award for this labourer who has been so useful for the Hermitage.

Antiquities Curator   Stefani

23 May 1884.

To His Excellency
A. A. Vasilchikov

Dear Sir, Aleksandr Aleksandrovich

I am honoured to inform Your Excellency that the Imperial Court Minister has rejected Your application of awarding the jeweller Fabergé with the title of Supplier to the Imperial Court. He suggested You should make a special application to award him, Fabergé, for the services he rendered to the Imperial Hermitage.

Allow me to assure You, dear Sir, of my humble devotion and dedication.

V. Jurgens.[1]

So the first attempt of an application for the title 'Supplier to the Imperial Court' for Fabergé brought no result. A year later, however, the Cabinet resumed its efforts.

The CASE of the Imperial Court Ministry Chancellery
on granting the 'Supplier to the Imperial Court'
title to St. Petersburg merchant jeweller Carl Fabergé.

His Majesty's Cabinet has three Appraisers permanently employed. They have a priority in selling to the Cabinet objects needed by the Cabinet and also making such objects out of the Cabinet materials for stock.

Independent of the above mentioned Appraisers, the Cabinet

purchases precious objects from the jeweller Fabergé, who is also commissioned to produce for the Cabinet stock.

For 19 years, since 1866, the Cabinet has purchased from the jeweller Fabergé precious objects valued at 47,249 roubles. The artistic execution of objects made by Fabergé by his own designs, as well as his very moderate prices, have always attracted our attention and very recently his Russian-style brooch received the Supreme approval.

Taking into consideration all of the above, as well as the fact that in September 1884 the jeweller Fabergé was invited to help the Appraisers with their work in the Commission specially formed for the acquisition of Imperial regalia and diamonds of the Crown, and for nearly five consecutive months he worked in this Commission free of charge, I am honoured to address myself to Your Excellency with an application of granting the jeweller Fabergé the title of 'Supplier to the Imperial Court' with the right of bearing the State coat of arms in his shop's sign.

Note – According to the rules existing at the Imperial Court Ministry the State Coat of Arms is granted to:
1. Cabinet Appraisers upon appointment.
2. Persons who have been supplying the Imperial Court for no less than 10 years.

The Cabinet State Secretary   N. Petrov
24 April 1885

St. Petersburg 2d Guild Merchant
Carl Gustavovich Fabergé
Store at 18 (Kononov House) Bolshaya Morskaya
The store has existed since 1840.
St. Petersburg   To Ober-Hofmarshall
1 May 1885

His Majesty the Emperor has granted his Supreme permission to St. Petersburg 2d Guild Merchant jeweller Carl Fabergé, with a store at 18 Bolshaya Morskaya, to bear the title Supplier to the Imperial Court with the right to bear the State Coat of Arms in his shop's sign.

I am honoured to inform Your Excellency of this Supreme will, which has already been reported to the St. Petersburg City Authorities.

Imperial Court Minister   Count Vorontsov-Dashkov[2]

These documents shed new light on Fabergé's early period in that they verify when and in what capacity he started working at the Court. The very favourable appraisal given to him by the high officials at the Imperial Hermitage is further evidence of his unique skill, conscientiousness, and industriousness. While working with old objects he mastered restorer's skills and was able to uncover the techniques and artistry of the jewellers of the past. It was not by chance that he was called 'learned jeweller'. Besides, at last we can clarify whether he himself worked as a jeweller. These materials testify that he designed and made jewellery, and was quite successful at it. Willing to earn the Court's good graces, or probably through his innate modesty, Fabergé, according to the Antiquities Curator Stefani, presented no bill to the Hermitage throughout all these years. The Cabinet, at the same time, quite willingly enjoyed his services, especially since his prices were always 'very moderate'.

In the early 1880s Fabergé was receiving wide public recognition, the striking proof of which was his success at the 1882 Pan-Russian Industrial Exhibition in Moscow. *Niva*, one of the most popular magazines of the time, dedicated an article to Fabergé (fig. 1). Interestingly, contemporaries perceived him as 'a discoverer of a new era' in jewellery.

Among the jewellery makers there is a man who made it a point to bring the business back to its lofty stand. We mean the well-known St. Petersburg jeweller Fabergé. Willing to elucidate the style of jewellery *objets d'art*, to impart them with artistry, Mr Fabergé addressed himself to a classic source of art and beauty – to Ancient Greece and its images. He had a lot to draw from – being the Imperial Hermitage jeweller he received permission to copy the best of the Ancient Greek art they have there. . . .

Mr Fabergé has been able to reproduce Greek art. Right now his showcase at the Exhibition in Moscow displays a multitude of excellent samples. In addition to various small pieces – bracelets, earrings, and rings – general attention is quite deservedly attracted by two full sets. Especially remarkable is the one whose original dates back to the era of Pericles. Looking at it one can make judgements of the Greek goldsmiths' work about 2 thousand years before our time. The work is marked with such delicacy that only when viewed through a magnifying glass does it disclose all its virtues. Seven masters worked for 120 days to make just one necklace. One master would have had to work for no less than 2 years and 4 months. This explains the price of the necklace: 3,100 roubles; and earrings: 400 roubles. Looking at the earrings among other things, we saw a few

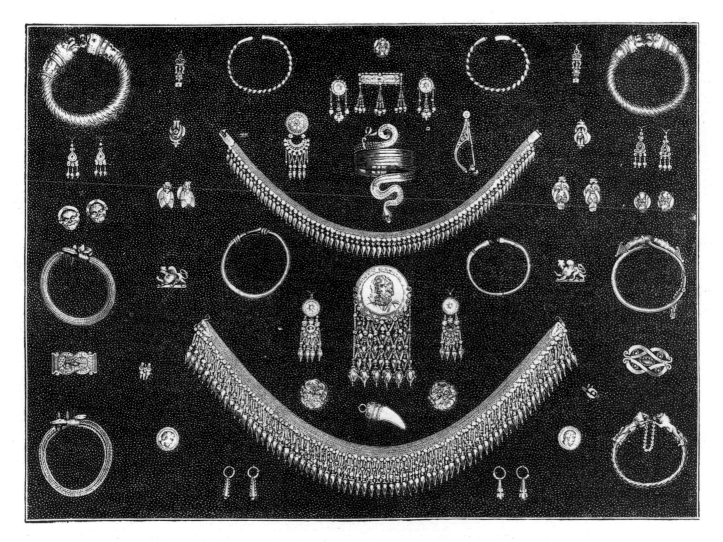

Московс. Промышл.-Худож. Выставка. Ювелирныя изделія К. Фаберже, копіи съ древнегреческихъ золотыхъ изделій (400 л. до Р. Х.) найденныхъ въ Керчи, въ Крыму и находящ. въ Эрмитажѣ въ СПБ. Съ фотогр. грав. Гельштейнъ.

dots on top of one of the ornamental figures; a magnifying glass showed that each of these dots consisted of three small 'bombs' of granulation. People did not have magnifying glasses at that time, so one should believe that their masters must have had extraordinary eyesight.

As we see, Mr Fabergé opens a new era in the art of jewellery. We wish him all the best in his efforts to bring back into the realm of art what once used to be a part of it.

We hope that from now on, thanks to our renowned jeweller, the value of the objects will be measured not only by the value of the precious stones, not by wealth alone, but by their artistic form as well.

One cannot, however, ignore the fact that Fabergé's showcase abounds with stones: among others, Cape diamonds (up to $23\frac{3}{4}$ carat) as well as stones from India and Brazil. A special rarity, though, is a remarkable sample of a Siberian stone that was given the name Alexandrite to honour the deceased Emperor. The stone was discovered not more than 20 years ago and up to this point only small samples were found. The new stone is valued much higher than Peruvian emerald. It has a dark olive-green colour in daylight and shines red in the evening. Mr Fabergé set it into a ring priced at 2,000 roubles.

Apart from their high artistic value and archaeological interest, the Kerch gold finds are characterised with astonishing technical execution. Amongst them are objects which we are unable to imitate in spite of all the perfection of our instruments; they seem impossible to manufacture without auxiliary optic devices. Fabergé, whose workshop has existed since 1842, has been able in 12 years to train enough workers so that under his guidance they could make this collection of copies for the Moscow Exhibition, a collection which attracted everybody's attention and was lauded by Their Majesties. Her Majesty honoured Fabergé by buying a pair of cuff-links with images of cicadas which, according to Ancient Greek belief, bring luck.[5]

The article makes it clear that Fabergé's creations were seen as *objets d'art*, unlike most of the other mass-produced jewellery that was filling the gold and diamond stores. Moreover, his work was interpreted as innovative. He was moving along those trends of historicism that were being actively worked out in the West at the time. In this case the style was Neo-Greek, one of the so-called archaeological styles. And last but not least, the journalist's words support the general opinion of Fabergé objects as being technically perfect. This opinion was quite widespread in the last decades of the firm's existence. Fabergé, however, always cared about quality no less than he did about artistic integrity.

The magazine review makes another important remark: Fabergé's collection was lauded by Their Majesties, and one of the items was even purchased by the Empress, who, by doing so, demonstrated her good disposition. And although by that time Fabergé had, for more than fifteen years, been associated with the Imperial Hermitage and had been supplying his objects to the Imperial Cabinet, and his name had obviously been known to the Imperial Family, the gesture was a nearly official recognition of Fabergé as Court Jeweller.

The magazine *Illustrirovannoye Opisanie Vserossijskoi Khudozhestvennoi Vystavki* (Illustrated Catalogue of the Pan-Russian Industrial Exhibition) lists other items exhibited by Fabergé. 'Especially good is a hibiscus flower priced at 8,500 roubles: around a large yellow diamond there are flower petals made out of tiny pink diamonds; among other things striking with their exquisite ornamentation are: a necklace, a diamond set of flowers, a parure with opals, a *sévie* out of various stones and a leaf brooch'. On 15 May 1883, Fabergé was awarded for this collection a Gold Medal to be worn on a St. Stanislas ribbon.

From about that time on, Fabergé received more and more commissions from the Court, especially since the Imperial Cabinet needed to increase its stock of precious objects because of Alexander III's Coronation. The Cabinet account books list Fabergé objects more and more frequently: chest crosses, brooches, golden objects, 'diamond rings with the date of Their Majesties' Coronation'. Until the fall of the Empire, Fabergé would invariably be involved in every major event at the Court. For the occasion of transporting Alexander III's body from Livadia (in the Crimea) to Petersburg, he made a *chiffre* with Alexander III's monogram and Imperial Crown, and ten other items. In 1896, preparing for Nicholas II and Alexandra Feodorovna's Coronation, Fabergé created about 150 various objects, from bracelets and brooches to crosses and snuff-boxes, and he was awarded the Order of St. Stanislas, 2d class, for this work. By that time he had long held official status at the Court. Since 1885 he had been 'Supplier to the Imperial Court', and in 1890 he became H&HM Cabinet Appraiser, a position that gave Fabergé priority in obtaining commissions.

Starting in 1890 the number of his commissions grew rapidly. That year the Cabinet was preparing for the upcoming trip of the Heir to the Crown Tsarevich Nicholas Alexandrovich to the Far East on the cruiser *Pamiat Azova*. This was an important diplomatic mission, during which time he visited a number of states in the South Pacific, and it obviously required a multitude of gifts of varying levels. In the course of the trip more objects were sent to the cruiser since the stock was being rapidly depleted. The Cabinet therefore had to turn repeatedly to the jewellery makers. The final accounts of the trip were made by the Cabinet only in 1896.

Fabergé was one of the main recipients of the orders. He made his objects from materials supplied by the Cabinet as well as drawn from his own sources. In addition to six diamond-set snuff-boxes made from their own supplies, the Cabinet selected two more snuff-boxes, two panagias with emeralds and aquamarines, two bracelets with emeralds and diamonds, seventeen silver cigarette cases with golden eagles, various diamond-set buttons, cuff-links, pins, and three brooches – altogether about 15,500 roubles worth of objects.[4]

Producing objects intended to become diplomatic gifts was to become an important part of Fabergé's work. In 1894 the Turkish Sultan was presented with a large watercolour portrait of the Tsar that was then placed in a silver frame made by the firm in the Louis XVI style.[5] Four years later a jardinière with figurines, four vases, and a diamond-set nephrite *kovsh* were fabricated for the same Sultan.[6] In 1900, for the twenty-fifth anniversary of his reign, the Sultan was given 'the Cabinet stock griffin with a clock and a photograph of His Imperial Majesty, set by jeweller Fabergé with diamonds, rubies and roses, and valued at 2,500 roubles'.[7]

Three years earlier, in 1897, the ship *Kostroma* arrived in Nagasaki with gifts from the Russian Tsar for the Emperor and Empress of Japan. All the objects were made by Fabergé. The trunks contained a 'Neptune' punch-bowl, two candelabra, a jade griffin with a clock, a presentation dish, a set of 'antique' dishes, a cabaret that included a tray with twelve *tcharki* and decanter, a nephrite casket, and a Louis XV gold and *moiré* pink enamel hand mirror. In transport the jade griffin was broken and sent back to St. Petersburg. As a substitute Fabergé made a Renaissance agate vase in a gilded frame for the same price of 3,000 roubles.[8]

In the same year, 1897, the Cabinet ordered presents for the Chinese Emperor and his Court. Fabergé offered six diadems with a price range from one to ten thousand roubles (four of

these were rejected), a crystal bowl with an engraved silver cockerel, three silver vases with crystal insertions, two crystal decanters, and a plateau. In addition he suggested five, small gold-and-stone scent bottles and a hat-pin set with a diamond, a ruby, and diamond roses.[9]

One day in 1898, Empress Alexandra Feodorovna invited Fabergé to appraise the objects presented to her by the wife of the Chinese Ambassador Liu Yu. As a reciprocal gift she ordered from Fabergé two five-light candelabra shaped as rose-buds and decorated with ruby-eyed dragons.[10]

Quite an extensive bill was presented by Fabergé to the Cabinet following the visit in 1897 of President Félix Faure of France. Among other objects the bill listed a 'red enamel diamond-set snuff-box with a miniature of His Majesty', a snuff-box with H.I.M.'s monogram, an eagle cup, and a writing desk set.[11] Gifts as nearly as great in value were presented to His Majesty the Emir of Bukhara in 1913: a nephrite cigarette case with a diamond-set, crowned cypher 'N II' and a silver clock with a Dmitri statuette.[12]

No less of a problem for the Cabinet were the endless foreign trips undertaken by Imperial Family members. Some of them were diplomatic missions that demanded serious preparation from the Cabinet. The Cabinet required a seemingly endless stock of precious objects for the nearly annual trips of Empress Maria Feodorovna to Copenhagen and London, for summer vacations of the whole family in Livadia, in the Crimea, in the Finnish skerries, or in French or German resorts. Germany was most frequently visited by Their Imperial Majesties. The files related to the Emperor and Empress' trips to Darmstadt in 1896 and 1897 have been preserved. For these trips Nicholas II personally selected two nephrite vases of 900 roubles each and a jug with gilded coins for 700 roubles, which were to become race prizes. At about the same time nephrite vases were presented to Lord Pembroke and Sir Arthur Binet [Paget] and a paperknife for 600 roubles for Lord Edward Clipton [?].[13] In 1897 the servants and the court of the Duke of Mecklenburg-Schwerin were presented with twenty-seven Fabergé objects.[14] Fourteen Fabergé items were bought especially for a trip to Berlin in 1913. Imperial Chancellor von Bethmann-Hollweg received a silver box costing 1,200 roubles.[15] During his trip to Japan in 1915, Grand Duke Georgi Mikhailovich presented Count Terauci [?], the Korean Governor-General, with a gold cigarette case.[16] In 1916, for Grand Duke Boris Vladimirovich's trip to Persia, the Cabinet 'released various precious objects', including items by Fabergé. Silver *kovshi* with the State coat of arms were given to Princess Faer ad Doule [Abdul?], the Shah's aunt, to Mullah Shariat Zadeh of Resht [?], and to Mirza Khan, Chief of the Russian Department at the Foreign Ministry.

To implement Your Majesty's Supreme order of 3 November, gifts were sent to Tiflis to His Imperial Highness Boris Vladimirovich, to be presented to His Majesty, the Shah and to the Heir of the Persian Throne: a large Old Russian style engraved silver vase, priced at 6,500 roubles, made by Fabergé, for the Shah; and a nephrite beaker with a mounting of precious stones made by the same jeweller and valued at 3,200 roubles.[17]

Unfortunately, the Cabinet files relating to private trips by members of the Imperial Family do not always contain information as to the recipients of particular objects. More information does exist on their domestic trips. Not infrequently in this case, the files contain complete lists of addresses, with the name of the object next to the name of the recipient. These range from servants to local railroad officials, to police or gendarmerie officers. Sometimes, however, more significant figures are found as well. Records relating to His Majesty's trip to Livadia in 1914, for example, indicate that Victoria Louise, Duchess of Braunschweig, received an aquamarine-and-diamond brooch in commemoration of her child's baptism.[18] On the same occasion Princess Elena of Serbia, mother of newborn Prince Vsevolod Ioannovich, was presented with a pendant brooch set with diamonds and an aquamarine, worth 1,475 roubles, nearly twice as much as the previous one.[19]

Fabergé was involved in making presents both for the baptism of Grand Duchess Irene Aleksandrovna and for her wedding, as well as for the wedding of the Grand Duke of Hessen-Darmstadt and Princess Victoria, and for the wedding of Grand Duchess Xenia Aleksandrovna and Grand Duke Aleksandr Mikhailovich. In fact, all facets of Imperial Family life – from births to burials, with their festivities, receptions, travels, griefs, and joys – are reflected in the Cabinet records and filed jewellers' bills.

The Tercentenary of the Romanov House in 1913 resulted in numerous orders for Fabergé. The invoices reveal that the work consisted of a multitude of uniform items rather than intricate, complicated, unique objects. The thick folder entitled 'On Orders to Jewellers and Others, of Precious Objects, Mitres and Miniatures; and also On Alteration of the Cabinet Stock Objects' has files of bills with long lists of cuff-links, brooches, tie-pins, pendants, and cigarette cases.[20] They were all meant for official presents, since they all were decorated with Romanov griffins, eagles, or Monomakh crowns. In addition Fabergé made twenty badges with the inscription 'For accompanying the Emperor's train'. A special order was placed for V. V. Andreev's Grand Russian Orchestra musicians 'who played on 5 May this year at the Tsarskoe Selo Palace for the Emperor: 47 tie-pins with Tercentenary emblems from the jeweller Fabergé, 25 roubles a piece and 8 pins with balalaikas from the Morozov Trade House, 30 roubles a piece'.[21] Also, '12 pairs of cuff-links from the Cabinet stock, 135 pins from the jeweller Fabergé (25 roubles a piece) and 43 brooches from the jeweller Fabergé (25 roubles a piece) for a musical concert at the Supreme banquet on 21 May this year at the Kremlin Palace in Moscow'.[22] The brooches were made of gold with rose diamonds and decorated with Monomakh crowns. The pins had the Monomakh crown and Romanov griffins. And of course, there were frames, cups, and *kovshi* with eagles and Imperial Crowns – the usual array of items for officialdom.

In the meantime, the Imperial Family's private life was following its routine and little seemed to interrupt its flow. Nothing could stop Maria Feodorovna from her annual trips to Copenhagen and London. In the 1890s, apart from various jewellery items, Fabergé's bills list more and more silverware and hardstone objects. In 1893 the following was sent to Copenhagen (the numbers in front are the firm's inventory numbers):

N46413. Varicoloured enamel bracelet, 225 roubles; N35159 Bracelet, 340 roubles; N46504 Diamond ship brooch, 315 roubles; Steel enamel brooch, 170 roubles; Nephrite elephant, 75 roubles; N398 *Bonbonnière* with a coin, 54 roubles; N43931 *Kovsh* with a coin, 95 roubles; Mushroom, 55 roubles; N44429 Little tray with a coin, 75 roubles; N348 Kovsh with a coin, 45 roubles; Cup with an eagle, 400 roubles; N275 Bears cabaret, 1200 roubles; Two eagle jugs, 600 roubles; Jade elephant, 550 roubles.[23]

A few objects from this list evoke associations with Fabergé objects known through catalogues. Some of the following items were presented during the trip of HIH Tsarevich Nicholas to London in 1894: Lord Sheffield, Equerry of the Prince of Wales, received a silver helmet valued at 700 roubles; Sir John Probin, Chamberlain of the Prince of Wales, was presented with a bratina for the same price; Mr Douglas, the Prince's yacht navigator, was given a match holder valued at 75 roubles; and Sir Bradford, a London police officer, received a glass and a cup valued at 175 roubles.[24]

One of the special features of the Fabergé business was that it combined two, in fact different, trades. On the one hand the firm produced jewellery with precious stones, enamels, and objects of vertu: snuff-boxes, *bonbonnières*, cigarette cases, and various baubles. On the other hand it fabricated a lot of silverware, including sets, services, vases, bowls, and prize cups. The firm's growing activity in this direction is reflected in the documents of the 1890s and 1900s. The Hermitage archives have a bill with a list of 'Louis XVI silverware (88 *zolotnik*) made by the jeweller Fabergé in 1894 at the order of the deceased Emperor Alexander III for the now reigning Emperor Nicholas II with the monogram N.A. and a crown'.[25] The service included a footed flower vase and stand, four circular fruit vases, four candelabra with fifteen lights each, four *bonbonnières*, eight champagne coolers, and eight *compotières*. In the early 1900s a vase for champagne, a meat-dish cover, a saucepan for hazel grouse, soup bowls, and a soup tureen were brought from the Anichkov Palace to the Winter Palace. All these objects must have come from the same Nicholas Alexandrovich service. Baron Foelkersam, in his *Opisi Serebra Dvora Imperatorskogo Velichestva* (Catalogue of Silver in His Imperial Majesty's Court), mentions that the Hermitage Treasury had a large, gilded banquet service and various table decorations as well as objects from Anichkov Palace and a signed silver clock.[26]

It is known that Fabergé, as a rule, made his objects for the Court following 'designs which had received the Supreme approval'. A few of these designs have been preserved in the Hermitage. Among them are some objects from an Empire-style service with swans and sphinxes, a large Louis XVI *surtout de table* with the monogram 'O.A.', and a large rococo *surtout de table* with the same monogram. These must be the designs and services mentioned in the folder entitled 'Service made by Fabergé priced at 50,000 roubles' for Grand Duchess Olga

Aleksandrovna's wedding. The file contains documents relating to two Fabergé services: '29 pieces of 88 percent silver Louis XVI service (707 pounds, 93 zol.)'. It was ordered by the deceased Emperor Alexander III and made by Fabergé for 50,000 roubles. The service includes a flower vase, 4 candelabra, 4 fruit vases, 8 *bonbonnières*, 4 *compotières* and 8 champagne vases'. This description best fits the service made in 1894 for the wedding of Grand Duchess Xenia Aleksandrovna. A similar service, at the same price, was made in 1908 for the wedding of Grand Duchess Olga Alexandrovna: 'The Supreme Order to Fabergé for a dinner service. The design must be presented for preliminary approval. [Signed] Baron Frederiechs'. The presented drawings were 'acknowledged by Empress Maria Feodorovna to be not attractive. Upon Her return from Denmark she will give Her instructions according to which the jeweller Fabergé will have to make these designs'. The bill presented by Fabergé stated: 'Engraved Louis XVI Surtout de table with the monogram O.A. Oxide. Cost: 50,000 roubles'.[27]

If, by the mid-1880s, Fabergé had executed commissions for less than 10,000 roubles, then twenty-five years later this sum had grown substantially. By way of comparison, his competitor Bolin had, in 1886, 30,000 roubles worth of orders from the Imperial Cabinet. The growth of Fabergé's importance to the Court is traceable through brief records of the Chamber Department of His Majesty's Cabinet in 1914.

The Cabinet storehouses had 2,164,679 roubles 86 kopecks worth of objects by 1.1.1914 and 2,069,032 roubles 67 $\frac{7}{8}$ kopecks worth by 1.1.1915. Including 10,443 precious objects with an overall value of 1,504,864 roubles 50 kopecks; 81,985 roubles 78 $\frac{7}{8}$ kopecks worth of gems; 2,737 stone items with an overall value of 480,542 roubles 39 kopecks; 3 furs valued at 1650 roubles.... The considerable increase of the number of precious objects in stock (from 526,994 roubles 27 kopecks to 1,504,665 roubles 52 kopecks) was caused by intensive purchases from 1909 to 1913. In 1909 alone the Cabinet ordered from its various suppliers objects which had received previous Supreme approval: from the jeweller Bolin for 40,000 roubles, from the jeweller Ivanov for 45,000 roubles and from the jeweller Fabergé for 120,000 roubles.[28]

Obviously, by the end of his career Fabergé became the Court's leading supplier, overtaking the major trade houses of Bolin, Ivanov, and Morozov.

While searching through the archives for bits and pieces of information on Fabergé and his career at the Court, we found a whole file that contained chronological information on the famous jeweller's activities. On 16 October 1910, Eugène Fabergé applied to the Court Ministry with a request to grant Carl Fabergé, Supplier to His Imperial Majesty's Court, the title of 'Jeweller to the Court'. The petition was first considered on 12 November and a month later a positive answer was received.[29]

To His Excellency, Head of
the Chamber Department of
His Imperial Majesty's
Cabinet

REPORT

The Carl Fabergé firm was founded in 1842 by Gustav Petrovich Fabergé. Carl Gustavovich joined the business in 1864 and in 1872 took it over. Through Carl Gustavovich's energy and artistic taste the firm has, especially in the last 25 years, considerably expanded.

The firm exhibited its products at the 1882 Pan-Russian Exhibition in Moscow and was awarded a Gold Medal.

On 1 May 1885 Carl Gustavovich was awarded the title of 'Supplier to the Imperial Court'. The same year he took part in the Art and Industry Exhibition in Nuremberg where he also received a Gold Medal and a very favourable response. The 1888 Art and Industry Exhibition in Copenhagen also brought him a Gold Medal.

In 1887 Fabergé opened a branch and soon a factory in Moscow with 200 workers. The St. Petersburg and Moscow branches together employ 500 workers, which makes the firm the biggest in its field in Russia and one of the biggest in the world.

On 29 August 1890 Carl Gustavovich Fabergé was appointed Appraiser of His Imperial Majesty's Cabinet and on 1 November 1890 he was granted Hereditary Honorary Citizenship.

In 1896 the firm took part in the Pan-Russian Exhibition in Nizhny Novgorod and was awarded the State Coat Of Arms (State Emblem). In 1897 the firm took part in the Nordic Exhibition in Stockholm where Fabergé was granted the title 'Jeweller to the Court of His Majesty, the King of Sweden and Norway', which was recently confirmed by King Gustav V of Sweden.

In 1900 the firm had a major display at the *Exposition Universelle* in Paris where Carl Gustavovich was elected a member of the Jury. The French Government awarded him with the Cross of the *Legion d'Honneur*. To date he has received no award from the Russian Government.

In the same year, 1900, a branch in Odessa was opened.

Since 1901, by means of a number of commercial trips, the firm extended its sales to London and in 1903 a store was opened in London. The business there grows every year. All of the British Royal House are among the firm's regular customers. The Dowager Queen and the reigning King and Queen personally visit the store.

Since autumn 1908 the firm has ventured a number of commercial trips outside Europe, mostly in Asia: India, China and Siam. In Siam we were the first Russian trading company.

Carl Gustavovich Fabergé is privileged to have for many years been a supplier to Their Imperial Majesties. He is repeatedly invited for personal negotiations.

The Carl Fabergé firm is also privileged to list among its clients many foreign Royalty: the King and the Queen of Great Britain, the King and the Queen of Italy, the King and the Queen of Greece, the King of Spain, the Tsar of Bulgaria (in 1902 the Tsar, then Prince, Ferdinand awarded Fabergé with the Commanders Cross for Civilian Services; His Highness expressed a most favourable estimate of the artistic activities and aesthetic taste of Carl Gustavovich), the German Crown Princess, the King of Sweden, the King of Norway, the Heir to the Austro-Hungarian Throne et al.

Carl Gustavovich Fabergé never sought awards or distinctions but was nevertheless awarded with Gold Medals and Orders: the Order of St. Stanislas, 3d class on 25 February 1889; the Order of St. Anne, 3d class on 5 April 1892; the Order of St. Stanislas, 2d class on 20 June 1896. The latter was granted to him after His Majesty's Coronation and since then, that is for nearly 15 years, he has received no awards or distinctions, except for the title of 'Manufacturing Councillor', which was granted to him on 1 January 1910 at the request of his four sons.

It was only recently that I found out that the title of 'Supplier to the Imperial Court' is not identical with the title of 'Jeweller to the Court'. Therefore, taking into consideration all of the above and mainly the fact that C.G. Fabergé has already indeed for long been the Jeweller to the Imperial Court, having a personal relationship with Their Imperial Majesties, I am honoured to address myself to Your Excellency and humbly request that the title 'Jeweller to the Court' be awarded to Carl Gustavovich Fabergé.

On behalf of myself and my brothers Agathon, Alexander, and Nicholas Fabergé

Eugène Carlovich Fabergé.

The brothers also enclosed information on themselves.

Eugène Carlovich Fabergé
was born in May 1874 and joined his father's business in 1894.
Member of the Jury at the Nordic Exhibition in Stockholm in 1897. In
1898 served as an Expert for the appraisal of the Crown gems with
V.V. Sipiagin, the Head of Chamber Department.

In 1900, during the *Exposition Universelle* in Paris, the French
Government awarded him with the rank and badge of an Officer of
the Académie. In the summer of 1902 Prince Ferdinand of Bulgaria
personally awarded him the 'Chevalier Cross, Order of St. Alexander'.

He repeatedly fulfilled Their Imperial Majesties and Highnesses'
commissions and was invited for appraisals to His Majesty's Cabinet.
Agathon Carlovich Fabergé was born in January 1876, joined his
father's business in May 1895. At the *Exposition Universelle* in Paris in
1900, Agathon was awarded a Gold Medal from the French
Government.

In 1908 he served as an Expert for the appraisal of the Crown gems.
He repeatedly fulfilled Their Imperial Majesties and Highnesses'
commissions.

He was invited to appraise the deceased Grand Duke Aleksei
Aleksandrovich's collections of precious objects and permanently
worked as an Expert in the Imperial Hermitage Jewellery Gallery.

In view of the more than 15 years of very productive activities of E.
and A. Fabergé, it seems appropriate to apply for Imperial awards for
the brothers Eugène and Agathon Fabergé.

His Majesty's Cabinet.
The Imperial Court Hofmeister
Novoselski
12 November 1910

Having acquired the title 'Jeweller to the Court', Fabergé
reached the highest point of his Court career. Apart from his
talents as an artist and businessman, Fabergé had another
special gift: a sense for and an understanding of people. This
significantly aided him in selecting artists, designers, and
masters for the firm and in understanding the demands and
tastes of his high-ranking clientele. Prone as she was to
exaltation, the Empress often called him 'sweet Fabergé' and
even during the war, in a cable to her husband at Stavka, she
remembers her jeweller in the following way: 'Fabergé has just
brought your adorable egg for which I thank you a thousand
times. The miniatures are wonderful and all the portraits are
excellent. Alix'.

Figure 2. Installation photograph of the exhibition *Artistic Objects and Miniatures by Fabergé*, which took place at the von Dervise House in March 1902.

Figure 3. Installation photograph of the exhibition *Artistic Objects and Miniatures by Fabergé*. In the background is a clock presented by members of the Imperial House to Maria Feodorovna and Alexander III on their twenty-fifth wedding anniversary (cat. 4). On the mantelpiece is a silver set which belonged to Grand Duchess Xenia Aleksandrovna.

Fabergé was recognized as a European-level jeweller during the 1900 *Exposition Universelle* in Paris. His fame reached its pinnacle at home when the famous exhibition entitled *Artistic Objects and Miniatures by Fabergé*, sponsored by Empress Alexandra Feodorovna, was opened in March 1902 (fig. 2).

Novoye Vremya, a St. Petersburg newspaper, in its review of the exhibition at the von Dervise House on the English Embankment, had as many compliments for Fabergé as it had ecstatic listings of the high-ranking visitors.

Today, Friday, 8 March, at 4 pm, at the von Dervise House on the English Embankment, Her Imperial Majesty Empress Alexandra Feodorovna and Their Imperial Highnesses Grand Duchesses Maria Pavlovna, Elizaveta Feodorovna, Maria Georgievna, Grand Duchess Elena Vladimirovna and Grand Duke Georgi Mikhailovich previewed an exhibition of artistic objects, ancient miniatures and snuff-boxes by Fabergé which is due to open tomorrow.

The exhibition, held for the Imperial Women's Patriotic Society Schools, features precious art objects belonging to Their Imperial Majesties, the Emperor and Empress, and other members of the Imperial House.

The exhibition has been held under the auspices of Her Imperial Majesty, Empress Alexandra Feodorovna. The objects exhibited are of interest to the public if only because they are not to be seen at any other time and they are all art masterpieces. One room has been dedicated exclusively to Their Majesties' objects.

Among the exhibits here is a silver swan, presented to the Imperial Family on the day of their Imperial Majesties' wedding, a rare collection of miniature portraits of the Russian Emperors and other members of the Imperial Family, a silver mantelpiece clock with diamond-set hands, presented to the deceased Emperor Alexander III and Empress Maria Feodorovna by Members of the Imperial Family for the 25th Anniversary of Their Majesties' wedding; and a collection of Easter eggs belonging to Their Majesties, Empresses Maria Feodorovna and Alexandra Feodorovna [fig. 3]. Alexandra Feodorovna's collection has an egg with a concealed miniature spray of lilies-of-the-valley enclosed in moss. The lilies-of-the-valley are made of pearls, with nephrite leaves; the moss is woven out of the finest gold thread. Another egg has a whole miniature golden train of the Trans-Siberian Railroad inside. One of the train cars is an exact replica of the church car. A portrait of the Emperor by Mr Benkendorf is also excellent. Among the precious artistic objects belonging to Empress Maria Feodorovna, a carved nephrite statuette of a Chinese man with ruby eyes and ruby belt stands out.

Beautiful objects were made for the Imperial Hermitage and exhibited at the *Exposition Universelle* in Paris: a pearls and gems flower basket, a rose egg with pearls, a gold mounted album with rubies, a clock, and a fan. Miniature crowns of their Majesties and the Monomakh Crown are exact replicas of the Imperial Regalia.

Another room and part of the main hall exhibits jewellery of the Grand Duchesses Maria Pavlovna, Elizaveta Feodorovna, Aleksandra Iosifovna, Elizaveta Mavrikievna, Maria Georgievna, Xenia Aleksandrovna, Olga Aleksandrovna and Elena Georgievna, Grand Duchess of Saxe-Altenburg, and luxury items from the collection of Grand Dukes Vladimir Aleksandrovich, Kirill Vladimirovich, Aleksei Aleksandrovich, Sergei Aleksandrovich, Konstantin Konstantinovich, Nikolai Nikolaievich, and Georgi Mikhailovich.

Among the nobility and aristocracy exhibiting their objects here are the Vice-Chairwoman of the Women's Patriotic Society, Empress Alexandra Feodorovna's Hofmeisterin Princess Galitsin (a miniature collection), Countess Vorontsov-Dashkov; Princess Yusupov, Countess Sumarokov-Elston; the wives of: Ober Hofmarshall, (Princess Dolgoruki); Ober-Hofmeister (Mrs Vsevolzhski); Countesses Heiden and Sheremetev; the wife of French Ambassador Marquess de Montebello; Mrs Durnovo, Mrs Polovtsev, Mrs Hall, Mrs Von Etter; Countesses Orlov-Davydov and Benkendorf, Princesses Kurakin and Vassilchikov, Princes Orlov and Odoievski-Maslov, and others.

Novoye Vremya, 9 March 1902

A second article, which appeared the next day, further described the exhibition.

A ceremonial opening of an exhibition of artistic objects by Fabergé, ancient miniatures and snuff-boxes, belonging to the members of the Imperial Family and private persons took place today at 2½ hours at the von Dervise House (on the English Embankment). The exhibition is a benefit for the Schools of the Women's Patriotic Society.

At about three Their Imperial Majesties, the Emperor, Empresses Maria Feodorovna and Alexandra Feodorovna, Their Imperial Highnesses the Heir, Grand Dukes Vladimir Aleksandrovich with his daughter Grand Duchess Elena Vladimirovna, Andrei Vladimirovich, Aleksei Aleksandrovich, Sergei Aleksandrovich with his wife Grand Duchess Elizaveta Feodorovna, Grand Duchess Elizaveta Mavrikievna, Grand Dukes: Nikolai Nikolaievich, Mikhail Nikolaievich, Georgi Mikhailovich with his wife Grand Duchess Maria Georgievna, Grand Duchesses: Xenia Aleksandrovna, Olga Aleksandrovna with her husband Prince Oldenburg, Petr Aleksandrovich and Elena Georgievna, Princess of Saxe-Altenburg, Duchess of Saxony. Many foreign Ambassadors and diplomatic representatives, Court and St. Petersburg aristocracy were also present at the opening ceremony.

After examining all the exhibits Their Majesties and Their

Highnesses proceeded to the buffet where the charity sales were conducted by Princesses Orlov, Cantacuzene and Beloselski-Belozerski, Mrs Voieikov, Countess Kleinmichel, Mr Voieikov and Mr Knorring. Here the members of the Imperial Family were treated with champagne and at about four they left the Exhibition.

Yesterday we already described the most important objects belonging to Their Majesties and Their Highnesses. One can add that among these objects there are miniature gold replicas of the Coronation Coach and a steam yacht. The objects which stand out in the Empress Maria Feodorovna's collection are a group of miniature family portraits of the Emperor, Empress Alexandra Feodorovna, the Imperial sons and daughters and the grandchildren of Her Majesty Empress Maria Feodorovna. The miniatures are enclosed in a heart-shaped frame of precious stones propped on a stand. Each portrait, which is less than a silver five-kopeck coin in size, is covered by a ruby [?]. In the wonderful collection of Easter eggs is an egg with miniature portraits of the Imperial Family. Another egg has a diamond pelican, the Empress Maria's emblem, on top, and screens with miniature images of all the institutions the Empress is patronising inside. Yet another gold egg has a model of Gatchina Palace, the Empress's winter residence. Notable in the Imperial Heir's collection are a compass and a watch. Grand Duke Vladimir Aleksandrovich's and Grand Duchess Maria Pavlovna's showcase features a gold *kovsh*-shaped bratina with precious stones and images of various animals. Among the objects belonging to Grand Duchess Elizaveta Feodorovna are an exquisite gold fan with images of spring and a sumptuous vase with precious stone flowers. Of Grand Duchess Aleksandra Iosifovna's objects, especially remarkable is a swan of pearls and diamonds.

A miniature portrait with an à la Greuze small head catches one's eye in Grand Duke Georgi Mikhailovich's and Grand Duchess Maria Georgievna's showcase. Grand Duchess Xenia Aleksandrovna's objects, including a magnificent silver service with Empire vases, are all in the first room. An artistically made fan painted by Solomko is the gem of Grand Duchess Olga Aleksandrovna's collection.

In the same first room one showcase was given to the miniatures of Elena Georgievna, Princess of Saxe-Altenburg, Duchess of Saxony. A plenitude of objects belonging to various Grand Dukes and Duchesses fill the room. Especially remarkable is Princess Yusupov's collection of snuff-boxes and miniatures. One of them is a sapphire mouse with ruby eyes and diamond tail. Many beautiful objects are in the collections of Duke N.M. Leuchtenberg, General Durnovo, Count Fersen, and others.

That the exhibition was a success was obvious already on opening day when 3,000 roubles in entrance fees were collected. Tomorrow and until 14 March the entrance fee is 1 rouble 10 kopecks.

Novoye Vremya, 10 March 1902

Р. С. Ф. С. Р.

ЗАМЕСТИТЕЛЬ

ОСОБОУПОЛНОМОЧЕННОГО

ВЕТА НАРОДНЫХ КОМИССАРОВ
по
УЧЕТУ И СОСРЕДОТОЧЕНИЮ
ЦЕННОСТЕЙ

3 июля 1922 года

№ 1403

г. Москва, Тверская ,
Настасинский, 3.

Тел. 2-69-96.

К о п и я. -

М А Н Д А Т.

Дан сей эксперту Гохрана Агафону

Карловичу ФАБЕРЖЕ в том, что он команди-

руется в г.Петроград для участия в рабо-

тах по экспертизе изъятых из Петрогр. му-

зеев ценностей.

Работу предлагается проводить под

руководством и в контакте с Директором

Эрмитажа тов. ТРОЙНИЦКИМ и представите-

лем Особоуполномоченного Совнаркома тов.

ПРИВОРОТСКИМ.

Изложенное подписями и приложением

печати удостоверяется . -

Подлинный подписали:

ЗАМОСОБОУПОЛНОМОЧЕННОГО
СОВНАРКОМА: Базилевич

Секретарь : Соболев

С подлинным верно :

Figure 4. Mandate given to the State
Guard expert Agathon Fabergé.

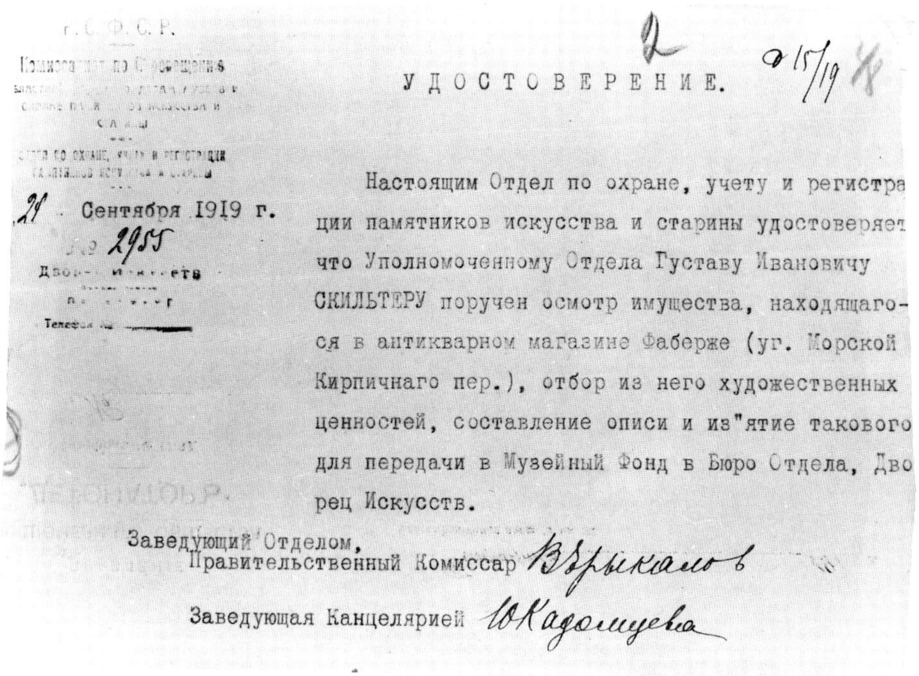

Figure 5. Certificate issued on 21 September 1919 to G. I. Skilter, a representative of the Department for Preservation, Recording, and Registration of Objects of Art and Antiques, authorising him to examine and select objects at the antique shop of Agathon Fabergé on Bolshaya Morskaya Street.

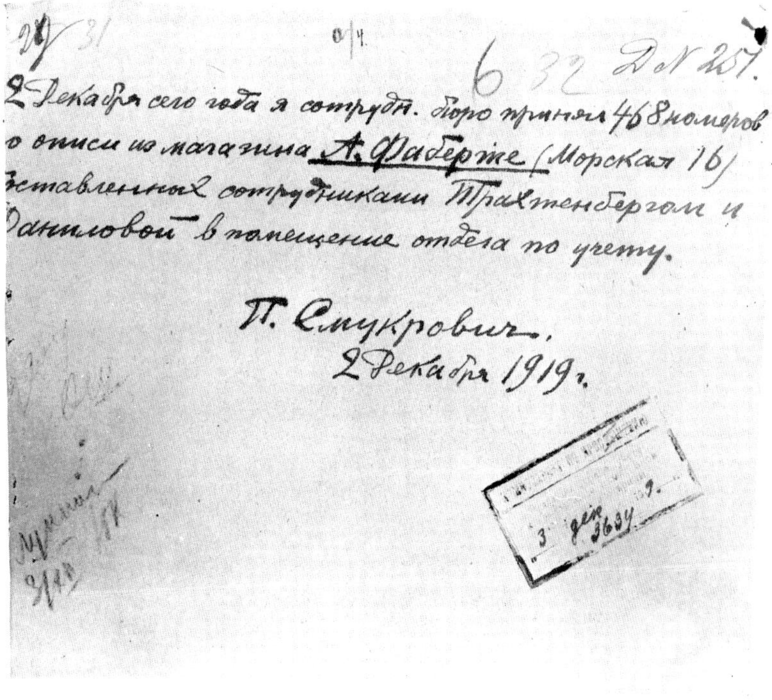

Figure 6. This document concerns the transfer of objects from Agathon Fabergé's shop to the Museum Fund.

No less admiration was expressed in the *Niva* magazine review.

The exhibition, although squeezed into a very limited space, features so many riches, so many marvellous, extraordinarily artistic objects that one would not know where to fix one's glance. . . . The last room and part of the last but one are full of the works of art belonging to the Imperial Family. It is difficult to imagine anything more spectacular and at the same time exquisite. . . .

Of special interest are the two showcases with objects belonging to Their Majesties Empresses Maria Feodorovna and Alexandra Feodorovna. Most of the items in these showcases are precious Easter eggs by the jeweller Fabergé: one of them has a superbly executed gold replica of the Gatchina Palace, no more than a *vershok* [4.45 cm] high. Very original looking are the folding eggs with albums of miniature portraits of the Imperial Family and images of the Patriotic and Pavel Institutes. . . .

The same room has larger objects belonging to the members of the Imperial Family: a huge silver swan and a mantelpiece silver clock with a diamond cypher on top of it and diamond hands. The clock is surrounded by silver cast *putti*.

Quite a few exhibited objects belong to the Grand Duchesses: how beautiful are the miniature hardstone animals from the collection of HH Grand Duchess Xenia Aleksandrovna! Charming is the fan made by the artist Solomko and belonging to Grand Duchess Olga Aleksandrovna.

Niva, no. 12 (1902), p. 234

By the 1900s Fabergé had acquired not only wealth but also substantial standing in society. He had become a respected authority in his professional milieu. Fabergé was interested in art education, and in 1903 he organized a competition for members of the Russian Society of Art and Industry, of which he was one of the founders. In 1912 the Society held a 'Court Jeweller Carl Fabergé Competition'. One of the winners was Franz Birbaum. Many prominent artists and architects collaborated on his projects and designs, including F. Schechtel, K. Schmidt, I. Galnbeck, E. Malyshev, G. Savitski, and V. Vasnetsov, as well as many others who were well known in their time but whose names are less familiar today.

Carl's sons socialized with collectors, lawyers, and professors. Unlike their somewhat shy father, they were refined aesthetes, ever surrounded by antiques and books, and travelling both in Europe and in the Orient. They represented a new generation, and backed by their father's wealth and reputation, they felt very self-assured.

Figure 7. Inventory of items from the collection of Carl Fabergé, 24 Bolshaya Morskaya Street, for transfer to the Museum Fund.

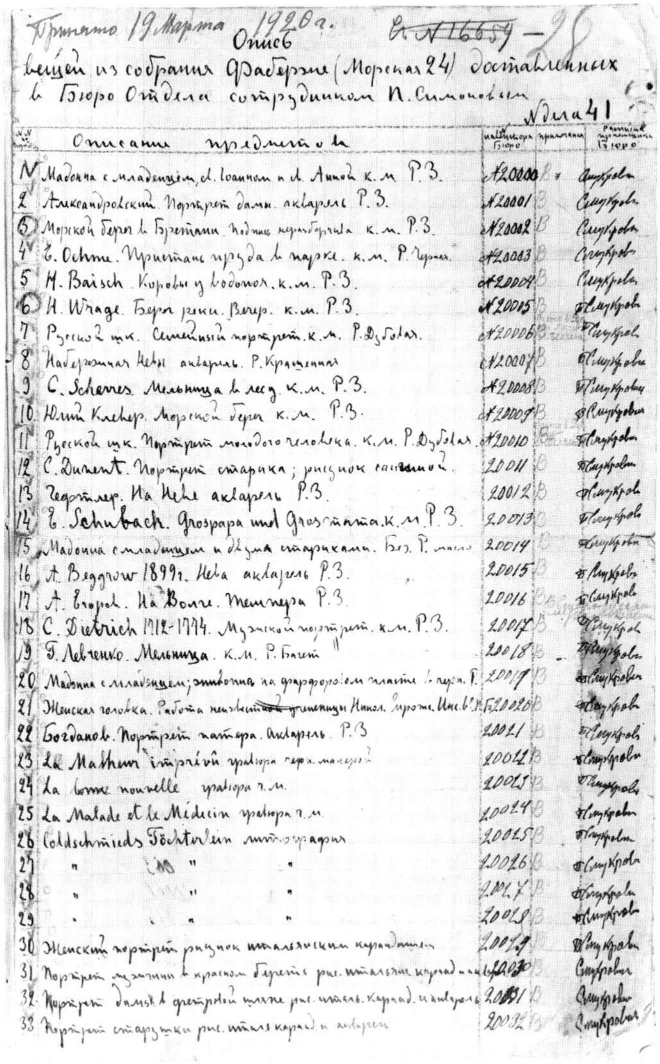

Thanks to the newly accessible archival sources much is known of Fabergé and his firm. Yet the firm's history still conceals a number of secrets (fig. 4). One of the documents of the Petrograd Commune in March 1919 has it that 'the owners of the firm fled, having hidden the documents and the instruments'. How true is this? In November of the same year, nine carts with Fabergé collections, including two trunks with the archives, were brought to the Hermitage (figs. 5–7). We do not know what happened to the trunks. They might have found their way into the storages of the Extraordinary Commission (*Cheka*), which was later transformed into the People's Commissariat of the Interior (NKVD). Even today these two abbreviations evoke morbid associations. Or the archives of the Court Jeweller might have been demolished as having no historical or cultural value for future generations, that is, for us.

1. Russian State Historical Archive (RSHA; formerly The Central State Historic Archive [CSHA]) f. 472 op. 38 del. 7 pp. 41–44.
2. Ibid., del. 38 pp. 1–5.
3. *Niva*, no. 40 (1882), pp. 952–54.
4. RSHA f. 468 op. 7 del. 414.
5. Ibid., op. 8 del. 148.
6. Ibid., del. 326.
7. Ibid., del. 414.
8. Ibid., del. 283.
9. Ibid., del. 275.
10. Ibid., del. 295.
11. Ibid., del. 290.
12. Ibid., del. 1336.
13. Ibid., del. 246.
14. Ibid., del. 282.
15. Ibid., del. 1343.
16. Ibid., del. 1391.
17. Ibid., del. 1400 pp. 12, 13.
18. Ibid., del. 1367.
19. Ibid., del. 1358.
20. Ibid., del. 1334.
21. Ibid., del. 1345.
22. Ibid.
23. Ibid., del. 101 p. 7.
24. Ibid., del. 150 p. 7.
25. State Hermitage Archive, f. 1 op. V, 1908, del. 46 p. 38.
26. Baron A. E. Foelkersam, *Opisi Serebra Dvora Ego Imperatorskogo Velichestva* (St. Petersburg, 1907), pp. 615, 719. Foelkersam mistakenly identifies the name of the sculptor as Aulert instead of Aubert.
27. RSHA f. 468 op. 8 del. 648.
28. Ibid., op. 44 del. 1394 pp. 1, 3.
29. Ibid., f. 472 op. 43 del. 130.

A Few Remarks Regarding Imperial Easter Eggs

Marina Lopato

Every Fabergé scholar has tried to add to the study of Fabergé's Imperial Easter eggs and to fill in the gaps in our knowledge. I would like to offer a few remarks, primarily concerning the first Imperial Easter eggs, in order to correct some existing inaccuracies.

It is generally accepted that the first Easter egg was created in 1885 on the order of Alexander III, a gold-and-white enamel egg containing a golden hen, now in the FORBES Magazine Collection in New York. A careful reading of the relevant record,[1] however, reveals inconsistencies between the record and the Forbes egg. The record reads: 'white enamel egg in a crown, decorated with rubies, diamonds and rose-cut diamonds'. The firm's invoices and the Imperial Cabinet's account books, which register payments, normally never fail to mention the surprise inside each egg or to indicate another characteristic or peculiarity. Yet the record concerning the 1885 Easter egg lists all the details, except the hen. At the same time, the records for the 1886 Easter present, which were usually documented by the date of the next year, lists nothing but a 'hen picking a sapphire egg out of the basket'. Fabergé's invoice, however, describes the same item as a hen and a sapphire (fig. 1). Neither of these descriptions tallies with the Forbes egg. This author would like to suggest that the extant list is incomplete.

There is no apparent reason why N. Petrov, the Head of the Chamber Department and the Chief of the Cabinet, began his entries in 1889, a few years after the first egg was created, nor does he mention that the 1885 egg was the very first one made. Petrov writes laconically, 'Her Imperial Majesty's gifts for the Holy Easter . . . made in 1885 . . .' and continues until 1889 (fig. 2). (The 1889 Easter egg was as yet unknown since the entry is dated 8 February, that is, before Easter.)

It is not to be excluded that Fabergé produced a first Imperial Easter egg on his own without an explicit order from the Cabinet. This might explain why Petrov remembered and mentioned only those that were officially registered in the Cabinet's account books. These are suppositions only, which have not been confirmed by any documentary evidence. If we assume that Fabergé made his first Imperial Easter egg a year previous to Petrov's accounting (i.e., in 1884), then each egg that is preserved, or recorded by Petrov, would fit into its own niche.

1. Lopato 1991, pp. 91–94.

Figure 1. Invoice of 2 April 1886 sent by
Fabergé to H.I.M. Cabinet for the golden
hen that was intended as an Easter present
to Maria Feodorovna.

The artist's development would then have been the following: After the 1884 copy of an eighteenth-century model (the naturalistic egg in the Forbes collection) comes a second, equally plain white egg made for Easter 1885, embellished with precious stones as described by Petrov. With the third egg of 1886, the master rejected the formula of the white egg as such, which limited possibilities of search for an appropriate shape, and added a semblance of action in that a hen picks up an egg from the basket. Thereupon follows the transition from the hen-egg type to more complicated compositions. The 1887 Easter gift is described as 'an Easter egg with a clock set with diamonds, sapphires, and rose-cut diamonds', which is normally associated with the Blue Serpent Clock egg (H.S.H. Prince Rainier of Monaco). However, neither the indicated price of 2,160 roubles (normally objects of this type with such rich decoration cost more than 6,000 roubles) nor the style of the object corresponds to such an early date.

For 1888, the records list an egg: 'Angel pulling a chariot with an egg'; 'Angel with a clock in a golden egg'. That is, the clock is in the golden egg mounted on the chariot. As we see, the composition here is more complex. There is no record for an 1889 egg, but the Resurrection egg would fit into this niche as one of the early Imperial Easter eggs characterised by simple ideas and equally simple, straightforward imagery of the kind associated with children's toys made by a jeweller rather than with jewellery objects.

A breakthrough did not occur until 1890 when Fabergé made a 'gold egg of pink enamel, in the style of Louis XVI' (according to his invoice to the Cabinet). Judging by this brief description, it was a jewelled object that contained no surprise. It was only the shape that pointed to the fact that it is an Easter egg.

In this author's opinion, the privately owned 'Ribbed blue enamel egg' and the Forbes Spring Flowers egg dated 1890 (or 'before 1899') should not be included amongst the Imperial eggs since they bear inventory numbers. None of the other Imperial Easter eggs was given an inventory number by the firm for obvious reasons.

Unfortunately, the documentary evidence, which we usually tend to trust implicitly, sometimes adds a certain confusion, as in the case of the Uspensky Cathedral egg dated 1904. A copy of the original Fabergé invoice preserved in the documents of the

Imperial Court Ministry is dated 7 June 1906. In the same manner, the Love Trophy egg is dated by a copy of an invoice for the Imperial Easter egg of 21 April 1907, although it seems to be identical with an egg described by Franz Birbaum in his memoirs: 'In the year when the Heir was born the egg resembled a cradle, decorated with garlands of flowers with the first portrait of the Heir in a diamond-set medallion inside'. (The Tsarevich Alexei was born on 30 July 1904, which means that the egg was made for Easter 1905.) To complicate matters, the Fabergé invoice of 21 April 1907 speaks of a 'miniature of the Imperial children'. The miniature of the portrait of the Tsarevich is mentioned in the same copy of the invoice as being contained in a different Easter egg of green enamel with wreaths of roses (Rose Trellis egg). Birbaum's memory probably confused the two Easter eggs.

There are other cases where documentary evidence contradicts itself. For instance, inventory lists of the Kremlin Armoury, Moscow, say that the so-called Egg with Revolving Miniatures was presented to Tsarina Alexandra Feodorovna in 1895, while other sources mention the date of 1896. To make things more complex, there are two other eggs known to have been made for the Easter of 1896 and both are dated with great confidence. It is necessary to remind the reader that Nicholas II commissioned two such souvenirs for each Easter – one was intended for his mother, the other for his wife.

No less strange is the case of an egg described in a Fabergé invoice as 'gold egg Empire with 9 miniatures'. This must be the egg known as the Pelican egg, which has eight miniatures and an engraved date of 1897. But the 1897 invoice is for two other eggs: the Forbes Coronation egg (cat. 110), which is also dated, and 'the egg of mauve enamel with 3 miniatures', for which the surprise might well be the Forbes Heart Surprise frame (cat. 22). In such cases we might have to accept that there were years when Fabergé produced three eggs.

If we are to base our knowledge on dated Easter eggs – and they are the only precise criteria available – we notice that invoices can be a year or even two later. To be more precise, we are talking about the copies of invoices which Fabergé used to give to the Business Department of the Ministry of the Court regarding the objects for which he never received payment. Some of the copies, though, refer to the Easter eggs dated the same year as the invoice.

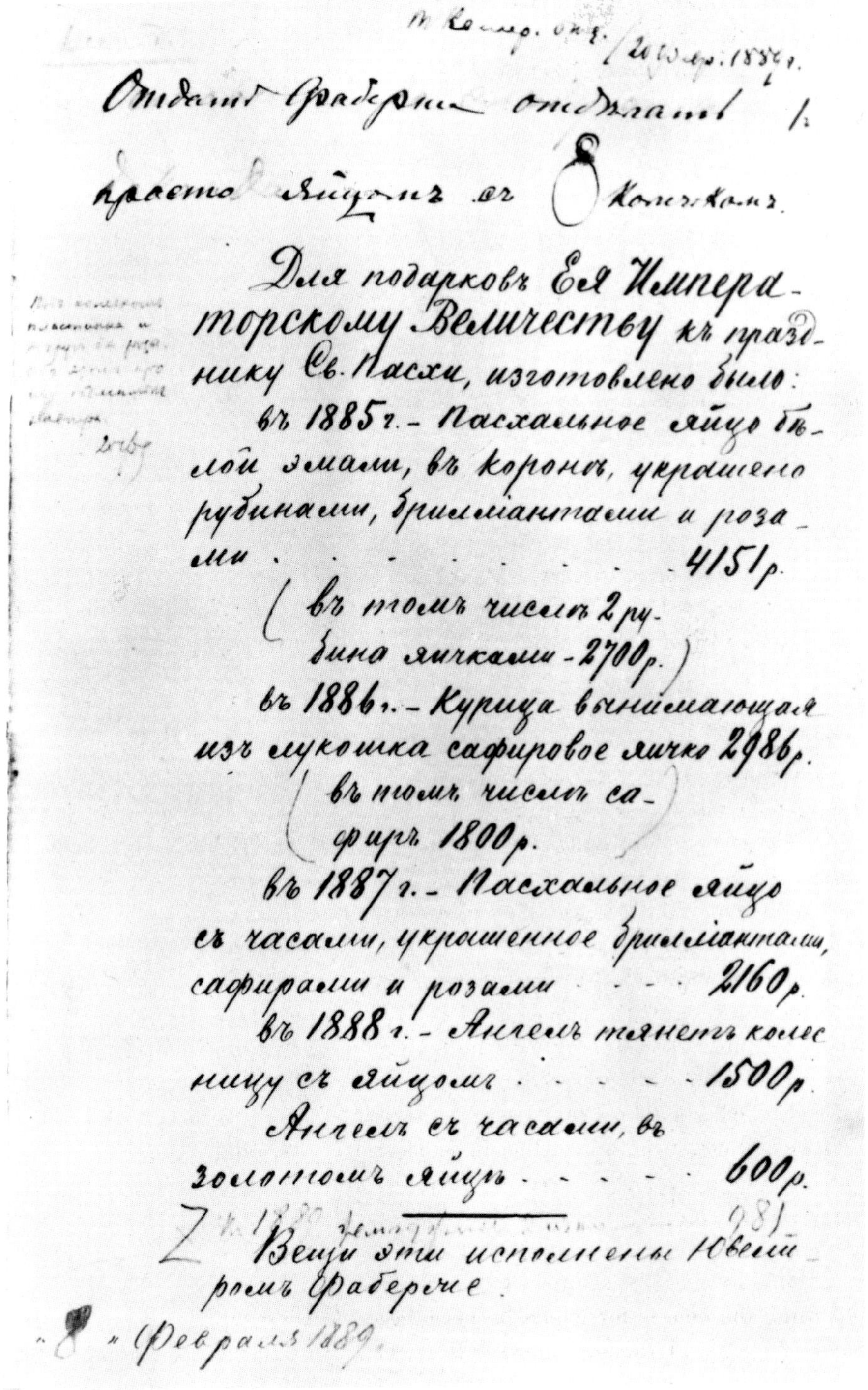

Отдать Фаберже отделать
простое яичко съ [рисунок яйца] колечкомъ.

Для подарковъ Ея Импера-
торскому Величеству къ празд-
нику Св. Пасхи, изготовлено было:

въ 1885 г. — Пасхальное яйцо бѣ-
лой эмали, въ коронѣ, украшено
рубинами, бриллиантами и розами . . . . 4151 р.

(въ томъ числѣ 2 ру-
бина яичками - 2700 р.)

въ 1886 г. — Курица вынимающая
изъ лукошка сафировое яичко 2986 р.

(въ томъ числѣ са-
фиръ 1800 р.)

въ 1887 г. — Пасхальное яйцо
съ часами, украшенное бриллiантами,
сафирами и розами . . . . 2160 р.

въ 1888 г. — Ангелъ тянетъ колес-
ницу съ яйцомъ . . . . . 1500 р.

Ангелъ съ часами, въ
золотомъ яйцѣ . . . . . 600 р.

981

Вещи эти исполнены Ювели-
ромъ Фаберже.

8 Февраля 1889.

Figure 2. Note by State Secretary
N. Petrov regarding the first Easter eggs,
which the Tsar commissioned Fabergé to
produce as presents to Maria Feodorovna.

Imperial Easter Eggs: A Technical Study

Carol Aiken

Figure 1. The interior of the top of the Fifteenth Anniversary egg (cat. 30). Tabs around the openings in the shell secure the miniature paintings which are mounted from the inside. FORBES Magazine Collection.

Figure 2. The eggshell and trellis cagework of the Fifteenth Anniversary egg. FORBES Magazine Collection.

Throughout his full range of work, Fabergé skillfully combined a diverse array of materials. Although the methods and techniques that achieved the combinations are not usually apparent, they are among the primary features that distinguish the creations of Fabergé from those of his contemporaries. Joins were rarely soldered when mechanical fasteners could be employed. Metal tabs, slender pins, and threaded shanks with small nuts were used routinely to unite the apparently seamless facades of the most complex Fabergé assemblies.

Objects assembled with pins and tabs could be disassembled, if necessary, for maintenance or to correct damages. Whether or not disassembly was an intentional feature, it provided assurance that all materials could be maintained to the highest standards. This, in turn, led to fewer restraints in the initial choice of materials. Fabergé delighted in combining precious materials with those of little intrinsic value. Nowhere is the combination of diverse materials used more effectively than in the Imperial Easter eggs.

Numerous books and articles describe the Easter eggs commissioned by the Imperial Family, as well as the few made for other wealthy individuals.[1] Although each egg is unique, many materials and techniques were used repeatedly in the commissioned eggs. One common thread in the creation of the commissioned eggs was a preliminary period of detailed and meticulous planning. Sketches were prepared. Discussions were held among the goldsmiths, silversmiths, enamellers,

jewellers, lapidary workers, and stone cutters who would contribute their talents to a finished creation. It is reported that some of the eggs, or at least the surprises placed within them, took years to complete.[2]

The Eggshells

The eggs aptly demonstrate Fabergé's ability to interpret, adapt, and transform historic styles into original works of art with an added dimension. More often than not, the eggs were associated with surprises contained within their shells. Access to the surprises varied. A number of the eggs are constructed in two halves that are hinged together, opening when the upper half is lifted, or in some examples, folding down when a clasp is released. When closed, many of the eggs appear impenetrable, carefully designed so that the lips between the halves are covered by decoration. Angular borders of the Rose Trellis egg and the Swan egg conform to the intersecting linear decorations on the surfaces of these eggs. The halves of the Tercentenary egg meet in gently undulating waves. The lip of the top half of the Alexander Palace egg has been precisely shaped to conform to the miniature portrait frames set in the lower half of its shell. Alternatively, prominent bezels readily indicate the divisions in the shells of many of the Easter eggs. Not every egg was made to open, however. Some surprises are displayed through transparent shells. Others emerge from closed shells, powered by key-wound mechanisms.

The enamelled shells display Fabergé's ability in *en plein* enamelling, that is, the smooth covering of comparatively large, flat surfaces. He adapted this difficult technique to the curved surfaces of the Easter eggs, preparing the gold or silver eggshells by a process of engraving known as *guilloché*. Either by hand or by machine, assorted patterns of lines were cut into the metal before the enamel was applied. Through the enamel these lines are visible as subtle decorative patterns. The lines reflect and scatter any light striking the enamel, creating a sensation of movement beneath its smoothly polished surface.

The colours of the enamelled eggshells were chosen from an extensive palette of coloured enamel.[3] Colours could be modified through a variety of techniques, including the initial choice of a gold or silver ground. During enamelling, a finely powdered vitreous pigment was applied to a metal ground and then fired at a high temperature. Each layer of the resulting glassy enamel was polished before the next layer was applied. Layers were built up, sometimes six or eight deep, until the desired richness of colour and thickness of enamel had been achieved. By varying one or two of the layers from the others, opalescent and iridescent effects could be obtained. The lustrous pink of the Duchess of Marlborough egg consists of a first layer of orange-yellow enamel on gold, followed by several layers of slightly translucent pink. Tones in the completed shell vary from a warm, transparent pink to an almost opaque mauve as light strikes its surface from different angles. The characteristic milky quality of some of the translucent enamels on other eggs, especially the white colours, was obtained by balancing mixtures of transparent and opaque enamels. Matte opaque enamel was used only once, on the shell of the mauve-colored Swan egg. Another departure from the usual techniques is found on the shell of the Cross of St. George egg, whose opalescent enamelled shell has an underpainted trellis in a laurel leaf pattern.

Unless enamel is also applied to the back of the supporting metal, uneven stresses build up during the process of enamelling. The stresses can lead to distortion of the metal support, causing subsequent cracking and loss of the enamel. To prevent this problem, a layer of contra-enamel is applied on the back of the metal support. Since it was rarely a distinguished colour, and it was never finished by polishing, the contra-enamel in the Easter eggs was not intended to be seen. Exposed interiors of the enamelled shells were usually covered with fitted velvet linings. Once in a while, however, the inner shell was given a spectacular finish. The shell of the Spring Flowers egg is lined with an insert of polished gold. Inside the Peter the Great egg is a brilliant yellow enamel on a *guilloché* ground, a difficult technical feat because the engraving, enamelling, and polishing were all carried out on a small concave surface.

Inside the Fifteenth Anniversary egg (cat. 30), the metal of the shell is covered with a pale green transparent enamel. Maker's marks are found on both halves of the egg under the contra-enamel. Red dots in the enamel designate the sites of pins used to attach separate domed ends (fig. 1). Portraits of the Imperial Family are mounted in panels of translucent oyster enamel with white enamel borders. The larger, rectangular scenes from the life of the Tsar are framed in matching white enamel borders. All the enamel fields and borders are applied

Figure 3. A detail of the Peter the Great eggshell. Swags in textured gold *à quatre-couleurs* embellish bulrush heads set with square-cut rubies on either side of the openings for miniature paintings. The Virginia Museum of Fine Arts, Lillian T. Pratt Collection.

Figure 4. A detail of the shell's interior of the Peter the Great egg. Foil covers the backs of the rubies set in the bulrush heads. Pins secure the swags as well as the enamelled banners, which provide legends for the miniature paintings. The separate bottom of the egg is secured mechanically with metal tabs. The Virginia Museum of Fine Arts, Lillian T. Pratt Collection.

directly to the egg's shell (fig. 2). Inside the shell, clean margins (without contra-enamel) surround the openings that contain the miniature paintings. Soldered to the bare metal of the margins are toothed frames that hold the paintings securely in place (fig. 1). Shaped silver backings, placed behind each painting, provide protection for the miniatures and contribute to the structural strength of the eggshell.

The Exterior Decorations

The mounts that were added to a naked shell not only determined a particular artistic or historic style but also helped create themes that introduced or reinforced the significance of the surprise within. Some of the more substantial additions to the shells, while decorative, also served as pedestals, bases, and supporting legs. The materials of the decorations were often determined by their functions.

Gilded bronze (ormolu) was used occasionally in the Easter eggs, both for its intrinsic beauty and its inherent strength, as a substitute for gold. The apparent delicateness of the stems and the more robust legs of the Lilies-of-the-Valley egg (cat. 23) are ormolu, as are the leaves that are enamelled in a transparent green. In the same egg, the sepals of the flower blossoms are of gilded silver (vermeil), which has a more lustrous surface than ormolu. Vermeil was also used to make the frames of the miniature portrait surprises that emerge from the egg.

For purely decorative effects, Fabergé frequently employed coloured golds. By combining precise proportions of pure gold

to other pure metals, colours in a range of intensities were created. The traditional yellow, green, red, and white golds, used together since the eighteenth century when the combination was known as gold *à quatre couleurs* (fig. 3), were joined in Fabergé's repertoire by the blue, orange, and grey coloured golds which were more difficult to attain.

To enhance metal surfaces, Fabergé regularly used texture, effectively combining dull or matte finishes with polished ones. Multicoloured golds with a range of textured surfaces were regularly employed in the fabrication of decorative borders, swags, and applied motifs. Striking examples of the results that could be obtained are demonstrated in the colourful and sumptuous decoration of the Serpent Clock egg. The highly embellished, smoothly polished easel that supports the heart-shaped surprise of the Pansy egg offers another stunning example of these combined techniques.

Continuous, overall decoration, usually described as cage-work, enhances a relatively large number of the eggs. Alone or combined with other features, the cages were created in a wide range of materials. Single-coloured, chased gold is used with great effectiveness on the Tercentenary egg and the Tsarevich egg. A rococo-scroll pattern in gold, set with brilliant diamonds, distinguishes the Pamiat Azova egg. A green gold trellis, with enamelled, double-headed eagles embellished with diamonds, is mounted on the yellow-green enamelled *guilloché* shell of the Coronation Coach egg (cat. 110). Cagework composed of scallops of diamonds is mounted on the deep blue enamelled surface of the Pine Cone egg. Intersecting lines of diamonds cover the bowenite shell of the Diamond Trellis egg and form a trellis on the pale green enamelled shell of the Rose Trellis egg. Woven through the diamond trellis of the latter egg are opaque light and dark pink enamel rose blooms with gold stems and green leaves. The roses are enamelled on gold that is slightly domed to provide a lush, three-dimensional blossom. The gold leaves have slightly raised veins that do not disturb the smooth surface of the enamel but do provide subtle color changes within the leaves.

The majority of surface decorations, from cagework and multicoloured gold swags to the leaves and sprays of flowers on the Lilies-of-the-Valley egg, are secured to the egg shells by small pins. These pins, soldered on the backs of the mounts, are placed through holes in the shells and then bent over, against the shell's inside surface, to hold the decorations firmly in place (fig. 4). George Stein, who made the model of the coronation coach concealed within the Coronation egg, described how the egg was completely submerged in a tank of water while the holes were being drilled through the enamelled metal shell.[4] Submersion was an extra precaution taken to protect the drill from becoming too hot and breaking or damaging the enamel surface.

The second row of diamond-set crosses on the enamelled trellis of the Fifteenth Anniversary egg are key pins with straight prongs. When the pins are removed, the egg separates into two unequal halves. The trellis is made of eight individual pieces. Six straight segments around the mid-section of the egg are combined with two cages that cover either end of the egg (fig. 2). The cages are secured with diamond-set crosses whose prongs have been bent over inside the egg. The straight trellis segments are secured with three prongs originating from the back of each segment. Garland cages constructed of straight sections were joined together with solder. These joins are visible on the inside of the baskets, but not on the superbly chased and enamelled exterior. The complexity of this decoration clearly demonstrates the need for meticulous planning in the initial stages of creating an Easter egg. It also demonstrates the richness of effect that can be realised through a combination of decorative techniques.

Figure 5. Detail of the heart-shaped surprise from the Pansy egg. Private collection, United States.

Figure 6. Detail of the mechanism inside the heart-shaped surprise from the Pansy egg. A series of springs and levers cause the openings over the miniature portraits to open in unison. Private collection, United States.

The Surprises

Among the surprises are miniature models in precious materials, pieces of jewellery, and images of people, places, and events that were important to the Imperial Family. Some surprises are displayed through the transparent shells of the eggs in which they are contained. Others are independent creations that can only be viewed or, in some cases, operated after removal from an egg. When the contents are hidden from view, it is usually necessary to open the outer shell of an egg. Hinges attach the movable portions of the shell, and the top of the egg can become a lid. The sides may become flaps that fold away, back, or down, depending on the locations of the hinges.

The covers of concealed miniatures normally have spring-loaded hinges, designed to fly gently open when a small button or catch is released. The heart-shaped frame surprise of the Pansy egg contains eleven minute but detailed miniatures, none more than 6 mm high. They are covered with individual, monogrammed covers that open in unison at the push of a ridged button on the bottom of the frame. A mechanism inside the egg is based on a simple series of levers and springs that unite the separate covers (figs. 5, 6).

Nothing was too large to be reinterpreted as a surprise and placed within an Easter egg. The Gatchina Palace and surrounding grounds, complete with trees, lamp posts, and statues, were recreated in chased and textured gold *à quatre-couleurs*. Tiny slabs of rock crystal were placed between the hollow walls of the palace to reflect light, creating an impression of real glass panes in the diminutive residence. In addition, the monument of Peter the Great, commissioned from Falconet by Catherine the Great, inspired a miniature surprise. A roughly finished sapphire represents the original 1000–ton granite base. When the lid of the Peter the Great egg is opened, the statue rises into position from the lower shell of the egg, and gently lowers as the lid is closed. The movement is controlled by a simple mechanism, engaged by opening and closing the hinged lid. A pin in the hinge controls a length of chain that is attached to a platform on four springs. When the chain is shortened, it pulls down the platform, compressing the springs so that the statue is lowered. When the chain is released, the platform rises, releasing the statue in a smooth and even upward movement (figs. 7, 8).

Figure 7. Detail of the hinge-operated lever that controls the chain which lowers the platform in the Peter the Great egg. The Virginia Museum of Fine Arts, Lillian T. Pratt Collection.

Figure 8. Detail of the springs and the tube-shaped guides under the platform in the Peter the Great egg. The Virginia Museum of Fine Arts, Lillian T. Pratt Collection.

The very simple mechanisms used on occasion were obviously designed in response to the specific needs of the eggs in which they are found. A basic geared mechanism raises and lowers the surprise inside the Lilies-of-the-Valley egg. Three miniature portraits – of Tsar Nicholas II and his two eldest daughters, Olga and Tatiana – rise out of the egg. When fully engaged, the counterweighted miniature frames assume a fan shape, so that each portrait is visible. The Imperial crown that surmounts the Tsar's portrait becomes the finial on top of the closed egg when the pictures are hidden inside. The geared mechanism that raises and lowers the miniatures 'floats' in the

Figure 9. The mechanism that raises and lowers the miniature portrait surprises in the Lilies-of-the-Valley egg (cat. 23). FORBES Magazine Collection.

bottom of the egg, supported by an ovid-shaped cradle that forms the framework for the gears. The contours of the cradle conform to the inner surface of the egg. A shank connects the controlling knob outside the shell to the mechanism within, but the mechanism itself is not attached to the egg's shell. The rectangular bezel that is visible at the lip of the top opening through which the surprise emerges caps a deep internal 'chimney'. The chimney guides the surprise, helping to maintain the proper alignment of the pictures (fig. 9).

Several of the eggs contain clocks. The movements are wound with keys, which are generally inserted in holes in the backs of the eggshells. One exception is the chased gold knob that winds the clock in the Duchess of Marlborough egg. The movement is engraved with the name Hy. Moser & Cie. It was made by the firm of Henry Moser & Cie, a Swiss company that normally supplied the movements for Fabergé clocks.[5] Several Easter eggs have clocks with a horizontal band of numerals that rotates past a fixed point to indicate the hour. On both the Duchess of Marlborough egg and the Serpent Clock egg, this point is the arrow-shaped tongue of a snake coiled around the base of the clock. The Chanticleer egg and the Cuckoo Clock egg both contain clocks with traditional round dials, and they both conceal animated birds that emerge from the top to crow or sing on the hour. The Orange Tree egg also holds a small bird with lovely iridescent feathers and an ivory beak. When the bird emerges from the top of the tree and begins to sing, the mechanism concealed in the foliage below causes the beak to open and close while the head moves back and forth, effectively imitating lifelike movements.

Perhaps the most famous of the moving surprises is the Coronation coach, a miniature replica, 9.3 cm long, recreating in gold and enamel the coach used in the 1896 Coronation proceedings of Nicholas II and his wife (cat. 369). Details were faithfully copied from the original vehicle. Curtains were engraved directly on rock crystal windows. The decorated door handles, smaller than grains of rice, turn to latch and unlatch the doors. When the doors are open, a pair of folding steps can be let down. The coach is suspended on movable straps that swing as freely as did the leather originals, so that the body of the coach sways on the chassis as the coach rolls forward.

The most intricate, articulated surprises are powered by key-wound mechanisms. Several of these were inspired by life-size eighteenth-century Swiss automatons, but the model train in the Trans-Siberian Railway egg is a faithful copy of the actual engine and its cars of the Trans-Siberian Express. A working model, the hinged train folds section by section into a velvet-lined compartment inside the egg. On the shell, the map of the rail route and a three-sided heraldic eagle finial allude to the surprise inside. In the best tradition of the Fabergé Easter eggs, this egg and its surprise are representative of a group of unique objects that unfailingly delight the eye, please the mind, and speak to the heart.

1. Among the publications with the most comprehensive descriptions and illustrations of Imperial and non-Imperial Easter eggs are Snowman 1962–64, Solodkoff 1984, Habsburg 1987, and San Diego/Kremlin 1989.
2. Details of the Coronation coach and the peacock are discussed in Solodkoff 1988, p. 30, and Snowman 1953, pp. 72 and 87.
3. Snowman 1953, colorplate III. One of the original charts showing colours of enamel and *guilloché* patterns on small numbered silver squares is illustrated.
4. Ibid., p. 56.
5. Cf. Solodkoff 1988, pp. 98–99, for a discussion of the association between Moser & Cie and Fabergé.

New Light
on the Workshop of
Henrik Wigström

Ulla Tillander-Godenhielm

with the assistance of Michael Wynne-Ellis

There we all stood, silent, with aching hearts, looking at the empty workshop around us. It was like being at a funeral, as though we had lost a close and dearly loved relative.[1]

This is how the young journeyman engraver Jalmari Haikonen described the last moments at the Fabergé workshop in Petrograd after the Bolsheviks had ordered its closure in early 1918. These poignant words by one of the craftsmen working for this legendary company may well express the feelings of his employer, the accomplished and dedicated Henrik Wigström, workmaster of the House of Fabergé.

Henrik Wigström had come to St. Petersburg in 1878 and six years later went to work for M. E. Perkhin, Fabergé's workmaster and head of the company's goldsmiths department. So great was Perkhin's faith in the talented Wigström that he bequeathed the workshop to him rather than to his own son. When Perkhin died in 1903, the workshop passed into the possession of Wigström (fig. 1).

In 1918, prevented from carrying on his business and unwilling to remain in the troubled capital, Wigström returned with his family (fig. 2) to his native land, to Ollila, Kivennapa, in Finnish Karelia, where he had his *résidence secondaire*. As this was a fully furnished dacha, there was little need to take more than the bare essentials with him.[2]

Remembrances of times past
Among the essentials, however, Wigström packed an album of photographs of close friends and relatives, and another folio-sized volume bound in half-leather. This contained almost a thousand illustrated drawings of *objets d'art et de fantaisie*, from eggs to jewellery, made between 1911 and 1916 in his workshop at the House of Fabergé.

What persuaded Wigström to take the stock book with him? Glancing through the pages today one realises that it is a superb record of some of the finest items from Fabergé's prime. Was it just for the memories it contained, or did Wigström perhaps dream of returning? Or did it contain another, more personal association, one that has yet to be discovered?

Whatever the case, a few years after his return Wigström gave the book to a close friend and neighbour.[3] These were difficult times in Finland for repatriates from St. Petersburg. Relations with the Soviet Union were anything but friendly, so

1. Henrik Wigström, St. Petersburg, *c.* 1900.

2. Wigström's children, St. Petersburg, *c.* 1900.

3. A gilded silver and red enamel box with incurvate sides (cat. 263) shown next to the drawing of the piece on page 211 of Wigström's book.

people talking about their former life and work in Russia were treated with suspicion. In exile, Wigström became taciturn and retiring, living quietly at Ollila until his death in 1923. Enforced inactivity obviously weighed heavily upon someone as creative and energetic as Wigström, so perhaps it was frustration that drove him to give the book away.

Now, seventy years later, we can be very grateful that this book of drawings found pride of place on the neighbour's bookshelf. Surprisingly, its owner never thought of showing it to anyone, especially in view of the tremendous publicity surrounding the name of Fabergé during the past two decades.

The book also provides a valuable complement to the stock and sketch-books of Albert Holmström, hitherto the only documentary record from a Fabergé workshop in existence. A. Kenneth Snowman had the good fortune to discover Holmström's books in 1986 and has since published a number of informative articles about them.[4] These have greatly added to our understanding of how the House of Fabergé operated at the workshop level, and they have thrown much new light on the company's production. Due to its similarity, the Wigström book offers an important new source of material from another Fabergé workshop.

The workshop of August Holmström and his son Albert produced most of Fabergé's jewellery. Mikhail Perkhin's workshop – and from 1903 on, Henrik Wigström's workshop – concentrated on objects of function and fantasy, and only to a lesser extent on jewellery. As shall be seen, however, these workshops were never strict compartments, for they produced each others' specialties whenever necessary. In any hierarchy of the Fabergé workshops, that of Perkhin/Wigström certainly came first, for it was there that the most demanding commissions, such as the Imperial eggs, were made. Perkhin, after all, was the chief master goldsmith of the company and under Wigström, Fabergé experienced its most rapid period of growth and expansion.

The purpose of the book
A dynamic and progressive workshop such as Wigström's, which crafted a wide variety of objects, required good pictures of models to which to refer in the course of manufacture. And if those pictures were arranged systematically, they would serve as a first-class reference work. Nowadays, cameras and copying

machines serve this purpose, but in St. Petersburg at the turn of the century they were still laboriously sketched by hand on the basis of the artist's original drawings.

In Wigström's stock book, objects have been classified by type, starting with perfume bottles and finishing with photograph frames and writing utensils. Each item has been carefully drawn in full scale and then coloured. The few explanatory notes concern technique, materials, or ornamentation. Exceptions, such as a handful of platinum objects, have been appended with pencilled notes. Objects made from hardstone occasionally have a note next to them specifying the material, i.e., nephrite, rhodonite, and so on. What is more interesting, however, is that all hardstone objects have been marked with a code indicating the cost of the lapidary's work. So far that code remains a mystery.

The Holmström books contain detailed information on the metals, gems, and the hours and cost of labour involved, most of which is missing from Wigström's book. This would indicate that the book's main purpose was to serve as a production tool or guide. Such a reference work would be of little use without a numbering or dating system. Beneath each drawing is a five-digit production number and the date when the piece was finished.

This production number, however, should not be confused with the inventory number, which was scratched on each piece as it was entered into the records. Mr Paul Schaffer has been able to verify this on the basis of a number of extant objects, one of which is the gilded silver and red enamel table box (fig. 3) illustrated on page 211 of the stock book. This carries the production number 13175 and was finished on 25 September 1912.[5] The actual piece, which was produced for the English market, has the inventory number 22683 scratched on it.

Another such piece is the large nephrite *kovsh* (fig. 4) illustrated on page 263, the gold handle of which is decorated with classical motifs flanked by two caryatids. It is numbered 13379 and price coded *zdy* (the cost of the lapidary's work on the nephrite). Following its completion (19 December 1912), the piece was sent down for pricing and entering into the records. Only then was the inventory number 23166 scratched on this magnificent item.

Perhaps Wigström's book was just one in a series used in the workshop, but we have yet to discover how many there were

4. Nephrite kovsh with a gold handle decorated with classical motifs on an opalescent white enamel background. L: 23.5 cm, W: 12.1 cm. Initials of Wigström, assay marks of St. Petersburg 1908–1917, inv. 23166, London import marks for 1912. Shown against page 263 of Wigström's book.

5. Plan and profile drawing on page 259 of a large, gold-mounted oval *guilloché* enamel dish with moss agate centre standing on chased gold feet. The rim chased with leaf tips suggests an alternative decoration. Production number 13014, dated 27 April 1912. L: 17 cm.

6. A selection of cane handles on page 67. Two amusing knobs carved in chalcedony are in the middle row – one of two bears cuddling and another of a dragon (cf. Habsburg 1987, cat. 273, for the possible original in the State Hermitage, St. Petersburg).

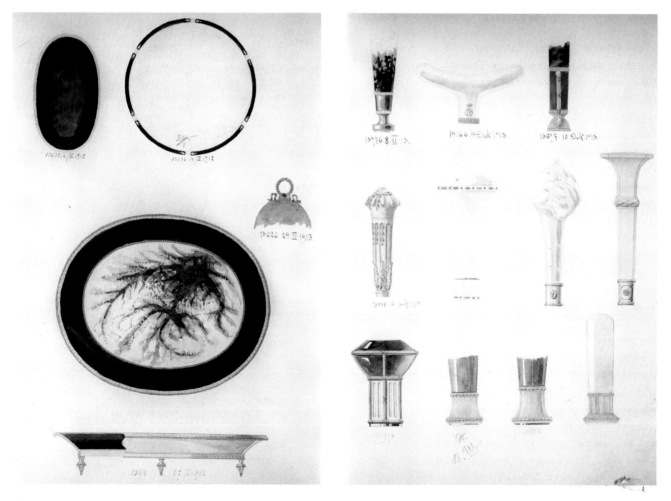

and the logic behind the order of sketches. When handling this massive tome (it measures 43 × 31 cm and weighs 4.2 kg), certain practical questions come to mind. If it was just one volume in a series, why does it not have an identifying number or a title on the spine? Imagine taking down from the shelf one hefty volume after another whilst searching for the right one! So possibly it was the first of its kind, the ambitious start to a new record of production, which ultimately proved too elaborate and time consuming. This assumption is supported by the fact that the book still exists. Why otherwise would Wigström – or perhaps his daughter Lyyli or son Henrik Wilhelm – have taken the book unless it had some very special meaning?

There is nothing particularly unusual about the book. It is an ordinary, half-leather book with brown cloth sides, purchased in St. Petersburg from the stationers Otto Kirchner, whose printed stamp still appears on the inside cover. Its heavy white pages have been numbered from 1 to 400. Sketches are on the right-hand side pages only, arranged according to article type, with several blank pages in between for later additions. The dates of the pieces illustrated, which run from January 1911 to 1916, are not in chronological order, and the majority fall within the years 1911 to 1913.

The production numbers run from 10109, for a small nephrite *kovsh* finished 16 May 1911, to 15604, for a lorgnette, drawn in pencil but not coloured, dated 1916. No sequence is evident in the production numbering, but this should not cause undue worry since the number was assigned when the piece was being planned.[6] Gaps also occur in the numbering, which adds to the general confusion as to the book's purpose. More time is required to study this question because, after all, the book only came to light a few months ago, in the spring of 1992.

The drawing technique
Objects have been drawn in their natural sizes, and an effort has been taken to produce a pleasing composition on most pages. It would appear that some pages were drawn at the same time, whilst others have been filled over a longer period. The pieces have been drawn in pencil and nearly all of them coloured in watercolours. Anyone familiar with Fabergé's work cannot fail to be delighted with the accuracy of these drawings.

Each item is well defined, and even the pattern of an engine-turned surface can readily be identified. The ornamentation is also easily recognisable, whether it be an applied band of laurel leaves, a *guirlande*, or a band of rosettes with dots of enamelling in between. The tiny rose diamonds of the thumbpieces on étuis and cases are clearly evident, as are the gems, whether a moonstone on a bell-push or a faceted amethyst set into a pendant. The material from which the piece has been made is never in doubt, and even the colours of the yellow, red, rosé, and green golds are true to life.

Quite evident are the hardstones, such as nephrite, bowenite, and rhodonite, and the striated or mottled agates, as is too the royal blue lapis lazuli. The moss agate plaques are there, likewise the bright red purpurines. It is quite impossible to mistake the sepia enamels set into their nephrite frames and cases (figs. 5, 6).

Who was the artist?

Although several illustrators were clearly at work, and we may one day know how many, it is doubtful that we shall ever discover their names. The artists also varied in skill. Most of the drawings made between 1911 and 1913 are of a high level. They are extremely accurate in line and colour and, through the skilful application of shading, have acquired a sense of depth. During 1915 and 1916 the job was obviously taken over by someone with less interest and talent. Perhaps by that time the book had lost its original purpose and had been superseded by another system in the workshop.

Four loose drawings are signed by Henrik Wigström, the signatures on which feature in a photographic montage (fig. 7).

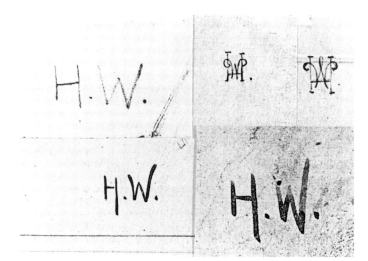

7. Montage of Wigström's signatures.

8. Design for a nephrite frame surmounted by gold ribbon cresting. Signed by Wigström. H: 11.6 cm.

One shows a nephrite frame surmounted by ribbon cresting in gold, complete with a miniature painting of a moustached gentleman (fig. 8). The other three depict mountings for evening bags. The illustration of the frame and one of an evening bag have been used as working drawings, as they are much folded, creased, and thumb-marked. The other two drawings appear not to have been used. All four have their counterparts in the stock book.

Wigström employed two of his children in the workshop. His eldest daughter, Lyyli (born 1885 in St. Petersburg), attended to the routine business affairs of the workshop after leaving school in 1902. She arrived early each morning, handing out the goldsmiths' boxes which had been kept overnight in the safe, as well as the gemstones and pearls delivered to the workshop from the company's central precious stones office. Wigström's son, Henrik Wilhelm (born 1889 in St. Petersburg), was apprenticed in 1905 and worked alongside his father until the workshop closed in 1918.[7] Neither Lyyli nor Henrik Wilhelm, however, can be identified as the illustrators.

Treasure hunt

Perhaps the most fascinating part of looking through the book is discovering drawings of existing pieces. The Napoleonic egg on page 189 is a good example. This, by the way, is the only Imperial egg in the stock book, and as few other Imperial commissions are featured, this indicates that they were recorded elsewhere.

The Napoleonic egg was presented by Tsar Nicholas II to his mother, the Dowager Empress Maria Feodorovna, in 1912 (fig. 9). This Imperial Easter gift, commemorating the centenary of Russia's victory over France, was made in the Empire style from gold with green enamelling. The body is surrounded with double-headed eagles and military symbols. It is now in the Matilda Geddings Gray Foundation Collection in New Orleans, Louisiana. Here, however, is a departure from the rule of true colours in the drawing. In the book the egg is a bluish green, whereas the actual piece is Empire green.

The Imperial egg appears in the centre of the page surrounded by five ovoid boxes or *bonbonnières*, one in white chalcedony and four in nephrite. Also on the page is a red gold gadrooned egg that opens on hinges to reveal a miniature painting of a figure resembling an early eighteenth-century

9. Drawing on page 189 showing the Napoleonic Easter egg that Tsar Nicholas II presented to his mother in 1912. H: 11.6 cm. The page also includes five gold-mounted ovoid *bonbonnières* – one in chalcedony, the others probably of nephrite – and a red gold gadrooned egg (H: 7 cm) that opens to reveal a miniature portrait.

10. Drawing on page 251 of a boat-shaped nephrite bowl in the Thai Royal Collection. H: 7.5 cm.

12518 23/VII 1911

Polish hetman.[8] Each has a production number and was finished around Easter 1912.

Three objects from the Royal Thai Collection are also drawn in the book. One is a small, boat-shaped bowl in nephrite, decorated in white enamel at the rim. The gadrooned stem, round base, and handle are in the shape of mythical birds. Cabochon rubies are set into the rim of the bowl and are also used for the eyes of the birds. The drawing in the Wigström book (fig. 10) gives the date of completion as 23 July 1911 and the production number 12518.[9]

Another piece from the same collection in Wigström's book is a nephrite box, the sides of which are carved with a lotus petal motif. It stands on four gold feet in the shape of small elephants. The lid is inset with a sepia-painted panel depicting the Temple of Dawn. The drawing, however, gives neither date of completion nor production number, but as all the other items on the same page were finished in 1914, it can be assumed that this is from the same year (fig. 11).

A small (width 11 cm) evening bag in the Thai Collection, with a mounting made by Wigström in 1912, also appears. Enamelled in light blue, it has a decor of laurel swags and is set with rose diamonds. Two moonstones decorate the clasp.

Several other pieces in the Thai Collection bear a close resemblance to drawings in Wigström's book. One is an *objet de fantaisie*, a gold *bonbonnière* in the shape of a miniature sleigh. The seat is enamelled on a engine-turned ground. The drawing indicates green upholstery, whereas in the actual piece it is white. It was finished on 8 December 1911 and carries the production number 12232.

Among the other *objets de fantaisie* made to surprise and delight the beholder, Fabergé's famous conversation pieces, is a salt-cellar in the shape of a miniature bidet, which is now part of the India Early Minshall Collection at the Cleveland Museum of Art in Cleveland, Ohio (cat. 260). A drawing of this piece, dated 26 May 1915, bears the production number 12417 (fig. 12). The actual piece in the museum is scratched with the inventory number 25256. This gold bidet in the Louis XVI-style has a nephrite seat, hollowed out and lidded. The lid and both sides of the back are decorated with sepia and opalescent transparent enamel over an engine-turned ground to simulate brocade. The front side of the back is bordered with half pearls. It was originally sold by Fabergé's London branch.[10]

11. Drawing on page 219 of a nephrite box in the Thai Royal Collection that stands on four gold feet shaped as small elephants. W: 9.3 cm.

12. Drawing on page 205 of a Louis XVI-style salt-cellar shaped as a miniature bidet. The actual piece is in the Cleveland Museum of Art in the United States (cat. 260).

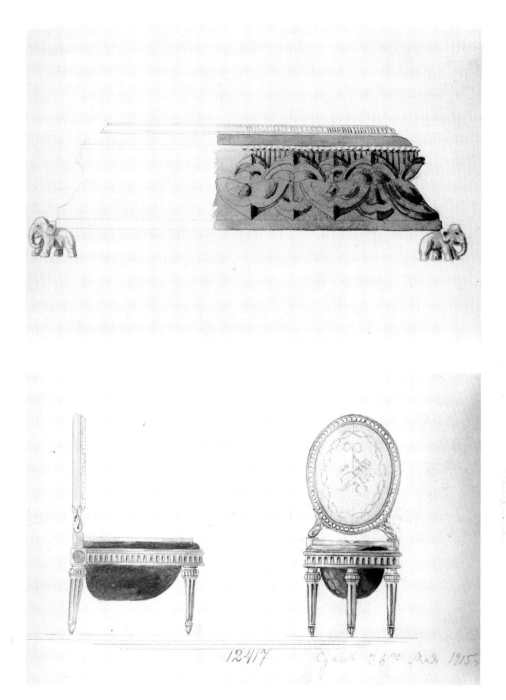

Another exquisite piece in the same genre – a *bonbonnière* in the shape of an Empire fauteuil – is now in the esteemed FORBES Magazine Collection in New York (fig. 13). It is made from gold with a backrest enamelled in translucent lime green over a *repoussé* ground and chased with sea-horses flanking a ribbon-tied laurel wreath. The hinged seat, *repoussé* and chased with sphinxes, was also enamelled translucent lime green. Also enamelled are the back of the backrest, in a translucent strawberry red over a ground engraved to simulate wood grain, the legs, and the green armrests supported by sphinxes. This fauteuil appears in the stock book alongside a number of conventional pillboxes. The undated drawing has no production number (fig. 14). The other items on the page date from 1911 and 1912.

Yet another intriguing object is a tiny painter's easel in silver-gilt with a plaque of moss agate to simulate a painting (figs. 15, 16). This oval panel is partially foiled and cut to suggest dusk over a misty lake seen through pine trees. Its gold bezel, matte black enamel reserve, and rectangular frame with leaf-tip decoration rest on a simple easel support. This item was featured in a Sotheby's auction in Geneva in 1990.

13. The enamelled gold *bonbonnière* shaped as an Empire-style fauteuil shown in figure 14. H: 7.5 cm. Signed by Fabergé, with 'CF' in Latin letters. Initials of Wigström, assay marks of St. Petersburg 1908–1917, 72 (*zolotnik*), inv. 22841, London import mark for 1911.

14. Drawing on page 207 of an Empire-style *bonbonnière* shaped as a fauteuil.

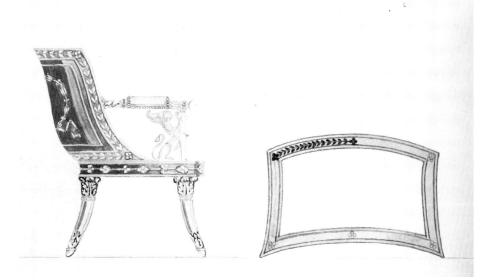

15. Drawing on page 345 of a miniature easel.

16. Miniature painter's easel shown in figure 15. Its plaque of moss agate is cut to suggest dusk over a misty lake.

17. Drawing on page 113 of the Cossack bodyguard of the Dowager Empress Maria Feodorovna (cat. 43). Figurine with overcoat of green jasper bordered with brown Caucasian obsidian, braids in gold, and double-headed eagles in black enamel. Hat, beard, and moustache of grey jasper, eyes of sapphires, and medals of gold and different enamels. H: 16.1 cm.

The stock book contains only one drawing of a hardstone figurine (fig. 17). A miniature of the Dowager Empress Maria Feodorovna's Cossack bodyguard appears on page 113. Underneath are two dates, indicating that two identical pieces were made, one finished 31 January 1912 and the other 25 April 1912. The January piece carries the production number 12995. Two such Cossack pieces are still in existence. One is in the Pavlovsk Palace Collection, with a provenance of the Alexander Palace in Tsarskoe Selo (cat. 43), the last home of Tsar Nicholas II and his family. The other was formerly part of the Hammer Gallery Collection and is discussed by Henry Bainbridge in his well-known book on Fabergé.[11]

Bainbridge, who was employed at the London branch and often visited St. Petersburg, recalls that when the Empress Alexandra Feodorovna and the Dowager Empress Maria Feodorovna went riding in their sleighs or motorcars, they were attended by one of two personal bodyguards, both Cossacks. Nicholas II commissioned Fabergé to make stone models of these guards, and as they were to be real portraits, the two Cossacks had to sit and be modelled in wax at the Fabergé studio.[12] The drawing in Wigström's book clearly proves that this is a portrait. A photograph from the 1920s of the Dowager Empress Maria Feodorovna in exile in Copenhagen shows her being assisted out of her car by her Cossack bodyguard. He looks remarkably like this hardstone figurine.[13]

The exquisite flower studies of Fabergé, most of them bearing the hallmarks of Henrik Wigström, are completely absent from the stock book, which would indicate that a special record was kept of them elsewhere. Likewise, the famous menagerie is almost completely missing, where only half of page 111 is devoted to drawings of 'winged creatures'. Most hardstone animals were made by lapidaries in Fabergé's other workshops, with Wigström supplying the gold legs, beaks, and gemstone eyes. Among these few drawings is a crowing cock, its head raised and beak open wide. This rather unusual piece, made from labradorite and white quartz, with a purpurine comb and wattles, was included in Christie's Geneva auction in May 1982. Other drawings depict a red-breasted male bullfinch (still extant), a blue and yellow tomtit, a goose, a black pigeon, and a carnelian owl (fig. 18).

On page 191 (fig. 19), the numerous drawings of miniature egg pendants offer many a happy reunion, including a

18. Page 111 shows drawings of various fowl: a crowing cock made of labradorite and white quartz with purpurine comb and wattles, a hardstone goose, a carnelian owl, a blue and yellow tomtit, a black pigeon, and a red-breasted male bullfinch.

19. Detail of page 191 showing miniature egg pendants and amusing egg-shaped owls, pigs, and elephants.

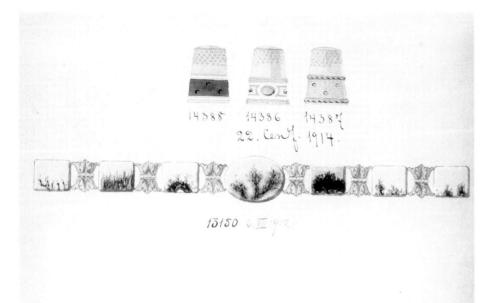

20. Detail of page 91 showing three thimbles and a drawing of a bracelet with gold-mounted moss agate plaques linked by chased gold acanthus bundles.

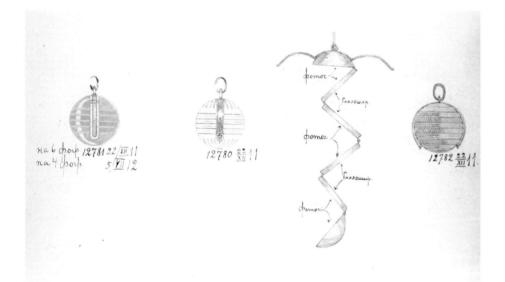

21. Drawings on page 75 of spherical gold and enamel lockets. One unfolds to reveal hinged panels that could contain up to ten miniature portraits or photographs.

22. Drawings on page 73 of two snowflake pendants made of gold, with rose diamonds set in platinum on a rock crystal ground (cf. cat. 179–181).

23. Drawing on page 11 of an octagonal gold box enamelled in salmon pink with the name *Dmitri* set with rose diamonds beneath an oval miniature.
L: 8.7 cm, W: 6.3 cm.

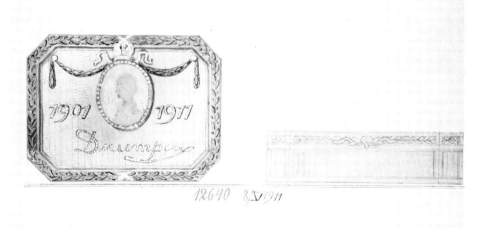

24. Drawings on page 337 of a pale blue *guilloché* enamel desk set designed for a lady with the initials 'OR'.

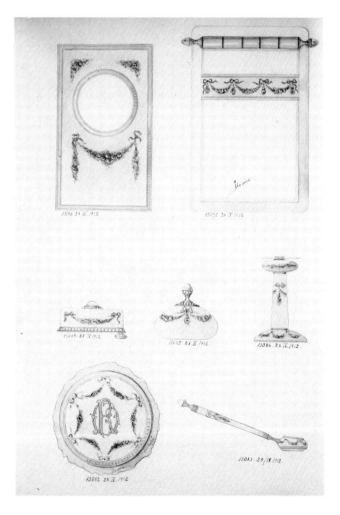

kingfisher now in the FORBES Magazine Collection in New York. Among these imaginative and exquisite eggs are some that border on the grotesque. In others, roosters and hares emerge from eggshells, an Easter theme also known from porcelain figurines. It could not have been easy for Fabergé's designers to satisfy the demand for ever more fanciful miniature eggs. This page, in addition, offers an opportunity to study Wigström's pricing code. Eggs made partly from hardstone have above them the coded price of the lapidary or some other subcontractor.

Although Wigström's workshop did not specialise in jewellery, the book nevertheless contains six, mainly incomplete pages of jewellery and trinkets. A half-page of belt buckles and cape clips also features badges, tie-pins, and cufflinks intended as Imperial presentation pieces. A range of delightful thimbles is mingled with gold rings with the motif of a snake swallowing its tail, as well as ordinary men's signet rings. Also evident is an exquisite gold bracelet with seven moss agate plaques, six oblong and an oval centre piece, linked by chased gold acanthus bundles (fig. 20). In addition is an imposing pectoral surmounted by an Imperial crown, no doubt made for a church dignitary, and several jewelled crosses for ladies. Among the lockets is an unusual spherical type, enamelled *en plein* on an engine-turned ground, that unfolds to reveal several hinged panels that hold as many as ten miniature portraits or photographs (fig. 21).

Page 73 of Wigström's book offers a real surprise: two pencilled snowflake pendants of the type associated with Holmström's workshop and its designer Alma Pihl-Klee (fig. 22). This is surely evidence of the close connection between Fabergé's different workshops.

Custom-made pieces
In addition to the orders from His Imperial Majesty's Cabinet, with Imperial cyphers and monograms set beneath the Romanov crown, Fabergé made several frames, cases, boxes, *kovshi*, and other objects adorned with crowns of lesser status and set or engraved with monograms. The presentation cufflinks, tie-pins, and badges commissioned by the Imperial Cabinet primarily date from 1913, the tercentenary of the Romanov dynasty.

On page 75 appears an oval brooch, enamelled white on an

engine-turned ground and set with Roman letters forming the name Serge. The brooch is surmounted by an Imperial crown, as well as by a large gold cross with the name Xenia engraved in Cyrillic letters. Both names were probably ordered in honour of members of the Royal Family. The exquisite box on page 11 (fig. 23) bears the name Dmitri in Cyrillic facsimile hand-writing in relief, set with rose-cut diamonds beneath an oval. A rose diamond, entoured miniature painting depicting a young lady in profile is surmounted by an Imperial crown. Flanking the portrait are the years 1901 and 1911, also set in diamonds. The oblong case (8.7 × 6.3 cm) has cut corners and is enamelled *en plein* in salmon pink on an engine-turned ground. The rim of the case has a green enamelled foliate decor. Finished at the workshop on 8 November 1911, the case was given the production number 12640. A study of the Romanov genealogy and the Almanach de Gotha has failed to produce a likely candidate for the elusive Dmitri.

A desk set on page 337 (fig. 24) was made for presentation to a lady with the initials 'OR'. Finished on 28 April 1912, it consists of a photograph frame, stand for a note pad, bell-push, gumpot, taper holder, round box, and seal in the shape of a bed warmer. The set would appear to be from silver-gilt, enamelled in light blue, with an applied decor of floral garlands in varicoloured gold.

It is a well-known fact that cigarette cases were the main article that Fabergé produced at the time. Wigström's book contains drawings of 149 designs on 17 pages. Some are repeated, two or three cases being made from the same design with, perhaps, only a change in colours. These pages offer an excellent opportunity to study the spectrum of design available for this popular Fabergé item.

About half are dated 1911, the rest 1912, with none at all between 1913 and 1916. During these years cigarette cases were produced in considerable numbers, so probably a separate stock book was kept just for them. Only three Imperial presentation cases are shown: one for Christmas 1911, bearing the Imperial cypher 'N II' in Cyrillic letters surmounted with the Imperial crown (fig. 25); and two plain gold cases made in March 1912, with diamond-set, doubled-headed eagles in the centre.

The interesting case is illustrated on page 143 (fig. 25). Made from varicoloured gold with snakes in gold and silver intertwining around a centre plaque, the case has an inscription suggestive of Arabic. Bearing the production number 12646, it was finished on 1 December 1911 and measures 10.1 × 6.7 cm.

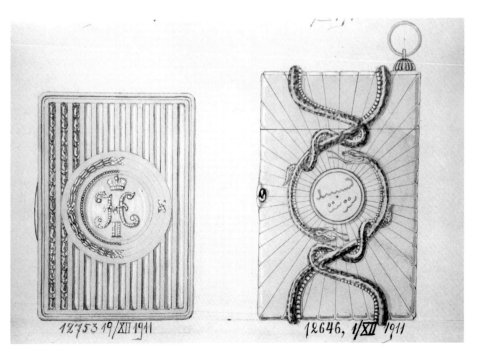

25. Drawings for two cigarette cases: an Imperial presentation case with the cypher 'N II', and another in varicoloured gold inset with an Arabic inscription and two entwined snakes. The original, commissioned by M. Luzarche d'Azay, is in the Musée des Arts Décoratifs, Paris (cat. 286).

The young journeyman engraver Jalmari Haikonen worked for Wigström from October 1915 until the workshop was closed three years later. That part of his memoirs dealing with this period offers wonderful insight into life at the workshop.

There were about ten men employed making cigarette cases. These were made in a wide variety of models and shapes, and from many different materials. Most of them were from 56 zolotnik gold, a few from 72 zolotnik. Cases in varicoloured golds were very popular, yellow gold being combined with red, rosé and green gold. Decorating them was a laborious and time-consuming job, and the majority were engraved over the whole surface, either by hand or on the guilloché machine. There could be up to forty cases waiting to be engraved at any one time. . . . After engraving most cases were enamelled. Several layers of transparent enamel were applied so the engraving could still be seen underneath.

Haikonen recalls that engraving decorations was a slow process, and that once, in 1917, he spent two months working on a particularly elaborate design. Fortunately he kept the design, which is still in his family, and by a lucky coincidence the original cigarette case has also been discovered.[15]

On the subject of his fellow workers, Haikonen is very informative. 'One of the engravers was an old man of 82, who had joined the company when he was 25. He reckoned he was quite content with his lot, and all the other craftsmen felt the same. Everyone liked working in this workshop'.[16] Working at a bench behind Haikonen was an old man of 72, who always kept to himself. He had been working, day in and day out, banging the same silver tea-glass holder with his chasing hammer for over two months. This is a charming example of the humane way in which a faithful old retainer, long past his prime, was allowed to stay on.

Haikonen relates how Wigström's son, Henrik Wilhelm, told him that the best way to learn was to study the work of the other journeymen. The employers never ceased urging journeymen to take their time with their work, to be careful and painstaking in practice, as a piece executed hastily could never be perfect. They should persevere and be diligent, but they should never hurry unduly. Haikonen tells an amusing anecdote to illustrate this philosophy. Apparently the workshop toilet had four seats, and one day Haikonen found himself sitting next to Henrik Wigström. Suddenly another man rushed in and seconds later rushed out again. 'Dear me', exclaimed the master. 'Even here one must take one's time. Everything takes time'.[17]

Each time an important piece was finished the workshop held a little ceremony to allow everyone to admire it. Wigström and a manager walked between the benches with the piece, stopping before each craftsman and saying, 'Look at this superb thing, it's finished now'. This simple act did much to motivate the craftsmen and strengthen their sense of fellowship. Haikonen describes one ceremony in particular. 'One day, around New Year 1916, they showed us a truly exceptional piece, a magnificent cigarette case in platinum commissioned by the Tsar himself'. Haikonen relates that he had the remarkable good fortune to observe the making of this case from the beginning. It weighed a good pound, and the top was decorated with the Imperial cypher – a large 'N II' set with diamonds – and jewelled double-headed eagles appeared in all four corners. The case was a present from the Tsar to his father's cousin, the Grand Duke Nikolai Nikolaievich, on his sixtieth birthday. 'All the craftsmen were allowed to admire this fine Imperial commission. It lay inside a red leather case with the Romanov coat of arms on top. Afterwards we journeymen started guessing at the price and came to the conclusion that it must have cost all of 50,000 gold roubles'.[18]

Although Haikonen's memoirs provide valuable information about life in Henrik Wigström's workshop, there is no mention of the stock book or how, in general, products were recorded. The stock book was obviously nothing more than a tool used in production, part of a recording system the exact meaning and scope of which we are only beginning to understand. Nevertheless, a fragment of this system has come down to us in the form of this delightful and edifying book of drawings. Our admiration for the House of Fabergé grows as we see the skill and talent that went into each object and the almost endless variations on them. Once time permits a deeper study, it will undoubtedly further our understanding and knowledge of Fabergé's production, in much the same way as the Holmström stock books have already done.[19]

1. Jalmari Haikonen. Lappeenranta, Finland. Unpublished memoirs, passim.

2. Information supplied by the family of Henrik Wigström.

3. Ibid.

4. A.K. Snowman, 'Two Books of Revelations', in Habsburg 1987, pp. 47–60. Also A.K. Snowman's article 'Two Books of Revelations. The Fabergé Stock Books', in *Apollo* (September 1987, pp. 150–61).

5. The 'old style' Julian calendar prevailed in Russia until 1918, when the 'new style' Gregorian calendar was adopted. All dates in Wigström's stock book are given in the 'old style'. The thirteen-day difference between the two calendars can give the impression that something was sold in London before it was finished in St. Petersburg.

6. The jewellers A. Tillander of Helsinki, founded in St. Petersburg in 1860, still uses a system whereby each piece is given a production number at the planning stage and an inventory number upon completion, which is entered into the records and scratched on the object. The production number series does not run chronologically because the pieces are finished at different times.

7. U. Tillander-Godenhielm, 'Personal and historical notes on Fabergé's Finnish workmasters and designers', in Tillander, *Carl Fabergé and his contemporaries* (Helsinki, 1980), pp. 29–33.

8. Tom C. Bergroth of Turku has studied this drawing and is of the opinion that it depicts an early eighteenth-century Polish hetman or nobleman. He further suggests that, as the egg was finished in 1912, it was made to commemorate a bicentenary. The picture of the facing panel is not shown in the drawing.

9. Krairiksh, passim. Illustrations of the boat-shaped nephrite bowl seen in figure 10 and the nephrite box in figure 11 appear on pages 113 and 197, respectively, of Krairiksh's book.

10. Hawley, 1967, p. 32.

11. Bainbridge, 1949, p. 113.

12. Ibid., p. 113.

13. Archives of Åhlen et Åkerlund, in Staffan Skott, *Romanovs* (Viborg, 1990), p. 129.

14. Haikonen memoirs, passim.

15. U. Tillander-Godenhielm, 'Bolšaja Morskajan suomalaiset kultasepät' (The Finnish goldsmiths of St. Petersburg), in K. Kaurinkoski et al., *Pietarin kultainen katu* (The golden street of St. Petersburg), (Helsinki, 1991), pp. 112–16.

16. Haikonen memoirs, passim.

17. Ibid.

18. Tillander-Godenhielm, 'Bolsaja Morskajan suomalaiset kultasepät', pp. 112–16.

19. See Snowman, 'Two Books of Revelations', *Apollo*, pp. 150–61.

Fabergé: The Moscow Workshops

Anne Odom

In the vast literature about Carl Fabergé, scarcely ten pages have been written about his Moscow workshops.[1] Both Henry Charles Bainbridge and Franz Birbaum[2] in ther memoirs refer to the high quality of design and craftsmanship, which, in their opinion, saved from oblivion the production of the Moscow workshops. These views, however, are so obscured by their enthusiasm for the technical virtuosity and creative imagination of Fabergé himself and his workmasters in the Petersburg workshops that their praise of the Moscow production has gone unnoticed.

Most experts on Fabergé consider the opening of the Moscow workshops merely a good businessman's attempt to cultivate a new market, namely, the increasingly wealthy Moscow merchants, which it certainly was. It is time, however, to put the objects made in the Moscow workshops in their proper historical perspective, because this new enterprise turned out to be more than just a smart business venture. Moscow produced many objects in the same classical styles as those made in the Petersburg workshops, but they also fabricated significant pieces in the Neo-Russian style. These may not have appealed to an international clientele or to the aristocrats of St. Petersburg, but in the luxury arts, they are among the few expressions of the creative ideas of Moscow artists at the turn of the century. By pursuing this style, Fabergé left an important legacy of work, virtually ignored to date, which is truly Russian to the core.

The production of Neo-Russian pieces in the Moscow workshops needs to be seen in the broader context of the cultural schism that existed between Moscow and St. Petersburg. Although the Russian revival began in St. Petersburg as a court style in the 1830s, by the 1880s Moscow had become the centre of its development. Fabergé's trademark Neo-Rococo and Neo-Classical pieces were part of a more widespread artistic reaction, especially in St. Petersburg, to what were considered the national excesses of Moscow design. In the hands of Moscow artists and craftsmen, the Russian style went through various phases, but the stylistic dichotomy between the cities persisted.

When Fabergé opened his Moscow workshop in 1887, the jewellery/silversmith business in that city was dominated by two very large firms, those of Pavel Ovchinnikov and Ivan Khlebnikov, both of which had been founded considerably earlier, and a large number of smaller firms, often led by highly talented silversmiths. Although Ovchinnikov and Khlebnikov, in particular, produced a wide range of silverware, they were most famous for their enamels in the Old-Russian style. In opening his Moscow workshop, Fabergé brought imaginative design to the competition.

For a better understanding of the importance of Fabergé's enterprise in Moscow, it is useful to review what is known about its management, workshops, and designers. An advertisement reports the opening of a shop on Kuznetski Most in House No. 4 of the Merchants Society on 1 February (13 February n.s.) 1887.[3] The workshops were at Verkhne-Bolshoi Kiselnyi Lane, House San Galli, No. 4.[4] Allan Bowe headed the Moscow operation as Fabergé's partner. An Englishman born in South Africa, Bowe was assisted by his brothers, Arthur, who later set up the Fabergé branch in London, and Charles.[5] Bowe's management was known as efficient and commercially successful. In 1900 he also took on the management of the newly opened Odessa shop. Fabergé clearly thought well of his manager, writing in 190l, 'My friend Allan Andreevich Bowe is my assistant and first manager – he showed himself to advantage being the manager of all my business at the Moscow factory and at the branches in Moscow and Odessa for 14 years'.[6] A presentation tray (cat. 231) from the Forbes collection has the dates '1890' and '1895', a portrait of Allan Bowe and the Roman numeral 'V'. It is inscribed 'To the much respected Allan Andreevich from sincerely grateful employees'. The meaning of the dates on the tray remain unresolved. It is difficult to imagine what other reference this could be than to Bowe's service, although the newspaper advertisement and the comment by Fabergé referring to fourteen years make 1887 as the year he began to work for Fabergé quite clear.

Bowe's partnership with Fabergé ended in 1906 when Otto Jarke replaced him as manager.[7] Jarke was followed by Andrea Marchetti, an expert in silver and gems,[8] and by 1912 the workshops were headed by Fabergé's son Alexander,[9] until their close in 1918.

There were two departments in the Moscow factory: one for silver and one for jewellery. The silver department, headed by Mikhail Cherpunov, was the largest, producing primarily silver and cutlery for the table. The silver workers, as was commonly the case, were divided into two categories: those who made services, samovars, and other tableware, and those who produced cast pieces – candelabra, statues, and clocks. According to Birbaum, several reasons accounted for placing silversmithing in Moscow rather than St. Petersburg. For one, Moscow's production was extensive and well organised. Because the former capital had long been a centre for silversmiths, craftsmen were available; good schools for training were available; and more significantly, the salaries were lower.

Despite Moscow's advantages, the most important silver commissions generally went to Julius Rappoport, Anders Nevalainen, or Stephan Wäkeva, Fabergé's chief silversmiths in Petersburg. The quality of silver produced in those workshops was still higher than that made in Moscow. All three worked occasionally for the Moscow workshops in a relationship that is not clear; their marks can be found with the Moscow mark of Fabergé. The great mass of table silver, however, was turned out in Moscow. The magnitude of this operation is revealed in the statistic that eight engravers were employed carving monograms alone.[10] Birbaum also says that the quality of Moscow silver tableware was superior to foreign, due in part to a large selection of punches and presses made for this purpose. According to Kenneth Snowman, large pieces, such as *bratini*, *surtouts de table*, and samovars, were sent to other silversmiths because of excessive demand. These works carried a Fabergé mark as long as the design was by Fabergé.[11] The Moscow factory also turned out huge numbers of silver mounts for glass vases, pitchers, decanters, and serving bowls. It is not known who supplied the glass, or to which factory Fabergé supplied the mounts, but some of the glass was possibly foreign.

The jewellery department was under the management of Oskar Pihl, a Swedish Finn. He apprenticed in August Holmström's jewellery workshop in Petersburg and married Holmström's daughter. Pihl was succeeded after his death in 1897 by a Pole named Mitkievich. Bainbridge, in his book on Fabergé, refers to a third department for objects of fantasy, which he says was headed by the jeweller Gustav Jahr. It is possible, though, that this is the same Jahr (Yahr) who operated his own workshop in Moscow, was a supplier of the Ovchinnikov firm, and in 1904 began to supply Cartier with *guilloché* enamels.[12] If so, he did not run a section for Fabergé but was an independent jeweller. Although he at no time

1. Frame, carved wood, Aleksei Zinoviev, Talashkino, *c.* 1905. Hillwood Museum Library.

2. Frame, silver and enamel, Feodor Rückert/Fabergé, 1908–1917. Miniature copy of *Fetching Water* by Ivan Kuliukov. Private collection.

worked exclusively for Fabergé, the main supplier to Fabergé of enamelled objects in the Russian style was Feodor Rückert.

Both Bainbridge and Birbaum list a number of designers for the Moscow workshops: Mikhail Ivanov, Baron Nikolai Aleksandrovich von Klodt (1865–1915), Feodor Ivanovich Kozlov (born 1884), Lett, Jan Lieberg-Nyberg, Navozov, and several others. Baron von Klodt taught at the Moscow School of Painting, Sculpture, and Architecture and was a member of the Union of Russian Artists.[13] Kozlov entered the Stroganov Central School of Technical Drawing in 1896 and finished in 1906.[14] Little is known about the others. Von Klodt and Kozlov did not work exclusively for Fabergé; whether any of the others did is not clear. Aleksei Prokofievich Zinoviev (1880–1941) may have also briefly been a designer for Fabergé. He entered the Stroganov School in 1894 and upon graduation worked for the Moscow branch of Fabergé. In 1903, at the age of twenty-three, he went to Smolensk to head the school at Talashkino, the art community founded by a wealthy patroness of the arts, Princess Tenisheva.[15] Zinoviev designed many pieces during his tenure at Talashkino, including a wooden frame (fig. 1) that possibly inspired a frame by Feodor Rückert (fig. 2). Zinoviev may have remained an important connection between the designers at Fabergé and the latest innovations at Talashkino. When Allan Bowe retired in 1906, the employees presented him with a portable oak desk in the Neo-Russian style, similar to objects being designed at Talashkino (fig. 3).[16]

That some of Fabergé's designers, and possibly some of the silversmiths as well, studied at the Stroganov School is significant. The training of artisans and craftsmen had reached a fairly sophisticated level by the turn of the century. Some silversmiths had their own schools; Pavel Ovchinnikov's was the oldest and largest. The Stieglitz School and the classes organized by the Society for the Encouragement of the Arts were in St. Petersburg. The Stroganov Central School for Technical Drawing in Moscow, founded in 1860 by combining two earlier schools, remained the most important. The Crystal Palace Exhibition in London in 1851 inspired a raft of technical art schools across Europe intended to improve the quality of the applied arts, and this was the mission of the Stroganov School as well.

Feodor Solntsev inaugurated the search for a native design vocabulary in Russia with the publication, between 1846 and

1853, of *Drevnosti rossiiskago gosudarstva* (Antiquities of the Russian State), six volumes of drawings of Russian armour, weapons, church plate, and objects in the Kremlin Armoury.[17] In the 1860s, led by Viktor I. Butovski, Director of the Stroganov School, students collected ornaments from manuscripts, church decorations, and textiles, which Butovski compiled into the volume *Istoriia russkago ornament s X do XVI stoletie po drevnym rukopisiam* (The history of Russian ornament from the X to XVI century from ancient manuscript).[18] These works, and others that followed in rapid succession, provided a grammar of Russian ornament used by porcelain manufacturers, silversmiths, glass houses, and woodworkers to create a Russian style, specifically, the Old-Russian style.[19]

3. Portable oak desk, wood and silver, Moscow, 1906. Presented to Allan Bowe upon his retirement.

4. Cat and owl door, carved wood, Elena Polenova, Abramtsevo, c. 1893. Hillwood Museum Library.

By 1900 the Russian style was being infused with Art Nouveau elements from the West, resulting in a *stil modern*, as the Russians called it. Actually, *stil modern* encompassed two trends in Russia. One was closer to a pure Western Art Nouveau; the other was a mixture of Art Nouveau and Russian motifs and colour, termed the Neo-Russian style. Abramtsevo, the estate that the railroad magnate Savva Mamontov had transformed into an artist colony outside Moscow, was the centre of the Russian equivalent of the Arts and Crafts movement.[20] Elena Polenova, who assisted Mamontov's wife in setting up a carpentry workshop (see fig. 4 for the cat and owl door she designed), began collecting folk art as examples for local craftsmen to follow. Soon she was creating her own designs with folk art as the basis, and this became the foundation of the Neo-Russian style.

Silversmiths had their own long, rich tradition of metalwork from which to draw, so they were not dependent on manuscript or folk motifs for indigenous design. That silversmiths were influenced by the Neo-Russian ornament emanating from Abramtsevo and Talashkino, however, is clear from the study of the objects. Links between the luxury arts and the Arts and Crafts movement have not been sufficiently explored because it is not immediately clear how they were formed.[21] They must have been through the technical schools, especially the Stroganov School, because soon these new ideas were perculating through design courses. Thus, designers and silversmiths trained in these schools from the mid-1890s on exerted a tremendous impact on design at the beginning of this century. That some of Fabergé's designers and artists studied at these schools, and especially at the Stroganov School, explains the high quality of its Neo-Russian design.[22] As Birbaum says, 'The first thing that distinguishes work produced by the Moscow firm is the predominance of the Russian folk style. One can disagree with many of its special characteristics, with the lack of purpose in its structure, the archaic, intentionally crude execution, but all these temporary defects are redeemed by the freshness of the design, and the cliché-free composition'.[23]

A direct connection of another kind apparently existed between the Stroganov School and Fabergé. The School produced and exhibited a ceramic ibis in 1902–1903 for the exhibition *Architecture and Applied Arts in the New Style*.[24] Ibises and ducks such as this, with Fabergé silver wings and ornament on them, are rare but do exist. Most often the birds have no mark. One, at least, appears to have a Stoganov School mark on the bird.[25]

It is difficult to draw conclusions about the production of jewellery or objects of fantasy in Moscow because little remains or can be identified as such. Thus, the following comments about style are largely devoted to the silver and enamel made in Moscow. By dividing the silver production of the Moscow workshops into the date divisions that can be made according to the changes in marks – that is, before 1896, 1896 to 1908, and after 1908 – it is possible to make some useful observations about the stylistic evolution that occurred from 1887 to 1917. For the purposes of this study, examples from museum collections and from the sales catalogues have been used.

It should come as no surprise that throughout the existence of Fabergé's Moscow workshops, the wares from Moscow reflect the styles of St. Petersburg. After all, if Moscow was producing the majority of the silver for the firm, it had to satisfy all its clientele, in Petersburg as well as Moscow. This explains the large amount of silver in the Rococo and Classical styles favoured in St. Petersburg, with most of the Rococo pieces made before 1896. The Rococo objects are stylistically not unlike those being produced in Mikhail Perkhin's workshop. The popularity of the Rococo style at this time stems, no doubt, from the Rococo revival taking place in France in the 1890s and the exchanges that led up to the Franco-Russian Alliance in 1894, which resulted in visits between the two countries and a French exhibition of luxury arts in Moscow and Petersburg in 1890.[26] It is significant that the silver tray, given to Allan Bowe in 1895, is Rococo in style. The employees of the factory would surely have given considerable thought to the style of a presentation gift to their factory manager.

Vestiges of Russian Realism remained, of course. Examples are the desk sets and smoking implements, such as the smoker's compendium in the shape of an *izba*, or peasant house, in the Forbes collection.[27] While this style was remarkably long lived with a broad appeal, the Art Nouveau pieces, particularly those that are closer to Western Art Nouveau, fall exclusively into the 1896 to 1908 time frame and are relatively few in number. This is also the case with the enamelled and hardstone objects in the Art Nouveau style made by Fabergé's Petersburg workmasters. Mounts for glass vases and pitchers were often in the Art

Nouveau style. A ceramic vase in a silver Fabergé mount in the Art Nouveau style (cat. 38) was among the personal possessions of Alexandra at the Alexander Palace in Tsarskoe Selo. Although Nicholas and Alexandra were not known as fashion setters, Alexandra's brother, it should not be forgotten, was Ernst Ludwig, Grand Duke of Hessen-Darmstadt. As one of the leading patrons of German *Jugendstil*, he supported the building of an artist colony in Darmstadt. Roman F. Meltser remodelled several rooms in the Alexander Palace for Nicholas and Alexandra in the Art Nouveau style.

Of all the styles produced by the Moscow workshops, none is more interesting than the Neo-Russian version of the *stil modern*. While not unique to Moscow, it attained a distinctive appearance there, which is immediately recognisable as Moscow, and in this style the Fabergé production was rivalled only by the ecclesiastical objects produced by Olovianishnikov & Sons. The Khlebnikov firm and several of the Artels (cooperatives) after 1908 produced some interesting *moderne* work, but not in large quantity. Henry Charles Bainbridge recognised Fabergé's contribution when he wrote that the Russian style 'as developed by Fabergé, was the result of the Craftsman's study of the mural decoration, documents, pieces of pottery and gold and silversmith's work of the time of Ivan the Terrible'. He considered this an 'outstanding contribution to Russian Art'. 'The Moscow house', he said, 'made use of this style almost *ad infinitum* in silver work of every kind, such as tankards, bratini, ikons (sic!), bowls, cigarette cases, etc., and in silver work associated with Siberian stones. These objects were made much use of as presentation gifts to Emirs and Khans, visiting foreign potentates, statesmen, etc.'.[28]

The sculptural groups produced by the Moscow firm have several interesting prototypes. The 'Ivan Kalita' bowl from the Forbes collection may have been inspired by Mikhail Vrubel's sculptures, created in the Abramtsevo ceramic workshop. More realistic than Vrubel's molded figures, Ivan is an integral form with his bowl. Russian heroic figures such as Ivan Kalita, Dmitri Donskoi, or those legendary warriors, the *Bogatyrs*, reappeared in Russian art as early as 1851, when Ignatii Sazikov exhibited several silver sculptures at the Crystal Palace Exhibition in London. In his statue of Dmitri Donskoi and his warriors (see fig. 5 for an example of one of those on display in 1851), Sazikov's figures, their armour, weapons, and helmets

5. Dmitri Donskoi, silver, Ignatii Sazikov,
1851. Hillwood Museum Library.

were faithfully copied from Solntsev's *Drevnosti* (Antiquities).

Sazikov's hero, Dmitri Donskoi, lying wounded under a tree with a comrade nearby, provides some of the same upward dynamic that is found on a *kovsh* in the Forbes collection (cat. 232). While Sazikov's sculpture is much more realistic, and the Forbes *kovsh* has incorporated Neo-Russian ornament into the front of the *kovsh* and at the tip of the handle, the Forbes *kovsh* is undoubtedly a direct descendant of the Sazikov piece.[29] These sculptures were probably not produced at the factory much before 1903, and they continued to be made until World War I.

Other *kovshi*, smaller in size than the one mentioned above and without the figures, but with similar archaic ornament around the edges and along the handle, can be found in sales catalogues. The ornament along the side of a *kovsh* can give the impression of wood carving along the gunwale of a Viking ship, as imagined in one of Nikolai Roerich's paintings,[30] or it is like the angular scrolls used by Feodor Shekhtel for the design of the wrought iron fence around the Derozhinskaia House (1901) in Moscow and the fabric design in the interior. Silversmiths frequently made use of this type of ornament, often set with semiprecious stones, on icon *oklads* (covers). A page of designs for eighteen *tcharki* (fig. 6) gives an idea of the infinite number of design possibilities that could be achieved with interlace, gadrooning, rosettes, and granulation, all of which are found in ancient Russian silverwork,[31] but used here in a modern interpretation.

A presentation, portable oak desk (fig. 3),[32] given to Allan Bowe by his employees at the time of his retirement in 1906, stands in remarkable contrast to the silver tray presented to him in 1895. Similar angular scrolls decorate applied metal corners, and birds are enclosed in roundels on the blotter cover and in partial roundels on the hinges of the box. Just as the Rococo tray reflected the output of Fabergé's Moscow workshops in 1895, so this desk was in the latest style of 1906.

It is worth mentioning that, judging from the sales catalogues, the number of presentation pieces produced by the Moscow workshops is enormous. These are not the grand silver wedding anniversary presents which the Tsar or other members of the Imperial Family presented to each other. Those were more likely to have been made in St. Petersburg.[33] In addition to the objects made to present visiting dignitaries, mentioned by Bainbridge, the Moscow workshops fabricated

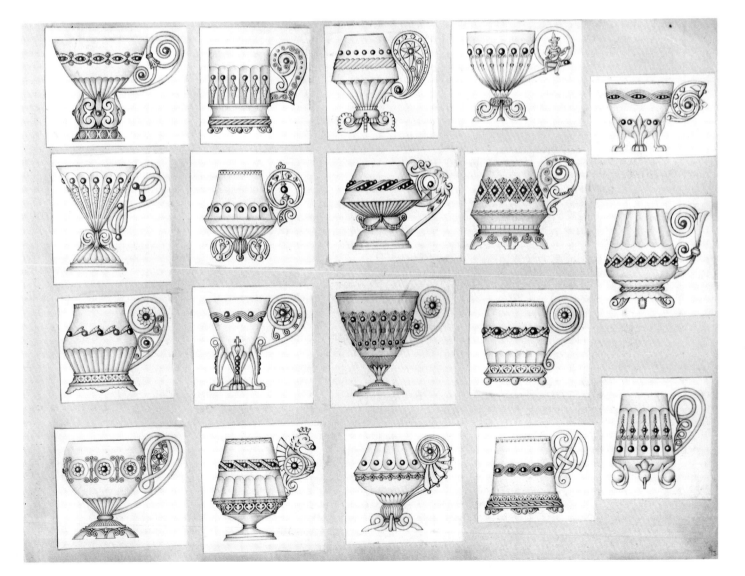

retirement gifts from employees to their directors, silver wedding anniversary presents of middle-class families, and prizes for various competitions. Just as Americans went to Tiffany to buy a silver vase for a similar occasion, so Muscovites went to Fabergé.

A single colour, opaque enamel decoration also distinguishes silver objects made in the Moscow workshops. Sometimes enamel covers the entire surface as a background to *repoussé* folk motifs, such as birds on either side of the tree of life.[34] *Repoussé* designs of big, blousy tulips and other flowers found in the seventeenth-century northern enamels from Solvychegodsk also appear.[35] At other times the enamel was used as a border decoration, with enamel squares alternating with silver ones, for example.[36] On occasion, small river pearls were affixed over a matte background of dark wine, medium blue, or dark green (cat. 216). The soft glow of the pearls against the flat matte colour, highlighted by the shiny silver, creates an elegant effect. Some of these, such as the *kovsh* in cat. 216, have stylised birds and animals enclosed in their handles in a manner reminiscent of some of the Scythian gold ornaments.

Fabergé also produced silver boxes with miniature paintings on the tops. Feodor Rückert could have supplied the artwork, although there is no evidence to date that he did.[37] These boxes are not to be confused with those in filigree enamel that Rückert supplied to Fabergé. Made of silver and simply decorated with semiprecious stones to imitate ancient caskets, they sometimes bear Neo-Classical ornament. One such box with Empire swans along the sides has a miniature painting that depicts the defeat of Napoleon, obviously made for the one hundredth anniversary of that event in 1912. The miniature is signed 'C. Berth', about whom, unfortunately, nothing is known.

Copies of the Viktor Vasnetsov illustrations in *The Prophecy of Oleg*, a special edition of the tale of that name, were used on several of these boxes. Of interest is one signed 'A. Borozdin',[38] for Aleksandr Borozdin (born 1880), who worked for a time in the icon workshop of Vasilii Pavlovich Gulianov, a source of icons for Fabergé.[39] In fact, an icon in the Pratt collection at the Virginia Museum of Fine Arts is also signed by Borozdin.[40]

A year later, in 1913, another box was undoubtedly made to commemorate the three hundredth anniversary of Romanov rule. It is in the shape of a seventeeth-century *larets*, or casket, and is studded with semiprecious stones.[41] The miniature painting on the top is a copy of Konstantin Makovski's *Choosing of the Bride*, painted in 1886.[42] It depicts an historical event in 1647, when Tsar Aleksei Mikhailovich ordered all the beautiful maidens of the realm be brought before him so he could choose one for his bride. These and other miniature paintings used by Rückert reflected the 'Boyarmania' that started in the 1880s – Vasnetsov and Makovski both painted their most imporant works before 1900 – and reached a fevered pitch at the time of the Tercentenary. Preferred paintings were romantic depictions of the bogatyrs of Kievan Russian and the life of the sixteenth- and seventeenth-century boyars, with their elaborate dress and richly ornamented palaces.

The master of miniature paintings on enamel was Feodor Ivanovich Rückert, who supplied Fabergé with most of his enamels in the Russian style. Rückert's association with Fabergé can be dated from 1887, when the Moscow workshops opened, to 1912, when a cup was produced to celebrate his twenty-five years with Fabergé (cat. 219). Rückert made many pieces for Ovchinnikov and Kurliukov in the 1890s and in the early years of the twentieth century, and later for Marshak in Kiev, but what he did precisely for Fabergé before 1903 is not clear. Very few pieces exhibit his early style of flowers, birds, and animals in pastel colours, with Fabergé overstamping his mark or with the Fabergé mark alone. Most of his work for Fabergé appears after 1908.

A *bratina*, clearly in Rückert's style, was presented by Nicholas II to the French admiral Germinet in 1902.[43] It is a surprise because the colours and style of the piece were not used by Rückert until slightly later. This could mean Rückert was experimenting with a darker palette quite early. (These kinds of determinations can be made by matching inventory numbers. After doing so, colour and style changes then become quite obvious.)

Most of the pieces made for Fabergé are in the Neo-Russian style. Rückert's son, Pavel Friedrikhovich (born 1883), entered the Stroganov School in 1899.[44] If he completed the full course, usually six years, he would have returned to work for his father around 1905. This could account for the design changes that are found in his work just before the mark changes in 1908. The *kovsh* (cat. 220) presented to Ludwig Olsen, Director of the Nobel Factory, by his employees in 1908 is a good example.

Rückert used the strong black colouring in his enamels for a brief period around 1907.

By 1908, Rückert not only employed a palette of dark blues, greens, greys, and browns, but he had also developed intricate wirework patterns. Filigree wires no longer separate colours but begin to form patterns of their own, with coils, cross hatching, and rarely, as seen with one box (cat. 214), wirework actually invading the miniature painting. In this box and in a similar one (cat. 215), the wirework is strikingly like a Gustav Klimt painting. Sometimes the geometric patterns of enamel and wire give the effect of the chip work on carved wooden implements made in the Abramtsevo carpentry shop (see fig. 4 for the chip work on the door).

Rückert also began to employ those motifs found on Abramtsevo and Talashkino wares, such as chickens, guinea hens, owls (as seen on the side pieces of a frame [fig. 2] and on a silver-and-enamel box [fig. 7]), horse handles, sunflowers, and cloud berries (fig. 2), triangular shapes like mountains (compare the ornament on the sides of the table in fig. 8 to the designs at the top of the box in fig. 7), and stylised pine trees which appear as part of the borders of Ivan Bilibin's illustrations.

Rückert united these Neo-Russian motifs with romantic paintings, combining two seemingly incompatible styles by means of colour, in which the enamelled colours of the box complemented the colour tones of the painting. He used highlights of white or red, such as the red feet of the swans and the red tongue of the dragon, to pick out the sunset of *Bogatyr at the Crossroads* (cat. 217). The enamelwork became a frame for the miniature in the manner popular for posters, theatre programs, fairy-tale covers, and menus.[45] He also designed frames. The similarity between a Rückert frame (fig. 2) and one designed by Zinoviev at Talashkino (fig. 1) gives an idea of the influences at work.

All the miniatures on Rückert's pieces (and he sold many independently and through Marshak) are copies of original paintings popular at the turn of the century. While the source paintings for all known miniatures have not been identified, enough have been found to substantiate this claim. Most popular were works by Vasnetsov and Makovski. While some of the Makovski paintings are little known today, several are in Western collections. *The Boyar Wedding* at Hillwood Museum

7. Box, silver and enamel, Feodor Rückert/ Fabergé, 1908–1917. Miniature copy of *Fetching Water* by Ivan Kuliukov. Private collection.

8. Table, carved and painted wood, Aleksei Zinoviev, Talashkino, c. 1905. Hillwood Museum Library.

in Washington, D.C., and *The Dressing of the Bride* at the DeYoung Museum in San Francisco, California, were often featured on Rückert boxes.[46]

Many of the paintings are totally unknown today, and the artists long forgotten. Sergei Solomko, who won a prize at the Chicago Columbian Exposition in 1893,[47] Klavdii Lebedev, Ivan Kuliukov (fig. 7), Mikhail Avilov, and Feodor Sychkov are not household names, even in the field of art history. They were popular painters who participated in the regular exhibitions, primarily at the Academy of Art; they were illustrators of books and posters, and their work was instantly recognisable at the time. Solomko, whose painting *Evening Walk* appears on a *kovsh* (cat. 218), served as an artist for Fabergé. He decorated a fan, which was a gift from Nicholas to his sister Olga at the time of her marriage in 1901 to the Duke of Oldenburg.[48] These artists are remembered today only on old postcards and these pieces by Feodor Rückert.

From this brief survey it is possible to see the remarkably rich and varied production of Fabergé's Moscow workshops. It ran the gamut of appealing to popular taste, following the latest trends in Neo-Russian design, and leading the Neo-Classical revival of the first decade of this century. The output of the Moscow workshops was always distinguished, as both Birbaum and Bainbridge noted, by fine craftsmanship and creative design. If the work produced in St. Petersburg represented *la belle époque*, the internationalism of Russia before World War I, that of Moscow symbolised the heart of the country, its Russian soul, along with the Western cultural layers that had been spread over it since the time of Peter the Great.

1. The author is grateful to the Fabergé Arts Foundation for supporting a curator exchange which provided the opportunity for research in the Russian archives. The author is also indebted to Jean M. Riddell for sharing her knowledge about Moscow enamels and to Wendy Salmond for her thoughtful comments on this work. Valentin V. Skurlov was very helpful in negotiating the way through the Russian archives.
2. Bainbridge 1966, and Birbaum 1993. The author would like to thank Marina Lopato for the opportunity to read the Birbaum Memoir before its publication in this book.
3. Advertisement in the *Moskauer Deutsche Zeitung*, illustrated in Snowman 1952, nos. 20, 21.
4. 'F. San Galli' was a metalworking-tinsmithing firm, founded in 1853, which grew rapidly, received the Imperial Warrant, and presumably by 1887 moved into larger quarters. *Iubileinoe istoricheskoe i khudozhestvennoe izdanie v pamiat 300-letiia tsarstvovaniia derzhavnago Doma Romanovykh* (Moskva, 1913). The firm is listed, but no page number is given.
5. Bowe is listed in *Vsia Moskva*, 1906, as General Allen Andreevich Bo. In 1907, the year after his retirement, he is listed with 'precious stones' after his name, meaning, presumably, he was an expert. It is possible that he became an expert in gems in South Africa, and that is one of the reasons that Fabergé hired him.
6. Quoted in V.V. Skurlov, 'The Odessa Branch of the House of Fabergé', in *The Great Fabergé* (Leningrad, 1990), p. 55.
7. Otto Gustavovich Iarke (Jarke) is listed in *Vsia Moskva*, 1906, as a merchant and an agent and chief bookkeeper of Fabergé. In that year he was active as a member of such societies as the Society of Russian-Photography, and the Society for Lovers of Drama, Art, and Literature. He was a veteran of the war with Japan. In 1907 he is listed as an agent and chief spokesman for Fabergé. He is no longer listed as being a member of these societies.
8. Andrei Karlovich Marketti (Marchetti) is listed in *Vsia Moskva*, 1906 and 1907, as working in the Fabergé firm. In 1907 he is listed also as secretary of the Italian Philanthropic Society.
9. In *Vsia Moskva*, 1912, Alexander Fabergé is listed with an address at House San Galli.
10. G.G. Smorodinova and B.L. Ulyanova, 'The Russian Master Goldsmiths', in Hill 1989, p. 29.
11. A. Kenneth Snowman, *The Art of Carl Fabergé* (London, 1955), p. 48.
12. Hans Nadelhoffer, *Cartier: Jewelers Extraordinary* (New York, 1984), p. 91.
13. *Vsia Moskva*, 1907, pp. 679, 163.
14. Central State Archive of Literature and Art, Moscow, f. 681 op. 1 del. 1151.
15. L.S. Zhuravleva, 'Kollektsiia rabot A.P.Zinovieva v sobraniiakh Smolenskogo muzeiia zapovednika i muzeia narodnogo iskusstvo v Mosvke', *Pamiatniki kultury, novye otkrytiia*, 1982 (Leningrad, 1984), pp. 469–77. The Fabergé firm is supposed to have gilded the dome of the church at Talashkino.
16. See Sotheby's, London, 20 June 1977, no. 187.
17. For more on Solntsev and the origins of the Russian style, see Anne Odom, 'Feodor Solntsev, the Kremlin Service, and the Origins of the

Russian Style', *Hillwood Studies*, no. 1 (Fall 1991). Fabergé himself made use of *Drevnosti*. One crystal plate was taken from a prototype in vol. 5, no. 2, and some of his hardstone *kovshi*, mounted in gold, were clearly inspired by examples in *Drevnosti*.

18. Several facts indicate the importance of these developments. In 1870, Butovski presented six porcelain plates with manuscript designs on them to the Musée National de Ceramique Adrien-Dubouche in Limoges (they are on exhibit there), and Butovski's *Istoriia* and other publications of the Stroganov School were exhibited at the Philadelphia Centennial exhibition in 1876. See *Ukazatel russakago otdela* (St. Petersburg, 1876), pp. 186–88.

19. For more on the development of the Russian style, see Evgenia Kirichenko, *Russian Design and the Fine Arts: 1750–1917* (New York, 1991).

20. For more on the Arts and Crafts movement at Abramtsevo and Talashkino, see ibid., and Wendy Ruth Salmond, 'The Modernization of Folk Russia: The Revival of the Kustar Art Industries 1885–1917', Ph.D. diss., University of Texas, 1989.

21. Margaret Kelly, in 'Fabergé Sculptural Silver and the Slavic Revival', *Fabergé Fantasies: The Forbes Magazine Collection* (Lugano, 1987), pp. 21–36, explores this connection, and G.G. Smorodinova and B.L. Ulyanova in Hill 1989, pp. 23–52, discuss the importance of the Stroganov School.

22. Valentin V. Skurlov, who has done a prodigous amount of work in the Russian archives, tracking workmasters, artists, and designers, pointed out in conversation with the author that many craftsmen moved from Petersburg to Moscow. This may be the case, but their movement does not seem to have altered the basic stylistic differences between the two cities.

23. Birbaum Memoirs, published here.

24. For illustrations, see *Mir Iskusstva*, no. 9 (1903), and Elena A. Borisova and Grigory Sternin, *Russian Art Nouveau* (New York, 1988), p. 216.

25. See Christie's, 18 April 1989, no. 78. The mark is listed as *S T*s in Cyrillic, which would not be right, although the *T*s might be a *U* in Cyrillic for *uchiliche* (school).

26. Debora L. Silverman, *Art Nouveau in Fin-de-Siècle France* (Berkeley, 1989), p. 161.

27. *Fabergé Silver from the Forbes Magazine Collection* (London, 1991), no. 20.

28. Bainbridge 1966, p. 132.

29. For a similar *kovsh*, see Sotheby's, New York, 19 June 1991, no. 184. This one has warriors standing at the foot of the handle. They are not integrated into the form of the *kovsh* as well as in the Forbes *kovsh*.

30. See Sotheby's, Geneva, 15 and 17 November 1988, no. 127, for such a *kovsh*. Another is in Habsburg/Solodkoff 1979, no. 44.

31. Christie's, London, 10 October 1990, no. 111. There is also an example in *Fabergé Silver from the Forbes Magazine Collection*, no. 32.

32. See Sotheby's, London, 20 June 1977, no. 187.

33. See cat. 70 for the tea set from the Hillwood Museum collection presented to Grand Duke Konstantin Konstantinovich and his wife for their wedding anniversary. It was made by the 1st Silver Artel, which succeeded Rappoport in St. Petersburg.

34. See *bratina* in *The Great Fabergé*, no. 83.

35. For an example of this, see a large, three-handled cup in Christie's, Geneva, 14 May 1991, no. 224. An especially archaic *bratina* appears in Sotheby's, Geneva, 13 November 1986, no. 465.

36. Hill 1989, no. 203.

37. In *Vsia Moskva* for 1901, he is listed as having a painting establishment as well as a silver workshop.

38. Sotheby's, New York, 13 and 14 December 1984, no. 504.

39. According to V.V. Skurlov in conversation with the author, Gulianov provided Fabergé with icons. For more on Gulianov, see *Khudozhniki narodov SSSR, Bibliograficheskii slovar'*, Tom 3 (Moscow, 1976), p. 243.

40. Lesley 1976, no. 243.

41. See Snowman 1955, no. 63. Snowman says the miniature copy 'by Haritonov', leaving it unclear whether the miniature is signed by Kharitonov, or whether there is a Kharitonov copy in the Tretiakov Gallery.

42. The painting, commissioned by William Schumann, the American jewellery merchant who had bought *The Boyar Wedding* in 1885, is now in the Museo de Arts Ponce in Puerto Rico.

43. Habsburg/Solodkoff 1979, no. 91.

44. Central State Archive of Literature and Art, Moscow, f. 667 op. 2 del. 7670. In his application for entry, he used the German version of his patronymic. Another son, Feodor Feodorovich (born 1888) studied at the school briefly in 1903 as a *liubitel* (literally, art lover), a part-time student.

45. A Bilibin poster of 1903 has a design that could be a Rückert wirework pattern. See Mikhail Anikst and Nina Baburina, *Russian Graphic Design, 1880–1917* (New York, 1990), no. 33.

46. See Anne Odom, 'A Key to the Past: Feodor Rückert's Miniature Picture Gallery', *Apollo* (January 1993), pp. 22–27, for a more complete study of the paintings. *Blind Man's Bluff* (cat. 214) was recently sold at auction in New York (Sotheby's, 20 February 1992, no. 84) and *The Boyar* (cat. 213) was on the cover of *Solntse Rossii* in March 1913, but its present whereabouts are unknown.

47. Solomko's prize winning painting is mounted on a Rückert box. See Sotheby's, New York, 18 December 1991, no. 149. A receipt attached to the box explains the painting.

48. See Snowman 1955, p. 115. For an illustration of the fan, see Bainbridge 1966, pl. 44.

Fabergé and the Paris 1900 *Exposition Universelle*

Géza von Habsburg

The Paris World's Fair of 1900 was planned to be the most lavish one of its kind ever held.[1] Preparations must have taken many years, since they involved a substantial modification of the capital's centre. Few are aware today that the Gare d'Orsay and both the Grand and the Petit Palais were built for this occasion. Both of these palaces, which were then situated on 'Avenue Nicholas II' (today Avenue Winston Churchill), were baptised thus as a gesture of friendship towards Tsar Nicholas II. Together with Tsarina Alexandra Feodorovna and President Félix Faure, the Tsar had laid the foundation stone of the Pont Alexandre III on 7 October 1896, another monument destined to be opened in 1900 as a symbolic underpinning of Russo-French entente. The visit of the Tsar and Tsarina had been heralded for the opening of the *Exposition Universelle* in order to inaugurate the bridge. The visit never took place: French papers attributed the Russian change of mind to Alexandra Feodorovna's concern for their lives. Instead the bridge was inaugurated by the Russian Ambassador, Prince Ouroussov.

The World's Fair covered 112 hectares, extending to the Champs Elysées, the esplanade of the Invalides, the Champ de Mars, and the banks of the Seine. The *Exposition* opened its doors on 14 April 1900 and closed on 12 November. Paris was in a frenzy. Seventy-six thousand exhibitors showed their wares, and fifty million entries were registered. Cléo de Mérode danced her Cambodian dances in the Asian Theatre at the Trocadero, and Sarah Bernhardt acted in Rostand's *L'Aiglon*, her star role.

The planning and construction of the Russian Pavillion and its contents at the Trocadero was a major undertaking. Mr de Kowalevsky, Director of the Department of Commerce and Manufacture, was President of the Imperial Commission, Mr A. de Raffalovich of the Ministry of Finance acted as its Vice-President, Prince Vincheslas Tenicheff as its General Commissar, and Mr Basil Wouyich as its Deputy Commissar. With a team of eighty-five members, the Commission succeeded in producing a most lavish *mise en scène*. Architect Meltzer recreated an entire city, with its kremlin, church, and all, to contain the *Palais de l'Asie Russe*. A village in its middle exhibited the smaller Russian rural industries under the patronage of Grand Duchess Sergei. This Russian village was peopled with typical workmen, craftsmen, cossacks, and

1. Fabergé's stand at the *Exposition Universelle*.

musicians, including the famous V. V. Andreev with his Grand Russian orchestra, whom Feodor Chaliapin visited.

Since the Moscow-Vladivostok line of the Trans-Siberian Express had been inaugurated that same year, Wagons Lits exhibited an original train, which was used as a public bar. Visitors could imagine a trip on the Trans-Siberian Express as a continuous panorama glided past the bar's windows. In the section of textiles, the firm of Sapozhnikov exhibited the coronation mantles of Tsar Alexander III and of Nicholas II. At the Invalides (*Industries Diverses*), a large map of France was shown, made by the hardstone cutting factory of Ekaterinburg and presented to the French Government by Tsar Nicholas II.

The exhibition of jewellery and goldsmithwork was shown as part of the Pavillion de l'Industrie on the Esplanade des Invalides, with foreign exhibitors presenting their work in the annex building *Section Etrangère*. Fabergé had been invited to participate as a member of the *Classe 95 (Joaillerie et Bijouterie)*, which was presided by Louis Aucoc fils (fig. 1). His works appeared *hors concours* alongside Commission members Frédéric Boucheron, René Lalique, and Henri Vever. As a member of the International Jury, he also showed works in the section *Classe 94 (Orfèvrerie)*, presided by Georges Boin, alongside Commission members Th.-Joseph Armand-Caillat and Emile Froment-Meurice.

At the House of Fabergé preparations for this major occasion were in full swing by 1899. The Tsar and Tsarina had permitted Fabergé to exhibit a selection of items from the Imperial Treasury, including a number of Imperial Easter eggs. Many works exhibited in Paris were later shown to the Russian public in 1902 at the Dervise Mansion (see descriptions of these items in Lopato, 'New Insights into Fabergé from Russian Documents.'). It was Fabergé's initiative to ask permission to reproduce some of the Imperial Regalia in miniature. A file 'On permission to jeweller Fabergé to produce for the purpose of exhibiting at the Paris Exposition of the miniature replicas of the Imperial regalia' was opened on 28 June and closed on 24 August 1899.[2]

Report.

Having the intention to make the miniature replicas of the Imperial crowns regalia (some of them) for the forthcoming Paris World's Fair, and not daring to do so without knowledge and permission of the Cameral Office of His Majesty's Cabinet, I report such is my intention and kindly request to grant me, if possible, permission to make such replicas.

28 June 1899   C. Fabergé

Note: His Excellency V.V. Sipiagin – I ask you to discuss the matter.
28.VII.99

Report

Jeweller Fabergé addressed the Cameral Office of His Majesty's Cabinet with a request to allow him to make for the forthcoming Paris World's Fair and to exhibit there the exact miniature replicas of some Imperial regalia (big Emperor's Crown, Sceptre and Orb). Such request of Mr Fabergé is submitted for the consideration of your Excellency.

28 July 1899   Director of the Chamberlain's Office of His Majesty's Cabinet in the rank of Imperial Court Equerry
V. Sipiagin.

Note: Imperial permission is granted, but not for sale.
Baron Frederiechs. 4. August 1899

Dear Sir, Carl Gustavovich,
I inform you that the Imperial permission is granted for your manufacturing the replicas of the Imperial Regalia.[3]

A note in the files of the Imperial Cabinet concerns the acquisition in 1902 of these replicas by His Majesty's Cabinet.[4] They have been on view at the Hermitage since that time (cat. 113).

In absence of a list of loans from Fabergé, we can only base our knowledge on the descriptions in contemporary reports (fig. 2, 3). Only a small number of Fabergé's exhibits were actually mentioned either in the press or in the jury's reports. Those that are described are the Pamiat Azova egg of 1891; the Lilies-of-the-Valley basket and the Lilies-of-the-Valley egg

2. Rørstrand vase with silver-gilt mounts shaped as water lilies. As exhibited at the *Exposition Universelle*. For a vase with similar mounts in the Pavlovsk Palace collection see cat. 37.

3. Nephrite Imperial presentation *kovsh* with Renaissance-style jewelled and enamelled gold mount. As exhibited at the *Exposition Universelle*. Topkapi Museum, Istanbul.

LES INDUSTRIES D'ART A L'EXPOSITION UNIVERSELLE DE 1900

ORFÈVRERIE

4. Imperial Pansy egg, presented by Tsar Nicholas II to his mother, the Dowager Empress, for Easter 1899. As exhibited at the *Exposition Universelle*. Private collection, United States.

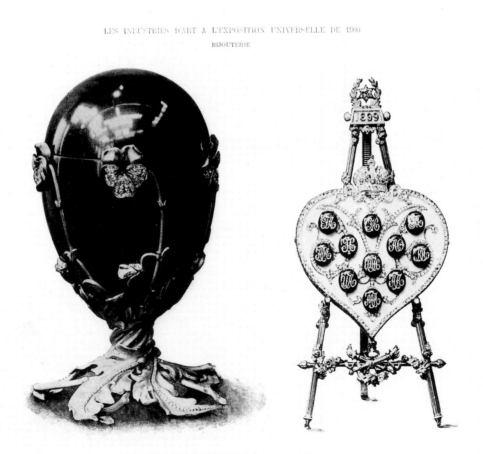

ŒUF DE PAQUES, EN NÉPHRITE, OR ET DIAMANTS

Offert par S. M. l'Empereur de Russie Nicolas II à sa mère l'Impératrice douairière
contenant un petit chevalet décoré du chiffre des membres de sa famille.
Exécuté par M. Fabergé (Russie).

(cat. 23), both of 1896; the Pansy egg of 1899; and the miniature replicas of the Imperial Crown Jewels of 1900; a carnet de bal, a group of flowers, and a candelabra and a large centre-piece, both in nephrite and mounted in bronze and silver.

The Jury of *Classe 94 (Orfèvrerie)* gave a very positive report on Fabergé's exhibits.

We have examined with pleasure the works presented by Mr Fabergé, the jeweller goldsmith, who, as member of the Jury of *Classe 95*, was *hors concours*. He showed us some interesting objects of goldsmith-work: a Louis XVI-style candelabra and a large decorative piece, in which the use of nephrite, bronze and silver and their decoration in the modern taste were worthy of praise, but what was most charming was his collection of precious objects, in gold and enamel destined to give satisfaction to the national tradition of presents, which both the great and the humble, the rich and the poor habitually give at the occasion of Easter.

The Collection of Easter eggs borrowed from the Imperial Treasure was quite exquisite.

These pieces stem more from the tradition of the jeweller than of the goldsmith, but the forms, and the decoration and above all the dimensions have made us classify them more as goldsmithwork rather than jewellery. The mounts are delicate, the secret compartments, the chasing, the enamels were truly remarkable.[5]

The Jury of *Classe 95 (Joaillerie et Bijouterie)* analysed Fabergé's exhibits as follows:

One cannot but express one's satisfaction when one can examine one by one in detail the jewels exhibited by the House of Fabergé. *Hors concours* as a member of the Jury, this is craftsmanship at the very limits of perfection, the transformation of a jewel into a true object of art. The perfect execution as well as irreproachable setting distinguish all objects exhibited by the House of Fabergé, whether it is this tiny imperial crown set with 4000 stones, or these enamelled flowers so perfectly imitated that they seem natural, or these numerous objects of fantasy, which have been examined at length by the Jury.[6]

In the same vein, traditionalists amongst the critics hailed Fabergé's art unreservedly as being stylistically and technically perfect, as Victor Champier observed.

In Russia there would be nothing to write about, were it not for the court jeweller, Mr Fabergé, who brings a most ingenious and artistic note. It is not so much in jewellery strictly speaking, in the diadems,

sparkling and lavish, in the stomachers and symbolic pendants that Fabergé shows the original talent of an innovator. It is mainly in his jewels of a more special nature, which are less made for personal adornment, and more for an intimate use, that he shows the rarest qualities of the inventor. Much admired at the World's Fair were, for instance, the exquisite objects made by Fabergé for members of the Imperial Family, and which, according to the custom of this land, are given at Easter: there are numerous little *chefs d'oeuvre*, of perfect execution and taste, which rejoiced the *connoisseurs*. Amongst these objects, one will gladly remember a certain nephrite Easter egg, which, opened by a spring, displays a mobile easel, in gold, enamel and diamonds: it is a present given by Tsar Nicholas to his mother the Dowager Empress. On the easel is placed a heart of enamel, and on this heart, between the design of a diamond-set cypher of the Empress, there appear other little enamelled hearts, each marked with an initial, which is that of the children and grandchildren of the widow of Alexander III. The idea is delightful, of great feeling, and is rendered with all imaginable charm. Two or three other presents of a similar nature are exhibited in the showcase of Mr Fabergé, [and] seemed to me of equal merit to this one.[7]

Louis Houillon regretted that there was but little worthy of note to report in the field of enamelled objects, which had not progressed since the 1889 exhibition. However, 'those exhibited in the showcase of Mr Fabergé, the great Imperial jeweller of Russia, should be mentioned. Boxes, bonbonnières and eggs covered in opalescent pink enamel, are beautiful and their milky hues harmonise well with the precious stones to which they are the background'.[8]

Jewellers and goldsmiths showing their works at the World's Fair belonged to one of two strongly opposed factions: traditional and modern. A few traditionalists continued in the vein of the period associated with Napoleon III, with flower sprays set with numerous diamonds. Boucheron exhibited objects of vertu not unlike those of Fabergé, in Louis XV and Louis XVI styles.[9] Chaumet's widely admired, heavy diamond jewellery was reminiscent of Agathon Fabergé's designs.

Fabergé's historicist styles were very much at odds with the general trend in Paris around 1900. The vast majority of craftsmen had designed their exhibits in the Art Nouveau style, which had made its appearance in France around 1895. Its main exponent, René Lalique, was celebrated by the French as the greatest jeweller of all time and awarded a Gold Medal and the Cross of the *Légion d'honneur*.[10] Lalique's showcase, with its winged, bat-like female figures, was one of the highlights of the World's Fair. E. Feuillâtre, Georges Fouquet, Henri Vever, and lesser jewellers, such as G. Falguières and Henri Teterger, followed his lead. The *Exposition Universelle* was the crowning of the French Art Nouveau style. Rare were the foreigners deemed worthy of mention by critics. Those who were included Tiffany and Gorham of New York, the Worshipful Company of Gold-and Silversmiths of London, Andersen of Norway, Shaper of Germany, and Ovchinnikov and Fabergé of Russia.

Hitherto it has been generally accepted that Fabergé was unconditionally fêted, that his objects were acclaimed without criticism, and that he was hailed as the greatest goldsmith of his time and duly decorated with the *Légion d'honneur*. However, to the devout champions of Art Nouveau, Fabergé's historicist works of art seemed backward. Indeed, the use of earlier French historical styles had been tacitly banned by all exponents of this new style. Fabergé's own acceptance of this idiom is first visible in the Lilies-of-the-Valley egg of 1898 (cat. 23). It is interesting to note that the foundation of the *Mir Iskusstva* (World of Art) movement, a union of artists and writers similar to the Arts and Crafts movement in Britain, occurred in the same year.[11] In Fabergé's oeuvre, Art Nouveau had but a short life span in St. Petersburg (further examples are the Pansy egg of 1899 and the Clover egg of 1902), while in Moscow its existence is evident much longer, particularly in the field of silver.

Coming from the camp of the exponents of Art Nouveau, the most incisive discussion by far of Fabergé's exhibits is provided by Rene Chanteclair, obviously a champion of the *style moderne*. 'Mr Fabergé of St. Petersburg shows a collection of *bibelots* worthy of interest: for instance a series of Easter eggs of gold and enamel, princely presents, without determined use, hiding their qualities in lavish showcases'.[12]

Chanteclair admired the leaves and blooms of the Lilies-of-the-Valley egg (cat. 23) as being 'of delicate taste', but criticised them as 'too closely adhering to the egg'. He would have preferred 'three feet, instead of four, leaves not terminated by banal scrolls, and that the egg should be set in assymetrical sprays'. The critic lauded the workmanship of the Lilies-of-the-Valley basket but considered it 'without artistic or decorative feeling. We have before us a colour photograph of nature, without the artist having impressed his own style upon it'.[13]

The Pamiat Azova egg[14] received the strictest verdict.

We do not like its patina, the exterior ornamentation of the egg, a little overdone, nor the rose-cut diamonds set in midst of the scrolls. Since Mr Fabergé remains a faithful admirer of French styles, we think that he could have easily chosen in each one of them, ornaments less obvious and more felicitous.

The surprise in the Pansy egg (fig. 4),[15] a heart-shaped frame is described as

charming, its mechanism ingenious, but, much like the other jewels, it has the characteristics and aspect of a toy, rather than a work of art, which is all the more to be regretted, since its execution, even though complicated, is irreproachable.

Chanteclair selected only an oyster-coloured carnet de bal in Louis XVI style painted with dendritic motifs (possibly cat. 13) for unrestricted praise. 'Its heather sprays [are] so dainty and exquisite, that one would attribute them to Fairy fingers'. But in the next breath Fabergé's flowers are described as being 'too faithfully copied from nature, not imparting any feeling of art nor taste: they are objects for a showcase, well crafted, but their use remains obscure'. A *kokoshnik*-shaped diadem[16] brought him pleasure only because of its ethnic connotations as a characteristic example of the Russian national style. 'It is regrettable that such specimens are not to be found in all countries, which are unfortunately losing all their originality'. Finally, the components of the miniature Regalia (cat. 113) were lauded for their workmanship and their settings.

Fabergé's attempts at Art Nouveau were deemed 'mediocre' by Chanteclair, who thought

a Russian craftsman acquires, through patience and perseverance, a praiseworthy quality of execution, but, as he is still imbued with national traditions, he hitherto ignores the principles of a new decoration, so that his ingenuity remains confined in reminiscences. . . . We regret that such perfection in craftsmanship was not employed in the creation of more original works of art, of a large daring piece.

These disparaging comments stand in stark contrast to Bainbridge's oft-cited remarks that he allegedly attributed to French goldsmiths when he praised Fabergé. '"Louis XIV, Louis XV, Louis XVI! Where are they now?" they said, and themselves replied: "In St. Petersburg, for we now call them 'Fabergé'. You are now all with Fabergé in St. Petersburg"'.[17]

In spite of the negative criticism coming from an Art Nouveau advocate, there is no doubt that Fabergé – in his first major showing in the West, which earned him a Gold Medal and the Cross of the *Légion d'honneur*, his son Eugène the rank and badge of an Officer of the Académie, and head workmaster Mikhail Perkhin a Bronze Medal[18] – deeply influenced the art of his more traditionally minded competitors. Up until the eve of the First World War, Fabergé cast a long shadow over the production of *objets d'art* of such important firms as Cartier and Boucheron in Paris, Friedlander in Berlin, Collingwood in London, and Köchert in Vienna.[19]

1. This author warmly thanks Princess Nathalie Narishkine and her assistant, Mlle Lucienne Reboul, for their kind assistance with his research in Parisian libraries.
2. The author also thanks Dr Marina Lopato for her kind permission to publish the documents from the Imperial Cabinet pertaining to the Imperial Regalia.
3. CSHA F. 468 op. 8 del. 371 p. 1ff.
4. CSHA F. 468 op. 14 del. 880.
5. Armand Caillat, *Extrait du rapport presenté au nom du Jury classe 94* (1903), p. 330.
6. Soufflot 1901, *Rapports du Jury international, classe 95, Joaillerie et Bijouterie*, p. 8. The report also mentions 'Fabergé Charles, joaillier de la Cour et estimateur près les Cabinet de S.M. l'Empereur'. The above quote comes a few pages further.
7. Champier 1902, pp. 232–33.
8. Houillon 1903, pp. 98–101.
9. For Boucheron's exhibits at the World's Fair cf. Gilles Nérat, *Boucheron* (Paris, 1988), pp. 56–59, and Habsburg 1987, pp. 336–37.
10. For René Lalique at the *Exposition Universelle* cf. MAD 1991, pp. 236 ff. Pol Neveux [*Art et Décoration*, no. 7, 1903, pp. 126–36] in his *Rapport* compares Lalique to Benvenuto Cellini.
11. For the *Mir Iskusstva* movement cf. Vsevolod Petrov, Alexander Kaminsky et al. *The World of Art Movement* (Leningrad, 1991).
12. Chanteclair 1900, pp. 61–74. All other quotes by Chanteclair are from this article.
13. Habsburg 1987, cat. 401.
14. Ibid., cat. 353.
15. San Diego/Kremlin 1989/90, cat. 11.
16. Illustrated in Chanteclair 1900, p. 63.
17. Bainbridge 1966, p. 38.
18. Exhibited San Diego/Kremlin 1989/90, cat. 29.
19. For Fabergé and his foreign competitors cf. Habsburg 1987, pp. 335–37.

Fabergé's London Branch

Géza von Habsburg

The discovery in 1979 of Fabergé's London sales ledgers[1] and one of his account books[2] was one of the few exciting *trouvailles* in the West before the recent opening of the archival sluices in Russia. They have provided an exceptional insight into the activity of a Fabergé branch that acted as one of his most successful sales points from 1907 until 1917, during the ten most prolific years of the firm's existence. They list the date of acquisition, name of buyer, description of object, inventory number, sales price in pounds, and cost in roubles. Their existence has facilitated numerous identifications of objects chiefly in British collections. The second ledger summarises intercompany expenses. Another source of information concerning the London branch of Fabergé is the chatty reminiscences of Henry Bainbridge, Fabergé's local representative. They are a mine of information, if somewhat longwinded, concerning Edwardian London.[3] Together they give an accurate picture of how Fabergé and Edwardian society interacted (fig. 1).

Fabergé must have been encouraged to open an office in London by Tsarina Maria Feodorovna, wife of Alexander III and sister of Queen Alexandra, who obviously doted on the Russian jeweller. She is known to have written, 'Fabergé is the greatest genius of our time. I also told him: *"Vous êtes un génie incomparable"*'.[4] There is little doubt that the first permanent premises at Dover Street were chosen with a view of offering the Queen a very private venue for her Fabergé acquisitions. 'It was for her that Fabergé made his modest gesture. The rooms were hers, so that she might come and go at her pleasure and see what Fabergé was doing at the time'.[5]

Following the immense success of the 1900 Paris *Exposition Universelle*, Fabergé assigned Arthur Bowe, one of the three Bowe brothers and previously his representative in Moscow, to open an office in Berner's Hotel in 1903. Operations were moved to Portland House, Duke Street, and then in 1906, to 48 Dover Street, where they remained until 1911. Following the death of King Edward VII, a last move took place to 173 New Bond Street.

While Bowe managed the establishment, Henry Bainbridge travelled to St. Petersburg for a six-month crash course in 1906–1907. Following the dissolution of the partnership with Allan Bowe in 1906, Eugène and Nicholas Fabergè visited London to assess the situation. In 1909 Nicholas took over the

Figure 1. Fabergé's Royal clientele gathered at Windsor, 1907. Left to right (seated): King Edward VII; Infanta Isabella of Spain; Beatrice, Princess Henry of Battenberg; Marie, Grand Duchess Vladimir of Russia; Queen Amelie of Portugal; Helene, Duchess of Aosta; Isabella, Maria Immaculata, Princess John of Saxony. (Standing): Princess Louise, Duchess of Fife; Arthur, Duke of Connaught; Queen Maud of Norway with Crown Prince Olav; Kaiser Wilhelm II of Germany; Victoria Mary, Princess of Wales; Princess Patricia of Connaught; George, Prince of Wales; King Alfonso XIII of Spain; Empress Augusta Victoria of Germany; Prince Arthur of Connaught; Queen Alexandra; Grand Duke Vladimir of Russia; Queen Victoria Eugenia of Spain; Louise Margaret, Duchess of Connaught; Princess Victoria; Prince John of Saxony.

direction of the London branch (a first salary was paid on 1 May 1909), where he remained until November 1916. In May they were joined by George Piggott, one of Fabergé's Moscow branch managers, according to an entry dated 17 May 1911: 'on a/c Mr Piggott's removal to London £157/17/11'.

By 1904 Fabergé's reputation was established in London thanks to Lady Paget's exhibition of his objects at a charity bazaar held in aid of the Royal Victoria Hospital for Children at the Royal Albert Hall. Queen Alexandra, who attended, purchased a jade scent bottle and an enamel-and-diamond cigarette holder.

The first entry in the London sales ledgers, dated 29 October 1906 and pertaining to twenty-two objects acquired by Queen Alexandra, was crossed out. The ledgers begin again a year later, on 6 October 1907. Between these two dates must have occurred the often-cited commission that was to be of great benefit to Fabergé. Mrs George Keppel, a friend of King Edward VII, suggested that Fabergé should portray the animals of Queen Alexandra's zoo at Sandringham. Modellers Boris Froedman-Cluzel and Frank Lutiger were dispatched from St. Petersburg, worked in secret at Sandringham, submitted their results to the King, and received the Royal assent. The cost of this commission was presumably included in a high charge to St. Petersburg on 14 October: 'Purchases to St. Petersburg. Note 49. Cost of goods sold in London to date £5240/5/3'. A large selection of animals from the Royal Collection at Sandringham was shown to the public for the first time at the Victoria and Albert Museum in 1977.[6]

The King and Queen were to remain amongst Fabergé's most loyal customers, spending an additional £3694/35 between the two of them up to 1911. Each year, after Bainbridge's return from his 'buying' trip to St. Petersburg, they reserved for themselves the right of first choice, vying with each other for this prerogative in order to acquire items as yet unseen. Edward VII's command to Bainbridge was, 'We must not make any duplicates'.

Edward VII's last visit occurred on 22 November 1909, when he bought the 'Model of a Chelsea Pensioner in purpurine black onyx, silver, gold enl. 2 sapphires' for £49/15[7] and two ducklings in brown agate and white onyx with gold legs to supplement the Queen's zoo for her birthday, on 1 December. After the King's death, Queen Alexandra did not return until 13

November 1911, when, in the company of her lady-in-waiting Charlotte Knollys, she spent £421/5 on thirteen items, including £20/10 on 'Dog, "Tige" obsidian'. Her last visit before Fabergé closed down took place on 20 December 1916, when she bought a 'box, silver enamel painting of Tsar's falconers' for £21. Queen Alexandra never met Fabergé. When she expressed the wish to make his acquaintance during one of his visits, the bashful master-craftsman allegedly fled London at once.

The Prince of Wales, later King George V, first visited Fabergé's on 20 December 1907, when he bought a 'polar bear wh calcedony on rock cryst pedestal' for £29. During his first visit as King, on 7 November 1910, he bought a 'box, nephrite, gold mts. ptd. enl. view of "Sandringham"' for £96/10. After his Coronation, his next visit occurred on 24 July 1911, when he spent £129 buying, amongst other items, an 'ashtray nephr lizard orletz tray & rock cryst' for £46/10. Both the King and Queen Mary remained faithful clients of the Russian craftsman. From Queen Mary, a great amateur of *objets d'art*, came the saying, 'There is one thing about all Fabergé pieces, they are all so satisfying'.[8]

The patronage of the British Royal Family was to be of invaluable service to Fabergé, for it brought in its wake all the elite of Edwardian society. Fabergé's toys for the rich were adopted as the perfect present for all and, in particular, for those in the highest places. Many emulated the King by taking the liberty to add to Queen Alexandra's rapidly growing collection. Such presents of a relatively inexpensive nature were acceptable gifts at Court, delighting the Queen, who would greet them with an 'Oh, how lovely'. Edward VII, more difficult to humour, was himself the recipient of numerous Fabergé walking-stick handles. He knew Fabergé's stock full well and could direct a prospective donor of some unwelcome present with 'Go to Fabergé's. They have a hippopotamus cigar-lighter in nephrite. If you wish to give me something, give me that. Besides, the lighter is half the price, and it is amusing'.[9]

Of course, Fabergé's objects were relatively inexpensive only to his very rich clientele. The cheapest items available were plain enamelled miniature Easter eggs at 10s., the price of a room at Claridge's. More lavish eggs cost upwards of £5. Plain silver cigarette cases started at £7, with more elaborate enamelled versions at £20. Hardstone boxes began at £35, gold cases at £47, and platinum cases at £120. Plain enamelled cuff-links sold for £7, enamelled pencils for £3/15. The popular nephrite elephants cost £11/15; other animals in rarer stones went up to £45 or more. Simple enamel clocks started at £27 but could cost up to £70. Flower sprays might cost as little as £20, with the most expensive priced at £117. Elaborate frames sold for as much as £135 ('Leo. de Rothschild: Frame, dk, blue enal. garlands in gold & platn.'). Silver commissions were highly priced ('Sir E. Cassel: Twelve Silver Bowls; chasings depicting growth of the British Navy £250'). Jewels, because of their intrinsic value, are the most expensive items in the sales ledgers ('James de Rothschild: Bracelet, plat, 6 chrissps. 457 brilliants £350'; 'Mrs H.M. Kelly: Earrings 2 brills & brills £725'; 'Mrs Mango: Brooch Pendant Diadem, 1 old amethyst cab & brills £875'). The highest price at Fabergé's, London, was paid by Mrs Wroham on 14 December 1909 ('Tiara, brills & roses in silver, platinum, £1400').

Fabergé's well-designed and useful objects of fantasy were the epitome of the Edwardian era. 'Nothing, whether of importance or of no importance, took place unless signalised by them'.[10] If, in Russia, Emanuel Nobel set the tone by offering his dinner guests objects from Fabergé in their napkins, in London it was Stanislas Poklewski-Koziell who was the most prolific giver. 'When he went off to country house parties he arrived loaded with things from Fabergé; two large suitcases filled with them'.

Not intended as a work of art, a gift from Fabergé's carried a message of goodwill and affection. These lighthearted objects were meant to be just that: a souvenir of a happy moment. Its purpose was fulfilled at the moment of its presentation. This explains why innumerable Fabergé objects acquired by one person have ended up in another's possession. They were not collected in the true sense of the word (with the exception of perhaps Queen Alexandra and Countess Torby). Carried around without much care, they were often left standing on side tables or mantelpieces, and they were sometimes broken or damaged. Many of the articles listed in the ledgers were returned as broken or needing repair.

Fabergé's sales ledgers underline the personal relationship that existed between the firm and its clients. There were virtually no 'cash sales', and only a few items were sold to an 'unknown gent.' or 'unknown lady', or to 'Mr X'. The names of foreign clients read like an European Gotha and include the Dowager Empress of Russia; Empress Eugénie; the King and Queen of Norway; the Kings of Greece, Denmark, Spain, and Portugal; the Queens of Italy and of Spain; Grand Duchess Vladimir and Grand Duke Boris of Russia; Prince Paul of Serbia; the Crown Prince of Roumania; the Duchess of Schleswig-Holstein; Princesses Cécile Murat, Polignac, Hatzfeldt, of Teck, Dolgorouki, Salm-Salm, and Thurn und Taxis; Prince de la Moscowa; the Aga Khan; Countess de Pourtales; Counts Széchény, Kinski, Károlyi, Benckendorff, and Blücher; and the Maharadja of Bikanir.

Fabergé adepts from among the Edwardian 'smart set' who were close to the King and Queen included Grand Duke Mikhail and Countess Torby (part of their collection may be viewed at Luton Hoo), Mrs George Keppel, the Hon. Mrs Ronald Greville, Lady de Grey, Lady Paget, Mrs Sackville West, Sir Ernest and Lady Cassel, Lord Revelstoke, and Lady Desborough. Other names that appear frequently in the sales ledgers include the Yznaga sisters from Cuba,[11] the Duchesses of Westminster, Portland, and Roxburghe; the Countesses of Dudley, Ilchester, and Howe; Ladies Brougham and Vaux, Savile, Desborough, Arlington, Cunard, Juliet Duff, Curzon, Gerard, Sassoon, Portarlington, Dufferin, and Cunard; Mrs Arthur Sassoon, Mrs Anthony Drexel, Mrs Koch de Gooreynd, Mrs Eckstein, Mrs Scaramanga; and a bevy of Rothschilds: Leopold, Albert, Edmond, Edouard, and Miss Miriam.

Some European Edwardians were married to their American counterparts. Consuelo Vanderbilt became Duchess of Marlborough (she acquired a fine Easter egg bearing her monogram at Fabergé's in St. Petersburg in 1902),[12] and Claire Huntington from Detroit became Princess Hatzfeldt and another of Fabergé's good clients. Others from the United States who joined the magic circle were Lady Violet Astor, Mr Waldorf Astor and Captain J.J. Astor of 4 St James's Square; Mr and Mrs Cornelius Vanderbilt; Jules Bache and Lady Bache Cunard; the Hon. Mrs Ivor Guest; Mrs Bradley-Martin; Mrs A.F. McCormick of Chicago; and Miss E. Ames of Massachusetts.

The sales ledgers are a mine of information about the London social scene. For example, Fabergé's figures for the fiscal year of 14 July 1913 to 13 July 1914 in London (fig. 2) indicate that 581 objects sold for a total of £15,541. These included 107 cigarette cases and cigar boxes (6 were sold on 24

Date.	Customer's Name.	Description of Goods.	Stock Number.	Selling Price.						S. L. Folio.	Cost Price.	
				Details.			Total.					
1913				£	s.	d.	£	s.	d.		Rbls.	Cop.
Nov 13	Sir E. Cassel	Blue-bells, blueish enarnd.										
		gold stem, green enl, roses										
		rock crys. vase, neph. ped.	2336	58	"	"					204.	
		Frame, neph. gilt sil. rim										
		(sil oxyde plaque of "Happy"	22026	32	10	"					90.	
		Pendant, rock crys. roses	16979	60	"		150	10	"	14	331.	
19	Mrs Hoover	Tea caddy, sil. filigree eno. 18715										
		Tea Shovel, " " 27491			nett	26	10	"	383	148.	
20	Grande Duchesse Vladimir	Group of 4 Rabbits in agate (one piece), roses	1465				50	"	"	340	237.	
"	H.M. Queen Alexandra	Pig, (smiling) satuarn	21501	14	"	"					36.	
		Cock, orletz, tourmaline	20979	20	"	"					50.	
		Pendant, chryso & diads	16902	55	"	"	89	"	"	1	262.	
"	H.R.H. Princess Victoria	Pendant, amethyst cab. 3 brills & roses in plat	17532				50	"	"	2	289.	
"	Miss McLellan (Lady Cooper's maid)	Brooch, mauve en: roses	13418	gratis			"	"	"	1	43.	
24	E.C. Foster Esq	3 Ice Servers & two (2) Compote Servers, gilt silver & filigree enamel	N.N.				nett	16	10	"	1	84.
25	Capt. E. Brassey	Bellpush, hollywood & gilt silver mounts, mecca	23678				8	5	"	33	46.	
"	Pcesse. di Teano	Bellpush, white bds enamel &c	23338				8	"	"	33	48.	
						Forward	£	398	15	"	R.	1878

December), 58 miniature Easter eggs (19 were sold to Grand Duke Mikhail Mikhailovich in Cannes at Easter), 20 pencils, 16 hardstone animals, 12 bell-pushes, 9 matchboxes, 10 frames, 10 clocks, 8 ashtrays, *8 necessaires*, 8 bonbonnières, 6 calendar blocks (all before New Year), and 3 flowers.[13] The lowest monthly total was for March (£746/3), the highest for December (£3246/15). In all, over 10,000 objects were sold in London, including 35 flowers and 4 hardstone figures. Fabergé's profit margin was generally 100 percent. To some of the best clients nett prices were accorded.

Bainbridge must have led a constant fight to obtain merchandise from the already overworked Russian workshops. His Edwardian clientele harassed him constantly with their orders. Bainbridge himself offered advice and suggested new themes. Special requests included Leopold de Rothschild's favourite gold-and-blue striped objects (cat. 166, 167), the silver models of his race horse St. Frusquin, and the lavish Renaissance vase (cat. 168) for which he paid on 12 April 1911 and presented, filled with orchids from his hothouses at Gunnesbury Park, on the occasion of the Coronation of King George V and Queen Mary on 22 June 1911 ('Cup rock crystal engraved gold 72 enamelled, different stones, nr. 18001, nett £430, cost price 2,705 roubles'). One very special keepsake was the exquisite blue enamel cigarette case, entwined by a diamond-set serpent, that was given by Mrs Keppel to Edward VII and returned by the thoughtful Queen Alexandra to Mrs Keppel in 1936. She in turn left it to Queen Mary at her death (cat. 165). Another was the model of Edward VII's favourite terrier 'Cesar', which was bought by Mrs Greville on 28 November 1910 and presented to Queen Alexandra.

Edwardians rarely shopped alone. Edward VII often came with Mrs Keppel; the Queen usually arrived either in the company of Edward VII, Princess Alexandra of Battenberg, Princess Victoria, or Miss Knollys. On 24 December 1912, Queen Alexandra and her sister, the Dowager Empress of Russia, came to finish their Christmas shopping with Mrs Cole of Sandringham, who received a tie-pin costing twenty-two roubles ('gratis'). King George V usually visited Fabergé's shop with Queen Mary (they bought things on separate and on joint accounts). The Goldschmidts (Baronne Albert) often came with the Rothschilds (Baronne Maurice). On 29 March 1912, Count Károlyi stopped by with his valet who received a 'brooch,

Figure 2. A page from Fabergé's London sales ledger dated 13–25 November 1913.

blue enal. 3 brills no. 82508 costing 34 roubles (gratis)'. Before Christmas, husbands and wives would often enter on separate days. French clients came in droves just before Christmas. These included the Baronne de Gunzbourg, Baronne Edouard and Baron Edmond de Rothschild, the Duchesse de Canastra, and the Princesses Murat de la Moscowa.

Shortly after the death of King Edward VII, the Dowager Empress visited on 9 June 1910. Grand Duke Boris stopped by on 20 June 1911 while attending the Coronation of King George V. Mrs Leeds became the firm's best client in its last two years, spending £2,766 in 1915. In a splendid Christmas shopping spree on 14 December 1916, she acquired twenty-six items for £1,130. She was outdone only by Mrs Mango, who, on 21 November 1916, spent £1,185 on twenty-three items.

Unusual entries in the ledgers include a payment on 13 July 1915 by a Lloyd's underwriter ('article stolen by Salvatori [sic] Ottorino: Pendant plat. 2 brills. square cut sapphire & platinum chain £288 nett'). A Mr Rosser (Salavatore Ottorino) had previously visited Fabergé's on 3 June 1915 and had acquired a 'Brooch (Safety-pin) gold 1 sapphire & brills no. 82794 £10 cost 51 roubles.' (Is that when the theft occurred?)

The firm's account books add a few details to Fabergé's well-documented test case against the Worshipful Goldsmiths' Company, which was tried in November 1910. At issue was an antiquated British law that obliged foreign silversmiths to have any enamelled silver items destined for sale in London sent to London for sale, pre-assayed, 'in the raw', to be returned for enamelling to their country of origin before being sent to London for sale. Fabergé apparently did not accept the logic of this law, requiring Bainbridge to travel to Russia in April 1910 presumably in order to report on the matter personally. He incurred heavy legal expenses (14 July 1911: 'Legal expenses Assay Trial' £1305/16/4), including a trip to London of expert witness Henrik Wigström (21 March 1911: 'Assay Trial a/c (Wigström Exps)' £52/12/7), but he lost the case. Henceforth, Fabergé's enamelled silver objects of under 91–zolotnik purity were subjected to this law. These are hallmarked according to British standards in Latin characters and can be readily identified in the London sales ledgers. All other imported Fabergé objects carry the usual Russian hallmarks.

Selling trips by staff members were often made to the Continent: 16 December 1909 to Paris; January – March 1910

to Rome ('Mr Houriet's ticket, passport, 2 bags & portfolio and cash on a/c £35'; 'Mr Houriet's life insurance £16'; 'cash lent by London branch £480'). The total sold to clients in Rome, including the Queen of Italy, was £1,984 with further orders for £1,063/14/5. Payments to the Rome account were made in February and March of 1911 (13 February: Rome a/c 'cash to M. Eugen' £47; 14 February: ditto £31/11/7; and 'to Rome a/c' £357). A trip to Paris on 8 December 1911 brought sales of £866/9.

A trip taken to Paris, the Côte d'Azur, and Rome from January through Easter of 1914 resulted in sales to some of their old London customers who were enjoying the better weather there. Grand Dukes Mikhail Mikhailovich and Mikhail Aleksandrovich bought seventeen miniature Easter eggs between them. In Cannes, the widow of Crown Prince Rudolph of Austria, née Princess Stefanie of Belgium, who had married Prince Lonyay in 1900, bought on 2 March a 'papercutter bird's eye wood rasp red enal 134 francs'. She was followed by her husband three days later (5 March: 'pencil, dk blue enal 148 francs').

The London base was also used to finance costly annual forays to the Orient, beginning in 1908 and ending in 1917. A total of over £9,000 was spent in over ten years, presumably to cover costs of trips to India, Bangkok, China, and Japan. Apart from the treasures housed at the Bangkok Royal Palace[14] and a few items from India in the collection of the Maharadja of Bikanir, another good London client, nothing sold to or ordered by Fabergé's clients in the East has surfaced in the West.

In 1915, the London shop received orders from Russia to close down its operations, as foreign capital had to be repatriated to finance the war effort. Nevertheless, trading continued until 9 January 1917 under Nicholas Fabergé and Bainbridge. The remaining stock of some two hundred objects was sold to the French jewellers Lacloche Frères and disposed of under their own name.

Two bills for Messrs. C. Fabergé & Co Ltd, Petrograd, have survived from Johnson, Mathey & Co of Hatton Garden, London, dated 16 January and 30 January 1917 for 9332.8 oz (290.911 kg) of standard silver sheets costing £1466/4/11 and for 6378 oz (198.382 kg) of silver skillets costing £969/19/9. These were packed in five cases and dispatched to Petrograd on board the S.S. *Titane* at a cost of £57/11/0. During the War silver must have been unobtainable in Russia.

The lawyer's firm of Rawle, Johnstone & Co was given power of attorney by Nicholas Fabergé in March 1917 to wind up the business and to assist in collecting outstanding debts. An elusive Mr Stones c/o Primrose Club was to act on behalf of Fabergé. Debtors included the Maclaine of Lochbiue (£17), Mrs Albu (£31/3/0), Captain Delme Radcliffe (£33), Comte Mouravieff (£112/17/5), Baroness van Pallandt Eerde (£96/9/6), Mr G. Wolkoff (£30/5/0), Grand Duke Mikhail (£140), and Queen Alexandra (£18/18/0). Most of these debts had been collected by 31 July 1917, with legal fees amounting to £35/2/8, paid by Henry Bainbridge on 11 September 1917.

1. The two leather-bound volumes, identified by this author in a hat box in the attic of the late Mrs Theodore Fabergé in Geneva, are now in the Fabergé Archive in Geneva. They were first published in Habsburg/Solodkoff 1979, pp. 140–42, and more recently in Solodkoff 1982, pp. 102–5.

The ledgers begin without preamble on 29 October 1906, skip a year, re-start on 6 October 1907, and break off on 9 January 1917. Entries from 14 April 1908 on are in Bainbridge's hand. Fabergé's first full fiscal year, after a first year of only nine months (October 1907 to 13 July 1908), begins on 14 July 1908 and ends on 13 July 1909.

2. Fabergé Archive, Geneva. The first entry is dated 30 November 1906, the last entry 13 February 1917.

3. Bainbridge 1966, pp. 78–109.

4. Solodkoff 1984, p. 78.

5. Bainbridge 1966, p. 28.

6. V&A 1977, pp. 13–16, 29–30, 32, and 35.

7. Habsburg 1987, cat. 385.

8. Bainbridge 1966, p. 109.

9. Ibid., p. 82.

10. Ibid., p. 86.

11. Objects by Cartier, including two fine flowers, and Fabergé were given by one of the Misses Yznaga to the Musée des Arts Décoratifs in Paris. Others were sold at auction in Geneva between 1979 and 1984.

12. Solodkoff 1984, p. 11.

13. Alexander von Solodkoff (Solodkoff 1982, p. 104) has computed similar figures for 1912–1913: 713 objects were sold for a total of £16,401. Amongst these were 91 cigarette cases, 71 miniature Easter eggs, 25 animals, 23 frames, and 8 table clocks.

14. Krairiksh 1984.

Fabergé Drawings in the Hermitage Collection

Karina Orlova &
Larisa Zavadskaia

The State Hermitage possesses a major collection of Russian gold, silverware, and jewellery. It fully represents the history of the Russian art of jewellery from times immemorial to the turn of the twentieth century, from the wonderful enamels of old Kiev to exquisite works by St. Petersburg and Moscow masters. Drawings are an inalienable part of this collection. Here one can find drawings by such renowned St. Petersburg jewellers as Carl Edward Bolin, Ludwig Breitfus, and Leopold Zeftingen. A considerable number of leaves are marked with Carl Fabergé's stamp.

The collection of Fabergé drawings counts about one hundred items and throws light onto several decades of the firm's activities. The Hermitage obtained all these drawings from the Museum Fund in 1929, but little more information concerning their provenance is known. Most of them are never-realised designs of silver toilet sets, ceremonial dinner services, cups, *kovshi*, mugs, table clocks, silver cutlery, and photograph frames. These drawings vary greatly, reflecting the different styles, fashions, tastes, and aesthetics of the firm's clients, but they all share one thing in common: perfection of execution and meticulous elaboration of minute detail.

Fabergé always lavished great attention on the designs of his objects. He paid considerable salaries: six to ten thousand roubles a year to artists to ensure original and new drawings from his masters. He had a comprehensive knowledge of Russian and European jewellery and expected the same from his artists. By the turn of the twentieth century the firm employed twenty designers. Among them were graduates of the Stieglitz School of Technical Drawing: Jan Lieberg, Feodor Grinberg, Oscar Mai, Leiser Strikh, Evgeni Jakobson, and Vasilii Zuiev. Many of these names are known only through archival documents: no drawing can be attributed to a particular artist.

The earliest of the drawings in the Hermitage collection date from the times of Alexander III – the 1880s. A drawing of a silver rectangular case decorated with turquoise and pearls (cat. 302) was signed by the Court Jeweller Carl Fabergé. He also signed a few sheets with drawings of ceremonial silver services. One of them is made in the rococo style with playful figures of putti and languid figures of nymphs (cat. 329), while others, in the Louis-XVI style, are more austere and restrained (cat. 333, 334). A few of the objects depicted in the drawings have the monogram of Empress Alexandra Feodorovna. Nicholas II must have planned to give a silver dinner service to his wife as a present for the tenth anniversary of their wedding or coronation, but apparently it was never executed. *Stolitsa i Usadba* in 1914 published a photograph of a few objects from a rococo dinner service by Fabergé. The service belonged to the Russian Ambassador in Berlin. The forms and decorations once elaborated by the firm's designers are traceable in these objects.

The drawings of a nephrite tray (cat. 303) and a large stone vase (cat. 304) bear the monograms of Russian Emperor Nicholas II and Empress Alexandra Feodorovna and those of German Emperor Wilhelm II and his wife Augusta Victoria. In 1906 the German Imperial couple celebrated their silver wedding anniversary. These two drawings are probably the traces of numerous projects for gifts from the Russian Imperial Family to their German counterparts. The drawing of the tray is signed 'K. Fabergé' and the drawing of the vase has an oval stamp in French of 'K. Fabergé. Court Jeweller. St. Petersburg'.

A number of drawings bear the same stamp in Russian in addition to the State Emblem. Some of them have notes in pencil indicating the size of the objects and their prices. All these cups, clocks, and kovshi must have been made in preparation for a major celebration, such as the Romanov Tercentenary.

In the early twentieth century, Russian jewellers often made use of subjects from national history, chronicles, myths, and legends. The figures of Old Russian warriors (cat. 338, 340) and girls in *kokoshniki* decorate various objects from the St. Petersburg and Moscow workshops. Historic characters are seen in the drawings of silver objects offered by Fabergé.

Not only were traditional *kovshi*, mugs, and cups used as gifts but photographs of members of the Imperial Family were also placed in ornate table frames. Many of the drawings have designs of such frames. Wooden frames were decorated with moulded silver and gilded applications in the shape of garlands, swags, bands, torches, and quivers with arrows. In the early twentieth century classicism became fashionable again, and masters working in applied artforms made wide use of architectural motifs from the periods of Catherine the Great and Alexander I. At the same time, Old Russian ornamentation acquired new significance. The idiom developed by the craftsmen of Talashkino and Abramtsevo was revived with new vitality by Fabergé's artists. Polychrome enamels, lush floral ornaments, and sparking gem tones all hark back to the works of Russian silversmiths of the seventeenth century.

Also of interest are written instructions as to optional changes in design: alterations to enamel colour, elimination of some of the ornamentation, selection of other materials for a specific detail of an object. Many drawings of the frames bear the rectangular stamp 'K. Fabergé. St. Petersburg' and the date of the submission of the drawing to the Minister of the Imperial Court for approval.

So far we have been unable to find a single object made after a design from our drawings in the literature. Apparently the firm's designers, when composing an object, combined elements from various drawings.

This is the first time that the collection of Fabergé drawings from the Hermitage has been published. We hope that this will allow Fabergé scholars to ascertain some doubtful Fabergé attributions and permit a more precise dating of other objects.

Fabergé's Houses in St. Petersburg

Boris Ometov

Bolshaya Morskaya Street in St. Petersburg was a true mecca for jewellery makers. At various times jewellers Bolin, Butz, Polvinen, Tillander, Bock, Ovchinnikov, and Dennisov-Uralski lived, worked, and/or had their stores here. As early as 1842 Gustav Fabergé, founder of the famous firm, settled in the house at 11 Bolshaya Morskaya (fig. 1).

That house, designed by the well-known St. Petersburg architect Pavel Petrovich Jacot (1798–after 1852), was built in 1837–1838. The architect's descendants owned the house until the beginning of the twentieth century, and it survives with minor changes. Mikhail Evlampievich Perkhin, Fabergé's principal jeweller, opened his workshop there in 1886.

The Fabergé family's next address was at 16 Bolshaya Morskaya, in the Ruadze-Kononov House (fig. 2). Built in the early 1850s by the architect R. A. Zhelyazevich, the house belonged to Hereditary Honourable Citizen I. A. Kononov, then to N. N. Gartong, a high-standing official at the Emperor's Court. Carl Gustavovich Fabergé lived there with his family and also opened a gold and jewellery store on the premises. His sons Eugène, Agathon, Alexander, and Nicholas grew up here.

As the firm expanded and the number of personnel grew, Carl Fabergé decided to start a kind of centre for the firm, with workshops and a big store in the same Bolshaya Morskaya. With this idea in mind, a piece of land with a house at 24 Bolshaya Morskaya was bought from Colonel V. P. Zolotov, and a new building was designed by the architect K. K. Schmidt.

Born in St. Petersburg, Karl Karlovich Schmidt (1866–after 1941) graduated from the Peterschule and then enrolled in the Physics and Mathematics Department of St. Petersburg University. He attended the course at the Imperial Academy of Arts for six years, finishing in 1893 with a Gold Medal. Karl Schmidt designed many mansions, apartments, and public and industrial buildings, including his own house (13 Khersonskaia Street, at 12 Perekupnoi Lane), 1901, and his own dacha in Pavlovsk (7 Second Krasnoflotski Lane), 1900s; G. A. Schulz's apartment building (22 Kuibyshev Street), 1901–1902; the Aleksandrovski Home for Women (45–51 Bolshoi Prospekt, Vasilyevski Island – 11 14th Line), 1897–1899; and O. V. Paley's Palace (1 Sovetski Lane in Tsarskoe Selo), 1910–1914. In 1909 he was elected an Academician for his work as an architect.

Karl Schmidt's mother was Carl Fabergé's cousin. Many

common interests, including philately, brought him close to the Fabergé family. Having carefully studied all the requirements for the new building of the St. Petersburg branch of the Fabergé firm, the architect decided to tear down all the structures on the plot and build a four-storey building with basements as well as four-storey wings with basements and garrets. The design obtained Imperial approval on 29 May 1899. By 1900 construction was completed.

The Gothic stylisation of the building stands out in this, one of the most fashionable and architecturally diverse streets of the northern capital (fig. 3). The grey-pink granite façade, with its polished and heavy red granite half-columns and its big windows, is crowned with triangular gables. The original plastered facades in the courtyards have also survived. Some of these were rusticated, while others were plastered. The four-storey courtyard wings, each with an additional garret, are of different heights, with the western wing being the highest. In its plan, the configuration of these wings is quite complicated, with numerous corbels and struts.

The ground floor housed the sale-room. On the upper floors and in the courtyard structures, workshops were equipped with the best technology available at the time. The very top floor was given to the art studio. Talented young designers, recent graduates from the Baron Stieglitz School, worked there under the direction of the firm's main designer, Franz Birbaum. Offices and Carl Fabergé's apartment were also located in the building.

Figure 1. The house of the architect P. P. Jacot at 11 Bolshaya Morskaya today. Gustav Fabergé founded his firm here in 1842. It later became the workshop of Fabergé master Mikhail Perkhin.

Figure 2. A contemporary view of the Ruadze Kononov House at 16 Bolshaya Morskaya. Here, Carl Fabergé had his apartment and the firm had its store.

Figure 3. The House of Fabergé in St. Petersburg at 24 Bolshaya Morskaya Street as it looks today.

Figure 4. The main staircase as it appears today, showing the preserved stained glass windows, iron railings, and ornamental moulding.

After the new centre was built, many workshops were moved to 24 Bolshaya Morskaya, including those of Mikhail Perkhin and Henrik Wigström, Albert Holmström, August Hollming, Alfred Thielemann, Victor Aarne, Hjalmar Armfelt, Andrei Gorianov, Anders Nevalainen, Feodor Afanassiev, and Vladimir Soloviev.

The entrance to the main staircase is located at the end of the west wing. One proceeds through the gates and the archway, the walls of which are faced with white and light green tiles, to the entrance hall on the lower landing. Lit with three tiers of stained glass windows in oak sashes, the staircase has been preserved with few changes (fig. 4). The Art Nouveau glass depicts white flowers and green-and-blue foliage entwined around a trellis growing through two of the three superimposed bays, the uppermost window showing only grey clouds in a blue sky. Limestone steps and landings are faced with intricately ornamented coloured ceramic tiles. The Art Nouveau railings on the staircase are of forged metal, while the walls in the staircase itself and in the landings are decorated with stucco borders. Also preserved on all floors are the original door frames cased in oak. Besides the main staircase, the building has two others: one in the southwest corner of the *carré* (the main square-form block) and the other in the central part of the east wing.

Unfortunately, the interiors of the Fabergé apartment, studio, and workshops were destroyed, and the layout of most of the rooms has been changed. Walls and, in some rooms, even ceilings were covered with wooden or plaster board tiles in the style of the 1960s. Only the magnificent plate glass windows with their oak sashes, some doors, and several windows suggest the high quality of the original work. Extant elements include the safe-lift, built by the Berlin firm of S. J. Arnheim, as well as the sliding metal grating on the courtyard windows.

Since the Revolution, the building has been used for various purposes. For some time it held apartments, and now it serves as the city telephone exchange, with the *Yakhont* (sapphire) jewellery store on the ground floor. It is our belief that, after careful study of archival and visual materials, some of the interiors of this fine building can be restored to their original splendour (fig. 5).

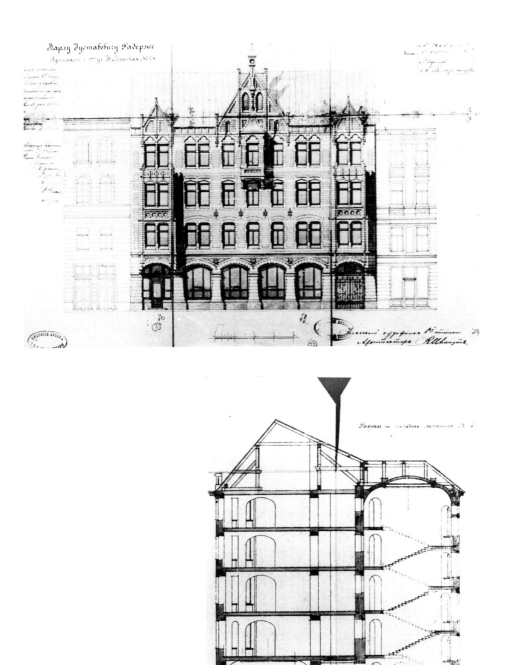

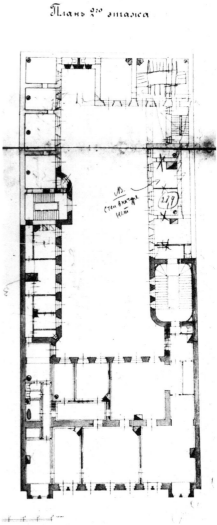

Figure 5. Architectural plans for Fabergé's building at 24 Bolshaya Morskaya. A) An original drawing of the main facade by Karl Schmidt. B) Original plan for the second floor. C) Cut-away view of the main staircase.

Figure 6. Main façade of Agathon Carlovich Fabergé's dacha in Levashovo today.

In 1883, Carl Fabergé purchased land for a dacha from Count V. Levashov. The site, picturesque and heavily forested, was located not far from the famous Vyazemski (Levashov) estate 'Aspen Grove'. In 1901, architect Karl Schmidt designed a two-storey wooden house. That same year the St. Petersburg Land Department approved the design and construction began. The walls were made of two rows of wooden beams, with gravel and broken bricks used as filling. The outside walls were then plastered and painted. The façades of the house, designed in an Art Nouveau style, were virtually undecorated.

In 1907 the new owner of the dacha, Agathon Carlovich Fabergé, decided to rebuild it. Ivan Andreevich Galnbeck received the commission for its design and construction. A graduate of the St. Petersburg Academy of Arts, Galnbeck had studied architecture in Europe for two years. He then taught at the Baron Stieglitz School of Technical Drawing, where he worked for virtually all his life. In 1904 he founded the Russian Society of Art and Industry and served as its first chairman. Carl and Agathon Fabergé were board members. Galnbeck designed and reconstructed more than ten buildings in St. Petersburg and around the city, including a Reformist Church school (36 Moika Embankment), 1899–1900; an Evangelical almshouse for men (Lesnaia Street), 1895; and a wing in the Levashov house (18 Fontanka Embankment), 1898.

His 1907 design for the Fabergé dacha, with its new two storeys, was approved by the St. Petersburg Land Department on 24 January 1908. Galnbeck kept intact most of the wooden dacha built by Schmidt. The western wall, where a stone wing was added, had to be disassembled. Another stone, two-storey wing, with a kitchen in the ground floor, was added to the north. He moved the main entrance with the porch in the eastern façade to substitute the oriel in the southern side. The entrance was decorated with a four-column, granite portico, and the entire house was raised onto a high granite base. Walls were plastered and painted white (fig. 6). A number of skylights enriched the dacha's silhouette. Various design patterns were used for the windows: some are rounded, while others have the curved, flowing contours characteristic of Art Nouveau.

Similarly, the interiors were stylistically diverse. After passing through the main entrance and by two pairs of red granite columns, one enters a vaulted hall. Its floor and walls, as well as the fireplace in the corner, are faced with marble. Through the six-fold door one enters the main hall, which leads to the main staircase. It is an impressive structure, with white marble steps framed by a wooden balustrade. The staircase leads into the first floor gallery, which is illuminated by a large three-tiered skylight (fig. 7).

Adjacent to the hall from the west is a drawing-room in which fragments of sculpting are preserved in the plastered moulding and in the decorated ceiling. The Concert Hall is the largest room on the ground floor. The floor here is on two levels,

Figure 7. A view of the dacha's main staircase displaying a collection of oriental carpets.

which are connected by a set of wooden steps with a well-designed metal balustrade. The upper floor is on the same level with the rest of the northern suite of rooms. Preserved ornamental sculpting of various plants and lyres with garlands recall the room's intended purpose of musical entertainment. A mosaic parquet floor and a carved marble fireplace complete the decoration of the hall.

North of the Concert Hall is an office, the floor of which is on two levels as well. The most interesting aspect of the office's decoration is a fireplace faced with genuine eighteenth-century Russian cobalt tiles decorated with various images, emblems, and inscriptions. A few other rooms in the house's eastern part have their sculpting preserved. Most fascinating in this part of the building is the dining-room, which has a terrace overlooking the entrance from the west and a big Italian window in the east. Two half-circular, tiled ovens with ceramic garlands are placed in the corners beneath the terrace. From the main staircase one enters the drawing-room, which has a balcony overlooking the main entrance.

The largest room on the first floor is the so-called Gemological Hall. This room, where Agathon Fabergé examined precious stones or gems, was illuminated by a skylight in the middle, as was the main staircase. The office adjacent to the Hall from the north led into a safe where gems were stored. A bathroom, toilet, and a bedroom with a brown tiled stove were located east of the Gemological Hall.

All of the building's interiors were furnished with excellent furniture of great artistic value. Paintings, portraits, and etchings adorned the walls. The house also contained painstakingly and lovingly assembled collections of Chinese and Japanese porcelain and sculpture.

A one-storey greenhouse with a skylight was later added to the northeast part of the building, where the kitchen was located. In later years, between 1908 and 1917, two more auxiliary structures were built: a coach-house and a two-storey dwelling for servants.

Oaks, elms, and pine trees were planted in the dacha's landscaped park. The park still boasts a few of the fir trees that were there at the time the original dacha was built. Legend has it that close to the main building was a gigantic oak tree planted by Carl Fabergé in 1901, when the corner-stone for the house was laid. Southeast of the dacha was a pond.

After the Revolution, in October 1918, Agathon Fabergé moved to Petrograd. (In 1927 he and his family secretly crossed the border and emigrated to Finland. He died in Helsinki on 10 October 1951.) The house, then used as a military barracks, was robbed and vandalised. Most of the interiors were demolished; furniture, paintings, and sculptures disappeared or were stolen (fig. 8). Just a few objects of applied art were saved and brought to the Vyazemski estate 'Aspen Grove'.

Various military organisations have since been quartered at the dacha. During World War II it housed a military hospital, and later a children's sanatorium. The building became dilapidated and virtually fell apart.

In 1989 the Fabergé dacha acquired the status of a national historic and cultural monument. That same year the State Inspectorate for the Protection of Monuments commissioned a design institute to prepare a feasibility study and a restoration design. It is hoped that the buildings and structures of the estate, as well as the landscaped park, will be restored in the coming years.

Already the process of restoration is underway on Bolshaya Morskaya, a street that has been called 'Jeweller's Walk' for the number of prestigious jewellery firms that once flourished there. The House of Fabergé, having been designated a historical monument, was the first to be surveyed under a planning grant from the J. Paul Getty Foundation in California. The restoration concept includes converting the structure to a museum and cultural centre that would highlight the artistic and entrepreneurial genius of the Fabergé firm. It is hoped that the House of Fabergé, once restored, will signal the renaissance of the historic centre of St. Petersburg.

Figure 8. The 1919 report concerning the robbing of Agathon Fabergé's dacha.[1]

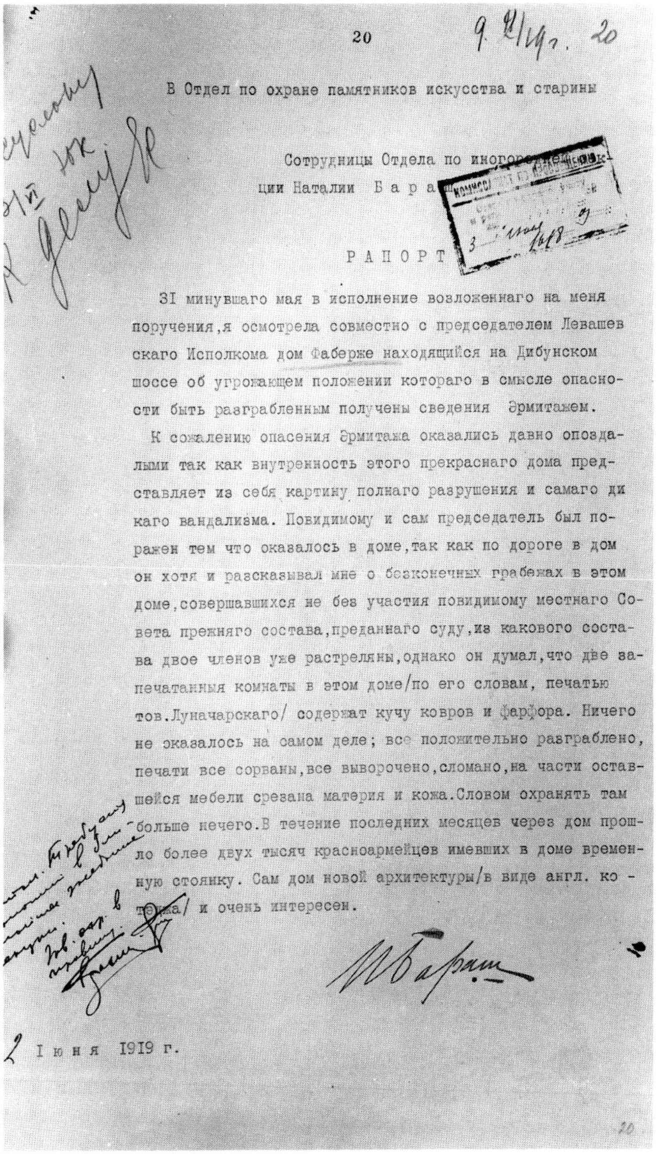

Note
1.

Department for Preservation
of Art and Antique Objects

From Suburban Section
Nataliya Barashkova

REPORT

On 31 of May this year in accordance with the mission entrusted to me, jointly with the Chairman of the Executive Committee of Levashovo, I examined the house of Fabergé located on Dibunskoe highway. The Hermitage had been informed of the condition that threatens the house, as there is a danger of it being robbed.

Unfortunately, it was too late for the fears of the Hermitage, as the interior of this wonderful house has been completely destroyed and now bears signs of the most ferocious vandalism. It seemed that the Chairman himself was shocked by what he saw in the house. On the way to the house he was telling me about endless robberies of the house that took place not entirely without the participation of the prior members of the local Council, who, as it seems, had been taken to the Court and two members had already been shot, but still he thought that two rooms which had been sealed in this house (as he put it, by the seal of Comrade Lunacharski) contained a lot of carpets and porcelain. In fact, nothing turned out to be left; absolutely everything had been robbed, the seals were gone, everything had been turned upside down, broken, fabric and leather cut off the pieces of furniture that stayed. To be short, there is hardly anything to be preserved. During the last months, more than two thousand Red Army soldiers went through the house, who were temporarily lodged in the building. The style of architecture of the house itself is new (looks like an English cottage) and is very interesting.

2 June 1919

Kshesinskaia's Memories

Galina Smorodinova

Mathilda Felixovna Kshesinskaia (1872–1971; fig. 1), an Imperial Theatre School graduate (1880–90) and an outstanding dancer at the Russian Imperial Ballet from the 1890s through the first decade of the twentieth century, was a protégé of Tsar Nicholas II and several Grand Dukes. The best ballet critics eulogised her. She was an object of worship for the next generation of dancers. After the Revolution, in 1920, she left Russia and in 1929 opened a dance studio in Paris. In 1921 she married Grand Duke Andrei Vladimirovich, Nicholas II's cousin.

The memoirs of Mathilda Felixovna Kshesinskaia, first published in extenso in Russian (Moscow, 1992), give a lively account of the Imperial Mariinski Theatre prima ballerina's life and milieu. Throughout the twenty-five years of her brilliant career, she enjoyed Tsar Nicholas II's patronage and was always surrounded by the love and devotion of the Imperial Court, Grand Dukes, and public in St. Petersburg, Moscow, Paris, and London.

Tributes of such adulation – gifts, items of luxury, decorations – presented by numerous admirers played a significant role in the ballerina's life. Her recollections of these objects are scattered throughout her memoirs and provide interesting material for enthusiasts and scholars of the Russian 'Silver Age'. They offer information as to which objects were presented, on what occasion, and when. They also serve as a source of information about the most famous jeweller of the Russian Empire, Carl Fabergé, and his firm.

For those familiar with Fabergé works in museums and private collections, and through illustrated publications, it is of value to discover how these objects existed, before they were alienated from their first proprietor and from the spirit of the time in which they were given.

Court Jeweller Fabergé is, with one exception, the only maker of gifts mentioned in this book. This exception is Ivan Khlebnikov, who worked on the bronze door for the chapel of the graves of Kshesinskaia's father and grandfather. And this is in spite of the fact that, in addition to Fabergé, a number of renowned jewellers then worked in Moscow and St. Petersburg. Fabergé's competitors – Bolin, Butz, Hahn, Koechli – by whom Kshesinskaia might have owned objects, pass nameless through her reminiscences.

In 1892, Tsarevich Nikolai Alexandrovich presented

* Mathilda Kshesinskaia, *Vospomininia* (Moscow, 1992). All subsequent references given in this essay are from this source.

Kshesinskaia with a gold bracelet set with a large sapphire and two large diamonds (p. 37).* On the occasion of her son's christening, 'a wonderful cross of dark-green Urals stone with a platinum chain' was given by Grand Duke Vladimir Aleksandrovich (p. 90). This could have been made in the workshops of the stonecarvers Alexei Kozmich Dennisov-Uralski or Avenir Ivanovich Sumin. They frequently supplied the Imperial Court with their objects, and their stones repeatedly received awards at various exhibitions. One might suppose that the gold garland with the names of Kshesinskaia's ballets engraved on the petals (p. 98) was made in G. Verzhbitski's workshop. He specialised in producing garlands, and he did receive commissions from His Imperial Majesty's Cabinet.

As a rule, actors of the Imperial Mariinski Theatre received 'Tsar's gifts' for their anniversaries. These were generally gold or silver objects, sometimes set with coloured stones, depending on the category of the gift, but invariably with a double-headed eagle or Imperial Crown (p. 75). Men were often awarded golden watches crafted by the Supplier to the Imperial Court, Pavel Buhré, who made nielloed or jewelled watches for His Imperial Majesty's Cabinet.

On the eve of the tenth anniversary of her performing on the Imperial stage, Kshesinskaia was not willing to receive such a gift, and she accordingly informed Tsar Nicholas II through her friend Grand Duke Sergei Mikhailovich. Instead, she was presented with 'a charming brooch in the shape of a coiled diamond snake set with a large sapphire, a symbol of wisdom, in the centre', which was chosen by the Empress herself (p. 75). This brooch could have been created by the firms of K. Bolin or A. Ivanov, the latter of which had for many years supplied the Court with various jewellery objects. Ivanov's workshop was famous for its diamond jewellery. M.I. Pyliaev, in his book *Precious Stones*, remarks that the wealth and variety of Ivanov's precious stones made him the leading jeweller.

For her twentieth anniversary in 1911, Kshesinskaia received as her Tsar's gift a 'remarkably fine and original' diamond eagle mounted in platinum with a pink sapphire pendant (p. 126). In the years from 1901 to 1916 the gold and diamond workshop of A.S. Beilin produced a number of gold chains, 'crown' diamond brooches, and diamond eagles. Diamond-set orders of various degrees were also made by C. Hahn and later by K. Blank.

1. Mathilda Felixovna Kshesinskaia was lauded as a leading ballerina of the Russian and European stage for over twenty-five years.

Judging by her memoirs, Kshesinskaia was close to Fabergé's firm and highly valued its work. Agathon, Carl Fabergé's son, was her good friend (p. 137). She had her most valuable and precious object, an icon with the Virgin of Czestochowa, which she had inherited from her father, mounted in silver at Fabergé's in order 'to save and preserve it' (p. 166), and she never parted with it the rest of her life. She felt comfortable enough to order not only an entire object but also a minor final touch, as she did when she requested her golden signature appear on a cigarette case that she presented to one of her admirers, G. Marr.

Kshesinskaia was given, and personally bought, many Fabergé objects. The gifts she received for her benefit performances were most important and memorable for the dancer – she always mentioned them in her memoirs. The celebration of her twentieth anniversary on stage is of special interest. On that day her friend and future husband Grand Duke Andrei Vladimirovich gave her a diamond-set tiara with six large sapphires. Prince Aleksandr Konstantinovich Shervashidze, a theater and stage set designer (1867–1968), created the tiara in an Egyptian style for the ballet *The Pharaoh's Daughter* (fig. 2), and Fabergé completed its fabrication (pp. 126, 117). Objects such as this were made in the workshop of A. Holmström and A. Hollming, who were well known for their work with diamonds and decorations.

Kshesinskaia described as a 'very valuable object' a present from Grand Duke Sergei Mikhailovich: 'a mahogany box in gold mounting from Fabergé. Inside, wrapped in a piece of paper, was a collection of yellow diamonds ranging from the smallest to quite large'. The ballerina ordered from Fabergé a 'remarkably beautiful corsage ornament' (p. 126).

Of special interest is a gift she received from the audience. Kshesinskaia offers a detailed description of it: 'a wonderful Louis XVI tea table by Fabergé with a full tea service [fig. 3]. The table's upper deck is made out of green nephrite and has a silver balustrade. The redwood legs are adorned with silver decorations. Underneath there is a deck for a pastry bowl which could be placed on top of the table when necessary' (p. 127). Two other Fabergé tables in the style of Louis XVI are known: a mahogany example made by Julius Rappoport and one of nephrite crafted in Moscow.

Elsewhere in her memoirs Kshesinskaia mentions an

2. Kshesinskaia poses in her costume for *The Pharaoh's Daughter*, wearing a tiara manufactured by Fabergé.

3. One gift from her many adoring fans
was a complete Louis XVI-style tea service
and table by Fabergé.

especially valuable 'large, pink rhodonite (orletz) Fabergé-made elephant with ruby eyes' given to her by Zhivotovski (p. 127). Fabergé stone objects were highly prized by her contemporaries. The State Historical Museum Archive has an inventory of the Yusupovs' St. Petersburg house, where Fabergé animals and birds were singled out as a separate category.

Silver-mounted crystal objects, most probably made by the Fabergé Moscow branch, were another common gift. For her twentieth anniversary on stage, Kshesinskaia received a crystal sugar bowl in a silver mounting. Five years later, she was given a crystal punch-bowl in a massive silver mounting with a huge silver ladle (pp. 127, 173).

Fabergé was renowned for his sensitivity to his client's whims. Kshesinskaia remembers a dinner she held in 1909 for her fellow ballerinas. One of the ballet aficionados present at the dinner took a plate and gathered silver and copper coins from the guests. Shortly thereafter the prima ballerina received from Fabergé a silver plate with an engraved inscription and the coins soldered onto it in memory of that night (p. 112). In this way Fabergé maintained an old tradition, known both in western Europe and in Russia, of incorporating medals and coins into silverware. The plate must have been made in the workshop of the firm's leading silversmith, Julius Rappoport.

Also fascinating is the information Kshesinskaia provides on her Easter gifts. She mentions an Easter present from Grand Duke Vladimir Alexandrovich 'in the shape of a large egg made out of lilies-of-the-valley with a Fabergé precious egg attached to it' (pp. 80, 95). In 1911, Grand Duke Andrei Vladimirovich gave her 'an original gift'. 'He sent a large straw egg with plenty of little packages inside. Among simple little things there were a few charming Fabergé pieces and a couple of diamond-set buckles' (p. 128).

Kshesinskaia also received Fabergé presents to commemorate more personal celebrations. For the tenth anniversary of their acquaintance, Grand Duke Andrei Vladimirovich gave her two large cabochon sapphires in a diamond-set mounting purchased from Fabergé (p. 121).

Not only did Kshesinskaia enjoy receiving gifts, she was a generous giver herself. She remembers: 'For a Christmas party I would make a Christmas tree. The celebration would start with a Christmas dinner after which the Christmas tree was lit and all the guests were given gifts which were normally made by Fabergé' (p. 86). Meeting her colleagues or distinguished artists was always an experience for her, and she liked giving them presents. In 1911 she gave American dancer Isadora Duncan 'a most beautiful agraffe made by Fabergé' (p. 124) .

In 1920, when she, Grand Duke Andrei Vladimirovich, and their son were fleeing Russia via Constantinople to Italy, she gave 'a couple of miraculously preserved Fabergé cuff-links' to the captain of the ship *Semiramide* (p. 222).

Kshesinskaia owned many Fabergé objects. She writes of a 'big collection of marvellous precious stones, artificial flowers and among them a little golden Christmas tree with tiny icicle-like diamonds on its branches. There were also many enamels objects, gold tcharkas and the already mentioned pink elephant' (p. 179).

The following quotation provides intriguing evidence of Kshesinskaia's close relationship with the Fabergé firm: 'I did not keep my large diamond objects at home, they were kept at Fabergé's' (p. 180). Even today a large safe can be seen at the Fabergé house at 24 Bolshaya Morskaya. Another large safe was at the dacha of Agathon Fabergé.

The Fabergé firm also offered its services when its clients were travelling. In 1911, Kshesinskaia was going to London and requested Fabergé to ship her fully insured jewellery there. Two copies of the inventory – one for Kshesinskaia, the other for Fabergé, with every item numbered – were made. In London, Kshesinskaia simply informed Fabergé's London office of the number of the item she wanted and a 'special agent-detective' (or two) would deliver it by the appointed time to a designated location at a theatre or elsewhere, stay there as a guard for as long as necessary, and then take it back to storage (p. 137).

Kshesinskaia lost all her possessions after the Revolution. Her mansion, taken over by the Bolsheviks in 1917, was plundered and vandalised, and used as headquarters for the Party and the Petrograd City Committees. In April 1917, Lenin, who had just returned from emigration, spoke from its balcony. Since 1957 the building has housed the Museum of the October Revolution.

The fate of the collections so dear to Kshesinskaia's heart is unknown. Accidentally she came across a few objects in Kislovodsk. Hopefully others will surface with time, based on published photographs and the details in her memoirs.

A Treasure Found in Solianka Street

Tatiana Muntian

In 1990 during reconstruction work in a typical old Moscow mansion at 13 Solianka Street, construction workers found two tin candy boxes wrapped in a decayed pre-Revolutionary poster (fig. 1). The boxes contained twenty-one fine gold-and-platinum jewels set with diamonds, sapphires, emeralds, and large white, grey, and black pearls. Part of this treasure is now in the Russian State Depository of Valuables (*Gokhran*). The Kremlin Armoury obtained thirteen of these objects from the turn of the century, which, except for a pair of earrings, were identified as the work of the renowned firm of Carl Fabergé.[1]

The site on the corner of Solianka and Pevcheski (now Astakhovski) Lane once belonged to Chevalier Pavel Petrovich Sviniin, Counsellor of State and a diplomat, man of letters, artist, and an art collector. After his death in 1839 and until the October Revolution, Sviniin's estate and premises became the property of the merchants Rastorguiev, a well-known Moscow family of the 1st Merchant's Guild, Hereditary Honourable Citizens, and very active in charity and public works.

In 1909 the building at 13 Solianka was sold at auction and acquired by Counsellor of State and 'Sugar King' Pavel Ivanovich Kharitonenko, one of the wealthiest men in Russia who headed the private company 'I. G. Kharitonenko and Son in Sumi'. It was agreed that one of the Rastorguiev sons, Dmitri Alekseievich, could stay in his old house in flat no. 60, where he maintained his firm's office.

The new owner and his wife chose not to live in the building they had purchased but instead renovated the house to their liking. Pavel Ivanovich died in 1914, and the company passed to his widow Vera Andreevna. In the last few pre-Revolutionary years 'P. I. Kharitonenko and Heirs' was managed by the family's friend, assistant Nikolai Mikhailovich Chuprov. His brother Zinovi Mikhailovich worked in the City House of Labour and had a flat in the building. Since the Chuprov brothers were obviously affiliated with the Kharitonenko family, the logical supposition is that at the time of the Revolutionary turmoils, the jewellery was given to these absolutely trustworthy persons. Searches were taking place around Moscow, and an unassuming employee of the House of Labour would not incite as much interest from the Revolutionary expropriators as would the well-known 'Sugar King' family. In 1918 the Kharitonenkos were forced to leave the country. Their property was nationalised, and their paintings distributed among various museums.

Figure 1. These two tin candy boxes, found at a construction site, contained a wealth of jewels set with diamonds, sapphires, emeralds, and large pearls.

Of the thirteen objects that found their way into the Kremlin, six bear the marks of Fabergé's Moscow branch: two pairs of earrings, which according to their marks were made between 1899 and 1908, as well as two rings and a tie-pin made later, between 1908 and 1917. A third pair of earrings set with two large sapphires bears the Cyrillic mark 'V. G.', possibly that of the jeweller Vilhelm Gabu, the owner of the Goldsmith and Goldwatch Depot in Nikolskaia Street. Other objects, including pendants, a brooch, and a bracelet, bear no marks. They are mostly of platinum or platinum alloys, which were not marked in Russia.

There is no doubt that these objects were made by Fabergé. They bear scratched inventory numbers that coincide with the names and numbers on the firm's carefully attached labels (fig. 2). They date from between 1899 and 1917, and some of them have their original price tags. A pair of gold earrings set with cabochon emeralds in a diamond setting (cat. 242) cost 6,000 roubles, and a silver pendant with diamonds and emeralds was priced at 18,000 roubles.

These prices were quite high. Clients of Fabergé who could afford such sums were the Imperial Cabinet, the aristocracy, and financial and industrial tycoons. As an example, Fabergé made a large diamond clasp priced at 8,762 roubles for a pearl necklace, worth 55,000 roubles, for the wedding of Grand Duchess Olga Aleksandrovna. Yet for the world-renowned jeweller, it was more important to make an object remarkable not so much by its price as by 'a new design' corresponding to 'all the fashion's erratic requirements'.[2] According to their advertisements, the firm produced objects of 'the newest and most fashionable designs', and the prices ranged 'from the most affordable to the most expensive'. Flawless diamonds of unusual cut and rare four-, five-, and eight-carat pearls worth 150 to 200 roubles per carat were used to produce these items of jewellery. Large valuable stones were set next to numerous, tiny rose-cut diamonds. Affixing these was a meticulous and painstaking process that considerably increased the cost. These objects were quite 'in the spirit' of the famous firm, which was considered a trend setter and was imitated by many jewellers of the time.

All the details of these objects were executed with extraordinary skill. The reverse of the rings are chased with rosettes and subtly engraved with ornamentation that can be seen only on close scrutiny. The stones are fixed almost invisibly to form smooth surfaces or intricate patterns. Neutrally coloured grey platinum emphasizes the beauty of the diamonds and pearls. Invisibly set calibrated stones were used in the making of the flexible pendant that was 'woven' out of dark blue sapphires. The lotus-shaped silver pendant is decorated with narrow, coloured strips of emeralds delicately set off by diamonds. The narrow platinum bracelet made of flexible links achieves its impression of weightlessness by the ribbon shape and by the juxtaposition of shining diamonds and matte pearls.

Geometric forms and flat surfaces prevail. Straight parallel lines and concentric rings are accentuated, making it possible to attribute the objects to the later period of the firm's jewellery production. Made in the early 1900s, they seem to anticipate some of the works made by Cartier in Paris and Tessier in England in the mid-1920s. The designers and jewellers of Fabergé, then the largest jewellery firm in the world, were at the avant-garde of artistic research at that time.

A concentric silver pendant with diamonds was fabricated after a design in an album belonging to August Holmström.[3] A brooch and a pendant from the treasure also relate to designs in this album, pointing to an origin in St. Petersburg. On the other hand, some of the items are similar to the designs by S. N. Adrianov, who worked with the Moscow firm in the early 1900s. Adrianov's designs are more original and richer in colour than the somewhat austere St. Petersburg compositions.

The clarity of compositional structure in most of the items pays homage to early twentieth-century Neoclassicism, which emerged in reaction to Art Nouveau. Although these objects lack the smoothly flowing lines and irregular contours characteristic of Art Nouveau, some of the style's features are distinctly noticeable, as in a silver pendant with a lotus motif, which was so popular in early twentieth-century art, with its interest in Oriental styles. Here, the floral naturalism of the previous decades has given way to the geometric, abstract compositions that marked the turn of the century.

When making these fashionable jewels, designers improvised with retrospective motifs: the sharp-toothed edge and concentric composition of a silver diamond-set pendant evoke memories of the Renaissance, while a pear-shaped, slightly baroque pearl framed by an elegant flower garland (cat. 240) is reminiscent of the seventeenth century. Such motifs are not slavishly imitated but are treated with great freedom in accordance with the ever-changing tastes of Fabergé's clientele.

These objects, a peculiar mix of Old World poetry and Art Nouveau, are also indicative of a new style that did not openly declare itself until the 1925 International Fair of Decorative Arts in Paris. Flat structures, invisible mounts, and the play of clearly defined forms were all features of the nascent Art Deco. Fabergé designers and jewellers, solidly based on the achievements of the past, were at the same time very sensitive to changing fashion, forever discovering and inventing new vistas in art.

1. All the jewels described in this article were first presented at *The World of Fabergé* exhibition, held at the Kremlin Armoury in Moscow in 1992, and illustrated in the exhibition's catalogue.
2. The brochure of the Fabergé firm from which these quotes are taken is preserved in the State Historical Museum, Moscow.
3. This album is with A La Vieille Russie in New York. The identification of the Moscow jewel in the album is due to Mr Paul Schaffer, to whom I am indebted for permission to publish this find.

Tracing Fabergé Treasures after 1918

Alexander von Solodkoff

Following the 1917 October Revolution in Petrograd, a 'Committee of the Employees of the Company K. Fabergé' was formed. It took over the management of the firm until November 1918, when Fabergé emigrated, with the aid of the British Embassy, first to Germany and then to Switzerland. With his departure the firm ceased to exist. Shortly afterwards the Jewellery Union (later also called *Leningradskoye Yuvelirnoye Tovarishchestvo*) settled in the Fabergé premises, inheriting the stock which included completed and unfinished items.

By 1918 the total of the Fabergé production was in the region of around 120,000 to 150,000 items, according to estimates based on inventory numbers and the recorded sales of items in the London branch, which totalled around 10,000 during a period of ten years.

The question arises, What happened to all these treasures after 1918? Were they neglected by the change of the political situation, the change of society, the change of fashion? Did these changes imply a difference in the appraisement of Fabergé *objets d'art*?

Apart from those pieces which were sold in London or those which were purchased by western European or American clients in St. Petersburg or Moscow, we are here mainly concerned with the fate of Fabergé pieces which were in the hands of Russians, including the Russian Imperial Family. These collectors of Fabergé can be divided into those who emigrated from Russia and those who stayed or were forced to stay in the Soviet Union.

Fabergé and the Russian Emigration

By 1922, about 1.5 million Russian refugees had fled the revolution and civil war, settling mainly in Berlin and Paris. More than 500,000 had gone to Germany by 1920, and most of these later settled in Paris, which in the 1930s became a mecca for Russian refugees. Others, about 250,000, travelled eastward crossing Siberia to the Far East.[1]

Many of the *émigrés* were from either the aristocratic or the wealthy bourgeoisie backgrounds that had most patronised Fabergé. Obviously, they took with them valuables and jewellery that would become useful when money was needed.

Here arises the problem that Fabergé articles were mostly not precious stone jewellery but decorative works of art. Understandably, diamonds or other jewellery were the first items to be sold by the refugees. This has been described in detail by Vladimir Nabokov in his memoirs, in which he accidentally mentions that his family despised Fabergé objects 'as emblems of grotesque garishness'. With regard to jewellery he states, 'Living expenses were to be paid by the handful of jewels which Natasha, a farsighted chambermaid, just before my mother's departure from St. Petersburg in November 1917, had swept off a dresser into a nécessaire'. The pigeon-blood ruby and diamond ring represented 'a whole period of emigré life for which that ring was to pay'.[2] Fabergé's enamelled vanity cases or hardstone animal carvings seemed to have been less tradable assets at a time when the market was concentrating on sales of precious stone jewellery.

The earliest recorded trace of Fabergé objects brought out of Russia by *émigrés* is that of six Easter eggs made for the gold-mining magnate Aleksandr Kelch. They appeared at the jeweller Morgan in Paris, as described by Léon Grinberg in his notes recording his purchases for the antiques gallery of his uncle Jacques Zolotnitzky. 'This clock [Chanticleer egg, now in the FORBES Magazine Collection], together with five other items in egg shape, all works by Fabergé, were purchased in the shop of Morgan on the rue de la Paix in 1920. For all six items we paid 40,000 francs. Morgan himself did not know to whom the eggs earlier belonged'.[3]

Small Fabergé objects, however, were apparently kept by the *émigrés* because, on the one hand, their trade value was regarded as insignificant. Still in 1938, according to an antiquaire such as Jacques Kugel, Fabergé items were sold by weight, which often meant that they were broken up and melted down for the stones or gold content. On the other hand, they received in the eyes of the *émigrés* an even increased nostalgic value due to the increasingly difficult circumstances of their lives.

This, for example, can be seen with the 1916 Imperial St. George Cross egg (The FORBES Magazine Collection, New York), which Grand Duchess Xenia had inherited from her mother, Empress Maria Feodorovna, and which she kept all her life. It was only sold after her death in 1961. Miniature Easter egg pendants, traditionally given as souvenirs, were among the small items of jewellery which were proudly worn on necklaces by *émigré* ladies in Paris at Easter. Apparently such large quantities of them were in hand that Countess M. was quoted as saying, 'We had so many – we kept losing them in the Métro'.

Apart from the sales value of Fabergé objects, one has to ask how they were appreciated in western Europe after the Revolution. 'I vaguely knew his [Fabergé's] name and that he had created elegant knick-knacks for St. Petersburg nobles but I certainly never guessed that thirty years later anything from his workshop would be considered a tremendous prize'. This was written by Loelia Duchess of Westminster, who had received a jewelled fan and a pale blue enamelled bell from Queen Mary and the Princess Royal as wedding gifts in 1930.[4] In 1934, however, Henry Bainbridge, formerly the director of Fabergé's London branch, was able to state, 'Today his creations, in the short space of sixteen years, have become classic. England is playing an important part in keeping his name and fame'.[5]

It is a well-known fact that Queen Mary was a most avid collector who patronised the Fabergé market. For instance, she acquired from Prince Vladimir Galitzine in September 1934 the table cigarette box with enamel miniature painting of the Peter the Great monument by Zuiev. Prince Galitzine, a former ADC to Grand Duke Nikolai Nikoliaevich, had emigrated to England and, in order to make a living, had started an antiques business in London on Berkeley Street, Mayfair, through which he and other Russian *émigrés* sold their valuables. It is interesting to note that the above-mentioned box was to be a gift to King George V by Queen Mary at Christmas 1934 (cat. 149).

Among other collectors in western Europe were Lady (Lydia) Deterding, the Russian wife of the oil trader Sir Henry Deterding, who, for instance, owned the Heart Surprise frame of 1897 (cat. 22, now in The FORBES Magazine Collection), and Countess Rosario Zouboff, an Argentinean heiress married to Count Sergei Plantonovich Zouboff. Under the date 13 May 1932 in Léon Grinberg's notes is found, 'Apart from this [furniture, paintings, and works of art] the Zouboffs bought a whole mass of various kinds of wonderful objects by Fabergé – bells, ashtrays, boxes etc. I remember for instance a small vase made of rock crystal from which grew a gold plant suspending precious little eggs, presents which were made at Easter (30,000 francs)'. This and many other of these items were later recorded with the provenance 'Grand Duke Paul' when they were sold by Christie's in 1974.[6]

Looking at the 1920s and 1930s, this period appears to have been the most difficult in *émigré* life. The more important Fabergé objects were sold, while the smaller, unsalable ones were kept also for nostalgic reasons as souvenirs of a bygone, better era. A turning point in the market for Fabergé apparently occurred in 1934, but it was only in the 1950s and 1960s that the *émigrés*, now of advancing age, or their heirs parted with their Fabergé pieces.

London auction sales catalogues show that hundreds of objects were sold, although they rarely disclose the Russian owner's name. A typical, in fact rather mysterious, example is recorded in the catalogue of Sotheby's London on 14 February 1957: 'The Property of Her Late Majesty the Empress Marie Feodorovna of Russia – Sold by Order of a Lady of Title'.

Fabergé in the Soviet Union
One of the rare accounts of the confiscation of jewellery by the Bolsheviks in 1917–1918 can be found in the recently published memoirs of Princess Ekaterina Meshcherskaia.

When banks were nationalised [27 December 1917], the opening up of safes posed great problems for the inexperienced people who had been charged with this task and who were to be responsible for the treasures contained therein. A special appeal was published, calling upon the owners of safe-deposit boxes in the banks to come forward with their keys. It was stated that part of the owners' 'decorative trivia' (jewellery with coloured precious stones) could be retained. In those days, the state was in desperate need of foreign currency, so the government was interested in acquiring only gold, not precious stones.[7]

In fact, all gold items were requisitioned and only 'small items covered with precious stones – costume jewellery – returned as having no currency value'. Although Fabergé items are not specifically mentioned in this account, there must have been some items among the 'watches, chains, cigar-cases, lockets, [and] medallions'. In the end it turned out that such small items of decorative jewellery had little value on the market which had been successfully cornered by the Bolsheviks.

Nobody was interested in our valuables. Russia was in the grip of famine and typhus. A piano could be exchanged for a handful of rye or a few potatoes. Pillows, blankets and sheets could be exchanged for a loaf of fragrant Ukrainian bread from the sharp dealers who rode the trains, but we had no bed linen to trade. All we had was a metal case full of 'baubles' nobody wanted.[8]

After the introduction of the NEP (New Economic Policy) by Lenin in 1921, a market for small jewellery seemed to have developed when these items could be sold in state-controlled commission shops. Yet again, the problem of how to value such items arose. The few people with knowledge who had not emigrated were recruited from the former staffs of jewellery firms. Amongst others, Agathon Fabergé, Carl's second son and formerly the firm's expert on precious stones, helped the commission set up by Academician Aleksandr E. Fersman to value the Russian Crown Jewels for the State Repository of Valuables (*Gokhran*) in 1922. For the same organisation, established by a Lenin decree on 3 February 1920, worked the former Fabergé workmaster Feodor Afanassiev from 1922 to 1926. He later did valuations for sales at the Moscow Jewellery Union (*Moskovskoye Yuvelirnoye Tovarishchestvo*).

Other state-run sales organisations were *Antikvariat* and *Torgsin* (All-Union Organisation for Sales to Foreigners), which existed from 1931 to 1936 with 550 shops throughout the country. In 1933 *Torgsin* published a guide for valuations under the title 'Receipt and Valuation of Precious Metals'.[9] Here we find numerous references to Fabergé objects, which had to be retained for later sale for hard currency to foreigners, and thus extracted them from the interior trade.

Among the works of the end of the 19th, beginning of the 20th century, items of exceptionally good quality by firms such as Fabergé, Khlebnikov, Ovchinnikov etc. should be retained all small items of unusual shapes such as vases, kovshi, cups, ashtrays, items for lady's dresses, writing desks – with coins or enamels – clocks, frames, figurines or other items of rare workmanship. Cutlery or services by the firm of Fabergé, even with repoussé works, should not be taken out. . . .

Special attention should be attached to silver that earlier had belonged to the Russian Tsars up to Nicholas II inclusive, to the Grand Dukes and their families (especially works by Fabergé). On these items will figure either the double-headed eagle or the owner's monogram under the crown.

Items that were at the time given to somebody as a gift by the Tsars, the Empresses or Grand Dukes should also be sorted out. –

Items with coats-of-arms or coronets or counts or princes should not be retained [for foreign sales].

This *Torgsin* guide shows that Fabergé objects, though only defined as 'precious metal' items, were still recognised, if merely for the purpose of the sale and requisition of hard currency. The phrasing of the guide, however, implies that the general knowledge about pre-Revolutionary *objets d'art* was at a rather low level.

As opposed to works of art which were still in private hands and sold at the state commission shops, Imperial property was confiscated and nationalised immediately following the October Revolution. Various organisations started to work on valuations, including *Gokhran*, the Moscow Jewellery Union, and such museums as the Kremlin Armoury in Moscow. *Antikvariat*, the organisation which mainly traded the goods for hard currency, was in the end responsible for the sale – at whatever price it deemed sufficient. This can be shown by examples from archive material which recently came to light in the Archive of the Armoury, Moscow.[10]

The valuation by the Armoury Museum for Imperial Easter eggs came to approximately 20,000 to 25,000 roubles per egg, the subsequent sale through *Antikvariat* being made at about a quarter or even less of this estimate. The 1903 Peter the Great egg (no. 17541), estimated at 20,000 roubles, was sold for 4,000 roubles in 1933 and is now in The Virginia Museum of Fine Arts in Richmond, Virginia. The 1914 Mosaic egg (no. 17459), valued at 20,000 roubles, went for 5000 roubles in the same year and is now in the English Royal Collection (cat. 29). Interestingly, the 1901 Flower Basket egg (no. 17550), now also in the English Royal Collection, found its way to *Antikvariat* from the Moscow Jewellery Union. The 1891 Pamiat Azova egg (no. 17543) was estimated at 20,000 roubles by *Antikvariat* due to the fact that the ship, represented *en miniature* as a surprise, had itself become part of Revolutionary history since mutinies by sailors had taken place on it. The estimate represented such a prohibitively high price that the egg was left unsold, and it is still in the Armoury Museum of the Kremlin.

The surprises of the Easter eggs are rarely mentioned in the archives, and it seems quite possible that they were separated from the eggs and sold individually by *Antikvariat* in order to achieve a higher sum in hard currency. Judging from the

1. Invoice/receipt from the Soviet authorities (People's Commissariat: Health Department) dated 26 November 1926: 'One cigarette case with cork, with 2 portraits of former Tsar's children, with brilliants and roses'. The price has been deleted. The cigarette case is now in The FORBES Magazine Collection.

detailed descriptions of Fabergé items made by the Soviet officials, giving the original names of the eggs, details of portraits, conditions, and provenance, it seems unlikely that these surprises were simply lost. Where, for example, is the 'Easel of white enamel with rubies, pearls and roses, 1 miniature of the Imperial children' of the 1907 Love Trophy egg, or the 'Diamond chain with medallion and miniature of H.I.H. the Grand Duke Tsarevich Alexei Nikolaievich' of the Rose Trellis egg of the same year?[11] Similarly, the Catherine the Great sedan chair automaton of the 1914 Catherine the Great egg, described by Empress Maria Feodorovna in a letter to her sister, had been removed (cat. 9).

It now seems speculative to try and trace other Imperial Easter egg surprises. A possible example could be the Heart Surprise frame (The FORBES Magazine Collection, formerly in the collection of Lady Deterding; cat. 22), which might be the surprise of the 1897 'Mauve egg with three miniatures' as recorded in the original Fabergé invoices.[12]

On the whole, the valuations by the Armoury and *Antikvariat* took into account both the historic value and the provenance. Dr Armand Hammer, one of the earliest and most successful business partners of the new Soviet regime, gave the following account about his policy in purchasing works of art: 'Among the priceless jeweled articles I was able to obtain by paying more than their intrinsic value in precious stones and gold is a collection of Easter eggs'.[13] Dr Hammer realised that the Imperial provenance could only be a bonus when later re-selling the items in the United States. He described in detail the 1912 Tsarevich egg made of lapis lazuli and diamonds, and containing a portrait of the Tsarevich, which he acquired from *Antikvariat*. 'This Easter gift was made by the Court Jeweler, Fabergé, who spent three years in designing and completing it. It came from the collection of Crown Jewels in the Alexander Palace. Inventory Number 17547. It is valued 100,000 gold roubles (about $50,000). (From the Hammer Collection)'.[14] The now-discovered archives state: 'Egg, lapis lazuli with portrait of Tsarevich Alexei. No. 17547. Sold for 8000 roubles (1930)'.

The valuations not only by the Soviet authorities and museums but also those by Dr Hammer show how speculative valuations of Fabergé objects can be. The intrinsic value is never of relevance with a Fabergé item; its appraisement is always based on the quality of the workmanship as well as the provenance. Obviously, this fact was already known around 1930.

Antikvariat sales of Fabergé were always made directly in the Soviet Union; they never appeared in the auction sales in London or Berlin. Similar to Dr Hammer, it was Emanuel Snowman of Wartski, London, who acquired Fabergé items in Russia, his first visit having been made in 1925. He purchased nine Imperial Easter eggs for later re-sale in London.[15] Other art dealers and private collectors, including the ambassadors Herbette of France, Count Brockdorff Rantzau of Germany, and Davies of the United States, subsequently followed the examples of Dr Hammer and Snowman.

When Fabergé items purchased from the Soviets turned up in London, it was obviously viewed with displeasure by *émigré* circles. As the *Times* of 26 November 1927 reported, these items were mostly 'things that were the intimate personal property of various members of the unfortunate Royal Family [*sic*] . . . things which the owners would have handled and treasured as personal belongings'. Prince Felix Yusupov gives in his memoirs an account of how his mother-in-law, Grand Duchess Xenia, the sister of Tsar Nicholas II, then living in Windsor, was asked by a collector, who showed her a recently acquired Fabergé jade box with crowned initials, whether she could tell whose initials they were. 'These are mine', the Grand Duchess replied, 'this is my property'. It was immediately taken by the new owner and put back into the cabinet.[16]

The sales of confiscated property could not be stopped legally since the Soviet Union was recognised by all western European states by 1924 and by the United States in 1933. Hereby its legal system, as well as the nationalisation of private property, had been accepted.

On 15 March 1934 the first Fabergé auction was held at Christie's in London. Its eighty-seven lots included two Imperial Easter eggs that must have come from a Soviet source. The Soviet Government sales policy for art, however, stopped officially in 1938.[17] By this time, the market for Fabergé objects was apparently established in the West. London auctions regularly included ever larger quantities of items from English, *émigré*, and formerly Soviet sources.

2. The 1892 Diamond Trellis egg, as illustrated in the Sotheby's, London, sales catalogue in 1960. It is shown with a silver base of three putti, apparently the same as illustrated in 1902 in an article on the Fabergé exhibition in St. Petersburg (cat. 361). The sales catalogue, however, states that the base bears English import marks for 1908. Egg and base have been separated since 1960.

3. Patch-box, steel grey enamel, gold mounts, signed Fabergé, H. Wigström, inv. no. 21 679, London import marks for 1911. Diam. 3.3 cm.
Provenance: Grand Duke Mikhail, bought at Fabergé's London branch for £9 on 14 December 1914.

Patch-box, raspberry red enamel, gold mounts, signed Fabergé, F. Afanassiev, inv. no. 20 239. Diam. 3.5 cm.
Provenance: Grand Duke Mikhail, bought at Fabergé's London branch for £8/5 on 30 April 1910. Thence by descent (Lord Ivar Mountbatten).

Ermitage Ltd., London

List of Imperial Easter eggs sold by the Soviet Government through Antikvariat, Moscow, and later re-sold in the West.

1925 to 1938: Imperial Easter eggs acquired by Mr Emanuel Snowman
1895 Rosebud
1897 Coronation (cat. 110)
1898 Lilies-of-the-Valley (cat. 23)
1900 Cuckoo
1905 Colonnade (cat. 20)
1906 Swan
1908 Peacock
1911 Orange Tree
1913 Winter

1930: Imperial Easter eggs acquired by Dr Armand Hammer
1893 Caucasus (5000 roubles)
1894 Renaissance (1000 roubles)
1895? Danish Palaces (1500 roubles) (cat. 5)
1896 Revolving Miniatures (8000 roubles)
1897? Pelican (1000 roubles)
1899 Pansy (7500 roubles)
1912 Tsarevich (8000 roubles)
1912 Napoleonic (5000 roubles)
1914 Catherine the Great (8000 roubles) (cat. 9)
1915 Red Cross with Miniatures (500 roubles)

1933: Imperial Easter eggs sold to unrecorded purchaser
1890 Spring Flower (2000 roubles)
1901 Flower Basket
1903 Peter the Great (4000 roubles)
1914 Mosaic (5000 roubles) (cat. 29)
1915 Red Cross with Resurrection Triptych (500 roubles) (cat. 129)

1934: 15 March, Christie's, London
1885 First Imperial egg
1887? Resurrection egg

1947: 10 July, Sotheby's, London
1911 Orange Tree egg (£1650)

1949: 8 February, Sotheby's, London (Collection of Sir Berhard Eckstein)
1913 Winter egg
1892 Silver Anniversary egg purchased by Mrs Marjorie Merriweather Post

1954 10 March, Sotheby's, Cairo (Collection of King Farouk)
1906 Swan egg

1960 5 December, Sotheby's, London
1892 Diamond Trellis egg

1961 27 November, Sotheby's, London (formerly in the Collection of H.R.H. the Grand Duchess Xenia and of Prince Vasilii Romanov)
1916 Cross of St. George egg (£11,000)

1973 20 November, Christie's, Geneva
1900 Cuckoo egg (SFr. 620,000)

1979 Forbes acquired from Wartski, London, two Imperial eggs – the 1897 Coronation [cat. 110] and the 1898 Lilies-of-the-Valley [cat. 23] eggs – for $2.16 million

1985 11 June, Sotheby's, New York
1900 Cuckoo egg ($1.76 million)

1986 Forbes privately acquired the 1895 Rosebud egg

1992 10 June, Sotheby's, London
1907 Love Trophy egg ($3.19 million)

1. M. Glenny and N. Stone, *The Other Russia* (London, 1990), pp. XVI, XX.

2. V. Nabokov, *Speak, Memory* (London, 1967), pp. 111, 253.

3. Solodkoff 1984, p. 42.

4. Loelia Duchess of Westminster, *Grace and Favour* (New York, 1961), p. 167.

5. Bainbridge 1934, p. 388.

6. Unpublished notes by Léon Grinberg in the possession of the author. Christie's, Geneva, sales catalogue, *Highly Important Works of Art by Carl Fabergé* (1 May 1974), lots 183–227 (The Property of a Lady of Title).

7. Princess Ekaterina Meshcherskaia, *Comrade Princess* (London, 1991), pp. 19, 21.

8. Ibid., pp. 23, 24.

9. Torgsin, *Priemka i otsenka dragotsennykh metallov, Rukovodstvo dlya skupochnykh magazinov Torgsin* (Moskva-Leningrad, 1933). Excerpts kindly provided by Mr V.V. Skurlov.

10. Arkhiv Oruzheynoy Palaty, f. 20 del. 21 (1930/1933). The author is grateful to Mr V.V. Skurlov, St. Petersburg, for kindly having provided details from hitherto unpublished archives.

11. Central State Historical Archives, f. 468 op. 14 del. 2610 (1907).

12. Ibid., f. 468 del. 1843 (1897).

13. Armand Hammer, *The Quest of The Romanoff Treasure* (New York, 1936), p. 216.

14. Ibid., p. 238.

15. A. Kenneth Snowman, 'Wartski and Fabergé', in Solodkoff 1984, pp. 125, 126.

16. Prince Felix Yusupov, *Mémoires (En Exil)* (re-edition 1990), p. 305. Cf. also Ian Vorres, *The Last Grand Duchess (Olga Alexandrovna)* (London, 1964), p. 184.

17. R.C. Williams, *Russian Art and American Money* (Cambridge, Mass., and London, 1980), p. 226.

Fabergé and America

Paul Schaffer

'All Thomas Colt, Jr., Director of the Virginia Museum of Fine Arts in 1947, knew was that a wealthy Mrs. John Lee Pratt had willed to the Museum her collection of the last Russian Czar's family trinkets. . . . When he unwrapped Mrs. Pratt's gift, he found: a world globe of topaz on a solid gold base; a rock crystal Easter egg rimmed with diamonds, . . . (*Life* Magazine, November 1947). The globe and the egg were advertised in 1939 for $2500 and $55,000, respectively. Their story suggests the fruitfulness of exploring the fate of Fabergé objects and their American collectors, both at the time Fabergé was still active, and from the Revolution to the post-war period, when public sales became more frequent and knowledge became more widespread.

It is true that the vast majority of Fabergé's clientele was composed of Europe's wealthy upper class, including royalty, but it also included more than one American who shopped before World War I, not only in St. Petersburg and in Moscow but also in London. Their acquisitions – with the exception of those made by Henry Walters of Baltimore, who, beginning in 1900, continued his interest in Fabergé after the Revolution – were for the most part limited to a few pieces, souvenirs of an exotic voyage or gifts for friends. They included purchases in St. Petersburg of the gold, enamel, and rock crystal sedan chair (The FORBES Magazine Collection, New York) selected by the junior J. P. Morgan, and the pink enamel Duchess of Marlborough egg (The FORBES Magazine Collection) acquired by Consuelo Vanderbilt in 1902. An elaborate gold and jewelled nephrite lotus form vase, possibly intended as a gift for H. M. King Chulalongkorn of Siam (exhibited A La Vieille Russie 1983, no. 310), was purchased by a Miss Morris of Philadelphia in August of 1903 in Moscow for the princely sum of 3250 roubles (fig. 1). Less important but probably more typical was a gold, ruby, and nephrite box (ALVR 1983, no. 168) obtained in London by Princess Hatzfeldt (the former Claire Huntington of Detroit, Michigan) in 1911 for £40.

These 'curio' collectors predated the collectors of the 1930s, such as Mrs Pratt, whose motivations included preserving the legacy of the Tsars, and the more focused collectors of the post–World War II period, which included Mr and Mrs Jack Linsky, Lansdell Christie, and Malcolm Forbes. They were influenced not only by the reputation of the House of Fabergé and the charm and quality of its wares, but also by the exposure Russian art was receiving in the West. According to the introduction to the catalogue of the Russian section of the World's Columbian Exposition held in Chicago in 1893, for example, 'It was the High Wish of His Imperial Majesty the Emperor, that the Russian exhibitors should profit of all aid and assistance to participate at the Exhibition', and indeed works by many of Fabergé's competitors, including Grachev, Hahn, and Klingert, were on view. As early as 1886, the firm of Anton Kuzmichev (silversmiths and enamellers) was exporting to the United States and selling through Tiffany & Co, as was the Kornilov Brothers Porcelain Factory after 1884, which also exhibited at the 1893 Columbian Exposition. The World's Fair held in St. Louis in 1904 included about six hundred paintings by contemporary Russian artists, apparently without much success, even though the 1900 *Exposition Universelle* in Paris had featured Fabergé's work and had furthered the interest in Russian art abroad. Contemporary fascination with Fabergé and with other forms of Russian art, especially the decorative arts, is not new. It had its genesis before the Revolution and was actively fostered by the Tsarist government, which tried to create an export market. Similarly, the young Soviet government would later look to the West for hard currency to finance its needs.

During the post-Revolutionary period, a trading market and an interest in collecting began to develop both in America and in Europe. Dealers involved became the dominant force in introducing Fabergé to the public. The primary traders in America, both in New York, were the Hammer Galleries from 1921, and Alexander Schaffer from the late 1920s. First individually and later as A La Vieille Russie, Schaffer used merchandise acquired in the Soviet Union to stimulate interest in Russian art among wealthy patrons who were attracted to the beauty of the art, sensitive to the tragedy of the Tsarist fall, and fascinated by its historical implications. The need for hard currency was paramount in the Soviet Union, and sales of works of art were effected by various governmental agencies responsive to inexperienced ministers who paid less attention to conserving the national heritage than to raising cash by selling the spoils of the aristocracy and the church to Western buyers.

Hammer and Schaffer purchased quantities of porcelain, icons, brocades, and memorabilia, as well as items in precious

Figure 1. Lotus-form nephrite vase by Fabergé workmaster Mikhail Perkhin, 1899–1903. Set with rubies and diamonds, the vase stands on a gold base enamelled opaque white and translucent red and green. It is shown here with its original label and price: No. 4400, roubles 3250. Height: 25.5 cm.

material, such as Fabergé, gold boxes, and antique jewellery. It has been suggested that the government was mocking the capitalists to whom they were selling, but the officials involved were trying to help in the rebuilding of their country, and the result was a relatively steady supply of merchandise. Overall, works by Fabergé, in addition to their artistic appeal, were important commercial items. As they were 'second-hand', barely being resold a decade or so after their manufacture, prices of objects were relatively reasonable. A merchant could buy quite a number of items for a modest sum and be assured of adequate stock.

Although it was not the main focus of the Soviet government, trade was active in Europe as well, with two previously established firms gaining new prominence by dealing in Fabergé and Russian art. Those firms were Wartski, from 1925 in London (run then by Emanuel Snowman, and later by his son A. Kenneth Snowman), and A La Vieille Russie (run by Jacques Zolotnitzky and his nephew Léon Grinberg), which re-settled in Paris around 1920 from Kiev. Zolotnitzky and Grinberg worked closely with Alexander Schaffer, who spent much time in Paris between the wars, eventually becoming partners. They began supplying Schaffer, as well as others, with Fabergé objects mostly purchased in the emigration. Through the hands of these four merchants, two in America and two in Europe, passed virtually all the important pieces which today are in major collections around the world.

Sales records of the post-Revolutionary period are sketchy, but a whole garden of Fabergé flowers or a menagerie of animals might be sold for $135 to $600 each. Silver items, except for the larger and more elaborate examples, were purchased by weight and were offered at reasonable prices. Gold and enamel picture frames could be had for $95 to $350, handles and clocks for around $65, a buckle for $15, a lorgnette in its original case for $67.50, and miniature eggs (those by Fabergé and others were similarly priced) sold for around $30 each. Also available were Gardner plates of the Order of St. Vladimir for $35 each, and a dozen *cloisonné* enamel spoons for $60 per set. Porcelain eggs with the monogram of Alexandra Feodorovna, now selling for $1500, were boxed and offered as gifts to favoured clients at Easter, and, as Fabergé had done, the brass and copper ashtrays manufactured during World War I (cat. 120, 121) were also offered as gifts. Specific examples of

more important pieces with the price history follow: a circular blue enamel presentation box with the monogram of Nicholas II (ALVR 1983, no. 218; cat. 101) was purchased in 1923 for $250, sold in 1930 for around $700, and resold in 1979 for $42,800; the twelve-panel pink enamel Easter egg now in the collection of Her Majesty the Queen (cat. 185) was sold in 1933 for around $850; the Coronation box (The FORBES Magazine Collection; cat. 105) was sold in 1937 for around $1700, with a profit of around $350; the rich *mujik* (Victoria and Albert Museum 1977, no. N 5) was sold in 1937 for $950, with a $200 profit; and a red enamel cigarette case (ALVR 1983, no. 118) was purchased in the mid-1930s for $54 and sold in 1975 for around $8000. Also illustrative are the deals not done: a smoky topaz vase (Helen B. Sanders Bequest, The Brooklyn Museum, Brooklyn, New York; ALVR 1983, no. 309) was turned down by A La Vieille Russie in 1938 when it was offered for $1350, and the *cloisonné* enamel tea set (Bainbridge 1966, pl. 36) was turned down in 1940 when offered by Fabergé's son in Paris for $1500. Lest these prices seem low, it should be remembered that in spite of the Depression, they were quite high, as they had been in Fabergé's time. A copy of the *New York Times* cost two cents, thirty-five cents bought lunch, and the Schaffers paid $150 a month rent for their gallery.

A discussion of Fabergé in the post-Revolutionary period should recognise that for many collectors of the time, Fabergé was but one of their interests. In reviewing the transactions and the major American collections of the period, it is clear that other items, especially precious icons and religious artifacts, commanded prices in excess of all but the most important pieces of Fabergé. Many icons were sold at prices ranging as high at $7500 for an elaborate silver and enamel triptych, and $4500 for a gilded silver and enamel icon of the Madonna with a pearl robe (both late nineteenth century, but neither by Fabergé), although the more usual seventeenth-century icons frequently sold for less than $100. The reason was that the later icons were more easily associated with the late Imperial Family than the earlier ones, and shared the appeal of the Imperial eggs.

Three major American collectors of the 1930s – Lillian Thomas Pratt, Marjorie Merriweather Post, and India Early Minshall – not only acquired Fabergé objects but also pursued other areas of Russian art. The Pratt Collection, now in The

Virginia Museum of Fine Arts in Richmond, Virginia, includes many icons. The Post Collection, now in the Hillwood Museum in Washington, D.C., possesses an enormous range of Russian material and is especially rich in icons and chalices. And the Minshall Collection, whose Fabergé is now in The Cleveland Museum of Art in Cleveland, Ohio, also comprised a rich assortment of Russian historical objects given to Case Western Reserve University in Cleveland. All three, therefore, were not simply collectors of Fabergé. They were fascinated, as were many others, by the tragedy of recent Tsarist history, and the icons and other memorabilia, including the Easter eggs from Imperial palaces and aristocratic estates, were tangible links to a storied past.

It took time before the Imperial eggs would reach their full value, as the $850 received in 1933 for the twelve-panel egg proved. Christie's sale of 16 March 1934 in London offered further evidence of this. Included in that dispersal of eighty-seven *objets d'art* by Fabergé, which presumably had been recently purchased in the Soviet Union, were two Imperial Easter eggs now in The FORBES Magazine Collection: the First Imperial egg and the Resurrection egg. Despite a glowing introduction to the catalogue by Henry Bainbridge, the first egg sold for £85 ($425) and the second for £110 ($550), but even more remarkable was lot 80, a jewelled, gold wine taster set with a pretty, but not valuable, sapphire of about three carats, which sold for £58 ($290), more than half the price of either of the eggs. It is immaterial that this *kovsh* was misattributed to Alfred Thielemann, rather than to the Tillander firm, as the quality is equal to that of Fabergé. The point is that when it reappeared at sale in 1991 (Sotheby's, Geneva, 16 May 1991, lot 246), the taster set fetched SF 8800 ($5800), not one half the price of an Imperial egg, but less than 1 percent of the recent sale of the Love Trophy egg, which sold for $3,190,000 at Sotheby's, New York, on 10 June 1992!

It was not necessary to wait until the 1990s to witness the change in perception that led to a reappraisal of Fabergé's best pieces – that was already noticeable in the late 1930s. A decade and an ocean made a significant difference. In 1928, after seven years, A La Vieille Russie, Paris, was finally able to sell a collection of seven eggs made for Barbara Kelch and Emanuel Nobel for FF 280,000, or about $1500 each. (The collection included the Pine Cone egg, which would sell in 1989 for SF

5,280,000 [$3,140,000].) In the early 1930s, the twelve-panel egg was purchased for $850, and the First Imperial egg and the Resurrection egg were sold for $425 and $550, respectively. Only a few years later, in the late 1930s, reflecting the extraordinary interest and awareness of the public in America (still home to the most avid of Fabergé collectors), prices would rise to ten to twenty times what they had been in Europe earlier in the decade.

Through the 1930s and early 1940s, the Hammer Galleries published a series of loose-leaf mail order catalogues which recorded the asking prices for all sorts of Russian art. In 1938, for instance, the Swan egg (which was sold to King Farouk and then purchased by A La Vieille Russie for E£6400 ($16,200) at the Egyptian Government sale in 1954, and resold to Dr Maurice Sandoz of Switzerland) was advertised for $25,000. In 1939, the Hammer Galleries offered the Rock Crystal egg with revolving miniatures (The Lillian Thomas Pratt Collection, The Virginia Museum of Fine Arts) for $55,000, and in 1940, the Caucasus egg for $35,000 (Matilda Geddings Gray Foundation Collection, New Orleans Museum of Art). It seems unlikely that they were paid as much as they asked, at least at the time the objects were advertised. The prices realised appear to have been much lower, as the Catherine the Great Easter egg (Hillwood Museum; cat. 9) was apparently offered for $18,500 and sold for somewhat over $10,000 around 1936. And the Peter the Great egg (The Lillian Thomas Pratt Collection, The Virginia Museum of Fine Arts), which had been purchased in the late 1930s by Alexander Schaffer, was something he never wanted to sell, his wife Ray recalls. To discourage Mrs Pratt, he revealed to her his cost and quoted her ten times what he had paid. (That amount was $1500, for which he earned the derision of his English colleagues for paying so much for what was only second-hand merchandise.) In the end, dealer and collector came to an agreement. Being a true collector, Mrs Pratt stretched her purse a little and paid for the egg in monthly installments. Events clearly proved her right, and The Virginia Museum of Fine Arts the richer.

Needless to say, $10,000 was a significant increase over earlier prices and underscored the artistic and historical merit of these pieces. Although business in less-expensive items proceeded more or less normally given the upheavals of the time, no major transactions seem to have been recorded during

World War II. On 10 July 1947, however, the Orange Tree egg (The FORBES Magazine Collection) was offered for sale by Sotheby's in London (lot 53, selling price of £1650 [$6600].) It eventually found its way into the collection of Dr Sandoz, from which, together with the Chanticleer egg, it was purchased by A La Vieille Russie some years later. Together with the Renaissance egg of 1894, they languished in Schaffer's collection for some time with more praises than purchases, but eventually, through different routes, all found a home in The FORBES Magazine Collection.

At first the late Malcolm Forbes only wanted to collect Easter eggs, and he had to be persuaded to venture beyond them. The result is the most important collection in the world now in private hands. American collecting has evolved from the casual buyer at the beginning of the century, followed by the 'amateur' of Russian items in general in the 1920s and 1930s, to the specialising collector we know in the second half of this century. As to the future of Fabergé in America, perhaps the best summary was made by Malcolm Forbes himself in his 'Fact and Comments' column in the 15 April 1973 edition of *Forbes* magazine. In considering new additions to his collection, Forbes confessed, 'I BUY THE WISDOM even if we didn't buy all the *objets* of it. Over the years, Forbes has accumulated a fabulous Fabergé collection. Recently we were discussing a couple of potential additions with Mrs. Alexander Schaffer of A La Vieille Russie, the prime house of Fabergé in this country. "When these were available to us once before several years ago, the price was about half what is now being asked. Now I wish we could have afforded them then." Said Mrs. Schaffer: "If you hadn't bought IBM when it was $50 a share, would you have refused to buy it when it was $100 a share?"' Sadly, Malcolm Forbes is no longer with us, but his wisdom remains.

'Fauxbergé'

Géza von Habsburg

If one were to believe experts and dealers today, no problems exist in the field of Fabergé scholarship. Yet this author, on his widespread quest for Fabergé works, has come across many thousands of objects bearing Fabergé hallmarks that are manifestly not by the Russian craftsman. As prices have risen to astronomical heights, the manufacture of fake Fabergé has become a very lucrative business.

All objects sold by the firm of Fabergé were hallmarked, if there was room to apply the necessary 'punches' without danger of marring the piece. All forgeries are therefore equally hallmarked with a set of 'punches'. Forgers before the 1970s frequently committed errors in applying the appropriate marks. Judging by the recent spate of fake Fabergé objects that have been produced on the basis of available scholarship, forgers have now attained well-nigh perfection in this sector. *Caveat emptor*: however perfect a set of Fabergé hallmarks is, since the death of Carl Fabergé it is no longer explicit proof of authorship.

Simultaneously we are faced with the problem of items that even in Fabergé's time were sold unmarked. These include animals, flowers, some hardstone figures, and jewellery. Only on exception were Fabergé animals hallmarked on their metal parts, and many were too small for engraved marks. Thus, without hallmarks and fitted cases Fabergé's animals become a matter of attribution. Similarly, flower stems were too delicate for hallmarking, and only a small percentage of Fabergé flowers was marked. Also, no law in Russia obliged the hallmarking of platinum jewellery, and since Fabergé's jewellery was mostly in this metal, little proof of authorship remains once the fitted case is lost or destroyed. In all these categories forgers have found their ideal medium.

As the jeweller's international fame gathered momentum following his exhibition at the 1900 Paris *Exposition Universelle*, foreign competitors began to adopt the *style Fabergé*. By imitating him, Cartier and Boucheron, as well as Collingwood of London, Friedlander of Berlin, and Köchert of Vienna, vied with Fabergé to gain access to his rich Russian and English clientele, which included many a Russian Grand Duke or Prince on their frequent visits to Paris and the Côte d'Azur, and virtually all of Fabergé's Edwardian clients, for whom Paris was an important port of call. Cartier's sales ledgers[1] list many names identical with those in Fabergé's books, from Queen

Alexandra (no. 586, '*poussin*'; no. 591, a pink quartz stork; nos. 642 and 670, two agate seagulls with ruby eyes) to Mrs Keppel, Lord Revelstoke, Ronald Greville, and Mrs Leeds. The Cartier ledgers mention 169 flower models, one of which was acquired from Fabergé (28 December 1909, '*achat Stopford. Fabergé 1 bleuet email*'). Stopford also sold to Cartier no. 1141, '*Fabergé 1 cochon en jade rose yeux en rubis*', as well as no. 1142, '*Fabergé renard en cornaline rouge yeux roses*'. In addition they mention over two hundred animals, many bought from the same Russian sources that supplied Fabergé, such as Ovchinnikov, Carl Woerffel (no. 1235, '*1 poule alabatre, crete pourpourine, bec en agate*'; no. 888, '*tomate [flacon colle] purpurine queue nephrite*'), and Dennisov-Uralski (no. 1280, '*perroquine lapis lazuli nephrite et jaspe*'). A few marginal drawings and some of Cartier's descriptions of animals are very reminiscent of those by Fabergé (no. 240, '*phoque obsidienne sur bloc de crystal de roche, yeux brillants*', sold to W. K. Vanderbilt on 26 March 1906; no. 396, '*pelican agate calcedoine pattes vermeil yeux roses*', sold on 16 June 1906; and '*renard enroule labardorite yeux brillants*', sold on 2 June 1907 to Prince Yusupov). The mysterious disappearance of these Fabergé look-alikes leaves no doubt that Cartier's early animal oeuvre is now irretrievably enmeshed with that of Fabergé, and it may well account for some of the stylistic anomalies in Fabergé's animal world. The same is probably true for some of Cartier's early flowers.

Posthumous 'Fabergé'

Following Fabergé's death in 1920, two of his sons, Eugène and Alexander, opened premises in Paris called 'Fabergé et Cie' in 1924, together with Andrea Marchetti, a hardstone specialist and branch manager of Fabergé Moscow, and Giulio Guerrieri of Lorie, the Moscow jewellers. According to Henry Bainbridge, Eugène 'carried on business as a jeweller and goldsmith, acting as agent for the sale of Fabergé's objects, and undertaking the repairing of them even to re-enamelling, with which he has had success'.[2] There is no doubt, however, that the firm also commissioned hardstone animal carvings from Idar Oberstein, a number of which were designed by Alexander. Igor Fabergé, the master's grandson in Geneva, discussed with this author his uncles' production in Paris of a number of world-famous pieces, some of which are illustrated in colour in authoritative books on Fabergé.

The name 'Fabergé', of which the copyright is now owned by Unilever, was licensed at one time to the jewellers Gerard of Paris. (A 'Fabergé' tennis trophy by Gerard was presented to Bjorn Borg in Monte Carlo in the 1960s.) Today the jeweller Viktor Mayer of Pforzheim has acquired the right to produce his own 'Fabergé', while Andrei Ananov in St. Petersburg, with a workshop of forty craftsmen, produces 'Fabergé by Ananov'.

Fabergé forgeries[3]

As early as 1934,[4] Bainbridge openly addressed the question of forgeries, obviously in answer to pleas for help from confused clients. In the United States, Fabergé forgers have been active since the late 1930s, when prices began their spiralling ascent and demand outstripped availability. Amongst these early forgeries are a large number of flower arrangements now on display in certain American museums. These are generally crude productions, invariably by the same hand(s), and presumably made in Idar Oberstein, Germany. Similar flowers exist in some private collections in the United States.

More ambitious forgeries began appearing in Europe in the mid-1950s, when colour photographs and drawings of hallmarks in newly published monographs gave craftsmen and their financiers models upon which to base their imitations. These forgeries are easy to identify since they are invariably straight copies of existing pieces. (As a rule, all of Fabergé's objects are unique, which is confirmed by the rare exceptions.) Again these are mainly hardstone figures, flowers, and animals.

According to Russian sources,[5] a spate of clever forgeries dating from the 1960s can be traced back to the Soviet Union. A certain Naum Nikolaievski in Moscow and his brother-in-law Vasilii Konovalenko in Leningrad are said to have specialised in selling genuine old pieces of Russian *cloisonné* enamel that were re-hallmarked, thus obliterating the original punches by superimposing Fabergé marks. More ambitious were their hardstone carvings of animals and figurines, which made their way into Western auction houses, in particular to Parke Bernet of New York. Their chief prey in Russia were members of the foreign diplomatic community, who paid cash in American dollars and smuggled out their acquisitions through diplomatic pouches, some with the intention of offering their goods for auction in London or Geneva. The arrest of fifteen people in

1969 and the ensuing lawsuit apparently ended with the condemnation of the ringleaders to years of hard labour in Siberia. As of the early 1980s, Vasilii Konovalenko, now deceased, was active as a sculptor in his own right in New York.

Residing in St. Petersburg today is a master forger whose name is mentioned with awe by Russian stonecarvers. Little is known about this mysterious craftsman who was involved in a major lawsuit and whose works tricked some of Russia's best experts. He is said to remain active as the head of a widespread ring of forgers whose reach stretches into the United States. Two hardstone figures by Russian forgers have graced the Fabergé showcase at the Kremlin Armoury for a number of years (for one example see cat. 298).

Workshops situated in Brooklyn and in mid-town Manhattan in New York are presently churning out substantial numbers of 'Fabergé' items of all kinds. The ring promoting these objects uses henchmen posing as newly emigrated Russians to ply its worldwide trade door-to-door. The suitcases of these traveling salesmen brim with harlequin sets of paperknives, all with Imperial coat-of-arms finials. They offer goods at a 'discount', do not 'guarantee' their wares, and leave no name cards or fixed addresses. Nevertheless, they have managed to hoodwink innumerable well-to-do American citizens. Members of this gang were recently caught red-handed in Zurich, travelling with one suitcase full of unmarked 'Fabergé' objects and another loaded with American dollars and the tools of their trade – a set of hallmarking tools.

The house style of this team of 'Brooklyn Forgers' in easy to identify: they work in both hardstones and *guilloché* enamel. Hallmarks and the quality of workmanship are generally first-rate. Their most obvious trademark is the over-utilisation of Imperial symbols. All their products are plastered with double-headed eagles and Imperial cyphers or monograms. (Such symbols, which imply Imperial ownership or presentation, are exceedingly rare on genuine Russian works of art.) Another characteristic is the over-use of Louis XVI-style laurel swags and swans. Perhaps the most subversive ploy used by this gang is channelling their wares back into Russia, from where they re-export them as genuine articles. A typical example, confiscated by Russian customs agents on its way out of the country, has been loaned by a Russian museum (cat. 299).

'Fauxbergé' has existed since the days of the master himself and his children. We live in THE century of gullible consumers and enterprising hucksters. The forging of Fabergé's art, which has attained monumental proportions, will continue to find a thriving market until the day that inexperienced buyers place their trust in the handful of truly recognised and qualified experts that can be found on both sides of the ocean.

1. I am grateful to Mme Betty Jais, Cartier's archivist, for giving me renewed access to the Cartier sales ledgers. My sources of information were the volumes 'Objets Pierre Dure' between 1904 and 1914. For Fabergé's clients in London cf. Habsburg, 'The London Branch', in this book.
2. Bainbridge 1966, p. 21.
3. Frank discussions of Fabergé forgeries can be found in Habsburg/Solodkoff 1979, pp. 149–51, and Habsburg 1987, pp. 343–46.
4. Bainbridge 1934, pp. 299–348.
5. Their story was published by Yuri Brokhin, 'The "Successor" to Fabergé', in *Hustling on Gorky Street* (New York, 1975), pp. 163–85.

Catalogue of Works

* Object shown in Paris and London only
** Object shown in London only
*** Object shown in St. Petersburg only

Alexander III and Maria Feodorovna

Fabergé's activity as a jeweller extends to the reign of Tsar
Alexander II. His production as a goldsmith began under
Tsar Alexander III and his wife, Tsarina Maria Feodorovna,
who actively patronised him. Featured here are items
associated with this Imperial couple, and, following the
death of Tsar Alexander III in 1894, with the Dowager
Empress.

1

MINIATURE HARP

Varicoloured gold, enamel, bowenite, diamonds, seed pearls,
crystal, ivory
H: 14.8 cm
Marks: Fabergé, initials of workmaster Mikhail Perkhin,
assay mark of St. Petersburg before 1899, 56 (*zolotnik*)

Miniature frame shaped as a harp standing on an oval bowenite
base, on two paw feet; red *guilloché* enamel body gilt with fleurs-
de-lys, the 'strings' applied with a miniature of Tsar Alexander II
in seed pearl border, suspended from a four-colour gold flower
swag.

Provenance: Presumably a presentation piece. The fleurs-de-lys
would point to a Royal French or Bulgarian connection.
Exhibitions: Lugano 1987, cat. 31, ill. p. 57; Paris 1987, cat. 31,
ill. p. 53.

The FORBES Magazine Collection, New York (FAB86015)

2

FRAME WITH NINE MINIATURES
Gold, silver
H: 21.5 cm W: 23.5 cm
Marks: Fabergé, initials of workmaster Victor Aarne,
assay mark of St. Petersburg 1899–1908,
initials of assay master Iakov Liapunov, 56 and 88 (*zolotnik*)

Triangular stand suspending nine oval miniatures from laurel leaf
garlands and crossed arrows, surmounted by an Imperial double-
headed eagle. The miniatures depict (left to right, top):
1. Tsar Alexander II
2. Tsarina Alexandra Feodorovna, wife of Tsar Nicholas I
3. Tsar Nicholas I
4. Tsar Alexander III

5. (bottom) Tsar Alexander III
6. Tsar Nicholas I
7. Tsar Alexander II
8. and 9. Tsar Alexander III
Miniatures 3, 7, and 9 are signed in Russian 'I. Goffert'; miniature
8 is signed in Russian 'Vegner'.

Provenance: An Imperial commission made to exhibit an already
existing collection of nine nineteenth-century portrait miniatures,
said to come from the Imperial apartments at the Alexander
Palace at Tsarskoe Selo.
Literature: Hawley 1967, no. 21.
Exhibitions: Hammer 1951, cat. 214; San Francisco 1964, cat. 122.

The Cleveland Museum of Art (The India Early Minshall
Collection, 66.460)

3

PRESENTATION TABLE CLOCK
Silver, bowenite, rubies, emeralds, pearls, gold, crystal, ivory
H: 28.6 cm
Marks: Initials of workmaster Julius Rappoport,
assay mark of St. Petersburg before 1899, 88 (*zolotnik*)

Bowenite body shaped as a commode with rococo silver mounts
and drawers, standing on four lizard-shaped feet, with female busts
at corners. Surmounted by a clock with white enamel dial and
gold hands, upheld by two putti, with flowering vase finial above
set with cabochon rubies, emeralds, and pearls. On the reverse,
crowned Russian monogram 'MF'; on the sides hinged panels
containing miniatures of Tsar Nicholas II and Tsarina Alexandra
Feodorovna.
    A photograph taken at the 1902 Fabergé exhibition at the von
Dervise House (cat. 361) shows a finial shaped as a bird with a
pearl in its beak.
    This is a Fabergé interpretation of a clock from the Imperial
collection at the Walters Art Gallery, Baltimore (cf. Habsburg
1987, cat. 664).

Provenance: Presented by Tsar Nicholas II and Tsarina Alexandra
Feodorovna to the Dowager Empress Maria Feodorovna.
Literature: Ross 1965, p. 65; Taylor 1983, p. 25; Habsburg 1987, ill.
p. 185.
Exhibitions: St. Petersburg 1902; Munich 1986/87, cat. 280.

Hillwood Museum, Washington D.C. (12.155)

4

ALEXANDER III TWENTY-FIFTH WEDDING
ANNIVERSARY CLOCK
Silver, onyx, diamonds
H: 71 cm
Marks: Fabergé's marks obliterated, initials
of workmaster Mikhail Perkhin,
assay mark of St. Petersburg before 1899,
inscribed 'L. Benoit del. Aubert sculps.
Fabergé fec. 1891'

Clock modelled with twenty-five silver
naked putti – to represent the number of
years commemorated – crowding around
dial and upholding torches, bows, quivers,
and playing various instruments. Onyx dial
with Roman numerals and inset with rose-
cut diamonds. Waisted clock case
vigorously chased with acanthus leaves,
scales, and fluting; stands on four paw feet;
surmounted by double-headed eagle
standing on (now empty) crowned laurel
wreath. Romanov griffin at base holds a
sword and two shields depicting Russian
Imperial and Danish Royal coat of arms
and is flanked by two cornucopiae. Stepped
rectangular green onyx base with curved
front; clock stands on a pediment chased
with foliage and husks. Reverse similarly
chased and applied with a cartouche-
shaped plaque engraved with names of
thirty-two donors in two columns.

Provenance: Presented 9 November/28
October 1891 by close relatives to Tsar
Alexander III and Tsarina Maria
Feodorovna on the occasion of their
twenty-fifth wedding anniversary;
Anichkov Palace (Blue Study Room).
Literature: Foelkersam 1907, pp. 615, 719.
Exhibitions: St. Petersburg 1902.

Private collection, United States

Franz Birbaum described the clock in his memoirs: 'A . . . silver chimney clock presented to Alexander III by members of his household on the occasion of his Silver Wedding. Around the clock face there is a group of about 25 flying cupids. The composition included the griffins of the Romanov coat of arms and the coat of arms itself. The wax model was made by the sculptor Aubert and is 1 arshin in height'.

This clock is visible in photographs of the 1902 exhibition held at the von Dervise House (see page 64) amongst items lent by the Dowager Empress Maria Feodorovna and is described as follows: 'The fireplace clock, made of silver with brilliant hands, presented to the late (resting in God's bosom) Emperor Alexander III and to Her Majesty the Empress Maria Feodorovna by the members of the Imperial family on the 25th anniversary of the Majesty's marriage . . .' ('Exhibition of Artistic Items and Miniatures', *Novoye Vremya*, 9 March 1902).

This was Fabergé's most important Imperial commission from the reign of Tsar Alexander III.

1. Grand Duke Konstantin Nikolaievich (1827–1892, son of Tsar Nicholas I)
2. Grand Duchess Aleksandra Iosifovna (1830–1911, born Princess of Saxe-Altenburg, wife of Grand Duke Konstantin Nikolaievich)
3. Grand Duke Konstantin Konstantinovich (1858–1915, son of Grand Duke Konstantin Nikolaievich, married to Elizaveta, Princess of Saxe-Altenburg
4. Grand Duchess Elizaveta Mavrikievna (1865–1927, wife of Grand Duke Konstantin Konstantinovich)
5. Grand Duke Dmitri Konstantinovich (1860–1919, son of Grand Duke Konstantin Nikolaievich)
6. Grand Duchess Aleksandra Petrovna (1838–1900, widow of Grand Duke Nikolai Nikolaievich, born Princess of Oldenburg)
7. Grand Duke Nikolai Nikolaievich (the younger, 1856–1929, son of Grand Duchess Aleksandra Petrovna)
8. Grand Duke Petr Nikolaievich (1864–1931, brother of Grand Duke Nikolai Nikolaievich)
9. Grand Duchess Militsa Nikolaievna (1866–1951, born Princess of Montenegro, wife of Grand Duke Petr Nikolaievich)
10. Grand Duke Mikhail Nikolaievich (1832–1909, youngest son of Tsar Nicholas I)
11. Grand Duchess Olga Feodorovna (1839–1891, wife of Grand Duke Mikhail Nikolaievich, born Princess Caecilie of Baden)
12. Grand Duke Nikolai Mikhailovich (1859–1919, son of Grand Duke Mikhail Nikolaievich)
13. Grand Duke Georgi Mikhailovich (1863–1919, brother of Grand Duke Nikolai Mikhailovich, later husband of Princess Marie of Greece)

14. Grand Duke Aleksandr Mikhailovich (1866–1933, brother of Grand Duke Nikolai Mikhailovich, later husband of Grand Duchess Xenia)
15. Grand Duke Sergei Mikhailovich (1869–1918, brother of Grand Duke Nikolai Mikhailovich)
16. Grand Duke Aleksei Mikhailovich (1875–1895, brother of Grand Duke Nikolai Mikhailovich)
17. Grand Duchess Olga Nikolaievna (1822–1892, daughter of Nicholas I, married Charles I, King of Württemberg)
18. Grand Duchess Olga Konstantinovna (1851–1926, daughter of Grand Duke Konstantin Konstantinovich, married George I, King of Greece)
19. Grand Duchess Vera Konstantinovna (1854–1912, daughter of Grand Duke Konstantin Konstantinovich, married Eugen, Duke of Württemberg)
20. Grand Duchess Anastasia Mikhailovna (1860–1922, daughter of Grand Duke Mikhail Nikolaievich, married Frederich Franz III, Duke of Mecklenburg-Schwerin)
21. Grand Duchess Ekaterina Mikhailovna (1827–1894, daughter of Grand Duke Mikhail Pavlovich [brother of Tsars Alexander I and Nicholas I], widow of Georg, Duke of Mecklenburg-Strelitz)
22. Duke Evgeni Maksimilianovich of Leuchtenberg (1847–1901, Fifth Duke, son of Grand Duchess Maria, eldest daughter of Tsar Nicholas I)
23. Duke Georgi Maksimilianovich of Leuchtenberg (1852–1912, Sixth Duke, brother of Duke Evgeni)
24. Duchess Stana (Anastasia) Nikolaievna of Leuchtenberg (1867–1935, daughter of King Nicholas I of Montenegro, wife of Duke Georgi, later wife of Grand Duke Nikolai Nikolaievich)
25. Duchess Maria Maksimilianovna of Leuchtenberg (1841–1925, married Wilhelm, Prince of Baden)
26. Prince Aleksandr of Oldenburg (1844–1932, married Princess Evgenia Maksimilianova of Leuchtenberg)
27. Princess Evgenia of Leuchtenberg (1845–1925, wife of Prince Aleksandr Petrovich)
28. Prince Petr Aleksandrovich of Oldenburg (1868–1924, son of Prince Aleksandr Petrovich, married Grand Duchess Olga, daughter of Tsar Alexander III)
29. Prince Konstantin Petrovich of Oldenburg (1850–1906, brother of Prince Aleksandr Petrovich)
30. Duke Georgi Georgievich of Mecklenburg-Strelitz (1859–1909, son of Grand Duchess Ekaterina Mikhailovna)
31. Duke (Karl) Mikhail Georgievich of Mecklenburg-Strelitz (1863–1934, son of Grand Duchess Ekaterina Mikhailovna)
32. Duchess Elena of Mecklenburg-Strelitz (1857–1936, sister of Duke Mikhail Georgievich, married Albert, Prince of Saxe-Altenburg)

5*

DANISH PALACES EGG
Gold, enamel, emeralds, diamonds, sapphire, mother-of-pearl
H: 10 cm (without stand)
Marks: Fabergé, initials of workmaster Mikhail Perkhin,
assay mark of St. Petersburg before 1899
Fitted velvet case inscribed 1895

With panels of pink translucent enamel over engine-turned cross
pattern ground within palm leaf and rose diamond borders and
with cabochon emeralds at intersections. Cover with cabochon star
sapphire finial in rose diamond mount. Contains a gold ten-leaf
screen set with mother-of-pearl panels, each painted with ships
and palaces of the Dowager Empress Maria Feodorovna, signed
and dated 'K. Krijitzki, 1891'; each with ribbon cresting.

1. The yacht *Nordstern*
2. Amalienborg Castle, Copenhagen
3. Villa Hvidøre

4. Fredensborg Castle, the Summer Residence
5. Bernsthorff Castle, Copenhagen
6. Kronborg Castle, Elsinore
7. Alexandria, near Peterhof
8. Gatchina, near St. Petersburg
9. Gatchina
10. The yacht *Tsarevna*

Provenance: Presented by Tsar Nicholas II to the Dowager Empress Maria Feodorovna, Easter 1895; Mr and Mrs Nicholas H. Ludwig.

Literature: Snowman 1962, ill. 326, p. 85; Bainbridge 1966, pl. 85; Fagaly 1972, cat. 25; Habsburg/Solodkoff 1979, pp. 157, no. 12, ill. p. 160; Snowman 1979, ill. p. 95; Solodkoff 1984, p. 70f.; Habsburg 1987, ill, p. 271; Pfeffer 1990, p. 38; Hill 1989, no. 28.
Exhibitions: Hammer 1937, cat. 3; Hammer 1939; Hammer 1951, cat. 157; ALVR 1949, cat. 129; V&A 1977, cat. M 8; Munich 1986/87, cat. 537; San Diego/Kremlin 1989/90, cat. 6.

The Matilda Geddings Gray Foundation Collection, New Orleans Museum of Art

6

CIGARETTE CASE
Steel, gold, cotton
H: 9.8 cm W: 6.2 cm
Marks: Fabergé, initials of workmaster Mikhail Perkhin,
assay mark of St. Petersburg before 1899, 56 (*zolotnik*)

Steel case applied with gold rococo scrolls, tindercord with gold
chain terminal.

Provenance: Gatchina Palace, acquired from Central Storage of
Suburban Palaces, 1956.

The State Hermitage, St. Petersburg (Inv. ERO-8657)

7

MOURNING CROSS
Gold, enamel
H: 4.6 cm
Marks: Fabergé, initials of workmaster Mikhail Perkhin,
assay mark of St. Petersburg before 1899, 56 (*zolotnik*)

Made in memory of the death of Alexander III. Photograph of the
Tsar in a mourning frame; engraved with the date of his death on
the back of the cross.

Provenance: Catherine Palace in Tsarskoe Selo (Pushkin) until
1935.
Exhibitions: Elagin Palace 1989, cat. 53.

The State Hermitage, St. Petersburg (Inv. E-15595)

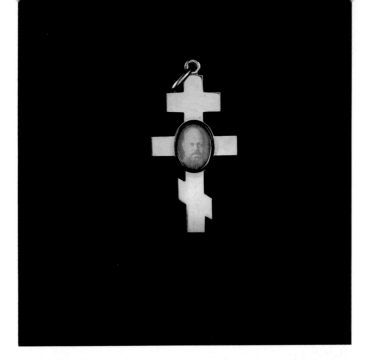

8***

REGIMENTAL GOLD SALT-CELLARS AND SPOONS
Platinum, gold, silver, marble
L: 9.7 cm; L of spoons: 3.4 cm
Marks: Fabergé, initials of workmaster Henrik Wigström,
assay mark of St. Petersburg 1899–1908, initials of
assay master Iakov Liapunov, 56 and 88 (*zolotnik*)

Shaped as a pair of regimental kettledrums with hinged covers,
applied with monograms of Peter the Great. Interior inscribed:
'The Horse Guardsmen to their Chief' and 'Krasnoe Selo. 8 August
1904'. Cups of spoons are of platinum and fold to form drumsticks.

Provenance: Dowager Empress Maria Feodorovna (Patron of the
Horse Guards Regiment).
Exhibitions: Kremlin 1992, cat. 12.

The Kremlin Armoury Museum, Moscow
(State Historical Cultural Reserve Inv. MR 869/1–2)

9*

CATHERINE THE GREAT EASTER EGG
Four-colour gold, enamel, diamonds, pearls
H: 12 cm, 17.1 cm (with stand) W: 8.9 cm
Marks: *Fabergé* (engraved) on inside of cover

Of Louis XV design, set at front and back with two large
rectangular panels painted by Vasilii Zuiev in *camaieu rose* with
allegories of Science and Art in the manner of François Boucher
within borders of seed pearls and white opaque enamel. Two
additional oval panels above and below and two to the sides are
similarly painted and then framed with two-colour gold borders
with diamond-set bowknots at the top and sprays of leaves at the
bottom. Spandrels are chased in four-colour gold with musical
trophies and laurel leaves on matte gold ground. Finial with
Russian cypher 'MF' under a portrait diamond, base with date
'1914' under a portrait diamond.

In a letter dated 8 April 1914, the Dowager Empress Maria
Feodorovna wrote to her sister Queen Alexandra: 'He [Tsar
Nicholas II] wrote me a most charming letter and presented me
with a most beautiful Easter egg. Fabergé brought it to me
himself. It is a true *chef d'oeuvre* in pink enamel and inside a *porte
chaise* carried by two negroes with Empress Catherine in it
wearing a little crown on her head. You wind it up and then the
negroes walk: it is an unbelievably beautiful and superbly fine
piece of work. Fabergé is the greatest genius of our time. I also
told him: *Vous êtes un génie incomparable*' (quoted from Solodkoff
1988, p. 24).

An automated sedan chair (ex-Clore Collection, Christie's,
Geneva, 13 November 1985, lot 30) fits the above description. Its
proportions and colours, however, do not seem to fit this egg as a
surprise. It is conceivable that Fabergé produced two versions of
this automaton.

Provenance: Presented to Dowager Empress Maria Feodorovna by
her son Tsar Nicholas II, Easter 1914.
Literature: Snowman 1962, pl. LXXXI; Ross 1965, p. 38; Taylor
1983, p. 33; Solodkoff 1984, p. 101; Solodkoff 1988, p. 33.
Exhibitions: Hammer 1937, 1939, 1943, 1951, 1952.

Hillwood Museum, Washington, D.C. (11.81)

10

'HVIDØRE' SEAL
Nephrite, two-colour gold, carnelian
H: 5.5 cm
Marks: Fabergé, initials of workmaster Mikhail Perkhin,
assay mark of St. Petersburg before 1899, 56 (*zolotnik*), inv. 50050

Table seal with ovoid nephrite handle partially encased in rocaille scrolls. Base with reed-and-tie rim; carnelian matrix cut with 'Hvidøre'.

The matrix was cut after the purchase in 1905 or 1906 of the Villa Hvidøre (White Ear) outside Copenhagen by Dowager Empress Maria Feodorovna and her sister, Queen Alexandra of England, both daughters of King Christian IX of Denmark, possibly as a haven for the former. In 1921, after her escape from the Crimea, Dowager Empress Maria Feodorovna lived at Villa Hvidøre.

Provenance: Dowager Empress Maria Feodorovna; Grand Duchess Xenia, her daughter; Prince Vasilii Romanov, her son, California.
Literature: Waterfield/Forbes 1978, ill. pp. 84, 140; Forbes 1980, pp. 5, 28, ill. p. 29; Solodkoff 1984, ill. p. 176; Kelly 1985, p. 23, ill. p. 22; Habsburg 1987, ill. p. 169.
Exhibitions: San Francisco 1964, cat. 104, ill. p. 32; Virginia/Minneapolis/Chicago 1983, cat. 43; Fort Worth 1983, cat. 100; Detroit 1984, cat. 93; Munich 1986/87, cat. 238; Lugano 1987, cat. 21, ill. p. 51; Paris 1987, cat. 21, ill. p. 47.

The FORBES Magazine Collection, New York (FAB77001)

11

IMPERIAL MINIATURE FRAME
Gold, enamel, ivory, gilded silver
H: 9.5 cm
Marks: Fabergé, initials of workmaster Mikhail Perkhin,
assay mark of St. Petersburg before 1899

Of shaped outline with rich, plum-coloured translucent enamel over *guilloché* sunburst ground. Oval miniature portrait of Tsarina Maria Feodorovna in a surround of four-colour gold sheaves of wheat, flowers, and ribbons. Ivory back and silver-gilt strut.

Provenance: Presumably a present from Tsarina Maria Feodorovna to her sister, Alexandra, Princess of Wales.
Literature: Bainbridge 1966, pl. 87; Snowman 1979, p. 135; Habsburg 1987, ill. p. 259.
Exhibitions: V&A 1977, cat. K 3; Cooper-Hewitt 1983, cat. 174; The Queen's Gallery 1985/86, cat. 20; Munich 1986/87, cat. 524; Zurich 1989, cat. 110.

Lent by Her Majesty Queen Elizabeth II

Nicholas II, Alexandra Feodorovna, and Their Children

Like his father, Nicholas as Tsarevich admired the work of Fabergé. His betrothal present to his beloved Alix came from Fabergé: a lavish pearl-and-diamond necklace. Following their Coronation, Nicholas and his wife Alexandra became the chief patrons of the jeweller. Fabergé's art played an increasingly important part in the Imperial Family's exchange of personal gifts.

12

IMPERIAL PRESENTATION BROOCH
Gold, diamonds, sapphire, ivory
H: 3.4 cm W: 4 cm
Marks: Initials of workmaster Mikhail Perkhin

Set with two oval miniatures of Tsar Nicholas II and Tsarina Alexandra Feodorovna, each in a frame set with rose diamonds, surmounted by diamond-set ribbon, an oval sapphire, and a rose diamond.

Identical, except for its mount, with cat. 60, also from Hillwood; both were probably presents to family members at weddings.

Provenance: Presented by Tsar Nicholas II and Tsarina Alexandra Feodorovna, probably 1894.
Literature: Taylor 1983, p. 28; Habsburg 1987, ill. p. 144.
Exhibitions: Munich 1986/87, cat. 124; Zurich 1989, cat. 185, ill. 158.

Hillwood Museum, Washington, D.C. (11.241)

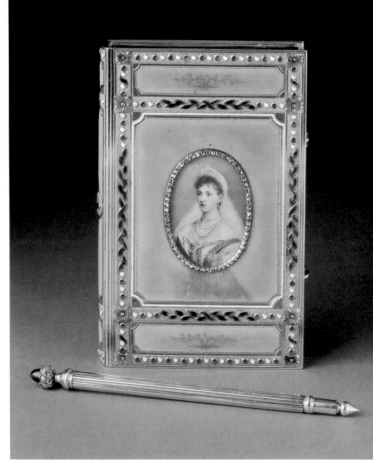

13

CARNET DE BAL

Gold, diamond, enamel, emerald

H: 10 cm W: 6.4 cm Diam: 1.3 cm

Marks: (Pencil) initials of workmaster Mikhail Perkhin,
assay mark of St. Petersburg before 1899, 72 (*zolotnik*)

Shaped as a Louis XVI *carnet de bal*, the cover applied with a
portrait in watercolour of Tsarina Alexandra Feodorovna within a
rose diamond frame, set in a panel of pink translucent enamel on
guilloché sunburst ground; the reverse similar, with central panel
imitated of moss agate. Further pink enamel panels to top and
bottom, each with dendritic motifs. Borders of granulated gold
enamelled with white and amber pellets and green foliage. Reeded
gold pencil with cabochon emerald finial in diamond-set mount.

Provenance: Tsarina Alexandra Feodorovna, circa 1894/96.
Literature: Ross 1965, p. 30; Taylor 1983, p. 24; Habsburg 1987,
ill. p. 252.
Exhibitions: ALVR 1983, cat. 214; Munich 1986/87, cat. 507.

Hillwood Museum, Washington, D.C. (11.77)

14

TRIANGULAR FRAME

Four-coloured gold, rubies, diamonds

H: 13.2 cm W: 10.1 cm

Marks: Fabergé's Imperial Warrant and initials, assay mark of
Moscow 1899–1908, initials of assay master Ivan Lebedkin,
56 (*zolotnik*), inv. 27280

Oval miniature of Tsarina Alexandra Feodorovna bordered in rose
diamonds suspended from a stand of three fluted yellow gold poles
forming a triangle. Cabochon ruby terminals tied with pink gold
ribbons, within a wreath of *quatre couleur* gold flowers.

Literature: Snowman 1962, pl. XIX; Hawley 1967, no. 56.
Exhibitions: ALVR 1961, cat. 189; San Francisco 1964, cat. 115.

The Cleveland Museum of Art (The India Early Minshall
Collection, 66.456)

15

CIRCULAR PRESENTATION BONBONNIÈRE
Gold, enamel, agate, pearls
Diam: 5.7 cm
Marks: Fabergé, initials of workmaster Mikhail Perkhin, initials of assay master Iakov Liapunov, assay mark of St. Petersburg 1899–1908, 56 (*zolotnik*)

Cover with an oval agate cameo carved with a profile portrait of Tsarina Alexandra Feodorovna, white on black ground, in a split pearl border set in a primrose yellow *guilloché* enamel box applied with radiating gold bands.

Exhibitions: Wadsworth Atheneum 1963; ALVR 1968, cat. 302; ALVR 1983, cat. 208.

Courtesy of A La Vieille Russie

16

PHOTOGRAPH FRAME
Gilded silver, two-coloured gold, enamel, bone
H: 14.3 cm
Marks: Fabergé, initials of workmaster Mikhail Perkhin, assay mark of St. Petersburg before 1899, 88 (*zolotnik*), inv. 58606

Shaped as a window, with red *guilloché* enamel pediment and frieze applied with laurel swags and acanthus motif; flanked by opaque white enamel half-columns with entwined green laurel sprays, with laurel wreath and ribbon cresting, bone back, and silver strut. Contains a photograph of Tsarina Alexandra Feodorovna and her daughter Tatiana, inscribed in Russian 'From Nicky and Alix. 1898'. The photograph has been wrongly identified as being of Grand Duchess Xenia Alexandrovna.

Provenance: Presented by the Imperial couple to Nicholas II's sister Grand Duchess Xenia Alexandrovna.
Literature: Habsburg 1987, ill. p. 176; Leningrad 1987, no. 149.
Exhibitions: Munich 1986/87, cat. 259; Zurich 1989, cat. 90; Helsinki 1989, cat. 10.

The State Hermitage, St. Petersburg (Inv. ERO-6761)

17

PRESENTATION BOX
Silver gilt, two-colour gold, enamel, porcelain, diamonds
L: 11 cm W: 9 cm
Marks: Fabergé, initials of workmaster Henrik Wigström,
assay mark of St. Petersburg 1908–1917, 88 (*zolotnik*)

Rectangular silver box with chamfered corners, of translucent pale
blue enamel over waved *guilloché* ground. Cover with circular
Imperial Porcelain Factory plaque dated 1909 painted in sepia
with a profile portrait of Tsarina Alexandra Feodorovna, with
green and red gold laurel leaf borders and rose diamond
thumbpiece.

Literature: Snowman 1962, ill. 96.
Exhibitions: Helsinki 1991.

Private collection, Finland

18

IMPERIAL PARASOL HANDLE
Bowenite, gold, enamel, diamonds
L: 6.5 cm

T-shaped bowenite handle, the sleeve of pink *guilloché* enamel
applied with crowned gold laurel swags and Russian monogram
'AF' set with rose diamonds on white *guilloché* enamel ground in
chased laurel leaf frame, with bead and tied laurel leaf borders.

Provenance: Tsarina Alexandra Feodorovna.
Literature: Waterfield/Forbes 1978, ill. p. 76; Solodkoff 1984,
ill. p. 169; Hill 1989, pl. 258.
Exhibitions: ALVR 1968, cat. 309, ill. p. 118; Virginia/
Minneapolis/Chicago 1983, cat. 33; Fort Worth 1983, cat. 84;
Detroit 1984, cat. 86.

The FORBES Magazine Collection, New York (FAB73004)

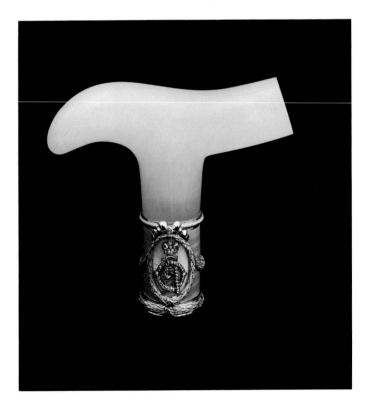

19

MINIATURE PINK FRAME

Four-colour gold, silver gilt, enamel, pearls, mother-of-pearl
H: 4.4 cm
Marks: Fabergé, initials of workmaster Victor Aarne, assay mark of
St. Petersburg 1899–1908, initials of assay master Iakov Liapunov,
56 (*zolotnik*), inv. 3076
Original fitted case stamped with Fabergé's Imperial Warrant,
St. Petersburg, Moscow, London

With arched top, of pink translucent enamel over *guilloché*
sunburst ground, applied with four-colour gold flower swags,
surmounted by ribbon cresting. Photograph of Tsarina Alexandra
Feodorovna in oval aperture with seed pearl surround. With
mother-of-pearl back and silver-gilt strut.

Literature: Kelly 1982/83, pp. 11, 13, ill. p. 12, fig. 17; Solodkoff
1984, ill. p. 171; Habsburg 1987, ill. p. 246.
Exhibitions: Virginia/Minneapolis/Chicago 1983, cat. 27; Fort
Worth 1983, cat. 50; Detroit 1984, cat. 65; Munich 1986/87, cat.
494, ill. p. 246; Lugano 1987, cat. 39, ill. p. 62; Paris 1987, cat. 39,
ill. p. 58.

The FORBES Magazine Collection, New York (FAB78007)

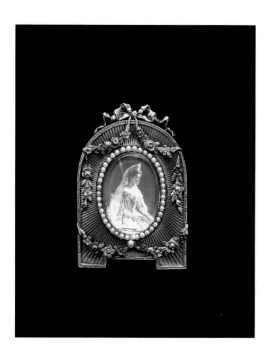

COLONNADE EASTER EGG

Bowenite, gold, enamel, platinum, silver gilt, diamonds
H: 28.6 cm
Marks: Fabergé, initials of workmaster Henrik Wigström,
assay mark of St. Petersburg 1899–1908, 56 (*zolotnik*)

'A clock of green grape-coloured ophite and pink enamel. The
enamel egg is encircled by a horizontal rotary clock face with
numbers made of rose diamonds. The egg is supported by 4 ophite
columns entwined with florals swags of varicoloured gold. The
columns are fixed on a base of the same stone. Golden figures of
4 girls (the Emperor's 4 daughters) sit on the steps of the base.
On the upper part of the egg is the figure of a boy (the Heir),
who is indicating the hour with a twig. In appearance the egg is
reminiscent of a large summer house with a colonnade under the
egg; between the columns there is a group of white silver kissing
doves' (Birbaum Memoirs).

Birbaum's recollection is almost perfect: there are in fact six,
not four, columns. (The Heir has since lost the twig in his hand.)
Birbaum mentions another egg shaped as a cradle, containing the
first portrait of the Heir, as being the one presented in 1905 to
mark the occasion of his birth. This might be the Love Trophy
egg (San Diego/Kremlin 1989/90, cat. 15).

Provenance: Presented by Tsar Nicholas II to his wife Alexandra
Feodorovna, probably Easter 1905; Queen Mary.
Literature: Bainbridge 1949/66, pl. 62; Snowman 1962, pp. 25, 96,
pl. LXXVII; Snowman 1977, pp. 49, 51; Habsburg/Solodkoff 1979,
p. 104, pl. 129; Snowman 1979, pp. 95, 96, 105, 121; Solodkoff
1984, pp. 91, 109; Solodkoff 1988, pp. 12, 44, 45.
Exhibitions: St. Petersburg 1902; V&A 1977, cat. K 24; Cooper-
Hewitt 1983, cat. 57; The Queen's Gallery 1985/86, cat. 177;
San Diego/Kremlin 1989/90, cat. 14.

Lent by Her Majesty Queen Elizabeth II

21

PETER THE GREAT BOX
Gold, enamel, rock crystal
D: 7.5 cm
Marks: Fabergé, initials of workmaster Henrik Wigström,
72 (*zolotnik*)

Louis XVI-style comfit box, the cover painted with Falconet's
statue of Peter the Great in *camaieu mauve* on pink ground.
Border of granulated gold enamelled with white opalescent pellets,
green foliage, and berries. Rock crystal base carved with crowned
Russian monogram 'AF'; sides with entwining laurel garlands.

An almost identical box with enamelled rather than crystal
sides and bottom is in the collection of H. M. Queen Elizabeth II.

Provenance: Tsarina Alexandra Feodorovna; Robert Strauss,
London.
Literature: Snowman 1962, pls. 113, 114, XXX.
Exhibitions: Wartski 1953, cat. 153, p. 15; ALVR 1983, cat. 202,
ill. p. 76; Lugano 1987, cat. 106, ill. p. 102; Paris 1987, cat. 106,
ill. p. 98.

The FORBES Magazine Collection, New York (FAB84015)

HEART SURPRISE FRAME
Gold, enamel, diamonds, pearls
H: 8.2 cm (closed)
Marks: *K. Fabergé* (inscribed on base)

Closed: heart shaped, of scarlet *guilloché* enamel applied with date '1897' set with rose diamonds. Stem of opaque white enamel gilt with laurel leaves; scarlet enamel base with two bands of rose diamonds and four pearls.
Open: shaped as a three-leaf clover, the 'petals' set with oval miniatures of Tsar Nicholas II, Tsarina Alexandra Feodorovna, and their daughter Grand Duchess Olga, in rose diamond frames on green *guilloché* enamel backgrounds.

The heart frame opens by deflecting a mobile sleeve at the top of the shaft. A spring mechanism in the shaft is triggered by pushing the central pearl in the base, causing the trefoil of miniatures to snap shut.

The date of this frame, obviously an Imperial gift, coincides with that of a lost egg described in the accounts of the Imperial Cabinet: '17 May 1897 egg mauve enamel with 3 miniatures 3,250 roubles' (CSHA f. 468 op. 13 del. 1843 p. 8. Cf. Solodkoff, 'Tracing Fabergé', of this catalogue). Further indication that this was a surprise from an Imperial egg is to be found in a Kelch egg dated 1902 (cf. Snowman 1962, ill. 389) containing a similar heart-shaped frame.

Provenance: Lydia, Lady Deterding, Paris.
Literature: Snowman 1964, ill. 103; Waterfield/Forbes 1978, ill. p. 61; Habsburg/Solodkoff 1978, p. 18, pls. 21, 22; Kelly 1982, ill. p. 6, fig. 6, p. 7, fig. 7; Solodkoff 1984, pp. 40, 41, ill. p. 170; Habsburg 1987, ill. p. 243; Hill 1989, p. 172, pls. 138, 139.
Exhibitions: Virginia/Minneapolis/Chicago 1983, cat. 16, ill. p. 8; Fort Worth 1983, cat. 52; Munich 1986/87, cat. 486; Lugano 1987, cat. 68, ill. p. 79; Paris 1987, cat. 68, ill. p. 75.

The FORBES Magazine Collection, New York (FAB78004)

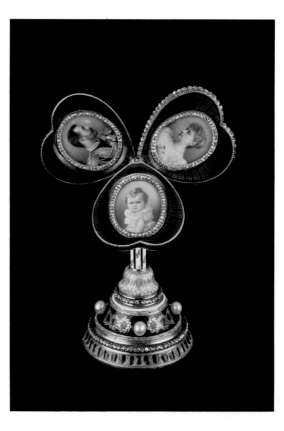

LILIES-OF-THE-VALLEY EGG

Gold, enamel, diamonds, rubies, pearls, rock crystal, ivory
H: 20 cm (open)
Marks: Initials of workmaster Mikhail Perkhin,
assay mark of St. Petersburg before 1899, 56 (*zolotnik*)
Original fitted case stamped with Fabergé's Imperial Warrant,
St. Petersburg, Moscow

Closed: gold egg in pink *guilloché* enamel, segmented with bands
of rose diamonds, standing on four foliate green gold cabriolet legs
set with rose diamond veins, surmounted by an Imperial crown set
with rose diamonds and two cabochon rubies.
Open: when a pearl button is turned, there appear in fan shape
three miniatures of Tsar Nicholas II and his two daughters, Grand
Duchesses Olga and Tatiana, signed by Zehngraf and bordered in
rose diamonds. Dated on reverse of miniatures: 5th April 1898.

Criticised by René Chanteclair (Chanteclair 1900, pp. 61–74),
this and the 'Pansy egg' (San Diego/Moscow 1989/90, cat. 11) are
the two strongest statements by Fabergé in the Art Nouveau style.

Provenance: Presented by Tsar Nicholas II to his wife, Tsarina
Alexandra Feodorovna, Easter 1898; purchased by Emanuel
Snowman for Wartski, London, c. 1927.
Literature: Chanteclair 1900, pp. 61–74; Bainbridge 1949, ills. 53,
54; Snowman 1953, p. 83, pl. XXV; Snowman 1962, p. 88, pl.
LXXIV; Bainbridge 1966, p. viii, pls. 52, 56; Habsburg 1977, ill. p.
55; Waterfield/Forbes 1978, p. 129, ill. p. 118; Forbes 1979, ill. p.
1237, pl. XVI; Snowman 1979, pp. 98, 140, ill. p. 98; Habsburg/
Solodkoff 1979, cat. pl. 15; Forbes 1980, ill. pp. 55 and on title
page; Solodkoff 1983, p. 65, ill. p. 62; Solodkoff 1984, ill. pp. 76,
127, 187; Kelly 1985, p. 14, ill. p. 25; Forbes 1986, ill. p. 52;
Solodkoff 1988, pp. 31, 34, 42, ill. p. 32; Hill 1989, pp. 14, 58, ill.
pl. 35; Pfeffer 1990, p. 55; Lopato 1991, p. 92, ill. p. 94.
Exhibitions: London 1935, cat. 585, p. 111; Wartski 1949, cat. 8, pp.
3, 10, ill. on frontispiece; Wartski 1953, cat. 285, pp. 4, 24–25; V&A
1977, cat. O 2, pp. 93, 132, ill. p. 101; Boston 1979, ill. on cover;
LACMA 1979; ALVR 1983, cat. 556, ill. p. 143; Fort Worth 1983,
cat. 190; Baltimore 1983/84, cat. 76; San Diego/Moscow 1989/90,
cat. 8, ill. pp. 24, 27, 48, 99.

The FORBES Magazine Collection, New York (FAB79003)

24

LILIES-OF-THE-VALLEY CIGARETTE CASE
Cork, gold, silver gilt, diamonds, ivory
H: 7.7 cm
Marks: Fabergé, initials of workmaster Mikhail Perkhin,
assay mark of St. Petersburg before 1899

Plain cork exterior, the cover applied with two miniatures of
Grand Duchesses Olga and Tatiana by Konstantin Makovski, each
in the centre of a flower set with rose diamonds. Gold lined
interior and diamond pushpiece. Interior inscribed in English:
'In remembrance/of Moscow/August 16 1898/fr. your loving/Alix'.

   The miniatures on this egg are very similar to those on the
Lilies-of-the-Valley egg (cat. 23), which Nicholas gave to his wife
the same year.

Provenance: Presented by Tsarina Alexandra Feodorovna to her
husband, Tsar Nicholas II, 1898.
Literature: Forbes 1986, pp. 56, 57.
Exhibitions: San Diego/Moscow 1989/90, cat. 28.

The FORBES Magazine Collection, New York (FAB85012)

25

NEPHRITE BOX AND COVER
Nephrite, gold, diamonds, rubies
W: 9 cm
Unmarked

Oval box on four scroll feet, the sides applied with gold laurel
swags suspended from rubies; lip inset with a band of rose
diamonds and rubies; domed cover surmounted by a pair of billing
doves set in rose diamonds.

   This is possibly an Imperial commission. The motif of the
billing doves is repeated in the Colonnade egg (cat. 20).

Literature: Bainbridge 1949, pl. 42; Ross 1952, ill. p. 5.
Exhibitions: ALVR 1949, cat. 277; San Francisco 1964, cat. 143.

The Walters Art Gallery, Baltimore, Maryland (57.913)

26***

CIGARETTE CASE

Gold, enamel, diamonds
L: 9.3 cm W: 6.3 cm
Marks: K. Fabergé, 72 (*zolotnik*)

Of oval section, with blue translucent enamel over *guilloché* sunburst, inset centrally in a lozenge with a miniature of the Tsarevich wearing a white fur hat, within a rose diamond-set border, further chased with laurel sprays, wreaths, and ribbons. With diamond pushpiece and inscription 'From Nicky to Mama' and date.

Provenance: Presented by Tsar Nicholas II to the Dowager Empress Maria Feodorovna.
Literature: Rodimtseva 1971, p. 12, ill. 5; Donova 1973; Solodkoff 1988, ill. p. 114.
Exhibitions: Elagin Palace 1989, cat. 115, ill. p. 105; Kremlin 1992, cat. 129.

The Kremlin Armoury, Moscow
(State Historical Cultural Reserve, Inv. MR 657)

27

TSAREVICH SEAL

Gold, enamel, bowenite, agate
H: 3.6 cm
Marks: Initials of workmaster Feodor Afanassiev, inv. 14.855
Original fitted case stamped with Fabergé's Imperial Warrant, St. Petersburg, Moscow

Egg-shaped bowenite handle, flaring gold stem in salmon pink *guilloché* enamel, base with laurel leaf border; agate matrix engraved with crowned Russian monogram 'AN'.

Provenance: Tsarevich Alexei Nikolaievich (1904–1918).
Literature: Snowman 1979, ill. p. 43; Habsburg 1987, ill. p. 144.
Exhibitions: V&A 1977, cat. K 32; Munich 1986/87, cat. 127; Zurich 1989, cat. 84, ill. p. 93; San Diego/Kremlin 1989/90, cat. 30.

Courtesy of Wartski, London

28

KARELIAN BIRCH FRAME
Karelian birch, silver gilt
H: 14 cm
Marks: Initials of workmaster Anders Nevalainen, assay mark of
St. Petersburg 1899–1908, initials of assay master A. Richter,
88 (*zolotnik*)

Polished birchwood frame applied with laurel wreath and a rosette
at each corner; wooden back and strut. Contains a photograph of
Tsarevich Alexei Nikolaievich, inserted by his mother, Tsarina
Alexandra Feodorovna, who further scratched in the back 'Spala
1912'.

Provenance: Presented by Tsarina Alexandra Feodorovna to her
sister, Princess Henry of Prussia, née Princess Irene of Hessen.
Literature: Waterfield/Forbes 1978, pp. 72, 132, 143; Kelly 1982/83,
ill. p. 10, fig. 14; Solodkoff 1984, p. 172; Forbes 1986, ill. pp. 56, 57;
Habsburg 1987, ill. p. 111.
Exhibitions: Virginia/Minneapolis/Chicago 1983, cat. 26, p. 12;
Fort Worth 1983, cat. 58; Detroit 1984, cat. 67; Munich 1986/87,
cat. 31; Lugano 1987, cat. 33, ill. p. 59; Paris 1987, cat. 33, ill. p. 54.

The FORBES Magazine Collection, New York (FAB76016)

29

MOSAIC EASTER EGG
Yellow gold, platinum, diamonds, rubies, emeralds, topazes,
sapphires, garnets, pearls, enamel
H: 9.2 cm
Marks: Engraved signatures 'C. Fabergé' and 'G. [*sic*] Fabergé,
1914' (on stand)

Platinum mesh body set with numerous calibrated precious and
semiprecious stones, with oval panels imitating *petit point* within
white enamel and split pearl borders. Cover with a moonstone
finial over Russian monogram 'AF'. The 'surprise' is a jewelled
and enamelled miniature frame painted with the profiles in
camaieu brun of the five Imperial children on an opalescent pink
enamel ground surrounded by green enamel husks and pearls,
surmounted by an Imperial crown set with rose diamonds. Reverse
enamelled with the names of the children, a vase of flowers, and
date '1914'. The oval base with vase-shaped white enamel stem is
set with rose diamonds, emeralds, and two suspended pearls.

The design books of Albert Holmström record the central motif of the panels in a brooch dated 24 July 1913. The design is by Alma Theresia Pihl, daughter of Fabergé's workmaster Oskar Pihl (cf. Helsinki 1980, p. 45).

Provenance: Presented by Tsar Nicholas II to his wife, Alexandra Feodorovna, Easter 1914; purchased by King George V and Queen Mary from Wartski, 1934.
Literature: Bainbridge 1949/66, pls. 51, 55; Snowman 1962, pp. 25, 106, pl. LXXIX; Snowman 1979, pp. 114, 115; Habsburg/Solodkoff 1979, pl. 136, p. 117; Snowman 1983, pp. 104, 105; Solodkoff 1984, pp. 64, 100; Habsburg 1987, pp. 278, 279 ill. p. 279; Solodkoff 1988, pp. 54–56.
Exhibitions: V&A 1977, cat. F 5; Cooper-Hewitt 1983, cat. 105; The Queen's Gallery 1985/86, cat. 164; Munich 1986/87, cat. 544; San Diego/Kremlin 1989/90, cat. 23.

Lent by Her Majesty Queen Elizabeth II

30

FIFTEENTH ANNIVERSARY EASTER EGG
Gold, enamel, diamonds, rock crystal, ivory
H: 13.2 cm (without stand)
Marks: Fabergé, initials of workmaster Henrik Wigström,
assay mark of St. Petersburg 1908–1917, 72 (*zolotnik*)
Original fitted case stamped with Fabergé's Imperial Warrant,
St. Petersburg, Moscow, London

'Red gold egg commemorating the fifteenth anniversary of
Nicholas II's Coronation: it is enamelled opalescent oyster with
heavy carved husk borders enamelled translucent emerald green
with diamond ties at the intersections. The surface is covered with
a series of paintings on ivory by Zuiev depicting notable events of
the reign; these are set under carved rock crystal panels and
represent:
1. The ceremonial procession to the Uspensky Cathedral
2. The actual moment of the Coronation
3. The Alexander III Bridge in Paris at the opening of which His
Imperial Majesty was present [Ed. This is incorrect. Cf. Habsburg,
'Fabergé and the Paris 1900 *Exposition Universelle*'.
4. The House in the Hague, where the first Peace Conference took
place, Huis ten Bosch
5. The ceremonial reception for the members of the first State
Duma in the Winter Palace
6. The Emperor Alexander III Museum
7. The unveiling of the Peter the Great monument in Riga
8. The unveiling in Poltava of the monument commemorating the
two hundredth year of the founding of Poltava
9. The removal of the remains of the blessed Serafim Sarovski'
(*Stolitsa i Usadba*, 1 April 1916).

The scenes depicted are flanked by miniature portraits of the Tsar,
of Tsarina Alexandra Feodorovna, and of their five children in rose
diamond frames, as well as the dates '1894' and '1911'. Finial with
monogram 'AF' under portrait diamond; culet with rose diamond
cluster.
  This egg commemorates the fifteenth anniversary of Tsar
Nicholas II's accession to the throne in addition to dates that were
personally significant in the family's history. They include the
laying of the foundation stone of the Pont Alexandre III in Paris
(cf. Habsburg, 'Fabergé and the 1900 Paris *Exposition Universelle*')
and the opening ceremony of the Duma on 27 April 1906, held in
the Throne Room.

Provenance: Presented by Tsar Nicholas II to his wife, Tsarina
Alexandra Feodorovna, Easter 1911.
Literature: Bainbridge 1933, p. 174; Snowman 1953, pp. 94–95,
ill. no. 330; Snowman 1962, p. 101, pls. 365, 366; Habsburg 1977,
p. 82; Waterfield/Forbes 1978, ill. pp. 24–26, 125, 140–42, and dust
jacket; Forbes 1979, ill. p. 1239, pl. XVIII; Habsburg/Solodkoff
1979, p. 158; Snowman 1979, p. 113, ill. p. 112; Forbes 1980, p. 5,
ill. p. 39; Marilyn Pfeifer Swezey, 'The Imperial Easter Egg of
1911: Russia During the Reign of Nicholas II', in Solodkoff 1984,
pp. 110–21; Kelly 1985, p. 14, ill. opp. title page; Forbes 1986, ill.
p. 54; Solodkoff 1988, p. 45; Hill 1989, pp. 14, 60, pls. 50, 51, and
title page; Cerwinske 1990, ill. pp. 55, 143; Pfeffer 1990, ill. pp. 93,
95.
Exhibitions: MMA 1967, cat. L.67.31.2; NYCC 1973, cat. 4, ill.
pp. 33, 35; V&A 1977, cat. L 7, pp. 72–73; Virginia/Minneapolis/
Chicago 1983, cat. 97, p. 16; Fort Worth 1983, cat. 193; Detroit
1984, cat. 136; Lugano 1987, cat. 120, ill. pp. 114, 115; Paris 1987,
cat. 120, ill. pp. 110, 111.

The FORBES Magazine Collection, New York (FAB66023)

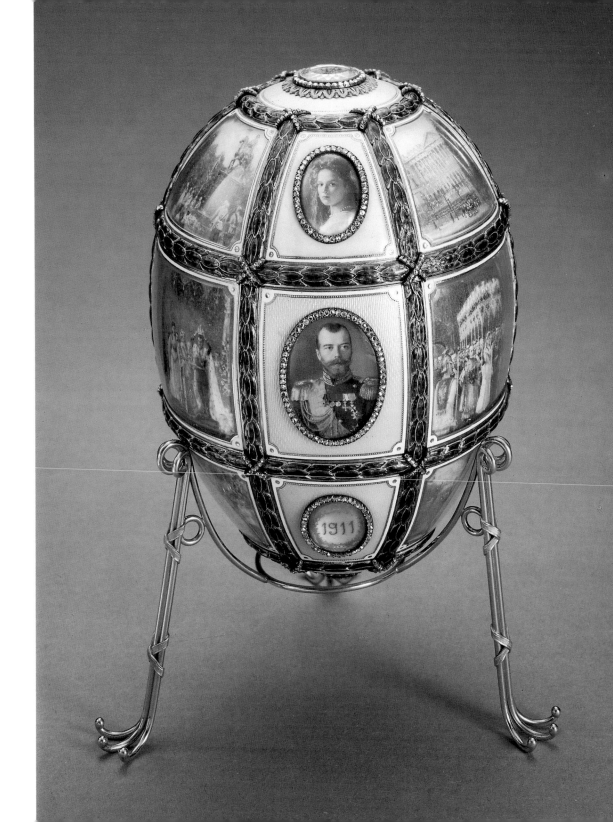

The Imperial Family at Home

Pavlovsk and Peterhof Palaces are the only Imperial homes that still house a number of works of art by Fabergé originating from the private apartments of Nicholas and Alexandra. The items at Pavlovsk are largely from Alexandra Feodorovna's rooms, the Mauve Room, and the Palisander Room at the Alexander Palace, Tsarskoe Selo. Contemporary photographs (cat. 359, 360) show a number of Fabergé pieces *in situ* and thus verify that the following items were in constant use by the Imperial Family. Tsarina Alexandra preferred the Art Nouveau style, for her family in Darmstadt actively patronised a colony of innovative Art Nouveau craftsmen.

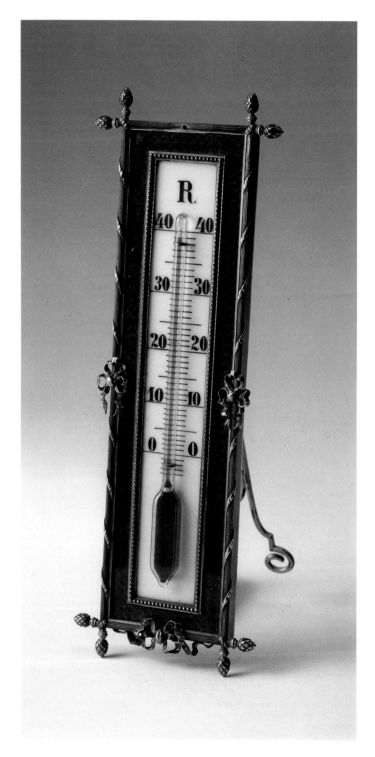

31

TABLE THERMOMETER
Silver, enamel, ivory, glass
H: 21 cm
Marks: Fabergé, initials of workmaster Victor Aarne, assay mark of St. Petersburg before 1899, initials of assay master Iakov Liapunov, 88 (*zolotnik*), inv. 56426

Upright rectangular, of pink *guilloché* enamel, borders as fluted staffs with ribbons and pine-cone finials; ivory back, silver strut, with Reaumur gradings on white porcelain plaque.

Provenance: Alexander Palace in Tsarskoe Selo.
Exhibitions: Elagin Palace 1989, cat. 7, ill. p. 66.

Pavlovsk Palace (Inv. Ts Kh-763–VII)

32

BOX SHAPED AS A LOUIS XV COMMODE
Bird's eye birchwood, velvet, glass, silver
H: 21.5 cm L: 22 cm
Marks: Fabergé's Imperial Warrant, assay mark of Moscow before
1899, 88 (*zolotnik*)

Of bombé shape, applied with silver rococo scrolls, the cover inset
with blue glass plaque and applied with a military trophy. Interior
lined in blue velvet, the cover with a silver plaque inscribed:
'To Her Imperial Majesty Empress Alexandra Feodorovna from
her loyal and devoted Orenburg Cossack Women'. The case was
presented containing an Orenburg scarf.

Provenance: Alexander Palace in Tsarskoe Selo (from the
Palisander drawing-room).
Literature: Kuchumov 1981, ill. 197.
Exhibitions: Elagin Palace 1989, cat. 107, ill. pp. 102, 103.

Pavlovsk Palace (Inv. Ts Kh-753–VII)

33

LOUIS XVI-STYLE VITRINE

Glass, silver

H: 32 cm

Marks: Fabergé, initials of workmaster Julius Rappoport, assay mark of St. Petersburg, 88 (*zolotnik*)

Shaped as a sedan chair, with classical decoration of Greek key pattern, stiff leaves, acanthus, fluted columns with pine-cone finials, laurel swags, and tied ribbons.

Provenance: Alexander Palace in Tsarskoe Selo (from Alexandra Feodorovna's rooms).

Exhibitions: Elagin Palace 1989, cat. 72, ill. p. 90.

Pavlovsk Palace (Inv. Ts Kh-9995–I)

34

NIGHT LAMP

Onyx, gilded silver, amethysts, silk

H: 26 cm

Marks: Fabergé, initials of workmaster Julius Rappoport, assay mark of St. Petersburg, 88 (*zolotnik*)

Standing on square onyx base with four paw feet, with ovoid onyx body flanked by fluted silver-gilt columns with artichoke finials; baluster silver top chased with palm leaves. White silk lampshade with cabochon amethysts in silver mounts to sides.

Provenance: Alexander Palace in Tsarskoe Selo (from Alexandra Feodorovna's rooms).

Literature: Kuchumov 1981, ill. p. 199.

Exhibitions: Elagin Palace 1989, cat. 69, ill. p. 87.

Pavlovsk Palace (Inv. Ts Kh-714–VII)

35

LAMP SHAPED AS AN AMPHORA

Onyx, silver, silk

H: 27.5 cm

Marks: Fabergé's Imperial Warrant, initials of workmaster
Julius Rappoport, assay mark of St. Petersburg 1899–1908,
initials of assay master Iakov Liapunov, 88 (*zolotnik*)

On circular base, with tapering body; silver mounts chased with
laurel leaves, flutes, and gadrooning, angular handles; silk shade.

Provenance: Alexander Palace in Tsarskoe Selo.
Literature: Kuchumov 1981, ill. p. 198.
Exhibitions: Elagin Palace 1989, cat. 70, ill. p. 88.

Pavlovsk Palace (Inv. Ts Kh-715–VII)

36

SILVER-MOUNTED OVERLAY GLASS BOWL

Glass, silver

Diam: 14.3 cm

Marks: Fabergé's Imperial Warrant, initials of workmaster
Julius Rappoport, assay mark of St. Petersburg before 1899

Circular Egyptian-style glass bowl with black overlay reserves
containing vultures; stands on three sphinx feet.

Provenance: Alexander Palace in Tsarskoe Selo.
Exhibitions: Elagin Palace 1989, cat. 64, ill. p. 86.

Pavlovsk Palace (Inv. Ts Kh-9980–I)

37

SILVER-MOUNTED DOULTON VASE
Pottery, silver
H: 20 cm
Marks: Fabergé's Imperial Warrant, assay mark of Moscow before
1899, 84 (*zolotnik*), inv. 7874

Red-glazed Doulton pottery vase decorated with frogs and
standing on three legs shaped as frogs; silver Art Nouveau mount
shaped as water lily pads.

Provenance: Alexander Palace in Tsarskoe Selo (from the
Palisander drawing-room; cf. cat. 360).
Exhibitions: Elagin Palace 1989, cat. 86, ill. p. 93.

Pavlovsk Palace (Inv. Ts Kh-6155–I)

38

DOULTON VASE WITH PEAPODS
Pottery, silver
H: 52 cm
Marks: Fabergé, initials of workmaster Victor Aarne, assay mark of
St. Petersburg 1899–1908, initials of assay master Iakov Liapunov;
vase stamped 'England 1654'.

Red-glazed pottery vase with pear-shaped body and elongated
neck; Art Nouveau silver mount of trailing peapods suspended
from rim.

Provenance: Alexander Palace in Tsarskoe Selo (from the
Palisander drawing-room; cf. cat. 360).
Exhibitions: Elagin Palace 1989, cat. 1, ill. p. 64.

Pavlovsk Palace (Inv. Ts Kh-749–VII)

39

SILVER-MOUNTED RØRSTRAND VASE
Pottery, silver gilt
H: 14.5 cm
Marks: Fabergé, initials of workmaster Victor Aarne, assay mark of
St. Petersburg 1899–1908, initials of assay master Iakov Liapunov,
88 (*zolotnik*), inv. 6240; vase marked in green 'Rørstrand' and with
three crowns.

Blue-glazed body with white-glazed pansy flowers to rim, with
foliate silver base and silver stems to flower heads.

Provenance: Alexander Palace in Tsarskoe Selo.
Exhibitions: Elagin Palace 1989, cat. 2, ill. p. 65.

Pavlovsk Palace (Inv. Ts Kh-4679–I)

40

SILVER PHOTOGRAPH FRAME
Silver, wood
H: 17 cm
Marks: Workmaster Anders Nevalainen, assay mark of
St. Petersburg 1899–1908, inv. 7181

Reed-and-tie border with ribbon cresting; wooden back and silver
strut. Photograph of Tsarina Alexandra Feodorovna, signed and
dated 1901.

Provenance: Alexander Palace in Tsarskoe Selo.
Exhibitions: Elagin Palace 1989, cat. 147.

Pavlovsk Palace (Inv. Ts Kh-1438–VII)

41

SOLDIER OF THE PREOBRAZHENSKI REGIMENT
Polychrome hardstones, gold, silver, sapphires
H: 17.7 cm
Marks: On the rifle: Fabergé, initials of workmaster Henrik
Wigström, assay mark of St. Petersburg 1899–1908, 72 (*zolotnik*),
inv. 24242
Original fitted case with red velvet and satin lining stamped with
Fabergé's Imperial Warrant, St. Petersburg, Moscow, London

The soldier stands 'at ease', a silver rifle at his side, his uniform
and cap of black jasper, purpurine, and gold, with jet boots, pink
and white quartz belt, pink jasper face and hands, and cabochon
sapphire eyes. His cap with a golden band is inscribed in Russian:
'For Tashkisen. 19 Dec. 1877'.

Provenance: Alexander Palace in Tsarskoe Selo.
Exhibitions: Elagin Palace 1989, cat. 19 (dust cover).

Pavlovsk Palace (Inv. Ts Kh-824–VII)

42

COSSACK

Polychrome hardstones, gold, silver, sapphires

H: 17 cm

Marks: On the sole of the right boot: Fabergé, St. Petersburg, scratched inv. 25104; on the sole of the left boot: 1914.

Cossack's coat made of lapis lazuli, with applied gold epaulettes and cartridge cases, and silver belt and dagger. Jet boots, obsidian hat, purpurine uniform and lining to hat, pink jasper face and hands, and sapphire eyes.

Provenance: Alexander Palace in Tsarskoe Selo.

Pavlovsk Palace (Inv. Ts Kh-823–VII)

43

PORTRAIT FIGURE OF KAMERKAZAK KUDINOV

Polychrome hardstones, sapphires, gold, silver

H: 19 cm

Marks: On the sole of the right boot: A. A. Kudinov 1912; on the sole of the left boot: Fabergé, St. Petersburg. Kamerkazak since 1878.

Cossack in a dark green jasper coat with brown jasper fur lining, gold braidings and seams, obsidian hat, and silver and enamel orders and medals to his chest. Beard of grey chalcedony, eyes of sapphires, boots of jet, and leggings of lapis lazuli.

   According to A. M. Kuchumov, this cossack was one of Nicholas II's personal guards at the Alexander Palace.

Provenance: Alexander Palace in Tsarskoe Selo.

Pavlovsk Palace (Inv. Ts Kh-822–VII)

44

SILVER ASHTRAY
Silver, enamel
Diam: 9.1 cm
Marks: Fabergé's Imperial Warrant,
assay mark of Moscow 1908–1917, 88 (*zolotnik*), inv. 32683
Original fitted case stamped with Imperial Warrant, Moscow,
St. Petersburg, Odessa.
Pencil inscription on bottom: 'For the train. 6 Dec. 1914'.

Plain silver ashtray; cuvetto with stylised laurel leaf wreath in
opaque white enamel.

Provenance: From Tsar Nicholas II's train, which was given in
1929 to the Museum of Peterhof and placed in Alexandria Park.
In this train outside Pskov, Nicholas II signed his abdication in
March 1917. From 1929 to 1941 the train was used as a museum
of the Romanovs' last days.
Exhibitions: Elagin Palace 1989, pp. 114, 135.

'Peterhof' State Museum-Reserve (Inv. PDMP 27, 27/I)

45

SILVER PAPERKNIFE
Silver
L: 20.7 cm
Marks: Fabergé's Imperial Warrant, assay mark of Moscow
1899–1908, initials of assay master Ivan Lebedkin, 84 (*zolotnik*),
inv. 23094
Original fitted case stamped with Fabergé's Imperial Warrant,
Petrograd, Moscow, London

Tapering blade with handle chased with fluting, anthemia, and a
medallion containing the crowned monogram 'NA' of Tsar
Nicholas II; reverse with date '1915'.

Provenance: From Tsar Nicholas II's train (cf. cat. 44).
Exhibitions: Elagin Palace 1989, cat. 112.

'Peterhof' State Museum-Reserve (Inv. PDMP 64, 64/I)

46

NICHOLAS II'S MAGNIFYING GLASS
Silver, agate, enamel, glass
L: 16.2 cm

Circular magnifying glass with agate handle, in gardrooned silver
mount with blue *guilloché* enamel, applied with laurel leaves,
crowned monogram of 'N II' and date '1898'.

Listed in the inventory of the Palace as being in its original
fitted case by Fabergé (Peterhof Palace Archive, inv. 255/58, p. 4).

Provenance: Transferred in 1917 from Nicholas II's Cabinet in the
Lower Palace of Nicholas II in Alexandria Park, Peterhof.

'Peterhof' State Museum-Reserve (Inv. PDMP 65)

47

DOUBLE PHOTOGRAPH FRAME

Silver gilt, enamel

H: 10.4 cm L: 7.3 cm

Marks: Fabergé, initials of workmaster Hjalmar Armfelt,
assay mark of St. Petersburg 1899–1908, 88 (*zolotnik*), initials of
assay master A. Richter, inv. 15563

On one side, dark blue *guilloché* enamel with reed-and-tie border
and rectangular photograph of Tsarevich Alexei wearing a straw
hat; reverse of white *guilloché* enamel with similar border and
oval photograph of Tsarevich Alexei in a sailor's uniform on the
yacht *Standart*.

The Imperial yacht *Standart*, with 5,480 tonnage, was built for
Nicholas II in Copenhagen in 1895 and cost 3,964,300 roubles.

Provenance: Transferred in 1917 from Dowager Empress Maria
Feodorovna's Cabinet in the 'Cottage' Palace in Alexandria Park,
Peterhof.
Exhibitions: Elagin Palace 1989, cat. 120.

'Peterhof' State Museum-Reserve (Inv. PDMP 191)

48

CIRCULAR PHOTOGRAPH FRAME
Birchwood, silver gilt, enamel
Diam: 15.5 cm
Marks: Fabergé, initials of workmaster Anders Nevalainen,
assay mark of St. Petersburg 1899–1908, 88 (*zolotnik*), inv. 15049

Pale blue enamel inner frame within gadrooned and stiff-leaf
borders, plain birchwood outer frame, back and strut. Contains a
photograph of Tsarina Alexandra Feodorovna with her son Alexei
sitting at a window in Tsarskoe Selo.

Provenance: Transferred in 1917 from Dowager Empress Maria
Feodorovna's Cabinet in the 'Cottage' Palace in Alexandria Park,
Peterhof.
Exhibitions: Elagin Palace 1989, cat. 37.

'Peterhof' State Museum-Reserve (Inv. PDMP 192)

49

RECTANGULAR PHOTOGRAPH FRAME
Palisander, silver gilt
H: 14.7 cm
Marks: Fabergé, initials of workmaster Mikhail Perkhin;
assay mark of St. Petersburg before 1899, 88 (*zolotnik*), inv. 57827

With plain silver mount and ribbon cresting. Contains a
photograph of Grand Duchess Anastasia.

Provenance: Transferred in 1917 from Dowager Empress Maria
Feodorovna's Cabinet in the 'Cottage' Palace in Alexandria Park,
Peterhof.
Exhibitions: Elagin Palace 1989, cat. 56.

'Peterhof' State Museum-Reserve (Inv. PDMP 198)

50

ROSEWOOD PHOTOGRAPH FRAME
Rosewood, silver gilt
H: 22.2 cm.
Marks: Fabergé, initials of workmaster
Hjalmar Armfelt, 88 *zolotnik*, assay mark
of St. Petersburg 1899–1908, initials of
assay master A. Richter, inv. 13644

Rectangular frame with silver-gilt
applications of laurel swags, ribbon bows,
and a wreath.

Provenance: Transferred in 1917 from
Dowager Empress Maria Feodorovna's
Cabinet in the 'Cottage' Palace in
Alexandria Park, Peterhof. Originally the
frame contained a photograph of Tsarevich
Alexei in a white suit and a bojar hat. It
was replaced after 1917 (Peterhof Palace
Archive, inv. 238/58, p. 275).
Exhibitions: Elagin Palace 1989, cat. 12.

'Peterhof' State Museum-Reserve
(Inv. PDMP 314)

51

PAPERWEIGHT
Lapis lazuli, silver
Base: 22.8 × 17.9 cm

Lapis lazuli base on two levels with two naturalistically chased fighting silver lizards.

Listed in the 1910 inventory as being by Fabergé and in original fitted case (Peterhof Palace Archive, inv. 239/58, p. 109).

Provenance: Transferred in 1917 from Dowager Empress Maria Feodorovna's Cabinet in the 'Cottage' Palace in Alexandria Park, Peterhof.

'Peterhof' State Museum-Reserve (Inv. PDMP 58)

52

EMPIRE-STYLE TABLE CLOCK
Jasper, silver
H: 17.5 cm W: 10 cm
Marks: Initials of workmaster Mikhail
Perkhin, assay mark of St. Petersburg
before 1899

Chocolate-coloured jasper clock case of
slightly tapering shape, standing on four
stud feet, applied with anthemia, sphinxes,
laurel swags, and staffs with pine-cone
finials. With white enamel dial, black
Roman numerals, and blued steel hands.

Provenance: Transferred in 1917 from Tsar
Nicholas II's Cabinet in the Winter Palace
to the Museum of the October Revolution
in the same Winter Palace; since 1938 in
the Museum of the October Revolution, in
M. F. Kshesinskaia's house; transferred to
Peterhof in 1974.
Exhibitions: Elagin Palace 1989, cat. 61, ill.
p. 85.

'Peterhof' State Museum-Reserve (Inv.
PDMP 501)

53
CYLINDRICAL VASE
Pottery, silver
H: 16.7 cm Diam: 8.8 cm
Marks: Initials of workmaster KB,
assay mark of St. Petersburg 1899–1908,
initials of assay master Iakov Liapunov,
84 (*zolotnik*), inv. 6119

Of purple-glazed pottery, applied with a
silver frog to the side, with gadrooned and
laurel leaf mounts.

Provenance: Transferred in 1917 from the
classroom of Nicholas II's daughters in the
Lower Palace in Alexandria Park,
Peterhof.
Exhibitions: Elagin Palace 1989, cat. 166.

'Peterhof' State Museum-Reserve (Inv.
PDMP 6I3)

54

CYLINDRICAL ROCK CRYSTAL VASE
Rock crystal, silver gilt
H: 8.2 cm
Marks: Fabergé, initials of workmaster Victor Aarne, assay mark of
St. Petersburg 1899–1908, initials of assay master Iakov Liapunov,
88 (*zolotnik*), inv. 8515

Of 'crak' type, standing on chased silver-gilt water lily pads.

Provenance: Transferred in 1917 from the classroom of Nicholas
II's daughters in the Lower Palace in Alexandria Park, Peterhof.
Exhibitions: Elagin Palace 1989, cat. 3, ill. p. 67.

'Peterhof' State Museum-Reserve (Inv. PDMP 622)

55

SMOKY QUARTZ VASE
Smoky quartz, silver
H: 37 cm
Marks: Fabergé, initials of workmaster Julius Rappoport,
assay mark of St. Petersburg before 1899, 88 (*zolotnik*)

Cuppa carved with a water nymph holding a shell, a dolphin at
her feet, rococo scrolls, and Art Nouveau foliage. Gilded openwork
base chased with scrolls and foliage.

Provenance: From the Winter Palace Collections, 1922.
Literature: Lopato 1984, pp. 43–49; Habsburg 1987, ill. p. 186.
Exhibitions: Leningrad 1984, cat. 23; Lugano 1986, cat. 118;
Munich 1986/87, cat. 282; Zurich 1989, cat. 33.

The State Hermitage, St. Petersburg (Inv. E-17576)

56

CYLINDRICAL VASE BY GALLÉ
Glass, silver
H: 25 cm
Marks: (Mount): Fabergé, initials of workmaster Julius Rappoport,
assay mark of St. Petersburg before 1899, 88 (*zolotnik*); (glass):
Emile Gallé, and a *Croix de Lorraine*

Triple overlay glass in yellow-green and violet-brown hues
decorated with yellow flowers; dark green buds and leaves stand
against a dark background. Silver base of acanthus foliage and
flowers.

Provenance: Winter Palace Collections.
Exhibitions: Leningrad 1974, cat. 234.

The State Hermitage, St. Petersburg (Inv. 23411)

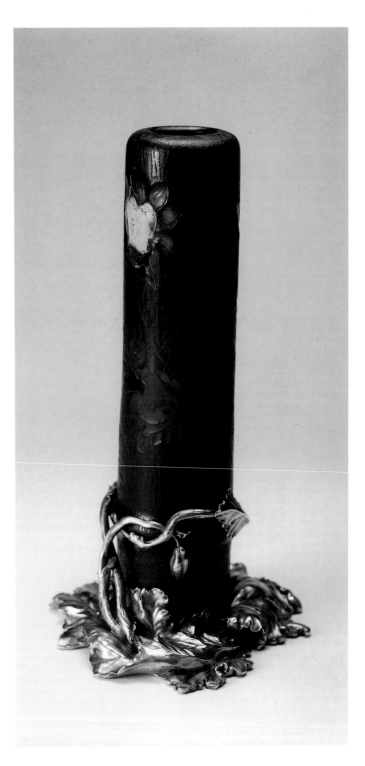

57
CONICAL 'VASE PARLANT' BY GALLÉ
Glass, silver
H: 20.5 cm
Marks: (Mount): Fabergé, initials of workmaster Julius Rappoport, assay mark of St. Petersburg before 1899, 88 (*zolotnik*); (glass): Gallé, Nancy

Quadruple overlay glass with opaline, pink, colourless, and black hues decorated with dragon-flies and lilies issuing from water. Inscribed on the edge: *'Végétation de Symboles'* and *'Palmes lentes de mes désirs. Nénuphars mornes des plaisir. Mousses froides, lianes molles . . . Maurice Maeterlinck'*. Everted conical silver base chased with waves and with two dragon-flies.

Provenance: Winter Palace Collections.
Exhibitions: Leningrad 1974, cat. 245.

The State Hermitage, St. Petersburg (Inv. 23410)

58

PEAR-SHAPED 'VASE PARLANT' BY GALLÉ

Glass, silver

H: 19.8 cm

Marks: (Mount): Fabergé, initials of workmaster Julius Rappoport, assay mark of St. Petersburg before 1899, 88 (*zolotnik*); (glass): Gallé, Nancy, France, 1896, and a *Croix de Lorraine*

Triple overlay vase in pink and violet-black hues decorated with a large flower, leaves, and swirling branches. Inscribed: '*En ses creusets le langage des fleurs et des choses/muettes Baudelaire*'. Silver base of ivy leaves.

Provenance: Winter Palace Collections.
Exhibitions: Leningrad 1974, cat. 228.

The State Hermitage, St. Petersburg (Inv. 23412)

Grand Dukes and Grand Duchesses

Many other members of the Imperial Family shared
Nicholas and Alexandra's love for Fabergé objects. Among
the constant donors and recipients of these *objets d'art* were
the Tsar's sisters Xenia and Olga and their husbands, and his
uncles and aunts, in particular Vladimir and his wife Maria,
and Sergei and his wife Elizabeth (Ella). Some of the Grand
Dukes also relied on Fabergé for tokens of their affections to
artists (see Smorodinova, 'Kshesinskaia's Memories', and
'Famous Clients', cat. 171–194).

59
RECTANGULAR PHOTOGRAPH FRAME
Silver, enamel, wood
H: 18.5 cm W: 27.9 cm
Marks: Fabergé, initials of workmaster Hjalmar Armfelt,
assay mark of St. Petersburg 1899–1908, 88 (*zolotnik*)

Of light blue enamel over *guilloché moiré* ground, applied with
laurel swags tied by a central ribbon, inner bead border and outer
reed-and-tie border. Contains under a bevelled glass a photograph
of the Tsar and his family.

The photograph shows (standing, left to right):
1. Grand Duchess Tatiana, daughter of Tsar Nicholas II
2. a lady-in-waiting to the Tsarina
3. Grand Duchess Victoria Feodorovna, wife of Grand Duke Kirill
4. Grand Duchess Olga, daughter of Nicholas II
5. Grand Duke Kirill, son of Grand Duke Vladimir Aleksandrovich
6. Marina, daughter of Grand Duchess Elena, future Duchess of
Kent
7. Olga, daughter of Grand Duchess Elena, future Princess Paul of
Yugoslavia
8. Grand Duchess Anastasia, daughter of Nicholas II
9. Elizabeth, daughter of Grand Duchess Elena
10. Grand Duchess Maria, daughter of Nicholas II
11. (seated) Grand Duchess Maria, wife of Grand Duke Vladimir
Aleksandrovich, mother of Grand Dukes Kirill, Boris, and Andrei,
and of Grand Duchess Elena
12. Tsarina Alexandra Feodorovna
13. Tsar Nicholas II
14. Grand Duchess Elena Aleksandrovna, wife of Prince Nicholas
of Greece
15. Grand Duke Boris, son of Grand Duke Vladimir
16. 'Bobtail' belonging to Grand Duchess Olga,
sister of Nicholas II
17. Grand Duke Andrei, son of Grand Duke Vladimir.

Literature: Habsburg 1987, ill. p. 247.
Exhibitions: Munich 1986/87, cat. 496.

Hillwood Museum, Washington, D.C. (12.179)

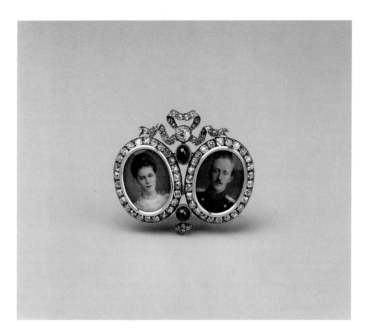

60
JEWELLED DOUBLE MINIATURE FRAME
Gold, diamonds, rubies
H: 3.5 cm W: 3.9 cm

Contains photographs of Grand Duchess Olga Aleksandrovna,
sister of Nicholas II, and of her husband Peter, Duke of
Oldenburg, each with a rose diamond border, surmounted by a
diamond-set bow, and with two cabochon rubies. Scroll-shaped
stand.

For a similar object, a brooch with miniatures of Tsar Nicholas
II and Tsarina Alexandra Feodorovna, also from Hillwood,
cf. cat. 12.

Provenance: Presented at the wedding of Grand Duchess Olga
Aleksandrovna (1882–1960) and Peter, Duke of Oldenburg,
on 9 August 1901.
Literature: Ross 1965, p. 27, Taylor 1983, p. 28.
Exhibitions: Hammer 1951, 1952.

Hillwood Museum, Washington, D.C. (11.75)

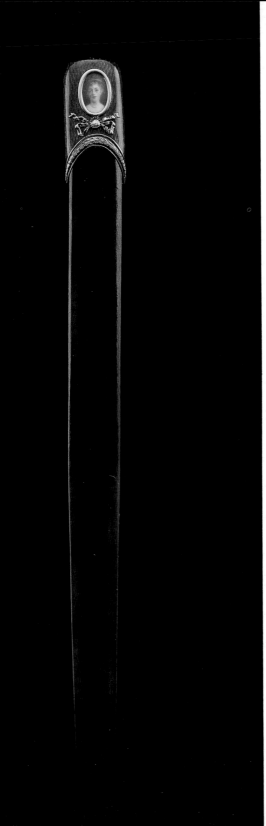

61

GRAND DUCHESS OLGA PAPERKNIFE

Nephrite, two-colour gold, enamel, diamond, ivory
L: 22.8 cm
Marks: Fabergé, assay mark of St. Petersburg 1899–1908, initials
of assay master Iakov Liapunov, 56 (*zolotnik*)
Original fitted case stamped with Fabergé's Imperial Warrant,
St. Petersburg, Moscow, Odessa

Long tapering nephrite blade with gold and strawberry red
guilloché enamel handle set with oval miniature of Grand Duchess
Olga Aleksandrovna; a gold tied bow and rose diamond beneath;
yellow gold laurel leaf mount.

Provenance: Grand Duchess Olga Aleksandrovna.
Literature: Waterfield/Forbes 1978, ill. p. 89; Solodkoff 1984,
ill. p. 176; Kelly 1985, ill. pp. 22, 23.
Exhibitions: Virginia/Minneapolis/Chicago 1983, cat. 44;
Fort Worth 1983, cat. 104; Detroit 1984, cat. 99.

The FORBES Magazine Collection, New York (FAB76005)

62

GRAND DUCHESS ELLA FRAME
Silver gilt, enamel, ivory
H: 10.3 cm
Marks: Fabergé, initials of workmaster Victor Aarne,
assay mark of St. Petersburg 1899–1908, 88 (*zolotnik*)
Original fitted case stamped with Fabergé's Imperial Warrant,
St. Petersburg, Moscow

Of yellow translucent enamel over *guilloché moiré* ground,
containing a photograph of Grand Duchess Sergei of Russia; oval
beaded bezel surmounted by a tied gold bow, crossed palm-leaf
sprays beneath, flanked by two rosettes; ivory back and silver strut.

Provenance: Presented by Tsar Nicholas II and Tsarina Alexandra
Feodorovna to Princess Irene of Hessen-Darmstadt (1866–1953),
who married Prince Henry of Prussia, brother of Emperor William
II. Grand Duchess Sergei, née Princess Elizabeth of Hessen-
Darmstadt (1864–1918), sister of Tsarina Alexandra Feodorovna
and of Princess Irene, married Grand Duke Sergei (1857–1905),
brother of Tsar Alexander III. The original note of presentation
survives and reads 'For dear Irine from Nicky & Alix'. In another
hand is written *'Bildnis von Ella'* (photograph of Ella).

Literature: John Herbert, ed., *Christie's Review of the Season 1983*,
p. 305; Kelly 1985, p. 8; Solodkoff 1988, p. 106.
Exhibitions: Lugano 1987, cat. 42, ill. p. 65; Paris 1987, cat. 42,
ill. p. 61.

The FORBES Magazine Collection, New York (FAB85002)

63

GRAND DUCHESS ELIZABETH LORGNETTE
Silver, enamel, glass
L: 12.6 cm
Marks: Fabergé, initials of workmaster Henrik Wigström,
88 (*zolotnik*)

Outer case in matte black enamel with opaque white enamel
borders, applied on one side with crowned initial 'E'.

Provenance: Princess Elizabeth of Hessen-Darmstadt, Grand
Duchess Sergei of Russia, sister of Tsarina Alexandra Feodorovna.
Literature: Solodkoff 1984, ill. p. 169; Kelly 1985, ill. p. 16;
Solodkoff 1988, ill. p. 106.
Exhibitions: Detroit 1984, cat. 83; Lugano 1987, cat. 44, ill. p. 65;
Paris 1987, cat. 44, ill. p. 61; London 1991, cat. 33, ill. p. 38;
Vienna 1991, ill. p. 67.

The FORBES Magazine Collection, New York (FAB84004)

64

PHOTOGRAPH FRAME

Gilded silver, enamel, maple wood

H: 16.7 cm

Marks: Fabergé, initials of workmaster Victor Aarne, assay mark of St. Petersburg before 1899, 88 (*zolotnik*), inv. 55942

Wooden pedestal with circular silver and mauve *guilloché* enamel frame above crossed torches and flower branch; tied ribbon cresting above. Contains a photograph of Grand Duchess Irina Aleksandrovna (1895–1970), daughter of Grand Duke Aleksandr Mikhailovich (1866–1933) and of Grand Duchess Xenia Aleksandrovna (1875–1960), granddaughter of Emperor Alexander III, niece of Emperor Nicholas II, and since 1914 wife of Prince Felix Felixovich Yusupov (1887–1967).

Provenance: Palace of Grand Duchess Xenia Aleksandrovna.
Exhibitions: Zurich 1989, cat. 88.

The State Hermitage, St. Petersburg (Inv. ERO – 6751)

65

CIRCULAR BOWL

Agate, gold, enamel, diamonds

Diam: 4.5 cm

Marks: Initials of Fabergé, assay mark of St. Petersburg 1899–1908

Hemispherical striated agate bowl, gold mounts enamelled with red lozenges and green foliage, set with rose-cut diamonds, angular handles with scroll ends.

Provenance: Grand Duchess Maria Aleksandrovna (1853–1905), sister of Alexander III and wife of Alfred, Duke of Edinburgh.

Madame Josiane Woolf, France

66

MUGHAL STYLE BOX

Gold, enamel, sapphire, rubies

H: 2.8 cm L: 2.3 cm W: 2.2 cm

Marks: Fabergé, initials of workmaster Mikhail Perkhin, assay mark of St. Petersburg before 1899, 56 (*zolotnik*), inv. 47449

Small rectangular *bonbonnière* with canted corners; cover with faceted sapphire applied with gold floral motif of rubies in gold setting; sides of white opaque enamel with gold and ruby flowers.

   Grand Duke Aleksei Aleksandrovich (1850–1908), fourth son of Tsar Alexander II and brother of Tsar Alexander III, was an Admiral and the Head of the Navy (1881–1905).

Provenance: Collection of Grand Duke Aleksei Aleksandrovich. Appraised and catalogued by Agathon Fabergé on 31 December 1908 (Hermitage Archive, f. 1 op. 5 del. 21, 1909, pp. 19–20): 'N 31. Gold bonbonniere with white enamel, in Indian style, with pale sapphire, set in gold. Made by Fabergé. 600 roubles'. *Exhibition*: Elagin Palace 1989, cat. 52.

The State Hermitage, St. Petersburg (Inv. E-307)

67

NAVAL PRESENTATION BOX
Silver gilt
L: 20.4 cm W: 14 cm
Marks: Fabergé, initials of workmaster Julius Rappoport,
assay mark of St. Petersburg before 1899

Rococo-style box chased with naval motifs of shells, tridents,
dolphins, and scrolls, with eight cartouches containing engraved
images of ships of the Russian Imperial Navy: *Pamiat Azova* and
Admiral Nakhimov on the cover, *Vladimir Monomakh* and
Admiral Kornilov to the front; submarines *Manchur*, *Koreiets*,
Sivuch, and *Bobr* to the sides. Cover applied with the crowned
cypher of Grand Duke Aleksei Aleksandrovich.

Provenance: Grand Duke Aleksei Aleksandrovich; acquired in 1940
from a state institution.
Exhibitions: Mikimoto 1991, cat. 18; Genoa 1992, cat. 16.

State Historical Museum, Moscow (Inv. 81749/ok 13664)

68

PRESENTATION CIGARETTE CASE
Gold, sapphire
L: 8.7 cm W: 6.1 cm
Marks: Initials of workmaster Eduard Schramm, assay mark of
St. Petersburg before 1899

Reeded and burnished gold case applied on one side with crowned
cypher of Peter the Great, the other with crowned cypher of
Grand Duke Konstantin Konstantinovich; cabochon sapphire
pushpiece. Interior inscribed in Russian: 'H.I.H. Grand Duke
Konstantin Konstantinovich' and the names of eighty-five other
members of the Preobrazhenski Regiment.
   Tsar Peter the Great was the founder of the Life Guard
Preobrazhenski Regiment; Grand Duke Konstantin
Konstantinovich was its Patron.

Provenance: Grand Duke Konstantin Konstantinovich (cf. cat. 69);
in the State Museum Fund until 1937.
Exhibitions: Mikimoto 1991, cat. 27.

State Historical Museum, Moscow (Inv. 61869/ok 5826)

69

COMMEMORATIVE POETRY ALBUM

Leather, *moiré* silk, mahogany, velvet, gold, silver, rubies, enamel
H: 17.8 cm W: 13 cm
Marks: Fabergé, initials of assay master A. Richter
Original fitted mahogany case with velvet lining

Silver-mounted brown leather binding applied with red and white
enamel plaque, with musical trophy inscribed 'Izmailov Leisure.
1884', monogram 'KR', date 'XXV', and with Art Nouveau foliage
and cabochon rubies. Interior of cover with white enamel
medallion and motto 'For Valour and Beauty', monogram 'KR',
and dates '1882–1907'. Contains forty pages of verse.

'KR' was the pseudonym of Grand Duke Konstantin
Konstantinovich (1858–1915). As President of the Russian
Academy, Head of the Military Schools, and Patron of the
Izmailov Regiment, as well as being a poet and a translator, 'KR'
was a prominent public figure. He was a friend of Peter
Tchaikovsky, who put to music numerous romances by 'KR'. For
twenty-four years, between 1891 and 1915, he owned Pavlovsk,
where he died on 2 July 1915.

'Izmailov Leisure' was a literary-artistic circle formed within
the Izmailov Regiment in 1882, but it soon outgrew its confines.
It was headed by the Regiment officers Lieutenant von Drentel
and Colonel Kesach. Grand Duke Konstantin Konstantinovich
played a significant role in the circle. Among its members were
Academicians A. F. Koni and N. V. Kotliarevski, prominent writers,
artists, actors, and musicians. 'Izmailov Leisure' dedicated evenings
to Gogol, Lermontov, Pushkin, Tiutchev, and Apukhtin.
The group staged theatre productions starring the famous actresses
Stravinskaia and Tomme. In 1907 the circle celebrated its
twentieth-fifth anniversary. The present album must have been
given as a gift on this occasion to the Regiment's Patron,
the poet 'KR'.

Pavlovsk Palace (Inv. Ts Kh-1486–VII)

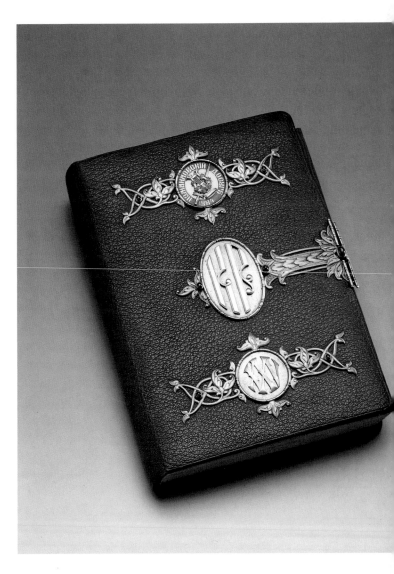

70

SILVER TEA SERVICE

Silver

Samovar H: 40.5 cm W: 27.9 cm Diam: 17.8 cm (base)

Small tray with samovar L: 41.9 cm W: 24.1 cm

Teapot H: 18 cm W: 20.3 cm Diam: 10.1 cm (base)

Coffee-pot H: 30.5 cm W: 26.6 cm Diam: 16.5 cm (base)

Cream jug H: 14 cm W: 10.8 cm Diam: 8.2 (base)

Sugar bowl H: 19 cm W: 19.1 cm Diam: 11.4 cm (base)

Slop bowl H: 13.9 cm Diam: 13.9 cm (top), 12.1 cm (base)

Large service tray L: 69 cm W: 45.7 cm

Marks: Fabergé's Imperial Warrant, assay mark of Moscow 1908–1917, Russian 'ICA' for the First Moscow Silver Artel, 88 (*zolotnik*); large service tray with Fabergé and workmaster's initials 'IW'

Teaset comprising samovar, stand, burner, teapot, coffee-pot, cream jug, sugar bowl, slop bowl, and two trays, all designed in the Empire style, with Roman tripod legs, paw feet, and winged lion's heads. Mouldings and borders with palmettes, laurel leaves, berries, and beads. Cover of samovar with crown in relief, Russian monogram 'IA', and facsimile signatures 'Olga', 'Vera', and 'Dmitri', the faucet with Roman numeral XXV, the base with date '1884–1909'. Large service tray by Fabergé not original.

Provenance: Silver wedding anniversary gift presented in 1909 by Grand Duchess Aleksandra Iosifovna (1830–1911), widow of Grand Duke Konstantin Nikolaievich, and her three children, Grand Duchesses Olga (1851–1926, Queen of Greece) and Vera (1854–1912, Duchess of Württemberg) and Grand Duke Dmitri (1860–1919), to her son Konstantin Konstantinovich (1858–1915) and his wife Elizabeth, Princess of Saxe-Altenburg (1865–1927); presented to Mrs Marjorie Post by her daughter Nedenia Rumbough (Dina Merrill).

Literature: Ross 1965, p. 77; Taylor 1983, p. 35.

Exhibitions: ALVR 1961, cat. 259.

Hillwood Museum, Washington, D.C. (11.241)

71

ROMANOV GRIFFIN
Silver, bowenite
H: 25.5 cm
Marks: Fabergé's Imperial Warrant, initials of workmaster Julius
Rappoport, assay mark of St. Petersburg before 1899, 88 (*zolotnik*)

Romanov griffin cast and chased in silver, upholding a sword
(shield missing), standing on stepped circular bowenite base.
Inscribed under the base in ink in Russian: 'Presented by Grand
Duke Georgi Mikhailovich on 7 March 1898 in memory of the
inauguration of Alexander III's Russian Museum'.

Provenance: Purchased in 1920 from I. I. Tolstoi.

The State Hermitage, St. Petersburg (Inv. ERO–5395)

72

GRAND DUKE KIRILL VLADIMIROVICH CUFF-LINKS
Gold, enamel, diamonds, rubies
W: 1.8 cm
Marks: Initials of Fabergé, initials of workmaster August
Hollming, assay mark of St. Petersburg 1908–1917, 56 (*zolotnik*)

Square, each link applied with an Imperial crown on white
translucent enamel over a *guilloché* sunburst; laurel leaf border.

Provenance: Grand Duke Kirill Vladimirovich (1876–1938), son of
Tsar Alexander III's brother Vladimir, a member of the Guard
Equipage, and father of Grand Duke Vladimir Kirillovich, recently
deceased.
Literature: Waterfield/Forbes 1978, ill. pp. 81, 139, and on cover;
Solodkoff 1984, pp. 22, 168; Kelly 1985, ill. p. 19; Forbes 1987, ill.
p. 16, fig. 12; Hill 1989, ill. on title page; Susan Jonas and Marilyn
Nissenson, *Cuff Links* (New York, 1991), ill. p. 43.
Exhibitions: Virginia/Minneapolis/Chicago 1983, cat. 37;
Fort Worth 1983, no. 74; Detroit 1984, cat. 75.

The FORBES Magazine Collection, New York (FAB75002)

73

CIRCULAR ROCK CRYSTAL FRAME

Rock crystal, gold, diamonds, rubies, ivory

Diam: 8.9 cm

Marks: Fabergé, initials of workmaster Mikhail Perkhin,
assay mark of St. Petersburg 1899–1908, 56 (*zolotnik*)

Rock crystal plaque engraved with laurel swags suspended from
tied bows, a laurel crown beneath. Rectangular aperture with
chased laurel border and rose diamond-set ties; outer border of
chased laurel leaves set with cabochon rubies, ivory back with gold
strut. Contains a photograph of Grand Duke Boris Vladimirovich
(1877–1943), brother of the above.

Literature: Thyssen 1984, no. 113, ill. p. 319.
Exhibitions: ALVR 1983, cat. 72; Zurich 1989, cat. 92, ill. p. 97.

Thyssen-Bornemisza Collection

74

TABLE SEAL WITH GRAND DUCAL COAT OF ARMS

Silver, milk glass, garnet

H: 6.3 cm

Marks: Fabergé, initials of workmaster Julius Rappoport,
assay mark of St. Petersburg 1899–1918, initials of assay master
Iakov Liapunov, 88 (*zolotnik*)

White opaline glass egg on a silver column base, tied with ribbon,
surmounted by a cabochon garnet.

Literature: Leningrad 1984, p. 41, cat. 104.

The State Hermitage, St. Petersburg (Inv. IP-1364)

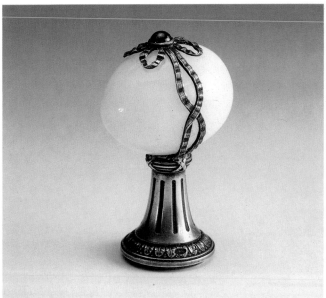

The Danish Relatives

King Christian IX and his wife Queen Louise were parents
of both Tsarina Maria Feodorovna and Queen Alexandra,
Fabergé's chief patrons. They received numerous presents by
Fabergé from their Russian daughter, from their son-in-law
Tsar Alexander, and from their grandson Tsar Nicholas.
Numerous examples of Fabergé's art are found both in the
private collections of H.M. Queen Margrethe of Denmark
and of Prince Henrik, as well as in the Chronological
Collection of the Danish Queen at Rosenborg Castle.

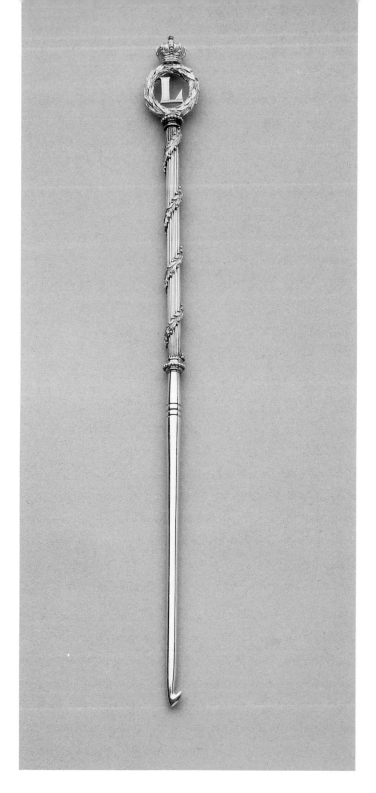

75
QUEEN LOUISE CROCHET HOOK
Gold
L: 17.8 cm
Marks: Initials of workmaster Erik Kollin,
assay mark of St. Petersburg before 1899, 56 (*zolotnik*)

Burnished two-colour gold hook with reeded handle entwined by a
laurel leaf and berry garland, surmounted by the crowned initial
'L' in a laurel wreath.

Provenance: Louise of Hesse-Cassel (1817–1898), wife of King
Christian IX of Denmark, mother of Tsarina Maria Feodorovna,
Queen Alexandra, King George I of Greece, and King Christian X
of Denmark.
Exhibitions: Lugano 1987, cat. 80; Paris 1987, no. 80.

The FORBES Magazine Collection, New York (FAB85004)

76

RECTANGULAR MINIATURE FRAME
Silver gilt, enamel, ivory
H: 8.8 cm W: 6.9 cm
Marks: Fabergé, initials of workmaster Mikhail Perkhin, assay mark of St. Petersburg before 1899, inv. 45117

Of pale blue *guilloché* enamel, containing an oval miniature of Queen Louise of Denmark facing right, with bead, laurel leaf, and reed-and-tie borders; ivory back.

Provenance: Empress Maria Feodorovna (1847–1928); her daughter Grand Duchess Olga Aleksandrovna (1882–1960), sister of Nicholas II.
Literature: Taylor 1983, p. 46.
Exhibitions: ALVR 1983, cat. 73.

Hillwood Museum, Washington, D.C. (12.178)

77

ROCOCO FRAME
Gold, nephrite, diamonds, seed pearls
H: 12 cm W: 8 cm Diam: 1.5 cm
Marks: Fabergé's Imperial Warrant, assay mark of Moscow before 1899, 56 (*zolotnik*)

Irregular shaped outline. Oval aperture set with seed pearls; outer scroll border with three rose diamond-set rosettes. Inscribed in upper cartouche: 'Sept. 8 1898 from VRI'. Contains a photograph of Queen Louise of Denmark.

Provenance: Presented to Queen Louise of Denmark by Queen Victoria; Queen Anne of Roumania.

Collection of Joan and Melissa Rivers

78

IMPERIAL REVOLVING FRAME
Silver gilt, bowenite, crystal
H: 22.8 cm
Marks: Fabergé, initials of workmaster Victor Aarne,
assay mark of St. Petersburg before 1899, 88 (*zolotnik*)
Original fitted case stamped with Fabergé's Imperial Warrant,
St. Petersburg, Moscow

Eight double-sided glazed photograph compartments with laurel
leaf frames, hinged on a central stand on three scroll feet,
surmounted by urn-shaped finial; stands on a circular bowenite
base with leaf-tip banding.

The sixteen original photographs include:
1. The Prince of Wales (1894–1972, later King Edward VIII)
2. King George V (1865–1936), Queen Alexandra (1844–1925),
Queen Mary (1867–1953), King Christian IX of Denmark (1818–
1906), and the Prince of Wales
3. Prince Aage of Denmark (1887–1940)
4. Prince Vigo of Denmark (1893–1970)
5. Princess Margaret of Denmark (1895–1962)
6. King Christian IX of Denmark
7. Queen Louise of Denmark (1817–1898) with her daughter
Thyra, Duchess of Cumberland (1853–1933)
8. King Christian IX, the Prince of Wales, and Princess Margaret
of Denmark
9. King George V, Queen Mary, and the Prince of Wales
10. King George V and Queen Mary
11. The Prince of Wales and Princess Margaret of Denmark
12. The Duchess of Cumberland with various members of her
father's Court
13. Queen Louise with her grandson, Prince George of Greece
(1869–1957)
14. Prince George of Greece
15. Queen Louise, her son Prince Waldemar (1858–1939), Prince
George, and King Constantine of Greece (1868–1923)
16. Queen Mary

Provenance: Tsarina Maria Feodorovna; the Danish Royal Family.
Literature: Kelly 1982/83, ill. pp. 2, 3, fig. 1, p. 5, fig. 5; Solodkoff
1984, ill. p. 170; Forbes 1986, ill. p. 57; Habsburg 1987, ill. p. 183;
Hill 1989, p. 170, pl. 132.
Exhibitions: Virginia/Minneapolis/Chicago 1983, cat. 29; Fort
Worth 1983, cat. 53; Munich 1986/87, cat. 278; Lugano 1987, cat.
41, ill. p. 64; Paris 1987, cat. 41, ill. p. 60; London 1991, cat. 4, ill.
pp. 12, 13; Vienna 1991, ill. p. 62.

The FORBES Magazine Collection, New York (FAB79012)

1,2,3,4

5,6,7,8

9,10,11,12

13,14,15,16

79

PAIR OF DANISH ROYAL WINE COOLERS
Silver gilt
H: 33 cm
Marks: Fabergé, initials of workmaster Julius Rappoport,
assay mark of St. Petersburg, 1892
Original fitted oak box (H: 85 cm W: 48.2 cm Diam: 40.8 cm)
with red velvet lining and silk, label stamped in Latin letters
'C. Fabergé' under Imperial eagle and in Russian 'St. Petersburg'.

Of cylindrical shape, standing on three ball feet, with three
elephant-shaped handles and three rococo cartouches engraved
with coats of arms and inscribed in French with the names of
donors from the Imperial and Royal Families of Russia, Hannover,
Denmark, Great Britain, Greece, and Sweden:

*Empereur Alexandre III, Impératrice Maria Feodorovna,
Cesarevitsch Nicolas, Grand Duc Georges, Grande Duchesse Xenia,
Grand Duc Michel, Grande Duchesse Olga; Duc de Cumberland,
Duchesse de Cumberland, Princesse Marie Louise, Prince Georges
Guillaume, Princesse Alexandra, Princesse Olga, Prince Christian,
Prince Ernest Auguste; Prince Waldemar, Princesse Marie d'
Orleans, Prince Aage Christian, Prince Axel, Prince Erick; Prince
de Galles, Princesse de Galles, Prince Albert Victor, Prince Georges,
Princesse Luise, Princesse Victoria, Princesse Maud; Roi des
Hellenes, Reine des Hellenes, Prince Royal des Hellenes, Princesse
Royale des Hellenes, Gde. Duchesse Alexandra Georgiewna, Grand
Duc Paul de Russie, Prince Nicolas, Princesse Marie, Prince Andre,
Prince Christophore; Prince Royal de Danemark, Princesse Royale
de Danemark, Prince Christian, Prince Carl, Princesse Louise,
Prince Harald, Princesse Ingeborg, Princesse Thyra, Prince Gustav,
Princesse Dagmar.*

Provenance: Joint present from the Russian Imperial Family and
the Royal Houses of Great Britain, Hannover, Greece, Denmark,
and Sweden to King Christian IX and Queen Louise of Denmark
on the occasion of their Golden Wedding Anniversary, 26 May
1892.
Literature: Willumsen Krog 1986, pp. 46ff.; Habsburg 1987, p. 132,
ill. p. 130; *Kunstkatte fra Zarernes Hof* 1990, cat. 201, ill. p. 94.
Exhibitions: Munich 1986/87, cat. 76.

Lent by Her Majesty Queen Margrethe of Denmark

Empereur Alexandre III
Impératrice Maria Fédorowna
Césarevitsch Nicolas
Grand Duc Georges
Grande Duchesse Xenia
Grand Duc Michel
Grande Duchesse Olga

80

DANISH ROYAL MONUMENTAL KOVSH
Silver gilt, enamel, quartzes
L: 82.2 cm
Marks: Fabergé, initials of workmaster Julius Rappoport,
assay mark of Moscow, 1892
Original fitted oak box (H: 96.8 cm W: 71.5 cm Diam: 82.8 cm),
with red velvet lining and silk, label stamped in Latin letters
'C. Fabergé' under Imperial eagle and in Russian 'St. Petersburg'.

Kovsh of traditional Russian shape. Sides chased with foliage and
scrolls forming cartouches containing a crowned interlacing
monogram 'C IX' and 'L', and date '26 Mai 1842–1892'. Front
with rococo cartouche containing the crowned coats of arms of
Denmark and Hessen; scrolling handle surmounted by the royal
Danish elephant with a blue enamel saddle cloth applied with a
monogram 'C IX' and 'L'. Turret-shaped howdah enamelled in
red and white, set with quartzes and with a seated blackamoor.

Provenance: Presented by Tsar Alexander III and Tsarina Maria
Feodorovna to King Christian IX and Queen Louise of Denmark
on the occasion of their Golden Wedding Anniversary, 1892.
Literature: Willumsen Krog 1986, no. 76; Habsburg 1987,
pp. 132–33, ill. p. 131; *Kunstkatte fra Zarernes Hof* 1990, cat. 202,
ill. p. 95.
Exhibitions: Munich 1986/87, cat. 77.

Lent by Her Majesty Queen Margrethe of Denmark

81

DOUBLE MINIATURE FRAME
Gold, enamel, diamonds, mother-of-pearl, silver gilt
H: 4.8 cm
Marks: Initials of workmaster Victor Aarne,
assay mark of St. Petersburg 1899–1908, 56 (*zolotnik*)

Two hinged red gold photograph frames of translucent royal blue
enamel over *guilloché* sunburst grounds containing photographs of
Prince Charles of Denmark and of Maud, Princess of Wales, each
within a border of rose diamonds. Standing on three stud feet,
applied with three-colour gold swags and six half pearls,
surmounted by ribbon cresting and central pomegranate finial,
with mother-of-pearl back and silver strut.

In 1896, Prince Charles of Denmark (1872–1957, King Haakon
VII of Norway 1905–1957) married Princess Maud of Wales
(1869–1938), youngest daughter of Edward, Prince of Wales, who
later became King Edward VII.

Literature: Snowman 1979, p. 135.
Exhibitions: V&A 1977, cat. K 11; The Queen's Gallery 1985/86,
cat. 18.

Lent by Her Majesty Queen Elizabeth II

The British Relatives

Through her visits to her sister Tsarina Maria Feodorovna, the Princess of Wales, later Queen Alexandra, became acquainted with Fabergé's work. The sisters exchanged his *objets d'art* as presents. After 1907, when Fabergé's art became available in London, Queen Alexandra was a regular client, buying chiefly for her own collection. Her husband Edward gave her innumerable objects, mainly hardstone animals. In the Edwardian Set, it was considered permissible to present little baubles from Fabergé to the Queen as well as to the King. Later, Queen Mary and King George enlarged the collection, adding two Imperial Easter eggs. Today the collection of H. M. Queen Elizabeth II comprises several hundred objects.

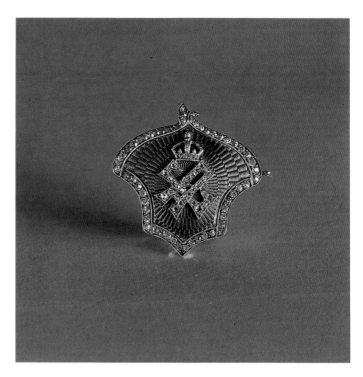

82

EDWARD AND ALEXANDRA BROOCH
Gold, enamel, diamonds
W: 4.1 cm
Marks: K. Fabergé

Of escutcheon shape applied with crowned entwined initials 'E' and 'A' set with rose diamonds, on steel blue *guilloché* enamel ground, with rose diamond border.

Provenance: King Edward VII (1841–1910) and Queen Alexandra (1844–1925).
Literature: Solodkoff 1984, p. 168; Kelly 1985, p. 16, ill. pp. 12, 16, 17; Habsburg 1987, ill. p. 141; Cerwinske 1990, p. 91, ill. p. 90 and on dust cover.
Exhibitions: ALVR 1983, cat. 383, ill. p. 111; Fort Worth 1983, cat. 73; Baltimore 1983/84, cat. 25; Detroit 1984, cat. 74; Munich 1986/87, cat. 106; Lugano 1987, cat. 88, ill. p. 90; Paris 1987, cat. 88, ill. p. 86; London 1991, cat. 36, ill. p. 39; Vienna 1991, cat. p. 76.

The FORBES Magazine Collection, New York (FAB83004)

83

SANDRINGHAM DAIRY FRAME
Gold, enamel
L: 7.1 cm
Marks: Fabergé, initials of workmaster Henrik Wigström,
assay mark of St. Petersburg 1908–1917, 56 (*zolotnik*), inv. 19770

Rectangular red gold frame with emerald green translucent
enamel border and opaque white enamel ties; contains an
opalescent pink enamel painting of the dairy at Sandringham.

Fabergé's animal models were displayed at the dairy for Edward
VII's inspection in 1908.

Provenance: Acquired at Fabergé's, London, by Princess Victoria on
14 November 1911 for £32 ('Frame, green en. white en. ptd. enl.
view of Qn. Alex.dras Dairy'); Queen Alexandra.
Literature: Bainbridge 1966, pl. 88; Snowman 1979, pp. 27, 29.
Exhibitions: V&A 1977, cat. H 7; Cooper-Hewitt 1983, cat. 139;
The Queen's Gallery 1985/86, cat. 335.

Lent by Her Majesty Queen Elizabeth II

84

KOALA
Agate, silver, emeralds, gold
L: 7.1 cm
Marks: Initials of workmaster Henrik Wigström,
assay mark of St. Petersburg 1908–1917, 88 (*zolotnik*)

Honey-coloured agate koala with gold-mounted cabochon emerald
eyes, on a chased silver branch.

Literature: Habsburg/Solodkoff 1979, ill. 108, p. 87; Snowman
1979, p. 71 (2).
Exhibitions: V&A 1977, cat. C 27; Cooper-Hewitt 1983, cat. 99;
The Queen's Gallery 1985/86, cat. 290.

Lent by Her Majesty Queen Elizabeth II

85
BEAVER
Nephrite, rose diamonds, gold
H: 5.5 cm

Upright nephrite beaver with gold-mounted rose diamond eyes.

Literature: Snowman 1979, p. 71 (8).
Exhibitions: V&A 1977, cat. C 28; Cooper-Hewitt 1983, cat. 179;
The Queen's Gallery 1985/86, cat. 252.

Lent by Her Majesty Queen Elizabeth II

86
OWL
Agate, diamonds, gold
H: 1.5 cm

Honey-coloured agate owl, its head turned to the right,
with gold-mounted rose diamond eyes.

Exhibited: V&A 1977, cat. D 38; Cooper-Hewitt 1983, cat. 116;
The Queen's Gallery 1985/86, cat. 118.

Lent by Her Majesty Queen Elizabeth II

87
'FIELD MARSHAL'
Aventurine quartz, sapphires, gold
L: 17.8 cm

Horse portrayed after nature, of reddish stone, with paler hoofs
and cabochon sapphire eyes in gold settings.
    This champion shire horse was one of the group of animals
modelled by Fabergé's craftsmen at Sandringham and carved in
hardstone in St. Petersburg.

Provenance: Birthday present to Queen Alexandra from King
Edward VII, 1 December 1908.
Literature: Snowman 1962, pl. XLII.
Exhibitions: V&A 1977, cat. B 14; Cooper-Hewitt 1983, cat. 73;
The Queen's Gallery 1985/86, cat. 248.

Lent by Her Majesty Queen Elizabeth II

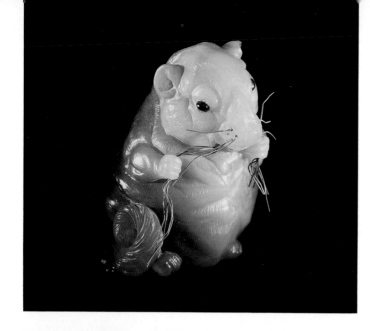

88

QUEEN ALEXANDRA'S DORMOUSE
Chalcedony, platinum, gold, sapphires
H: 6.3 cm

Dormouse seated upright, on its hind quarters, chewing at golden straws, with platinum whiskers and cabochon sapphire eyes.

Provenance: Acquired by Queen Alexandra at Fabergé's, London, 1911.
Literature: Snowman 1962, pl. XLII.
Exhibitions: V&A 1977, cat. B 25; Cooper-Hewitt 1983, cat. 168; The Queen's Gallery 1985/86, cat. 226.

Lent by Her Majesty Queen Elizabeth II

89

HORNBILL IN CAGE
Chalcedony, diamonds, gold, silver gilt
H: 9.2 cm
Marks: Initials of workmaster Mikhail Perkhin,
assay mark of St. Petersburg 1899–1908, 88 (*zolotnik*)

Pale and dark grey chalcedony carving of a hornbill with gold-mounted rose diamond eyes and gold feet in a silver-gilt cage with hinged door, two feeding bowls, and a drawer.

This is a good example of Fabergé's clever use of a stone's striations to indicate the beak and body of the bird.

Literature: Snowman 1962, ill. 238.
Exhibitions: V&A 1977, cat. D 33, p. 30; Cooper-Hewitt 1983, cat. 72; The Queen's Gallery 1985/86, cat. 140.

Lent by Her Majesty Queen Elizabeth II

90

VULTURE ON PERCH
Obsidian, sardonyx, diamonds, gold, silver
H: 4.8 cm
Marks: Initials of workmaster Mikhail Perkhin,
assay mark of St. Petersburg 1899–1908, 88 (*zolotnik*)

Obsidian bird with added translucent sardonyx head, gold-mounted rose diamond eyes and red gold claws, on a chased green gold perch and square base.

A fine example of Fabergé's skill at combining hardstones.

Literature: Snowman 1962, ill. 272.
Exhibitions: V&A 1977, cat. D 58, p. 33; Cooper-Hewitt 1983, cat. 85; The Queen's Gallery 1985/86, cat. 125.

Lent by Her Majesty Queen Elizabeth II

91

QUEEN ALEXANDRA'S PEKINESE
Fluorspar, diamonds, gold
L: 11.4 cm

Portrait model of Queen Alexandra's favourite Pekinese carved in pale green fluorspar, with gold-mounted rose diamond eyes.

Possibly linked to one of two acquisitons in 1908 of animal models from Alfred Pocock (cf. Habsburg, 'Fabergé and the London Branch').

Literature: Bainbridge 1966, pl. 99.
Exhibitions: V&A 1977, cat. A 17, p. 32; Cooper-Hewitt 1983, cat. 77; The Queen's Gallery 1985/86, cat. 240.

Lent by Her Majesty Queen Elizabeth II

92
ELEPHANT
Obsidian, gold, diamonds
H: 2.8 cm
Marks: Stamped with initials of Fabergé

Standing elephant with gold tusks and gold-mounted rose diamond eyes.

Provenance: Queen Elizabeth of Greece; Lance Reventlov.

Madame Josiane Woolf, France

93
BABOON
Chalcedony, sapphires
H: 5.7 cm

Baboon of grey chalcedony seated in an aggressive pose, with cabochon sapphire eyes.

Provenance: Queen Alexandra.
Literature: Bainbridge 1966, ill. p. 85; Habsburg 1987, p. 200.
Exhibitions: Munich 1986/87, cat. 344; Wartski 1992, cat. 137.

Courtesy of Wartski, London

94
LOBED DESK CLOCK
Rock crystal, gold, enamel, silver, diamonds, rubies
H: 12.6 cm W: 12.6 cm
Marks: Fabergé, initials of workmaster Mikhail Perkhin, assay mark of St. Petersburg 1899–1908, 88 (*zolotnik*)

Quatrefoil rock crystal plaque engraved with trophies within laurel leaf borders. White enamel dial with pierced red gold hands; translucent green enamel bezel chased with laurel leaves and rose diamond ties. Lobes divided by gold arrows with rose diamond bowknots centring on cabochon rubies. Reeded silver strut.

Provenance: Presented to Queen Victoria by Tsarina Alexandra Feodorovna; King George V.
Literature: Snowman 1962, ill. 146; Snowman 1979, p. 130.
Exhibitions: V&A 1977, cat. I 2; Cooper-Hewitt 1983, cat. 19; The Queen's Gallery 1985/86, cat. 59; Zurich 1989, cat. 103.

Lent by Her Majesty Queen Elizabeth II

95

PRESENTATION CIGARETTE BOX
Birchwood, gold, silver
L: 25 cm W: 13.5 cm H: 7.2 cm
Marks: Fabergé, initials of workmaster Hjalmar Armfelt,
assay mark of St. Petersburg 1908–1917, 88 (*zolotnik*), inv. 3374

Of polished birchwood, the cover centrally applied with a silver
laurel crown and the date '7 January/1917/8 February', flanked by
gold crowned initials 'GR' and 'M'; gardrooned borders, keyhole,
and four compartments.

Provenance: King George V (1865–1936) and Queen Mary
(1867–1953), born Princess of Teck; from the Leningrad Regional
Department Museum of Public Education, until 1926 in
Count Sheremetev's House, in the Fountain House.

The State Hermitage, St. Petersburg (Inv. ERO-6455)

96

PIVOT FRAME
Silver, oak, moonstones
H: 25.4 cm
Marks: Fabergé, initials of workmaster Hjalmar Armfelt,
assay mark of St. Petersburg 1899–1908, 88 (*zolotnik*)

Containing photographs of Tsar Nicholas II and George, Prince of
Wales, and (on reverse) of Tsarina Alexandra Feodorovna, under
bevelled glass within laurel leaf border. Silver mounted wooden
frame of mirror shape with ribbon bound fluted columns with
cabochon moonstone finials; stands on rectangular base with
chased leaf-tip border, surmounted by Imperial double-headed
eagle.

The photograph of Tsar Nicholas II with his cousin, the future
King George V of England, was taken at Cowes in 1909. They both
wear the navy blazer and white trousers of an English yachtsman.
Their family resemblance (their mothers were sisters, daughters of
King Christian IX of Denmark) was such that Princess Victoria
Louise, daughter of Kaiser Wilhelm II, wrote on the occasion of
her wedding in 1913, 'Only their uniforms told the difference
between them'.

Literature: Hill 1989, p. 172, pl. 135.
Exhibitions: AVLR 1949, cat. 172, p. 17; Lugano 1987, cat. 35, ill.
p. 60; Paris 1987, cat. 35, ill. p. 56; London 1991, cat. 6, ill. p. 17;
Vienna 1991, ill. p. 66.

The FORBES Magazine Collection, New York (FAB85034)

Other Royal Relatives

The tradition of presenting works by Fabergé at all occasions was adopted by many European Royal families, in particular amongst the German Royal families related to the Russian Tsars: the Hessens, Prussians, Hannovers, and Schaumberg-Lippes. Diplomatic gifts often took the guise of Fabergé creations, as did those offered to Kaiser Wilhelm II.

97

KAISER WILHELM II PRESENTATION CASE
Nephrite, gold, diamonds, ruby
L: 8.7 cm
Marks: Fabergé, initials of workmaster Mikhail Perkhin, assay mark of St. Petersburg before 1899
Original fitted red morocco case stamped with Imperial eagle and Fabergé's Imperial Warrant

Applied with diamond-set crowned cypher of Kaiser Wilhelm II within a gold frame of rococo scrolls and ribbons; reverse applied to one corner with gold rocailles and flowers, cabochon ruby pushpiece.

Literature: Booth 1990, ill. p. 135.

The FORBES Magazine Collection, New York (FAB93003), Courtesy of Ermitage Ltd., London

98

KAISER WILHELM II FRAME
Two-colour silver gilt, enamel, wood
H: 29.8 cm
Marks: Fabergé's Imperial Warrant, initials of workmaster Anders Nevalainen, assay mark of St. Petersburg 1899–1908, initials of assay master A. Richter, 91 (*zolotnik*)

Of translucent pale blue opalescent enamel on *guilloché* sunburst ground, applied with victor's laurel crowns at the corners; inner laurel leaf border, outer reed-and-tie border. Contains an original photograph of Kaiser Wilhelm II, signed and dated 'Berlin Feb. 1909'. Wooden back and silver strut.

Provenance: Presented by Kaiser Wilhelm II to an equerry of his uncle, King Edward VII.
Literature: Waterfield/Forbes 1978, ill. pp. 70, 143; Kelly 1982/83, pp. 9, 13; Solodkoff 1984, ill. p. 171; Kelly 1985, p. 16, ill. pp. 12, 17; Habsburg 1987, ill. p. 235.
Exhibitions: Virginia/Minneapolis/Chicago 1983, cat. 25, p. 12; Fort Worth 1983, cat. 41; Detroit 1984, cat. 55; Munich 1986/87, cat. 460; Lugano 1987, cat. 36, ill. p. 61; Paris 1987, cat. 36, ill. p. 57.

The FORBES Magazine Collection, New York (FAB76008)

99

KAISER WILHELM II CANNON
Nephrite, gold
L: 21 cm (with base)
Marks: Fabergé, initials of workmaster Mikhail Perkhin,
assay mark of St. Petersburg before 1899

A miniature replica of the 'Tsar Pushka' in the Kremlin.

Provenance: Presented by Tsar Nicholas II to his cousin Kaiser
Wilhelm II.
Literature: Habsburg 1987, ill. p. 191.
Exhibitions: Hanau 1985/86, cat. 231; Munich 1986/87, cat. 287.

Kasteel Huis Doorn, Doorn, The Netherlands

100

KAISER WILHELM II SILVER HELMET
Silver, silver gilt, semiprecious cabochon stones
H: 42.1 cm
Marks: Fabergé, assay mark of St. Petersburg 1899–1908

Cigar box shaped as a Russian helmet of the seventeenth century
similar to the 'Helmet of Jericho' at the Moscow Kremlin Armoury
by Nikita Davidov.

Provenance: Presented by Tsar Nicholas II to his cousin Kaiser
Wilhelm II.
Literature: Habsburg (K&A) 1987, p. 86; Habsburg 1987, ill. p. 128.
Exhibitions: Hanau 1985/86, cat. 105; Munich 1986/87, cat. 74.

Kasteel Huis Doorn, Doorn, The Netherlands

101

CIRCULAR PRESENTATION BOX

Gold, enamel, diamonds, ruby

Diam: 9 cm

Marks: Fabergé, initials of workmaster August Hollming, assay mark of St. Petersburg 1899–1908, initials of assay master Iakov Liapunov, 56 (*zolotnik*), French import marks 'ET'

Opalescent powder blue *guilloché* enamel box. Cover applied with crowned cypher 'N II' set with rose diamonds, on an oval white *guilloché* enamel plaque, within rose diamond border.

Provenance: Thought to have been presented by Tsar Nicholas II to Vilhelm, Duke of Sodermanland (1884–1965), son of King Gustav V of Sweden, and to Grand Duchess Maria Pavlovna (1890–1958) at the occasion of their wedding in 1908.
Exhibitions: ALVR 1983, cat. 218.

Courtesy of A La Vieille Russie

102

PRESENTATION FRAME

Holly wood, silver gilt, glass

H: 35 cm W: 23.5 cm

Marks: Fabergé, initials of workmaster Hjalmar Armfelt, 88 (*zolotnik*)

Rectangular pale yellow holly wood frame applied with central Royal crown; aperture with silver-gilt laurel border. Contains a glazed photograph of King Gustav V of Sweden, signed and dated 'Tsarskoe-Selo 1908'.

Provenance: Presented by King Gustav V of Sweden (1858–1950) to Count Vladimir Fredericks, Minister of the Imperial Court and household and aide-de-camp to Tsar Nicholas II during his visit to St. Petersburg on the occasion of the marriage of the King's son Vilhelm, Duke of Sodermanland, to Grand Duchess Maria Pavlovna in 1908.

Courtesy of A La Vieille Russie

103

PRESENTATION FRAME
Gold, pearls, enamel, ivory, gouache
H: 9 cm W: 6.7 cm
Marks: Fabergé, initials of workmaster Mikhail Perkhin,
assay mark of St. Petersburg 1899–1908
Original fitted case

Shaped rectangular frame of strawberry red *guilloché* enamel over
sunburst pattern, applied with four Bourbon lilies at corners and
surmounted by the Bulgarian Royal crown. Oval miniature
portrait of Ferdinand, Prince of Coburg, signed by Zehngraf.
Reverse with an ivory back stamped 'COURT OF H.I.H. GRAND
DUCHESS ELIZAVETA FEODOROVNA 304', with suspension ring and
gold strut.

Ferdinand, Prince of Coburg (1861–1948), ruled as King of
Bulgaria from 1908 to 1918.

Provenance: Presented by Prince Ferdinand of Bulgaria to Grand
Duchess Sergei (1864–1918), born Princess Elizabeth of Hesse-
Darmstadt, sister of Tsarina Alexandra Feodorovna; State Museum
Fund until 1927.
Exhibitions: Mikimoto 1991, cat. 3; Genoa 1992, cat. 3.

State Historical Museum, Moscow (Inv. 58678/ok 22562)

104

'FROG UNDER GLASS' BELLPUSH
Nephrite, silver gilt, enamel, diamonds
H: 8.3 cm
Marks: Fabergé, initials of workmaster Mikhail Perkhin,
assay mark of St. Petersburg 1899–1908, inv. 3605

Nephrite weather-frog with rose diamond eyes climbing a ladder
under a rock crystal 'glass'; cabochon garnet finial in silver-gilt
mount. Base with red *guilloché* enamel band between laurel and
fluted borders, on three stud feet.

Provenance: Sold to the Imperial Cabinet on 1 December 1900
('Electrical bell, nephrite frog, "glass" of rock crystal with red
enamel, one garnet and two roses, no. 3605 (1/2) 125 roubles' –
CSHA, f. 468 op. 14 del. 210); from the collection of
Prince George of Greece and Denmark (1869–1957),
cousin of Tsar Nicholas II, who accompanied him on a voyage
around the world on the cruiser *Pamiat Azova* in 1890–1891;
probably a Christmas present from the Tsar in 1900.

Literature: Solodkoff 1988, ill. p. 76; Booth 1990, p. 159.

Courtesy of Ermitage Ltd., London

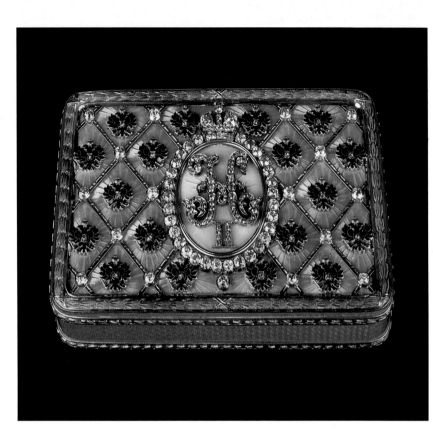

105
CORONATION BOX
Two-colour gold, enamel, diamonds
L: 9.5 cm
Marks: Fabergé, initials of workmaster August Holmström,
assay mark of St. Petersburg before 1899, inv. 1067
Original green morocco case applied with gilt Imperial eagle

Of yellow *guilloché* enamel; cover applied with cypher 'N II' set with rose diamonds on oval opalescent white enamel panel surrounded by rose diamonds and surmounted by a diamond-set Imperial crown. Further decorated with gold trellis and with rose diamonds at intersections containing black enamel Imperial eagles, each with a rose diamond. With wide laurel leaf border to the cover and waved *guilloché* panels to sides.

This item belongs to a series of objects presented in connection with the Coronation in 1896, all based on the colours and motifs of the Imperial Coronation mantle (cf. also cat. 110).

Provenance: Tsar Nicholas II; Mr Bomm, Vienna; Sidney Hill, Berry-Hill Galleries, London and New York; Arthur E. Bradshaw; Lansdell K. Christie, Long Island, New York.
Literature: Snowman 1962, ill. on frontispiece; Snowman 1963, pp. 244, 245; Snowman 1977, p. 55; Waterfield/Forbes 1978, pp. 51, 52, 130, 132, 135; Habsburg/Solodkoff 1979, p. 126, pl. 149; Snowman 1979, pp. 122, 125; Forbes 1980, p. 14; Kelly 1982/83, p. 10; Swezey 1983, p. 1210, ill. p. 1211; Solodkoff 1984/89, pp. 25, 27; Forbes 1986, ill. p. 57; Habsburg 1987, p. 255; Hill 1989, pp. 22, 140, pl. 120, and title page.
Exhibitions: Wartski 1949; ALVR 1961, cat. 93; Corcoran 1961, cat. 14; NYCC 1973, cat. 12; V&A 1977, cat. O 14; Boston 1979; Virginia/Minneapolis/Chicago 1983, cat. 7; Fort Worth 1983, cat. 26; Detroit 1984, cat. 37; Munich 1986/87, cat. 513; Lugano 1987, cat. 95; Paris 1987, cat. 95, ill. on cover; San Diego/Moscow 1989/90, cat. 27.

The FORBES Magazine Collection, New York (FAB66009)

The Coronation of Nicholas II, 1896

At this supreme occasion Fabergé easily outshone his competitors. Many of the finest presents given by Tsar Nicholas II came from the Bolshaya Morskaya shop. Characteristically, a number of them were designed in the Russian Imperial colours of yellow and black – the traditional colours of the Coronation mantles of the Tsar and Tsarina – with black double-headed eagles on a gold ground.

106

SQUARE IMPERIAL PRESENTATION CIGARETTE BOX
Gold, enamel, diamonds
L: 8 cm
Marks: Fabergé, initials of workmaster August Hollming,
assay mark of St. Petersburg 1899–1908, inv. 1208

Yellow gold box with translucent primrose yellow enamel over
guilloché sunburst and concentric rings, the sides studded with
pellets. Cover applied with central crowned initial of Nicholas II
set in rose diamonds flanked by four chased red and green gold
laurel wreaths centring on rose diamonds. Chased gold laurel
borders.

Literature: Bainbridge 1966, pl. 104; Habsburg 1987, p. 254.
Exhibitions: Wartski 1949, cat. 5; V&A 1977, cat. F 10; Cooper-
Hewitt 1983, cat. 192; The Queen's Gallery 1985/86, cat. 330;
Munich 1986/87, cat. 511.

Lent by Her Majesty Queen Elizabeth The Queen Mother

107

OCTAGONAL PRESENTATION BOX

Gold, enamel, diamonds

W: 8.2 cm

Marks: Fabergé, initials of workmaster Mikhail Perkhin, assay mark of St. Petersburg 1899–1908

Cover applied with crowned diamond-set cypher of Tsar Nicholas II in an oval diamond-set surround on a lozenge-shaped white *guilloché* enamel panel; spandrels of yellow *guilloché* enamel applied with black enamel double-headed eagles, gold laurel sprays, and rose-cut diamonds; sides of yellow *guilloché* enamel.

Provenance: Presented by Tsar Nicholas II; Sir William Seeds.
Literature: Bainbridge 1966, pl. 30; Snowman 1964, pl. IV; Snowman 1979, ill. p. 118; Habsburg 1987, ill. p. 255.
Exhibitions: Munich 1986/87, cat. 514.

The Board of Trustees of the Victoria and Albert Museum, London

108

ROUND PRESENTATION BOX

Gold, enamel, diamonds

Diam: 8 cm

Marks: Fabergé, initials of workmaster Mikhail Perkhin, assay mark of St. Petersburg before 1899

Circular *bonbonnière* of translucent primrose yellow enamel over *guilloché* wave pattern. Cover applied centrally with crowned cypher of 'N II' set in rose diamonds on oval white *guilloché* enamel panel within border of brilliant diamonds and surrounded by eight chased gold Romanov eagles each set with a rose diamond, with palm leaf borders. Interior inscribed in Russian: 'For Her Royal Highness Princess Elizabeth on the occasion of her Wedding with Hearty Congratulations. Zematov Bessarabia 27 February 1921'.

In the Imperial yellow colours of the Coronation mantle, probably first presented by the Tsar in 1896.

Provenance: Princess Elizabeth of Roumania (1894–1956), daughter of King Ferdinand I and Queen Marie, was married on 27 February 1921 to George II, King of the Hellenes (1890–1947). (Bessarabia was attached to Roumania by the Paris Treaty of 28 October 1920).
Literature: Habsburg 1987, ill. p. 254.
Exhibitions: Munich 1986/87, cat. 512.

Private collection

109

IMPERIAL WRITING PORTFOLIO

Silver gilt, diamonds, leather, watered silk

H: 33.5 cm

Marks: Fabergé, initials of workmaster
Mikhail Perkhin, assay mark of
St. Petersburg before 1899, 88 (*zolotnik*)

Rectangular, of beige morocco leather with
silver mounts; centre applied with crowned
cypher 'NII A' set in rose diamonds,
within a chased gold floral wreath tied by
a ribbon inscribed 'From the City of
St. Petersburg', in scalloped oval and
rectangular frames; corners with scrolling
acanthus foliage. Interior lined with ivory-
coloured silk.

Provenance: Presented by representatives
of the City of St. Petersburg to Tsar
Nicholas II and his wife Tsarina
Alexandra Feodorovna on 22 June 1896
on the occasion of their entry into
St. Petersburg during the Coronation
festivities.

Literature: Koronatsionnyi sbornik
(Coronation Collection), St. Petersburg:
Ministerstvo Imperatorskogo dvora, 1899,
vol. I, ill. p. 394; Waterfield/Forbes 1978,
pp. 84, 132, 135, ill. p. 83; Solodkoff 1984,
ill. p. 172; Forbes 1986, ill. p. 57; Hill
1989, p. 294, pl. 275.

Exhibitions: Fort Worth 1983, cat. 60;
London 1991, cat. 37, ill. 40; Vienna 1991,
ill. p. 78.

The FORBES Magazine Collection,
New York (FAB74002)

110

CORONATION EASTER EGG

Egg: Varicoloured gold, enamel, diamonds, velvet
H: 12.6 cm
Coach: Gold, platinum, enamel, diamonds, rubies, rock crystal
L: 9.3 cm
Marks: Initials of workmaster Mikhail Perkhin, assay mark of
St. Petersburg before 1899, 56 (*zolotnik*); the name Wigström
is roughly scratched into the inner surface of the shell

Egg: gold, with panels of translucent primrose enamel over
guilloché sunbursts, applied laurel leaf trelliswork, with black
enamel Imperial eagles at intersections, each with central rose
diamond. Cover with Russian monogram 'AF', culet with date
'1897', both under portrait diamonds; velvet-lined interior.
Coach: gold, red *guilloché* enamel, with rose diamond trellis to
sides, bevelled rock crystal windows, rose diamond Imperial eagles
to sides, and rose diamond crown finial.

The yellow ground and black Imperial eagles of this most
famous of Fabergé's creations again evoke the Coronation mantle
of Tsar Nicholas II. The perfect miniature replica of the
Coronation coach by George Stein took fifteen months to complete
and required many visits to the original for comparison (cf. the
original coach, cat. 369). A tiny egg, pavé-set with brilliants, once
hung inside the coach.

Provenance: Presented by Tsar Nicholas II to his wife, Tsarina
Alexandra Feodorovna, Easter 1897; purchased by Emanuel
Snowman for Wartski, London, *c*. 1927.
Literature: Bainbridge 1949, pl. 58; Snowman 1953, pl. XXIV and
dust jacket; Snowman 1962, pl. LXXIII and dust jacket (1974 ed.);
Bainbridge 1966, pl. 89 and dust jacket; Ricketts 1971, p. 105;
NYCC 1973, ill. p. 52; Snowman 1977, p. 55, ill. p. 51; Habsburg
1977, ill. p. 80; Waterfield/Forbes, pp. 52, 129, ill. p. 118;
Habsburg/Solodkoff 1979, pp. 105, 107, 158, pl. 126; Snowman
1979, p. 97; Forbes 1980, pp. 5, 14, 62, ill. p. 15; Kelly 1982/83,
p. 10; Solodkoff 1982, p. 103; Swezey 1983, pp. 1210–11, 1213;
Solodkoff 1984/89, p. 74 and ill. on dust jacket; Kelly 1985, ill.
pp. 14, 15; Forbes 1986, pp. 52–53; Habsburg 1987, pp. 272–73;
Forbes 1987 p. 11, ill. p. 14; Solodkoff 1988, ill. p. 35 and
dust jacket; Hill 1989, pls. 31, 32; Pfeffer 1990, ill. pp. 45, 47.
Exhibitions: London 1935, cat. 586, p. 111; Wartski 1949, cat. 6;
Wartski 1953, cat. 286; V&A 1977, cat. O 1, pp. 12, 93, ill. p. 101;
Boston 1979, ill. on cover; LACMA 1979; Virginia/Minneapolis/
Chicago 1983, cat. 95, p. 16, ill. p. 2; Fort Worth 1983, cat. 189;
Detroit 1984, cat. 134; Munich 1986/87, cat. 539;
Lugano 1987, cat. 119, ill. pp. 112, 113; Paris 1987, cat. 119,
ill. pp. 108, 109; San Diego/Kremlin 1989/90, cat. 7.

The FORBES Magazine Collection, New York (FAB79002)

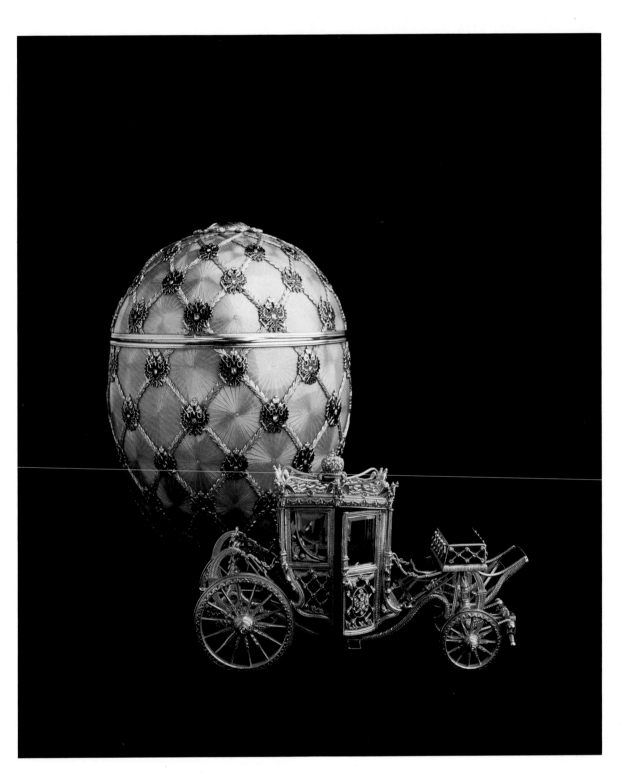

111

RENAISSANCE-STYLE ROCK CRYSTAL DISH

Rock crystal, silver, diamonds, enamel, gold
H: 39 cm W: 33 cm
Marks: Fabergé, initials of workmaster Mikhail Perkhin,
assay mark of St. Petersburg before 1899, 88 (*zolotnik*)

Oval dish formed of thirteen rock crystal panels cut with scrolling
foliage, the cavetto cut with the coat of arms of the City of
St. Petersburg and carved with flutes; granulated gold borders
chased and enamelled with stylised scrolling foliage in green, red,
and blue colours and set with rose diamonds. Reverse engraved in
Russian: 'From the Nobility of St. Petersburg, 1896'.

Based on a seventeenth-century dish in the Kremlin Armoury,
this piece was presented by the nobility of St. Petersburg to Tsar
Nicholas II on the occasion of his entry into St. Petersburg
following the Coronation in 1896.

Provenance: From the Diamond Chamber at the Winter Palace,
1922.
Literature: Lopato 1984, pp. 43–49; Habsburg 1987, ill. p. 187.
Exhibitions: Lugano 1986, cat. 118; Munich 1986/87, cat. 282;
Zurich 1989, cat. 22.

The State Hermitage, St. Petersburg (Inv. E-6388)

112

MONOMAKH CROWN BEAKER

Smoky topaz, gold, enamel, rubies, diamonds, emeralds
H: 22.2 cm
Marks: Fabergé, initials of workmaster Mikhail Perkhin,
assay mark of St. Petersburg before 1899, 56 (*zolotnik*)

Slightly tapering cylindrical hardstone beaker on flaring base with
three ball feet, the base with a wide band of Renaissance-style
champlevé stylised polychrome foliage set with faceted rubies,
rose diamonds, and cabochon emeralds; domed cover shaped as a
Monomakh *shapka*, with gardrooned gold mount, similar jewelled
band, and emerald bead finial.

The Monomakh crown was used at the coronation of the first
Romanov Tsar. Versions of this crown are preserved in the
Kremlin Armoury.

Exhibitions: ALVR 1983, cat. 308.

Courtesy of A La Vieille Russie

The *Exposition Universelle* of 1900

Fabergé's participation in the Paris *Exposition Universelle* of 1900 laid the foundation of his international fame. As the principal representative of Russian jewellers and goldsmiths, he exhibited many of his Imperial Easter eggs and objects of art from the collection of the Tsars. Generally acclaimed as one of the world's best craftsmen, Fabergé was distinguished with a Gold Medal and the Cross of the *Legion d'honneur* (see Habsburg, 'Fabergé and the Paris 1900 *Exposition Universelle*').

113

MINIATURE REPLICA OF THE IMPERIAL REGALIA
Gold, silver, platinum, diamonds, spinel, pearls, sapphires, velvet, rhodonite
Big crown H: 7.3 cm Diam: 5.4 cm
Small Crown H: 3.8 cm Diam: 2.9 cm
Orb H: 3.8 cm Diam: 4.4 cm
Sceptre H: 15.8 cm
Marks: Fabergé, initials of workmaster Julius Rappoport, assay mark of St. Petersburg 1899–1908, 88 (*zolotnik*); *K.Fabergé* on the base of big crown.

This work is an example of the combined creativity of two of the firm's masters. The regalia were probably made in August Holmström's workshop, while the silver bases and the decoration around the rhodonite column were made by Julius Rappoport. In 1912 Court Jeweller Agathon Fabergé gave the following appraisal: 'The Big Crown is made out of 1083 diamonds and 245 rough rose diamonds. The Small Crown out of 180 diamonds and 1204 rough (rose) diamonds. The Orb: 65 diamonds and 654 rough (rose) diamonds. The Sceptre: 1 diamond and 125 rough (rose) diamonds'.

Provenance: The regalia were made for the *Exposition Universelle* in Paris in 1900 and were purchased by Nicholas II shortly thereafter. Since 1901 they were kept in the Hermitage, in the Jewellery Gallery. In 1911 they were moved to the New Jewellery Hall of the Hermitage.
Literature: G. E. Liven, *Putevoditel po Kabinetu Petra Velikogo i Galeree Dragotsennostei* (Guide through the Peter the Great Cabinet and Jewellery Gallery), (St. Petersburg, 1902), p. 65; D. D. Ivanov, *Obyasnitelnyi putevoditel po khudozhestvennym sobraniyam Peterburga* (Explanatory Guide through the St. Petersburg Art Collection), (St. Petersburg, 1904), p. 154.
Exhibitions: Memphis/Los Angeles/Dallas 1992, cat. p. 135.

The State Hermitage, St. Petersburg (Inv. ERO-4745)

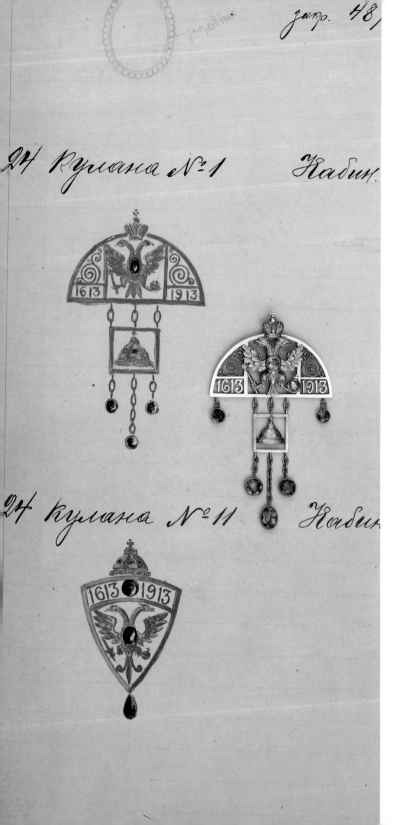

Japr. 48,

24 Купана № 1   Набин.

24 Купана № 11   Набин

The Tercentenary, 1913

The Romanov Tercentenary festivities in 1913 marked three hundred years of rule by the Romanov dynasty. Art produced to commemorate the occasion included the Romanov double-headed eagle or the Romanov griffin. Fabergé's workshops fabricated hundreds of objects with these symbols. Ironically, the Tercentenary marked the apotheosis and, at the same time, the swansong of the Russian Imperial Family.

114

JEWELLED GOLD TERCENTENARY PENDANT
Gold, amethysts, enamel
H: 5.75 cm
Marks: Initials of workmaster August Holmström
Original fitted blue morocco case gilt with double-headed eagle

Pendant brooch centres on a chased gold Romanov double-headed eagle flanked by gold scrolls and the white opaque enamel dates '1613' and '1913'. From it are suspended a Monomakh crown in an openwork square and five brilliant-cut Siberian amethysts.

According to Henry Bainbridge, 'In 1913 to commemorate the tercentenary of Romanoff rule, brooches of diamonds, stones of colour and pearls, in the shape of the Imperial Crown and emblems – all different, of course – were made for presentation to each of the Grand Duchesses and ladies of the Court. The designs for these were based on the original drawings which the Tsarina Alexandra Feodorovna prepared and sent to Fabergé for elaboration'. The pendant is illustrated here with Fabergé's design from Albert Holmström's design books.

Courtesy of Wartski, London

115

TERCENTENARY BROOCH

Gold, enamel, aquamarines, diamonds, ruby

Diam: 3.1 cm

Marks: Initials of workmaster Albert Holmström, assay mark of
St. Petersburg 1908–1917, inv. 4595

Circular openwork brooch with Monomakh crown at centre set
with a ruby and two rose diamonds, surrounded by three lozenge
shapes with dates '1613' and '1913', scrolls, and three aquamarines.

This brooch, and others of different designs, were presented to
the Grand Duchesses and ladies of the Court at the time of the
1913 Tercentenary celebrations.

Literature: Ross 1965, p. 53; Taylor 1983, p. 42.
Exhibitions: Hammer 1937, cat. 137; Hammer 1951, cat. 13.

Hillwood Museum, Washington, D.C. (17.84)

116

BROOCH FOR THE ROMANOV TERCENTENARY, 1913

Gold, silver, diamonds, glass

Diam: 2.2 cm

Of lobed and square shape centring on a diamond-set double-
headed eagle with green glass paste, within rose-diamond border;
gold outer border with scrolls and dates '1613' and '1913'.

The State Hermitage, St. Petersburg (Inv. VZ-1424)

117

PENDANT FOR THE ROMANOV TERCENTENARY

Gold, silver, diamonds, spinels

W: 5.7 cm

Marks: Initials of workmaster Albert Holmström,
assay mark of St. Petersburg 1908–1917, 56 (*zolotnik*)

Of semicircular shape, with central crowned double-headed eagle
set with rose diamonds and a spinel, flanked by gold scrolls and
dates '1613' and '1913'. From it are suspended a Monomakh's
crown set with three rose diamonds, and three spinels.

For Fabergé's designs dated 4 February 1913, see A.K.
Snowman, 'Two Books of Revelations', in Habsburg 1987, p. 49,
and cf. cat. 144 in this catalogue.

The State Hermitage, St. Petersburg (Inv. VZ-1439)

118

KREMLIN TOWER CLOCK
Rhodonite, silver, emeralds, sapphires
H: 29 cm W: 14.5 cm
Marks: Fabergé's Imperial Warrant,
assay mark of Moscow 1908–1917,
84 and 91 (*zolotnik*), inv. 16419 (?)

Shaped as a kremlin tower in the Neo-
Russian style; rhodonite body stands on
four lion feet and is decorated with
peacocks, scrolls, and geometric motifs, set
with cabochon emeralds and sapphires and
surmounted by a double-headed eagle.

The clock's style and date point to its
production for the 1913 Romanov
Tercentenary festivities.

Literature: Bainbridge 1935, pp. 87–90;
Bainbridge 1966, pl. 16; Hawley 1967,
no. 57.

The Cleveland Museum of Art (The India
Early Minshall Collection, 66.477)

119

ROMANOV TERCENTENARY BOX
Gold, enamel, diamonds, ivory
L: 10.5 cm
Marks: Fabergé

Of dark green translucent *guilloché* enamel over sunburst and
moiré grounds; cover applied with *accolé* miniatures of Tsar
Nicholas II and Tsarina Alexandra Feodorovna on ivory, set in a
rose diamond-set Imperial double-headed eagle. Inner border of
red *guilloché* enamel and chased gold laurel leaves and berries
between opaque white enamel bands, the spandrels applied with
rose diamond laurel crowns and ribbons. Base inscribed with a
commemorative inscription for the Romanov Tercentenary.

Provenance: Presumably presented by Tsar Nicholas II to Grand
Duke Mikhail Mikhailovich (1861–1929) on the occasion of the
Tercentenary festivities in 1913. Grand Duke Mikhail, grandson of
Tsar Nicholas I, married morganatically Sofia, Countess
Merenberg (1868–1927), since 1891, Countess of Torby. Their
descendants included Anastasia (Zia) (1892–1977), who married
Sir Harold Wernher.
Literature: Snowman 1962, ill. 137; Habsburg 1987, ill. p. 257.
Exhibitions: Wartski 1949, cat. 207; Munich 1986/87, cat. 517.

Lady Myra Butter and Lady Georgina Kennard

The 1914–1918 War

The 1914–1918 War brought the end of the Old Order. Initially it meant only a cutting back in the lavish commissions of the Imperial Family. Fabergé turned to producing objects with the theme of the Red Cross. Soon, however, his most skilled craftsmen were conscripted, and he contributed to the war effort by manufacturing grenades and shells for cannons in his Moscow workshops. Objects in copper, brass, and steel were made, many stamped with Romanov eagles and 'War'. Like so much of Russian life, the Revolution of 1917 was to sweep away both the Romanovs and the Fabergés.

120

THREE COMMEMORATIVE BOWLS
Silver; brass; copper
Diam: 10.8 cm
Stamped: 'K. Fabergé'

Each bowl embossed with a large Russian
Imperial eagle and inscriptions in Russian:
'War 1914'
    Such items were mass-produced by
Fabergé at the beginning of the 1914–
1918 War and were presented as gifts.

Exhibitions: ALVR 1983, cat. 7.

Courtesy of A La Vieille Russie

121

COMMEMORATIVE BOWL
Bronzed copper
Diam: 10.8 cm
Stamped: 'K.Fabergé 'and 'War 1914'
(in Russian)

The State Hermitage, St. Petersburg
(Inv. P – 1592)

122

COVERED POT
Copper, brass
H: 12.7 cm W: 13.3 cm
Marks: 'K.Fabergé', 'War', '1914'
(in Russian)

Covered copper pot with brass handles.
    This cooking pot is one of the many
utilitarian objects produced by Fabergé
during the war years.

Literature: Hawley 1967, no. 60.

The Cleveland Museum of Art (The India
Early Minshall Collection, 66.511)

123

CIGARETTE CASE

Silver

H: 9.9 cm W: 6.1 cm

Marks: Fabergé, assay mark of Moscow 1908–1917

Burnished, applied with circular plaque chased with double-headed eagle; inscribed in Russian: 'War 1914 1916'.

Exhibitions: Mikimoto 1991, cat. 31.

State Historical Museum, Moscow (Inv. 7228/ok 6899)

124

BEAKER

Nephrite, silver

H: 9.8 cm

Marks: Initials of workmaster August Hollming, assay mark of St. Petersburg 1908–1917

Applied with two circular silver medallions chased with double-headed eagle and an inscription in Russian: 'War 1914–1915. K. Fabergé'.

Exhibitions: Mikimoto 1991, cat. 30.

State Historical Museum, Moscow (Inv. 105665/ok 22987)

125

NEPHRITE MUG

Nephrite, silver

11.5 × 14.0 × 9.8 cm

Marks: Fabergé, initials of workmaster Albert Holmström,
assay mark of St. Petersburg 1908–1917, 84 (*zolotnik*)

Mug and handle carved from nephrite, applied to the front with
circular silver medallion embossed with Romanov Imperial eagle,
with inscription in Russian: 'War 1914' and 'K. Fabergé'.
Handle with four silver five-kopeck coins dated from 1899 to 1901.

The State Hermitage, St. Petersburg (Inv. ERKm – 1092)

126

WAR PRESENTATION BEAKER

Nephrite, silver

H: 9.7 cm

Marks: Initials of workmaster Henrik Wigström,
assay mark of St. Petersburg 1908–1917, 84 (*zolotnik*)

Of tapering cylindrical form, applied with a silver medallion
embossed with inscription in Russian: 'War', '1914–1915',
and 'K. Fabergé'.

Literature: Solodkoff 1984, p. 173, ill. pp. 6, 173.
Exhibitions: Fort Worth 1983, cat. 65.

The FORBES Magazine Collection, New York (FAB80002)

127

CIRCULAR RED CROSS BROOCH

Gold, enamel, diamonds

Diam: 2.6 cm

Marks: Initials of workmaster Mikhail Perkhin,
assay mark of St. Petersburg before 1899, 56 (*zolotnik*)

Red *guilloché* enamel cross in gold mount on opaque
white enamel field, with rose diamond border.

Exhibitions: ALVR 1983, cat. 380.

Courtesy of A La Vieille Russie

128

RHODONITE FRAME

Rhodonite, gold, enamel, diamonds, mother-of-pearl, silver gilt

H: 5.7 cm W: 4.5 cm

Marks: Fabergé, 88 (*zolotnik*)

Border of green enamel and white enamel dots, applied with
flower swags in two colours suspended from a gold bow; set with
three rose diamonds; mother-of-pearl back. Contains a photograph
of Grand Duchess Tatiana as a nurse.

   Grand Duchess Tatiana (1897–1918) assisted her mother as a
nurse in 1914–1915 at a hospital in Tsarskoe Selo.

Provenance: Mrs Augustus Riggs IV.
Literature: Taylor 1983, p. 46.

Hillwood Museum, Washington, D.C. (21.193)

129

RED CROSS EASTER EGG
Gold, silver, enamel
H: 8.6 cm
Marks: Fabergé, initials of workmaster Henrik Wigström,
assay mark of St. Petersburg 1908–1917, 72 (*zolotnik*)
White velvet case

White *guilloché* enamel exterior with red *guilloché* enamel crosses
to the front and back; contains miniatures of Grand Duchesses
Tatiana and Olga in Red Cross uniforms. Egg opens to form a
triptych icon, the centre panel painted by Prachov with the
Harrowing of Hell, the left hinged panel with St. Olga, the right
panel with St. Tatiana on gold grounds. Also enamelled with
crowned monogram 'AF' and date '1915'.

Two eggs on the theme of the Red Cross were produced by
Fabergé for Easter 1915. This piece was intended for Tsarina
Alexandra Feodorovna. Another, for Tsarina Maria Feodorovna,

and with a white and red *guilloché* enamel exterior, opens to
reveal a folding screen with portrait miniatures of Tsarina
Alexandra Feodorovna and her four daughters, all dressed as
nurses. At this time, while the Tsar and Tsarevich were at the
front in Stavka, the Tsarina and her daughters courageously
tended wounded soldiers in a hospital in Tsarskoe Selo.

Provenance: Presented on behalf of Tsar Nicholas II to Tsarina
Alexandra Feodorovna, Easter 1915.
Literature: Snowman 1977, ill. p. 76, p. 77, no. M 2; Forbes 1979,
pp. 1228–42, pl. XIII; Snowman 1979, p. 26; Forbes 1980, p. 68;
Solodkoff 1984, ill. p. 105.
Exhibitions: Hammer 1951, cat. 162; ALVR 1961, cat. 291; San
Francisco 1964, cat. 144; V&A 1977, cat. M 2; San Diego/Kremlin
1989/90, cat. 24.

The Cleveland Museum of Art (The India Early Minshall
Collection, 63.673)

Presentation Objects

Beginning in the 1890s, large numbers of Fabergé objects commissioned or acquired by the Imperial Cabinet were stored in a room in the Winter Palace for presentation by the Tsar, the Tsarina, the Dowager Empress, and members of the Imperial Family. All official occasions – from State visits and visits by members of other Royal Families, to weddings, birthdays, christenings, Easter, and Christmas – warranted a gift from Fabergé. On their regular travels to Copenhagen, London, and Germany, and on their excursions to Paris and Italy, members of the Imperial Family invariably took with them large numbers of presents from Faberge's. Imperial gifts were distinguished by the Romanov double-headed eagle, with portraits or cyphers of the donors. Presentation objects included traditional badges and medals, simple silver cigarette cases, and lavishly jewelled gold boxes. At the same time, many of the gifts received by the Imperial Family also originated from Fabergé.

130

JETON OF THE GUSTAV FABERGE STORE IN ST. PETERSBURG
Gilded bronze
Diam: 2.2 cm
Inscription in French (recto): 'G. FABERGÉ JOAILLIER BIJOUTIER A ST. PETERSBOURG'; (verso): 'GRANDE MORSKOY AU COIN DE LA KIRPITSCHNAJA Nº 18 MAISON ROUADZE'

Such jetons were given to a customer along with his purchase as a means of publicity and further expanding the business.

The State Hermitage, St. Petersburg (Inv. RM 8893)

131

MEDAL OF THE TSAREVICH AND GRAND DUKE ALEXEI NIKOLAIEVICH
INTERNATIONAL EXHIBITION OF LATEST INVENTIONS, 1909
Silver
H: 3.7 cm
Original fitted case stamped with Fabergé's Imperial Warrant, St. Petersburg, Moscow, Odessa

Circular medal with a crown, beneath which is an engraved portrait of the Tsarevich in military uniform and cap; reverse engraved with name of the exhibition. Suspended from a chain.

Provenance: Collection of the Imperial Family.

The State Hermitage, St. Petersburg (Inv. IO – 3043)

132

'BLUE CROSS' SOCIETY JETON
Silver gilt, enamel
H: 3.6 cm
Marks: Initials of workmaster Eduard Schramm, assay mark of
St. Petersburg 1899–1908, initials of assay master Iakov Liapunov

Lozenge-shaped badge with blue enamel cross, inscribed in
Russian: 'Blue Cross Society'; surmounted by a fireman's helmet.

For patrons of the Blue Cross Society, the National Society of
Aid to Firemen was established in 1897 with the purpose of
supporting firemen and their families in case of accident or death
while in service. The reverse bears the name of the donor and the
date. The jeton was usually worn on a watch chain.

Provenance: Numismatic collection of Tsar Nicholas II.
Literature: Shkabelnikov 1902, p. 69.

The State Hermitage, St. Petersburg (Inv. RM – 7060)

133

BADGE OF THE SOCIETY OF DISABLED SOLDIERS
Gold, silver, enamel
W: 5.3 cm
Marks: Initials of workmaster Alfred Thielemann, assay mark of
St. Petersburg 1908–1917, 56 (*zolotnik*)

Provenance: Numismatic collection of Tsar Nicholas II.

The State Hermitage, St. Petersburg (Inv. VZ – 309)

134

BADGE OF THE CAVALRY GUARD REGIMENT
Gold, silver, enamel
L: 5 cm
Marks: Initials of workmaster Alfred Thielemann, 56 (*zolotnik*)
Original fitted case with Fabergé's Imperial Warrant,
St. Petersburg, Moscow, London

Red and white enamel pennant applied with crowned monogram
'MF', suspended from a double-headed eagle; reverse with 'XXV'.

The badge was established on 2 March 1906 in honour of the
twenty-fifth anniversary of the patronage of Dowager Empress
Maria Feodorovna.

Provenance: Collection of the Imperial Family.
Literature: Andolenko 1966, p. 66.

The State Hermitage, St. Petersburg (Inv. IO – 3049)

135

Gold, enamel
H: 2.5 cm
Marks: Illegible workmaster's mark, 56 (*zolotnik*)

Egg-shaped burnished gold charm, on one side with crowned white enamel monogram 'AF', the other with Russian Imperial flag and '1914'.

Provenance: Presented by Tsarina Alexandra Feodorovna (1872–1918).
Literature: Solodkoff 1988, p. 58.
Exhibitions: Lugano 1987, cat. 125, ill. p. 119; Paris 1987, cat. 125, ill. p. 115.

The FORBES Magazine Collection, New York (FAB85006)

136

Gold, enamel, diamonds, sapphires
L: 3.2 cm
Marks: Fabergé, initials of workmaster August Hollming, assay mark of St. Petersburg 1908–1917
Original fitted red morocco case with gilt Imperial eagle

Hexagonal white *guilloché* enamel panel flanked by two squares with filigree scrolls and rose diamonds; centre with Imperial crown set with two cabochon sapphires and rose diamonds.

Provenance: Presented by Tsarina Alexandra Feodorovna to Miss Joan (Jouie) Bolestone, an English nanny (illustrated with original autograph postcard signed by the Tsarina, 1911).

Courtesy of Ermitage Ltd., London

137

ROCK CRYSTAL PAPERKNIFE

Rock crystal, gold, diamond

L: 17.5 cm

Marks: Russian initials 'KF', assay mark of 1899–1908

Original fitted case stamped with Fabergé's Imperial Warrant, Moscow, St. Petersburg. Contains pencilled dedication note in English: 'For dear Miss Jackson, with loving Xmas wishes from Alix 1900'.

With rounded ends, applied with a yellow gold laurel leaf mount, red gold ribbon, and set with a rose diamond.

Provenance: Given by Tsarina Alexandra Feodorovna to her nurse, Miss Jackson.

Literature: Habsburg 1987, ill. p. 161.

Exhibitions: Munich 1986/87, cat. 204; Wartski 1992.

Courtesy of Wartski, London

138

OVAL SILVER-GILT FRAME
Silver gilt, enamel, ivory, wood
H: 14.6 cm
Marks: Fabergé, initials of workmaster Anders Nevalainen,
assay mark of St. Petersburg 1899–1908, 88 (*zolotnik*)

Of red *guilloché* enamel, with miniature portrait on ivory of
Tsarina Maria Feodorovna, signed and dated 'V. Zuiev 1903';
wooden back and strut.

Provenance: Presented by Tsarina Maria Feodorovna to Princess
Alexandra Obolensky.

Courtesy of Ermitage Ltd., London

139

PRESENTATION BROOCH
Gold, silver, diamonds, sapphires
H: 4.3 cm
Marks: Initials of workmaster Alfred Thielemann, assay mark of
St. Petersburg 1908–1917, 56 (*zolotnik*), inv. 3229
Original fitted morocco case embossed with gold double-headed
eagle on cover

Varicoloured gold double-headed eagle with central sapphire
within a laurel leaf-and-tie wreath; three sapphires and rose
diamonds suspended below.

Provenance: Inna Grigorievna Samsonova (1877–1972), a graduate
of the Painting and Sculpture School in Moscow, taught drawing
at the Moscow Institute for girls of nobility. The brooch was
presented on the occasion of Tsar Nicholas II's visit at a drawings
exhibition.

The State Hermitage, St. Petersburg (Inv. VZ – 1391)

140

BROOCH WITH DOUBLE-HEADED EAGLE
Gold, silver, diamonds, sapphires
H: 4 cm
Marks: Inv. 2960

Diamond-set double-headed eagle on silver trellis, border of gold laurel leaves alternating with cabochon sapphires.

Provenance: According to its last owner, the brooch was presented to her mother at a reception at the Winter Palace for Gold Medal graduates.

The State Hermitage, St. Petersburg (Inv. VZ – 1466)

141

OCTAGONAL PRESENTATION BOX
Gold, diamonds, rubies
Diam: 8.4 cm
Marks: Fabergé, initials of workmaster August Holmström, assay mark of St. Petersburg before 1899, 56 (*zolotnik*)

Octagonal box of red gold; cover applied with central double-headed eagle set with rose diamonds, a central square diamond, and two rubies; engraved in the Empire style with garlands of leaves and daisies, the sides with sphinxes, a wreath and stars, a lotus and swans; base with a central wreath surrounded by swags of leaves and draped designs.

Literature: Ross 1965, p. 51; Taylor 1983, p. 23.
Exhibitions: Zurich 1989, cat. 14.

Hillwood Museum, Washington, D.C. (11.91)

142

SAMORODOK SILVER CIGARETTE CASE
Silver, gold, sapphire
L: 9.8 cm W: 6.3 cm
Marks: Fabergé's Imperial Warrant,
assay mark of Moscow 1908–1917, 88 (*zolotnik*)
Original fitted red morocco presentation case applied with gilt
Russian Imperial eagle

Applied centrally with gold Russian Imperial double-headed eagle,
with gold-mounted cabochon sapphire thumbpiece.

Provenance: A presentation letter, written in English, accompanies this box: '28th August 1911, Memorandum from Malborough House, Pall Mall, London S.W., To Mr. A. Beal. I am desired by Prince Obolensky, on behalf of The Empress of Russia, to send you the encosed [*sic*] silver case, as a Souvenir of Her Imperial Majesty's recent visit to England. Yours faithfully, J. Gordon Watson'.

Courtesy of A La Vieille Russie

143
RECTANGULAR PRESENTATION BOX
Gold, enamel, brilliant and rose diamonds
L: 9.5 cm W: 6.2 cm
Marks: Fabergé, initials of workmaster Mikhail Perkhin,
assay mark of St. Petersburg before 1899, 56 (*zolotnik*)

Red and green gold box engine-turned with dotted lines; cover
applied centrally with crowned Imperial double-headed eagle set
with rose diamonds on a translucent white enamel oval plaque
within a laurel leaf border; panels with outer yellow gold laurel
leaf border with red gold crossed bands; rose diamond thumbpiece.

Exhibitions: Helsinki 1988; Helsinki 1991.

Private collection, Finland

144
CASTENSKIOLD IMPERIAL PRESENTATION CIGARETTE CASE
Gold, enamel, diamonds, paste brilliants
L: 9.5 cm
Marks: Fabergé, initials of workmaster August Holmström,
assay mark of St. Petersburg before 1899, inv. 1159
Original red morocco fitted case with applied gilt Imperial eagle

Of royal blue translucent enamel over *guilloché* sunburst, centrally
applied with an Imperial crown set with rose diamonds and pastes;
elliptic diamond pushpiece. Interior inscribed: 'Ludwig
Castenskiold'.

Provenance: Presented by Tsar Nicholas II to Ludwig Castenskiold
(1823–1905), equerry of the Tsar's grandfather, King Christian IX
of Denmark.
Literature: John Herbert, ed., *Christie's Review of the Season 1983*,
p. 313; Solodkoff 1984/89, p. 25, ill. p. 27; Kelly 1985, p. 16, ill.
pp. 12, 17; Habsburg 1987, ill. p. 236.
Exhibitions: Virginia/Minneapolis/Chicago 1983, cat. 15; Fort
Worth 1983, cat. 29; Detroit 1984, cat. 40; Munich 1986/87,
cat. 462; Lugano 1987, cat. 98, p. 96; Paris 1987, cat. 98.

The FORBES Magazine Collection, New York (FAB82012)

145

IMPERIAL EAGLE PRESENTATION CIGARETTE CASE
Silver gilt, enamel, diamonds, sapphires
L: 9.7 cm
Marks: Fabergé, initials of workmaster August Hollming,
assay mark of St. Petersburg 1908–1917, 88 (*zolotnik*)

Of pale blue translucent enamel over *guilloché* sunburst ground,
applied with double-headed eagle set with rose diamonds and a
central faceted sapphire; sapphire pushpiece.

Provenance: Presented by Tsar Nicholas II.
Exhibitions: Lugano 1987, cat. 96, ill. p. 96; Paris 1987, cat. 96,
ill. p. 92.

The FORBES Magazine Collection, New York (FAB85021)

146

NICHOLAS II NEPHRITE BOX
Nephrite, gold, diamonds, ivory
L: 9.5 cm
Marks: Fabergé, initials of workmaster Henrik Wigström,
assay mark of St. Petersburg 1908–1917, 56 (*zolotnik*), inv. 4909
Original fitted case stamped with Fabergé's Imperial Warrant,
St. Petersburg, Moscow, London

Rectangular carved nephrite box; cover applied with a crowned
miniature of Tsar Nicholas II by Zuiev in a frame of rose
diamonds and a diamond-set laurel wreath; also enriched with a
diamond trellis set in silver; chased red and green gold laurel leaf
border.
    Tsar Nicholas II wears the uniform of the 4th Rifle Battalion of
Guards and the Cross of the Order of St. George, which he was
awarded in 1915.

Provenance: Presented by Tsar Nicholas II, 1915–1916; Mrs J.M.
Jacques, England; Lansdell K. Christie, Long Island, New York.
Literature: Bainbridge 1949, pl. 125(b); Snowman 1962, pl. 130;
Bainbridge 1966, pl. 127; Waterfield/Forbes, pp. 52, 54, 130, 132,
135, ill. p. 55; Snowman 1979, ill. p. 122; Solodkoff 1984, ill. pp.
26, 173; Kelly 1985, ill. p. 22; Hill 1989, pp. 22, 140, pl. 118.
Exhibitions: Wartski 1949, cat. 259; Wartski 1953, cat. 158; NYCC
1973, cat. 13, ill. p. 55; V&A 1977, cat. L 9, p. 73; ALVR 1983, cat.
216, ill. p. 79; Fort Worth 1983, cat. 28; Baltimore 1983/84, cat. 14;
Detroit 1984, cat. 39.

The FORBES Magazine Collection, New York (FAB66021)

147

NEPHRITE PRESENTATION BOX

Nephrite, gold, diamonds, enamel

W: 10.6 cm

Marks: Fabergé, initials of workmaster Henrik
Wigström, assay mark of St. Petersburg 1899–1908

Oval box; cover applied with diamond-set crowned
cypher of Tsar Nicholas II on an oval white *guilloché*
enamel panel flanked by two yellow gold laurel
wreaths in a rose diamond-set oval border.

Literature: Ross 1952, ill. p. 7.
Exhibitions: ALVR 1949, cat. 256; San Francisco 1964,
cat. 43, pp. 20, 49.

The Walters Art Gallery, Baltimore, Maryland
(Inv. 57.1047)

148

IMPERIAL PRESENTATION BOX

Gold, enamel, diamonds

L: 9.6 cm W: 6.4 cm

Marks: Fabergé, initials of workmaster Henrik
Wigström, assay mark of St. Petersburg 1908–1917,
72 (*zolotnik*)

Blue-grey *guilloché* enamel panels over sunburst
ground; cover set with a miniature of Tsar Nicholas II
in uniform, within a border of circular diamonds,
surmounted by an Imperial crown. White opalescent
enamel borders set with circular diamonds between
rose diamond borders; chased laurel leaf rim.

Provenance: Presented by Tsar Nicholas II to General
Trepov; given by Queen Mary to King George V on the
occasion of his birthday, 3 June 1934.
Literature: Bainbridge 1966, pl. 17; Snowman 1979,
p. 119; Habsburg 1987, pp. 257, 258.
Exhibitions: V&A 1977, cat. K 22, p. 51; Cooper-Hewitt
1983, cat. 194; The Queen's Gallery 1985/86, cat. 327;
Munich 1986/87, cat. 518.

Lent by Her Majesty Queen Elizabeth II

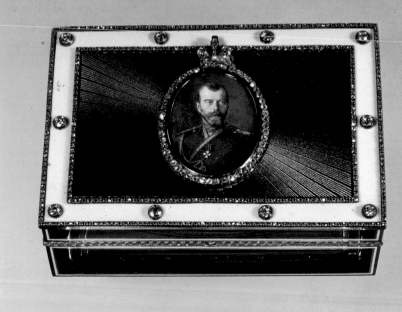

149

RECTANGULAR CIGARETTE CASE
Gold, enamel, diamonds
L: 9.2 cm
Marks: Fabergé, initials of workmaster Henrik
Wigström, assay mark of St. Petersburg 1908–1917,
56 (*zolotnik*)

Cover decorated with panels of opalescent oyster
enamel on waved *guilloché* ground; oval plaque painted
en grisaille and sepia with Falconet's monument of
Peter the Great, signed and dated 'Zuiev 1913' within
Vitruvian scroll border. Granulated gold mounts
enamelled with white opalescent pellets, red berries,
and green foliage. Thumpiece set with circular and
rose diamonds.

Provenance: Prince Vladimir Galitzine; presented by
Queen Mary to King George V, Christmas 1934.
Literature: Bainbridge 1966, pl. 17; Snowman 1979,
p. 119.
Exhibitions: V&A 1977, cat. K 24, p. 51; Cooper-Hewitt
1983, cat. 195; The Queen's Gallery 1985/86, cat. 326.

Lent by Her Majesty Queen Elizabeth II

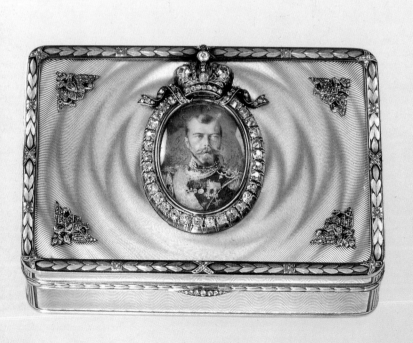

150

RECTANGULAR IMPERIAL PRESENTATION CIGARETTE BOX
Gilded silver, enamel, gold, diamonds
L: 10.1 cm
Marks: Fabergé, initials of workmaster Henrik
Wigström, assay mark of St. Petersburg 1908–1917,
72 (*zolotnik*)

Gold-mounted silver box decorated in pale mauve
translucent enamel over *guilloché* watered ground;
cover applied with oval crowned miniature of Tsar
Nicholas II signed by Rockstuhl, set with circular and
rose diamonds, flanked by four diamond-set double-
headed eagles. Green gold borders chased with laurel
leaves and with diamond-set ties and thumbpiece.

Literature: Bainbridge 1966, pl. 114; Habsburg 1987,
ill. p. 256.
Exhibitions: V&A 1977, cat. F 7; Cooper-Hewitt 1983,
cat. 194; The Queen's Gallery 1985/86, cat. 329;
Munich 1986/87, cat. 516.

Lent by Her Majesty Queen Elizabeth The Queen Mother

151

NEPHRITE CYLINDRICAL BOX

Nephrite, gold
H: 24 cm
Marks: Fabergé, initials of workmaster Mikhail Perkhin,
assay mark of St. Petersburg before 1899, inv. 531(?) 05

Cylindrical nephrite box standing on three pine cone feet, on
gadrooned gold base, applied with swirling bands of laurel leaves
and swags between borders chased with wave motifs; domed cover
carved with fluting, surmounted by chased yellow gold crowned
Imperial double-headed eagle.

Provenance: Presented by Tsar Nicholas II to Sydney Herbert, 14th
Earl of Pembroke, on the occasion of the Tsar's visit to Balmoral
in 1896.
Literature: Snowman 1962, ill. p. 275; Bainbridge 1966, pl. 8;
Habsburg 1987, ill. p. 188.
Exhibitions: Washington 1985/86, cat. p. 654; Munich 1986/87,
cat. 283.

Lady Myra Butter and Lady Georgina Kennard

152 *

IMPERIAL PRESENTATION KOVSH
Nephrite, gold, enamel, diamonds
L: 25 cm W: 13.5 cm
Marks: Fabergé, initials of workmaster Mikhail Perkhin,
assay mark of St. Petersburg 1899–1908, inv. 6926

Boat-shaped nephrite body; shaped gold handle chased with
rococo scrolls, inset with rose-cut diamonds, white enamel panels.
Centrally applied with crowned monogram 'N II' inset with
rose-cut diamonds.

Provenance: Presented by Tsar Nicholas II in 1906 to M. Boutiron,
French Ambassador to the Imperial Court; presented by
Mme Boutiron to the Musée des Arts Décoratifs, 1927.
Literature: Habsburg/Solodkoff 1979, ill. p. 43; Habsburg 1987,
ill. p. 190.
Exhibitions: Munich 1986/87, cat. 286.

Musée des Arts Décoratifs, Paris (Inv. 25990)

153

PRESENTATION DISH
Oak, silver, carnelians
Diam: 45 cm
Marks: Fabergé's Imperial Warrant, assay mark of Moscow
1899–1908, initials of assay master Ivan Lebedkin, 84 (*zolotnik*),
inv. 17657

Circular dish; centre applied with coat of arms of the city of
Libava and an inscription in Russian: 'TO THEIR IMPERIAL MAJESTIES
FROM THE CITY OF LIBAVA. 1903'. Rim applied with a siren,
peacocks, birds, and scrolling foliage set with cabochon carnelians.

Provenance: Presumably presented at a state visit of the Imperial
couple in Libava; Diamond Room of the Winter Palace.

The State Hermitage, St. Petersburg (Inv. ERO – 5424)

ИХЪ ИМПЕРАТОРСКИМЪ ВЕЛИЧЕСТВАМЪ

ЛИБАВА
1903

ОТЪ ВѢРНОПОДДАННАГО

КУРЛЯНДСКАГО ДВОРЯНСТВА

154

Oak, gilded silver
Diam: 50.5 cm
Marks: Fabergé, initials of workmaster August Hollming,
assay mark of St. Petersburg 1899–1908, initials of assay master
Iakov Liapunov

Circular dish; silver-gilt cavetto inscribed in Russian: 'TO THEIR
IMPERIAL MAJESTIES FROM THE DEVOTED KOURLAND NOBILITY. LIBAVA.
1903'. Rim applied with acanthus foliage.

Provenance: Diamond Room of the Winter Palace.

The State Hermitage, St. Petersburg (Inv. ERO – 5425)

155

PRESENTATION TRIPTYCH ICON

Silver gilt, enamel, rubies, emeralds, sapphires, pearls, birchwood
H: 32.8 cm W: 26 cm (open)
Marks: Fabergé, initials of workmaster Mikhail Perkhin,
assay mark of St. Petersburg before 1899, 88 (*zolotnik*)

Shaped as a cross-section of an Orthodox church. Centre painted
with figures of St. Nicholas, St. Princess Alexandra, and
St. Princess Olga above, within a frame of interlacing red and
green strapwork set with cabochon rubies, sapphires, emeralds, and
pearls. Wings painted with the Four Evangelists and two
Cherubim on panels of opaque blue enamel applied with gilded
geometric motifs. Exterior, panelled in birch, is applied with
inscription: 'From the Nobility of St. Petersburg, 3 Nov. 1895'.

This presentation piece is similar in design to a triptych icon
presented by Tsar Nicholas II to Prince Boris (later Tsar Boris III)
of Bulgaria at the occasion of his baptism (Habsburg 1987, ill.
p. 147).

Provenance: Presented to Tsar Nicholas II and his wife Alexandra
at the occasion of the birth of their first daughter, Grand Duchess
Olga (1895–1918), portraying their respective patron saints.
Exhibitions: Wadsworth Atheneum 1963; ALVR 1968, cat. 87;
V&A 1977, cat. O 6; ALVR 1983, cat. 311.

Courtesy of A La Vieille Russie

The London Branch

Fabergé's representatives arrived in London in 1904. Through the patronage of Queen Alexandra, Fabergé's premises rapidly became a focal point of Edwardian London. Gifts from Fabergé's were considered the ultimate in chic. The London sales ledgers virtually overflow with the names of Kings and Queens, American millionaires, heiresses, and the money barons of the world. From London, Fabergé's agents made selling trips to Paris, Rome, and the Côte d'Azur (see Habsburg, 'The London Branch', and 'The British Relatives', cat. 82–96).

156
RABBIT
Agate, diamonds
H: 3.4 cm
Original fitted case stamped with Fabergé's Imperial Warrant, St. Petersburg, Moscow, Odessa

Rabbit carved of grey-brown agate, seated on its hind paws, with rose-cut diamond eyes.

Provenance: Miss Yznaga, London.
Exhibitions: London 1935, cat. 588Z; Zurich 1989, cat. 142.

Madame Josiane Woolf, France

157
CAT
Chalcedony, diamonds, gold
H: 4.8 cm

Playful cat with an extended paw; carved of red-brown chalcedony, with rose-cut diamond eyes in gold mounts.

Provenance: Edward James Collection.
Literature: Habsburg 1987, ill. p. 206.
Exhibitions: Munich 1986/87, cat. 371; Zurich 1989, cat. 141.

Madame Josiane Woolf, France

158

CAPERCAILZIE COCK

Agate, diamonds, gold

H: 7 cm

Original fitted case stamped with Fabergé's Imperial Warrant, St. Petersburg, Moscow, Odessa

Displaying bird of carved honey-coloured banded agate, with rose-cut diamond eyes in gold mounts and chased gold feet.

Provenance: Miss Yznaga, London.
Literature: Habsburg 1987, ill. p. 372.
Exhibitions: London 1935, cat. 588B; Munich 1986/87, cat. 372; Zurich 1989, cat. 155.

Madame Josiane Woolf, France

159

DUCKLING

Chalcedony, diamonds, gold

H: 4 cm

Original fitted case stamped with Fabergé's Imperial Warrant, St. Petersburg, Moscow, Odessa

Standing carved yellow chalcedony duckling, with rose-cut diamond eyes in gold mounts and chased red gold feet.

Provenance: Miss Yznaga, London.
Exhibitions: London 1935, cat. 588H; Zurich 1989, cat. 157.

Madame Josiane Woolf, France

160

SQUIRREL

Carnelian, diamonds, gold

H: 4.7 cm

Original fitted case stamped with Fabergé's Imperial Warrant, St. Petersburg, Moscow, Odessa

Pouncing squirrel carved of honey-coloured carnelian, with gold-mounted rose-cut diamond eyes.

Provenance: Miss Yznaga, London.
Literature: Habsburg 1987, ill. p. 206.
Exhibitions: Munich 1986/87, cat. 374; Zurich 1989, cat. 145.

Madame Josiane Woolf, France

161

POUTER PIGEON
Chalcedony, rubies, gold
H: 5.3 cm

Carved of blue-grey and cream-coloured chalcedony,
with gold-mounted cabochon ruby eyes.

Provenance: Lady Juliet Duff.
Literature: Bainbridge 1949/68, pl. 76.

Madame Josiane Woolf, France

162

CHIMPANZEE
Petrified wood, diamonds, gold
H: 6.3 cm

Chimpanzee seated on its hind quarters on a circus stool, with
crossed arms; carved of greyish mauve stone, with gold-mounted
brilliant-cut diamond eyes.

Provenance: Lady Paget (described in Fabergé's London sales
ledgers as 'Chimpanzee, petrified wood, 24223, £55, 328 roubles').

Madame Josiane Woolf, France

163

MINIATURE GOLD SAMOVAR
Gold, palisander wood
H: 8.7 cm
Marks: Fabergé, initials of workmaster Henrik Wigström,
assay mark of St. Petersburg 1908–1917, 56 (*zolotnik*)

Spherical body on four stud feet, handles with palisander wood
mounts. Inscribed: '4 cups of tea – Palata' and 'Palata Buckhurst
Park Jubilé 9 Nov. 1933–7'.

Provenance: Lydia, Lady Deterding.
Literature: Snowman 1962, pl. 103; Habsburg 1987, p. 148.
Exhibitions: Munich 1986/87, cat. 144; Zurich 1989, cat. 60.

Madame Josiane Woolf, France

164

FEMALE TOAD
Bowenite, rubies, gold
L: 4.8 cm
Original fitted case stamped with Fabergé's Imperial Warrant,
St. Petersburg

Seated toad carved of highly polished bowenite, with gold-
mounted cabochon ruby eyes.
    After a Japanese netsuke model.

Literature: Habsburg 1987, ill. p. 205.
Exhibitions: Munich 1986/87, cat. 363; Zurich 1989, cat. 149.

Madame Josiane Woolf, France

165

ART NOUVEAU CIGARETTE CASE
Gold, enamel, diamonds
L: 9.3 cm
Marks: Fabergé's Imperial Warrant, assay mark of Moscow
1899–1908

Red gold case with translucent royal blue enamel over *guilloché moiré* ground; decorated on both sides with a snake inset with rose diamonds to simulate scales. Elliptical diamond as pushpiece.

Without doubt this is one of Fabergé's most imaginative creations, and it is an unusually well designed and executed piece from the Moscow workshops.

Provenance: Presented by Mrs George Keppel to King Edward VII, 1908; presented by Queen Alexandra to Mrs Keppel, 1936; presented by Mrs Keppel to Queen Mary (a note in Queen Mary's hand setting out its history is enclosed in the case).
Literature: Bainbridge 1966, pl. 70; Habsburg 1977, p. 71; Habsburg/Solodkoff 1979, dustcover and pl. 81; Snowman 1979, p. 51; Habsburg 1987, ill. p. 237.
Exhibitions: V&A 1977, cat. K 2; Cooper-Hewitt 1983, cat. 203; The Queen's Gallery 1985/86, cat. 313; Munich 1986/87, cat. 468; Zurich 1989, cat. 117.

Lent by Her Majesty Queen Elizabeth II

166

ROTHSCHILD MATCHBOX
Gold, enamel, diamond
L: 4.5 cm
Marks: Initials of workmaster Henrik Wigström, assay mark of
St. Petersburg 1908–1917, inv. 21769. London import marks for
1911–1912

Striped with narrow yellow and wide blue *guilloché* enamel bands,
with chased laurel leaf border and rose diamond pushpiece.

The yellow and blue bands were the Rothschild racing colours.
'Monsieur Leopold' commissioned numerous such items at
Fabergé's in London.

The matchbox figures in Wigström's design book as no. 12765
with the date '25 XI 1911' (see Tillander-Godenhielm, 'New Light
on the Workshop of Henrik Wigström').

Provenance: Baron Leopold de Rothschild, London.
Literature: McNab Dennis, fig. 17.
Exhibitions: MMA 1965; ALVR 1983, cat. 160.

Courtesy of A La Vieille Russie

167

ROTHSCHILD MINIATURE EASTER EGG
Gold, enamel, diamonds
L: 1.2 cm
Marks: Initials of workmaster August Holmström, 56 (*zolotnik*)

Diagonally striped with yellow and blue *guilloché* enamel bands,
set with rose diamonds

Provenance: Baron Leopold de Rothschild, London.
Exhibitions: ALVR 1983, cat. 518.

Courtesy of A La Vieille Russie

168
RENAISSANCE-STYLE VASE
Rock crystal, gold, enamel, rubies,
sapphires
H: 16.5 cm
Marks: Initials of workmaster Mikhail
Perkhin, assay mark of St. Petersburg
1899–1908, inv. 8011

Lobed rock crystal body cut with scrolling
foliage, British Royal coat of arms, and
date 'JUNE XXII MCMXI'. Stands on four claw
feet, with yellow granulated gold mounts
set with alternating cabochon rubies and
emeralds; enamelled with raised scrolling
foliage.
   Perkhin's initials date this vase to before
1903. This is presumably an item from
Fabergé's stock, engraved and sold in 1911,
to fulfil an urgent order from London.
Fabergé frequently used the Renaissance
style for official presents (cf. Habsburg
1987, p. 71).

Provenance: Acquired 12 April 1911 by
Leopold de Rothschild at Fabergé's
London ('Cup, rock crystal, engr., gold 72,
en diff. stones, no. 18011 nett £430 [cost
2100 roubles]') and presented by him to
King George V and Queen Mary for their
Coronation on 22 June 1911, filled with
home-grown orchids from Gunnesbury
Park.
Literature: Bainbridge 1966, pl. 90;
Snowman 1962, pl. XX; Habsburg/
Solodkoff 1979, pl. 151; Habsburg 1987,
pp. 184, 185; Solodkoff 1988, p. 112.
Exhibitions: V&A 1977, cat. F 4; Cooper-
Hewitt 1983, cat. 185, p. 101; The Queen's
Gallery 1985/86, cat. 150; Munich 1986/
87, cat. 279.

Lent by Her Majesty Queen Elizabeth II

169

CIRCULAR NEPHRITE TRAY

Nephrite, gold, enamel, diamonds

L: 33 cm

Marks: Fabergé, initials of workmaster Mikhail Perkhin, assay mark of St. Petersburg before 1899

Of shallow circular design; rococo-style handles chased and enamelled with strawberry *guilloché* enamel reserves; chased and matted gold scroll borders set with rose diamonds.

This is one of a group of such trays – the closest example being in the FORBES Magazine Collection – presented to the Imperial couple at the occasion of their Coronation in 1896 (see also cat. 303).

Provenance: Lady Ludlow.

Literature: Snowman 1962, ill. p. 279; Bainbridge 1966, pl. 22 (above); Habsburg 1987, ill. p. 189.

Exhibitions: London 1935, cat. 527; Wartski 1949, cat. 216; Washington 1985/86, cat. p. 654; Munich 1986/87, cat. 284.

Lady Myra Butter and Lady Georgina Kennard

170

BUTTERCUP SPRAY
Gold, enamel, diamonds, rock crystal
H: 16.8 cm

Modelled in gold, with translucent yellow enamel petals; each
flower with a central rose-cut diamond. Stands in a rock crystal
vase carved to simulate its water content.

Literature: Habsburg 1987, ill. p. 215.
Exhibitions: V&A 1977, cat. O 18; Munich 1986/87, cat. 393;
Zurich 1989, cat. 167.

Madame Josiane Woolf, France

Famous Clients

Princes, captains of industry, actresses, singers, and ballerinas – all figures from the *monde* and *demi-monde* – became Fabergé's clients. Tsars and Grand Dukes rewarded their favourites with presents from Fabergé. The London sales ledgers abound with the names of the rich and famous. Indeed, Fabergé considered the Nobel brothers equal only to the Tsars in their voracious collecting habits.

171***
DAFFODIL
Cachalong(?), nephrite, diamonds, gold, rock crystal
H: 27 cm

Petals carved from white cachalong, with a yellow and red enamel and rose-cut diamond centre, on a nephrite stem. Stands in a small rock crystal vase carved to simulate its water content.

Provenance: Until 1919 collection of A.K. Rudanovski, St. Petersburg.
Exhibitions: Leningrad 1974, cat. 20.

The State Hermitage, St. Petersburg (Inv. 14891)

172

CORNFLOWER AND OAT SPRAYS
Gold, enamel, diamonds, rock crystal
H: 19 cm

Two cornflower sprays with blue enamel petals and rose diamond pistils, and a spray of chased gold oats with loosely swinging seeds. Stands in a cylindrical rock crystal vase carved to simulate its water content.

Provenance: Prince Yusupov, 1922.
Literature: Habsburg 1987, ill. p. 218.
Exhibitions: Leningrad 1974, cat. 17; Helsinki 1980, cat. N 2, ill. p. 7; Munich 1986/87, cat. 398.

The State Hermitage, St. Petersburg (Inv. E – 13 353)

173

MINIATURE WATERING CAN
Nephrite, gold, enamel, diamonds
L: 10.5 cm
Inv. 4709
Original fitted case stamped with Fabergé's Imperial Warrant,
St. Petersburg, Moscow

Nephrite body; gold handle and nozzle in strawberry red *guilloché*
enamel with rose diamond borders.

A similar object, signed by workmaster Henrik Wigström, was
in the collection of King Farouk (cf. Sotheby, Cairo, 1954, cat. 149).

Provenance: Mme Elizabeth Balletta of the Imperial Michael
Theatre, St. Petersburg; Lansdell K. Christie, Long Island, New
York.
Literature: Snowman 1953, p. 262; Snowman 1962, p. 147, pl.
XXIX; Snowman 1963, ill. p. 242; McNab Dennis 1965, p. 234, ill.
8; Waterfield/Forbes 1978, pp. 44–45, 112, reprint p. 45; Snowman
1979, ill. p. 126; Solodkoff 1984, p. 165, ill. pp. 25, 165; Kelly 1985,
ill. p. 23; Forbes 1987, p. 13, ill. p. 15, fig. 8; Habsburg 1987, ill. p.
172.
Exhibitions: ALVR 1961, cat. 274, ill. p. 73; Corcoran 1961, cat. 11,
ill. p. 12; ALVR 1968, cat. 343, ill. p. 130; NYCC 1973, cat. 19, ill.
p. 63; V&A 1977, cat. L 11, p. 74; Virginia/Minneapolis/Chicago
1983, cat. 4, p. 11; Fort Worth 1983, cat. 10; Detroit 1984, cat. 12;
Munich 1986/87, cat. 245; Lugano 1987, cat. 65, ill. p. 76; Paris
1987, cat. 65, ill. p. 72.

The FORBES Magazine Collection, New York (FAB66008)

174

'BALLETTA BOX'
Gold, enamel, rose diamonds
L: 10.1 cm W: 7 cm
Marks: Fabergé, initials of workmaster Henrik Wigström,
assay mark of St. Petersburg 1908–1917
Original fitted red morocco case gilt with initials 'EB'

Rectangular *necessaire*; cover of translucent royal blue enamel over
engraved reeded ground, centrally applied with monogram 'EB'
set with rose diamonds in oval frame surrounded by trellis pattern
in rose diamonds. Sides and base with Louis XV-style *basse taille*
dark blue enamel floral festoons and ovals; base with central oval
medallion enamelled with anchor and initial 'A'. Contains pencil,
ivory pad, mirror, propelling pencil, lipstick tube, and two lidded
compartments.

Grand Duke Aleksei Aleksandrovich (1850–1908), son of Tsar
Alexander II, was Admiral-General and Supreme Chief of the
Russian Imperial fleet. Mme Elizabeth Balletta of the Imperial
Michaels' Theatre, St. Petersburg, was a favourite of the Grand
Duke. She owned a substantial collection of Fabergé objects, many
of which formed part of the Lansdell K. Christie Collection (cf.
Snowman 1962, pl. XVI). Others include the 'Balletta Vase',
(The Brooklyn Museum, New York) and a 'Begging Schnauzer'.

Provenance: Commissioned and presented by Grand Duke Aleksei
Aleksandrovich; Lansdell K. Christie Collection, Long Island,
New York.
Literature: Snowman 1962, pl. XVI; McNab Dennis 1965, pl. 19.
Exhibitions: Corcoran 1961, cat. 19; ALVR 1968, cat. 95.

Private collection

302

175

CARNET DE BAL

Gold, enamel, pearls, diamonds, moonstone
H: 7.3 cm W: 4.6 cm
Marks: Assay mark of St. Petersburg 1899–1908, initials of
assay master Iakov Liapunov, 56 (*zolotnik*)

Decorated with alternating opaque white and pink enamel stripes;
cover applied with Russian Imperial double-headed eagle set with
rose diamonds on an oval white *guilloché* enamel plaque within a
split pearl border, suspended from yellow gold laurel swags tied
with pink gold ribbons. Reeded gold pencil surmounted by a
cabochon moonstone. Interior with a gold plaque engraved in
French: '*Present de Sa Majeste L' Empereur Nicholas II, 2 Fevr.
1902*'.

Provenance: Presented by Tsar Nicholas II to Mme Elizabeth
Balletta of the Imperial Michael Theatre on the eve of a benefit
performance marking her tenth anniversary on the St. Petersburg
stage; Landsell K. Christie, Long Island, New York.
Literature: McNab Dennis 1965, fig. 19.
Exhibitions: Corcoran 1961, cat. 73; MMA 1965; ALVR 1968,
cat. 340; ALVR 1983, cat. 217.

Courtesy of A La Vieille Russie

176

NOBEL NECKLACE

Platinum, silver, diamonds, rock crystal
L: 33.3 cm
Original fitted case stamped with Fabergé's Imperial Warrant,
St. Petersburg, Moscow, London

Fifteen platinum links with ice crystal motifs set with rose
diamonds on rock crystal ground and with diamond-set borders,
flanking a platinum medal with two profile portraits set in a rose
diamond border. Inscribed on reverse in Russian: '1882–1912/
Mechanical Labour/Nobel'. Can be worn as separate bracelets.

Portrayed on the medallions are Emanuel Nobel and his father,
Ludwig. A rendering of this necklace/bracelet appears in the stock
books of Albert Holmström (Wartski, London). See also cat. 184.

Provenance: Presented by Dr Emanuel Nobel, nephew of the
inventor Alfred Nobel, to his stepmother, Edla Nobel.
Literature: Solodkoff 1984, ill. p. 168; Kelly 1985, ill. p. 18;
Habsburg 1987, ill. p. 142; Cerwinske 1990, ill. p. 99.
Exhibitions: Virginia/Minneapolis/Chicago 1983, cat. 39; Fort
Worth 1983, cat. 68; Detroit 1984, cat. 69; Munich 1986/87, cat.
115; Lugano 1987, cat. 92, ill. p. 92; Paris 1987, cat. 92, ill. p. 88.

The FORBES Magazine Collection, New York (FAB81004)

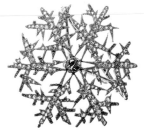

177

ICE CRYSTAL PENDANT

Platinum, rock crystal, diamonds

L: 3.6 cm

Lozenge-shaped with triangular top, centrally applied with simulated ice crystals set with rose diamonds on rock crystal ground, within borders set with rose diamonds.

    This work belongs to a series of such pendants designed for Emanuel Nobel, one of Fabergé's foremost clients, who offered such favours, epitomising Russian winters, at his dinner parties.

Courtesy of A La Vieille Russie

178

ICE CRYSTAL PENDANT

Platinum, diamonds, rock crystal

L: 2.7 cm

Marks: Inv. 98580

Ovoid, applied with simulated ice crystals on rock crystal ground, with horizontal band of rose diamonds and rose diamond border.

Courtesy of A La Vieille Russie

179

SNOWFLAKE BROOCH

Platinum, gold, diamonds

Diam: 3.2 cm

Marks: Initials of workmaster Albert Holmström

Snowflake with six points, of granulated platinum set with rose diamonds, with central brilliant diamond, mounted in gold as a brooch.

Literature: Habsburg 1987, ill. p. 141.
Exhibitions: Helsinki 1980, ill. 93, p. 93; Munich 1986/87, cat. 109; Zurich 1989, cat. 188.

Private collection, Finland

180

SNOWFLAKE BROOCH

Platinum, gold, diamonds

Diam: 1.9 cm

Marks: Initials of workmaster Albert Holmström, 56 (*zolotnik*)

Small flake with six points, of granulated platinum set with rose diamonds, mounted in gold as a brooch.

Literature: Habsburg 1987, ill. p. 141.
Exhibitions: Helsinki 1980, ill. p. 93; Munich 1986/87, cat. 110; Zurich 1989, cat. 189.

Private collection, Finland

181
CIRCULAR SNOWFLAKE BROOCH
Platinum, gold, diamonds, rock crystal
Diam: 2.9 cm
Marks: 56 (*zolotnik*)
Original fitted case applied with inscription: 'A Snowflake from Russia 1913'

Round rock crystal disc applied with six-point flake in granulated platinum set with rose diamonds, and a central brilliant-cut diamond, mounted in gold as a brooch.

Literature: Habsburg 1987, ill. p. 141.
Exhibitions: Helsinki 1980, ill. p. 93; Munich 1986/87, cat. 111; Zurich 1989, cat. 190.

Private collection, Finland

182
ICE CRYSTAL BRACELET
Platinum, rock crystal, gold, diamonds
L: 16.2 cm
Marks: Assay mark of St. Petersburg 1908–1917

Eight rectangular links of rock crystal and granulated platinum, each with a different ice crystal motif set with rose diamonds; each link separated by rose diamonds and three brilliant-cut diamonds.
 A similar necklace, separating into two bracelets, is in the FORBES Magazine Collection (cat. 176).

Private collection, Finland

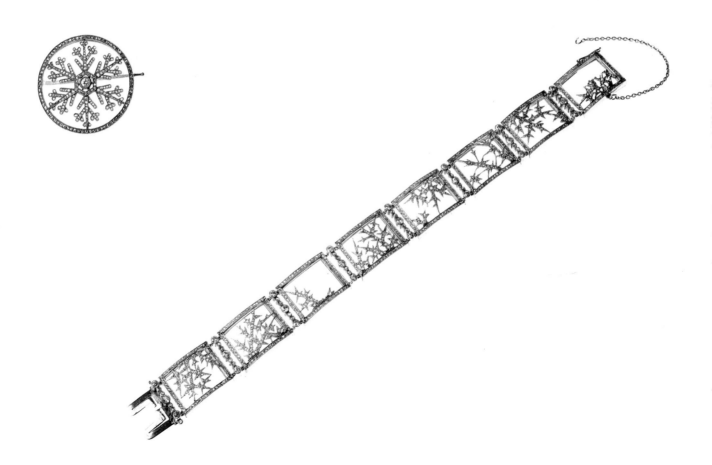

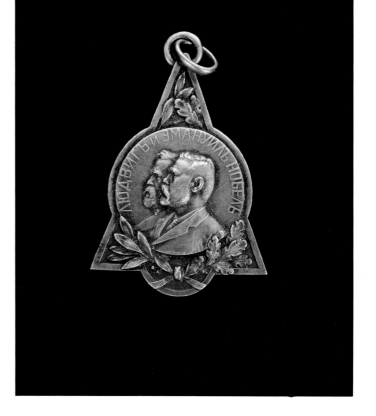

183

NOBEL COMMEMORATIVE PLAQUE

Bronze

H: 7.1 cm W: 10.3 cm

Original fitted case stamped with Fabergé's Imperial Warrant,
St. Petersburg, Moscow, London

Chased on one side with an allegorical figure and a view of an oil
field, the other with profile portraits of Emanuel and Ludwig
Nobel, a map of the Apsheron Peninsula indicating the Nobel oil
fields, and an inscription in Russian: 'IN MEMORY OF PRODUCING A
BILLION TONS OF RAW OIL BY THE NOBEL BROTHERS COMPANY BETWEEN
1879 AND 1906'.

Possibly produced by A.F. Vasiutinski (1858–1935), the leading
medal maker at the St. Petersburg Mint.

Literature: *Thirty Years of Nobel Brothers Oil Producing Company*
(in Russian), (n.d.), ill. between pp. 72 and 73.

The State Hermitage, St. Petersburg (Inv. RM – 14428)

184

JETON FOR THE FIFTIETH ANNIVERSARY OF THE LUDWIG NOBEL
MECHANICAL WORKS IN ST. PETERSBURG, 1912

Silver

H: 4 cm

Marks: Initials of workmaster Alfred Thielemann, assay mark of
St. Petersburg 1908–1917, 84 (*zolotnik*)

Triangular, inset with a circular medallion chased with profile
portraits of Ludwig and Emanuel Nobel placed above laurel and
oak branches and engraved with their names; reverse with name
of factory, date '1862–1912', and a trophy of Labour.

The State Hermitage, St. Petersburg (Inv. RM – 8191)

185

BONBONNIERE EASTER EGG
Gold, enamel, diamonds
H: 9 cm
Marks: Fabergé, initials of workmaster Mikhail Perkhin,
56 (*zolotnik*)

Gold egg with twice six panels of opalescent pink *guilloché* enamel over sunbursts and painted with *camaieu mauve* tied laurel sprays and dendritic motifs; panels bordered with opaque white enamel. Outer vertical borders of granulated gold, pink enamel rose blossoms, and green foliage; horizontal borders set with rose diamond bands, with diamond-set rosettes at intersections. Finial with monogram 'BK'; base with date '1899' under a portrait diamond. Contains a miniature enamelled egg as a surprise.

   This egg belongs to a series of six eggs which were made for Barbara Kelch, née Bazanova (cf. Habsburg/Solodkoff 1979, ill. p. 141). The other eggs are: 1898 Hen egg and 1904(?) Chanteclair egg (FORBES Magazine Collection); 1900 Pine Cone egg (Mrs Joanne Kroc, San Diego); 1901(?) Apple Blossom egg and 1903 Bonbonnière egg (both private collections).

Provenance: Presented by Aleksandr Ferdinandovich Kelch to his wife Barbara, Easter 1899; Zolotnitzky, Paris, 1921; Queen Mary.
Literature: Snowman 1962, pl. LXXXIII, p. 112; Snowman 1979, pp. 114, 115; Habsburg/Solodkoff 1979, p. 121; Solodkoff 1984, p. 122; Solodkoff 1988, p. 22.
Exhibitions: V&A 1977, cat. F 1; Cooper-Hewitt 1983, cat. 112; The Queen's Gallery 1985/86, cat. 165; Zurich 1989, cat. 198, pl. 47.

Lent by Her Majesty Queen Elizabeth II

186

COCKER SPANIEL

Opal matrix, rubies, gold

H: 4.5 cm

Original fitted case stamped with Fabergé's Imperial Warrant, St. Petersburg, Moscow, London

Carved seated spaniel with cabochon ruby eyes set in gold.

Provenance: Count von Blücher, Geneva.
Literature: Habsburg 1987, ill. p. 206.
Exhibitions: Munich 1986/87, cat. 373; Zurich 1989, cat. 140.

Madame Josiane Woolf, France

187

RECTANGULAR FRAME

Nephrite, gold, ivory

H: 13.5 cm

Spinach green frame, rectangular bezel with laurel leaf border; ivory back and gold strut. Contains a miniature of Princess Olga Orlova, signed by Zuiev.

Madame Josiane Woolf, France

188

OVAL MINIATURE FRAME

Gilded silver, gold, enamel, ivory

H: 13.5 cm W: 9.8 cm

Marks: Fabergé's Imperial Warrant, assay mark of Moscow before 1899, 84 (*zolotnik*), inv. 62268

Of deep yellow *guilloché* enamel over sunray pattern, outer translucent green enamel border of chased laurel leaves; applied with entwined four-colour gold flower swags and ribbon cresting; ivory back and silver-gilt strut. Contains a miniature of the celebrated courtesan Cléo de Mérode in diaphanous robes.

Literature: Snowman 1979, pp. 18, 138; Habsburg 1987, ill. p. 251.
Exhibitions: V&A 1977, cat. R 24; ALVR 1983, cat. 83; Munich 1986/87, cat. 505; Zurich 1989, cat. 86.

Madame Josiane Woolf, France

189

TRIANGULAR FRAME WITH PHOTOGRAPHS
Silver, wood, enamel, paper
H: 64 cm W: 67.5 cm
Marks: Fabergé, assay mark of Moscow

Silver-mounted triangular frame with rounded corners and outer reed-and-tie border. Centre with two oval photographs of I.I. Vorontsov-Dashkov and his wife, placed under the family's enamelled coat of arms; initial 'L' on ribbon of the Order of St. George, photographs of other members of the family, and dates '1858' and '1908' beneath, all within red *guilloché* enamel frame applied with swags. Outer border with Neo-Russian acanthus foliage contains circular medallions with photographs of Vorontsov-Dashkov's retinue. On stud feet; wooden back inscribed in Russian: 'To His Imperial Majesty's Governor of the Caucasus, General-Adjutant Count I.I. Vorontsov-Dashkov from members of his retinue on the occasion of the 50th Anniversary of his service. Adjutant-Prince A.Z. Chavchavadze. Officers. Tiflis. 25 March 1908'.

Illarion Ivanovich Vorontsov-Dashkov (1837–1916) served as General-Adjutant, General of Cavalry, a member of the State Council, and Governor of the Caucasus. He was married to Elizaveta Andreievna, née Shuvalova.

Provenance: Count I.I. Vorontsov-Dashkov; until 1930 in the Museum of Fine Arts.

State Historical Museum, Moscow (Inv. 69620/ok 6474)

190

YUSUPOV MUSIC BOX
Gold, enamel, silver, diamonds
H: 4.8 cm L: 8.8 cm W: 4.5 cm
Marks: Fabergé, initials of workmaster Henrik Wigström, assay mark of St. Petersburg 1899–1908

Shaped as a Louis XV snuff-box, set with six sepia enamel panels over *guilloché* sunburst grounds depicting Yusupov palaces, with additional panels of dendritic motifs and crowned initials 'F', 'Z', 'N', and 'F' at corners; thumbpiece as Roman numeral 'XXV' set with rose diamonds in foliate mount. When opened the box plays 'The White Lady' by François Boieldieu, the regimental march of the *Garde à Cheval*, Felix Yusupov's regiment.
The palaces are:
1. (top) Archangelskoe, outside Moscow
2. (front) Palace on the Moika, where Felix Yusupov and Grand Duke Dmitri later assassinated Rasputin
3. (bottom) Palace of Koreiz in the Crimea
4. (back) Yusupov Palace at Tsarskoe Selo
5. (left) Palace of Rakitnoe in the Government of Kursk
6. (right) Moscow residence.

Provenance: Presented by Felix and Nikolai Yusupov to their parents, Felix and Zenaïde, at the occasion of their twenty-fifth wedding anniversary, 1907.
Literature: Snowman 1962, pl. VIII; Habsburg/Solodkoff 1979, pp. 153–54; Taylor 1983, p. 27; Habsburg 1987, ill. p. 256.
Exhibitions: ALVR 1983, cat. 222; Munich 1986/87, cat. 515.

Hillwood Museum, Washington, D.C. (11.80)

191

YUSUPOV FRAME

Wood, velvet, gold, enamel, pearls, diamonds, ivory
H: 15 cm W: 7.5 cm
Marks: Fabergé, initials of workmaster Henrik Wigström

Rectangular backing with rounded corners covered in white velvet. Applied with an oval miniature of Princess Z.N. Yusupov, signed and dated 'V. Zuiev 1907', in a narrow gold frame enamelled in opaque white. Oval frame flanked with two sprays of lilies-of-the-valley set with pearls and gold leaves enamelled in green, tied with a diamond-set knot and suspended from a white enamel ribbon by a diamond-set ring. Reverse with a gold suspension ring and gold stand, covered with white *moiré* silk.

Princess Zenaïde Yusupov (1861–1939), married Count Felix Sumarokov-Elston, who took his wife's name by Imperial dispensation. She was also the mother of Felix Yusupov, one of Rasputin's assassins.

Provenance: Count Yusupov Collection; until 1932 in the State Russian Museum.
Exhibitions: Mikimoto 1991, cat. 12; Genoa 1992, cat. 12, p. 45.

State Historical Museum, Moscow (Inv. 73831/ok 6933)

192

SILVER ANNIVERSARY ICON

Silver, holly wood, pearls
H: 16.4 cm
Marks: Fabergé, initials of workmaster Hjalmar Armfelt, assay mark of St. Petersburg 1908–1917, 88 (*zolotnik*)
Original fitted case stamped with Fabergé's Imperial Warrant, St. Petersburg, Moscow, London

Silver-mounted icon of onion-dome shape, with Roman numeral 'XXV' as clasp; opens to reveal paintings of the Holy Virgin flanked by St. Sophia and St. Matthew. Reverse inscribed: 'Blessing from an old friend ZY/August 21, 1913'.

Saints Sophia and Matthew were the patron saints of Prince and Princess Cantacuzène, recipients of this icon.

Provenance: Presented by Princess Zenaïde Yusupov to Prince Mathias and Princess Sophie Cantacuzène at the occasion of their twenty-fifth wedding anniversary, 1913; Dino Yannopoulos, Philadelphia, Pennsylvania.
Literature: Kelly 1982/83, ill. p. 12, fig. 18; Solodkoff 1984, ill. p. 172; Kelly 1985, ill. p. 12.
Exhibitions: Virginia/Minneapolis/Chicago 1983, cat. 31, p. 13; Fort Worth 1983, cat. 61; Edinburgh and Aberdeen 1987, cat. 24, ill. in checklist; London 1991, cat. 11, ill. p. 22.

The FORBES Magazine Collection, New York (FAB81005)

193
RHINOCEROS
Jasper
L: 11.8 cm

Figure of a standing rhinoceros, of reddish variegated jasper.

Literature: Ross 1952, p. 7.
Exhibitions: ALVR 1949, cat. 256; San Francisco 1964, cat. 23.

The Walters Art Gallery, Baltimore, Maryland
(Inv. 27.0480)

194

HARDSTONE FIGURE OF GYPSY SINGER VARA PANINA
Russian hardstones, gold, silver, diamonds
H: 17.8 cm

Gypsy stands upright, hands folded, with swarthy aventurine
quartz hands and face, diamond eyes, gold earrings, and black
Siberian jasper hair; wears a striated jasper skirt, mottled green
quartz blouse, figured red-brown jasper shawl, purpurine kerchief,
and black calcite shoes. Around her neck on a gold chain is a
pendant formed of ten silver coins, each bearing an effigy of
Nicholas II.

This figure, the largest and most significant of Fabergé's
statuettes, is a portrait of the celebrated gypsy singer Vara Panina,
'famous for the extraordinary range and beauty of her voice, who
kept audiences entranced nightly at Moscow's Tzigane restaurant
Yar in spite of her lack of beauty. When her love for a member of
the Imperial Guard was unrequited, she dramatically took poison
and died on the stage in front of him singing "My heart is
breaking"' (Snowman, in V&A 1977, p. 92).

Literature: Snowman 1962, pl. XLVI; McNab Dennis 1965, fig. 14;
Habsburg/Solodkoff 1979, ill. p. 156.
Exhibitions: Corcoran 1961, cat. 91; MMA 1965; V&A 1977,
cat. N 11; ALVR 1983, cat. 482.

Courtesy of A La Vieille Russie

Commissions from Army, Navy, and Church

Similar to their civilian counterparts, Army regiments ordered punch-bowls and *kovshi* for anniversaries or departures of their officers. The Navy requested commemorative plaques to memorialise the launchings of their ships, while the Church had an insatiable appetite for icons, lamps, and panagias.

195
REGIMENTAL PRESENTATION TROPHY
Silver
H: 57 cm
Marks: Fabergé, initials of workmaster Julius Rappoport, 84 (*zolotnik*)

Spherical body supported by three double-headed eagles, on three cannons and cannon balls; rim chased with laurel leaf border, finial with a trophy of War.

Literature: Solodkoff 1984, ill. p. 173; Kelly 1985, ill. p. 12.
Exhibitions: Fort Worth 1983, cat. 64; Baltimore 1983/84, cat. 21; Detroit 1984, cat. 34; Edinburgh and Aberdeen 1987, cat. 1, ill. in checklist; London 1991, cat. 42, ill. p. 45.

The FORBES Magazine Collection, New York (FAB79005)

196
SILVER-MOUNTED GLASS
Silver gilt, glass
H: 10.4 cm
Marks: Fabergé, initials of workmaster Mikhail Perkhin, assay mark of St. Petersburg 1899–1908, 88 (*zolotnik*)
Original fitted case stamped with Fabergé's Imperial warrant, St. Petersburg, Moscow

Tapering glass, lower section mounted in silver on three ball feet, with a band of laurel crowns, one contains the crowned monogram 'N II', inscription above in Russian: 'From this glass Tsar Nicholas II drank to the health of the Regiment on 9. and 10. December 1898'; pierced sleeve of crossed arrows and laurel crowns above.

Literature: Ulyanova, p. 20.
Exhibitions: Zurich 1989, cat. 45, ill. p. 81; Mikimoto 1991, cat. 11; Genoa 1992, cat. 11, p. 107.

State Historical Museum, Moscow (Inv. 68257/ok 6777)

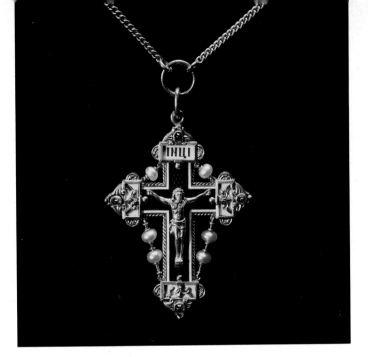

197***
REGIMENTAL PRESENTATION BOX
Silver and parcel-gilt
L: 27 cm W: 16.8 cm H: 28 cm
Marks: K. Fabergé, Imperial Warrant, initials of workmaster Julius
Rappoport, assay mark of St. Petersburg 1899–1908, 88 (*zolotnik*)

Front chased with a battle scene and engraved inscription in
Russian: 'Battle of Grokhovskoe'; sides with date 'February 13,
1892'; reverse engraved with 'The Uhlans of his Majesty to the
Sovereign Patron' and dates '1651' and '1903'. Surmounted by a
figure of an officer on horseback.

The battle scene depicts an attack of the First Division of
Chasseurs. The dates to the sides refer to a traditional holiday of
the Uhlan Battalion. In 1651 the title of the oldest regiment was
granted by the Tsar and the first Sloboda Battalions appeared in
the Ukraine. The year 1903 marked the one-hundredth
anniversary of the founding of the Battalion on 11 September
1803.

Provenance: Presented by the Uhlan Battalion to Tsar Nicholas II;
transferred to the Kremlin, 1922.
Exhibitions: Kremlin 1992, cat. 11

The Kremlin Armoury, Moscow (State Historical Cultural Reserve,
Inv. MR 5649/ok 11796)

198
PECTORAL CROSS
Gold, rubies, pearls, enamel, sapphires
H: 5.5 cm W: 4.1 cm Chain 35.5 cm long
Marks: Initials of workmaster August Hollming

Original fitted case, with applied silver plate with inscription in
Russian: 'Blessing to the Privates of L.G. [Life Guard]
Preobrazhenski Regiments'

Russian Orthodox crucifix with chased gold corpus on red *guilloché*
enamel ground, with chased scrolls and 'INRI' on white enamel
and cabochon sapphires at cross ends. Reverse inscribed in Russian:
'Spasi i Sokhrani' [Save].

Provenance: Acquired from the Military Historical Museum, 1933.
Exhibitions: Mikimoto 1991, cat. 42; Genoa 1992, cat. 30, p. 110.

State Historical Museum, Moscow (Inv. 68257/ok 6946)

199

BRATINA SHAPED AS A SHAKO OF THE 1907 LIFE GUARD SAPPER'S
BATTALION
Silver, wood
H: (Including feather plume) 39.5 cm (50 cm with stand)
Marks: Fabergé, initials of workmaster Hjalmar Armfelt,
assay mark of St. Petersburg 1908–1917, 84 and 88 (*zolotnik*)

Partially oxidised silver cap, applied at front with a star of the
Order of St. Andrew the Firstborn and a ribbon inscribed in
Russian: 'For the Balkan War in 1877'; chased silver braidings,
strap, and tassels. Removable champagne flute (with separate
wooden stand) shaped as a feather plume.

This *bratina* was probably made for the 1912 centenary of the
Life Guard Sapper's Battalion, which had been formed in 1812.
The Imperial Family patronised this battalion. Tsar Nicholas II
became its patron in 1906; Tsarevich Alexei, Grand Dukes Mikhail
Aleksandrovich, Boris Vladimirovich, Nikolai Nikolaievich, and
Petr Nikolaievich were listed as officers.

Provenance: Silver Storage vault of the Winter Palace.
Exhibitions: Leningrad 1981, cat. 502; Lugano 1986, cat. 130;
Helsinki 1989, cat. 10.

The State Hermitage, St. Petersburg (Inv. ERO – 5002)

200

PLAQUE COMMEMORATING THE LAYING OF THE KEEL OF THE
CRUISER *RIURIK*
Silver
L: 15.4 cm H: 10.3 cm
Marks: Fabergé, initials of workmaster Anders Nevalainen,
assay mark of St. Petersburg 1899–1908

Rectangular silver plaque engraved with drawing of the *Riurik*,
inscribed in Russian: 'Cruiser "Riurik" with 15200 tons of tonnage
and 19700 ind. power. Begun in Barrow-in-Furness (England) in
the works of Vickers and Co. on 9(22) August 1905.' Reverse
inscribed: 'Administrative head of the Navy Ministry General
Adjutant F.K. Avelan. Chairman of the Technical Council General
Adjutant V.F. Dubasov. Head of the Main Shipbuilding
Department Counter-Admiral A.R. Rodionov. Principal
Shipbuilding Inspector Lieutenant General N.E. Kuteinov.
Shipbuilding Inspector Engineer K.A. Tennison'.

The *Riurik* was launched on 17 November 1906 and participated in action in 1908. As part of the Baltic Navy she was actively involved in warfare during World War I and was discharged in 1922.

Such plaques were inset in each ship as a kind of passport and presented to dignitaries participating in the ceremony at the laying of the keel.

For a similar plaque in the Hillwood Museum see Taylor 1983, ill. p. 26.

Provenance: Presented to the Central Navy Museum by the Vickers Works, 1907.

Central Navy Museum, St. Petersburg (Inv. 6966)

201

PLAQUE COMMEMORATING THE LAYING OF THE KEEL OF THE
BATTLESHIP *CESAREVICH*
Silver
L: 14.8 cm H: 10.7 cm
Marks: Fabergé, initials of workmaster Victor Aarne, assay mark of St. Petersburg 1899–1908, initials of assay master Iakov Liapunov, 91 (*zolotnik*)

Rectangular silver plaque engraved with a drawing of the battleship and inscribed in a combination of Russian and French: 'Construction of "Cesarevich" was begun on 26 June 1899 at the Société Anonyme des Forges et Chantiers de la Méditerranée shipyard in "La Seyne" with Mʳ Lagane as superviser'. Inscribed on verso: 'At the time of His Imperial Highness Grand Duke General-Admiral Aleksei Aleksandrovich's management of the Navy and Vice Admiral Tyrtov's management of the Ministry of the Navy. In the presence of 1st Rank Captain Grigorovich and Ship Engineer Boklevski.'

The *Cesarevich* was launched in 1903, damaged by Japanese destroyers in Port Arthur in February 1904, and discharged in 1922.

Provenance: Acquired through the USSR Consul General in Geneva, 1983.

Central Navy Museum, St. Petersburg (Inv. 49574)

LOUIS XV-STYLE TRIPTYCH ICON
Silver gilt, enamel, diamonds, wood
H: 22.3 cm W: 20.7 cm (open), 8.1 cm (closed)
Marks: Fabergé, initials of workmaster Mikhail Perkhin,
assay mark of St. Petersburg before 1899, 88 (*zolotnik*)

Painted with the Raising of the True Cross by Emperor
Constantine and his mother St. Helena. Setting is a rococo
archway flanked by two fluted columns surmounted by the dove of
the Holy Ghost on a pink *guilloché* ground, a diamond-set cross
above, and a diamond-set trellis over pink *guilloché* enamel
beneath. Left wing with St. Alexander Nevsky and two Cherubim,
right wing with St. Mary Magdalen and two Cherubim, each in a
cartouche bordered by rose diamonds set in panels of pink
guilloché enamel and a diamond-set trellis. Inscribed on reverse of
right panel: 'To Leonid Kolchev, Prebendary and Archpriest,
Confessor to Her Majesty in pious remembrance from Xenia and
Olga' and '1866–1916'.

Provenance: Presented by Grand Duchesses Xenia (1875–1960,
who married Grand Duke Aleksandr Mikhailovich) and Olga
(1882–1960, who married Duke Peter of Oldenburg), sisters of
Tsar Nicholas II.
Literature: Snowman 1962, pl. LXXXV; Taylor 1983, p. 31.

Hillwood Museum, Washington, D.C. (54.29)

JEWELLED GOLD PANAGIA
Gold, enamel, diamonds, sapphires, rubies, pearls
H: 13.6 cm W: 8.5 cm
Marks: Fabergé, initials of workmaster Henrik Wigström,
assay mark of St. Petersburg 1908–1917, 56 (*zolotnik*), inv. 19428

Crowned oval pendant icon, centre with enamelled effigy of Christ
Pantocrator in the Byzantine manner. Wide border with segments
alternately set with cabochon sapphires and rubies, raised gold
scrolls set with rose diamond 'flowers', with seed pearls at
intersections. Hinged crown set with two cabochon rubies and rose
diamonds, suspended from a gold double-link chain.

Based on an eleventh-century medallion decorating an icon of
Archangel Gabriel from the Djumati Monastery in Georgia, today
in The Metropolitan Museum of Art, New York.

Exhibitions: ALVR 1983, cat. 312.

Courtesy of A La Vieille Russie

Silver from St. Petersburg

The production of silver objects and services formed one of Fabergé's chief sources of income. Made in St. Petersburg by the silver factories of Julius Rappoport and of the Wäkeva family, Fabergé's output included large silver *surtouts de table*, which formed part of the dowry of the Grand Duchesses.

204

FROG-SHAPED SILVER SPIRIT LAMP
Silver, garnets
H: 10 cm
Marks: Fabergé's Imperial Warrant, initials of Julius Rappoport, assay mark of St. Petersburg 1899–1908, inv. 7811

Frog humoristically portrayed, seated on its hind quarters, with cabochon garnet eyes. Its protruding tongue forms the wick.

Madame Josiane Woolf, France

205

ASHTRAY SHAPED AS A WOODCOCK
Silver
L: 14 cm
Marks: Fabergé, initials of workmaster Julius Rappoport, assay mark of St. Petersburg 1899–1908, 88 (*zolotnik*), inv. 3374

Naturalistically chased as a seated bird, with a hollow opening in its back.

Provenance: Strelna Palace; transferred from Central Storage of Suburban Palaces, 1956.
Exhibitions: Leningrad 1981a, cat. 500.
The State Hermitage. St. Petersburg (Inv. ERO – 8672)

206

SPIRIT LAMP SHAPED AS A MINIATURE SAMOVAR
Silver
H: 13.5 cm
Marks: Fabergé, initials of workmaster Hjalmar Armfelt, assay mark of St. Petersburg 1899–1908, inv. 13198

Shaped as a typical Russian samovar, with ivory handles; inscribed in Russian: 'Court Jeweller K. Fabergé St. Petersburg'.

The State Hermitage, St. Petersburg (Inv. ERO – 4320)

207

SILVER YACHTING TROPHY
Silver
H: 39.7 cm
Marks: Fabergé, Imperial Warrant, initials of workmaster Julius
Rappoport, assay mark of St. Petersburg 1899–1908, initials of
assay master Iakov Liapunov, 88 (*zolotnik*), inv. 5072
Original fitted oak box with purple velvet and silk lining stamped
with Fabergé's Imperial Warrant, St. Petersburg, Moscow; applied
with a silvered copper plaque on the cover, inscribed in Russian:
'Nevsky Yacht Club. The Prize from His Majesty for a Yacht Race
on 22 July 1898 in Peterhof. Perkun Yacht. Counts F.G. and E.O.
Berg'.

In the manner of an eighteenth-century *Münzbecher*, partially gilt
silver trophy of baluster shape, on three scroll feet; domed cover
surmounted by a double-headed eagle; cover and body inset with
coins of the seventeenth and eighteenth centuries.

Donated by Nicholas II, the trophy was used as the award for
the annual yacht race in Peterhof since 1898. The Peterhof Port of
the Nevsky Yacht Club was founded on 30 May 1898.

The Counts Berg had their estates in Estonia, Lithuania, and
Finland. Feodor Gustavovich and Kirill (Erik) Feodorovich Berg
were members of the Nevsky Yacht Club since 1895 and 1897,
respectively.

Exhibitions: Elagin Palace 1989, cat. 68.

'Peterhof' State Museum-Reserve (Inv. PDMP 656, 656/I)

208
COCONUT CUP
Coconut, silver gilt
H: 27 cm
Marks: Initials of workmaster Stephan Wäkeva,
assay mark of St. Petersburg before 1899

Coconut carved with rococo scrolls on a reeded ground and three
circular medallions with relief profiles of Catherine the Great,
Peter III, and a double-headed eagle; silver-gilt base similarly
decorated. Domed cover surmounted by a double-headed eagle.

 This is a copy of an eighteenth-century original in the Kremlin
Armoury Museum, Moscow.

Provenance: A.I. Marchasmin Collection.
Exhibitions: Mikimoto 1991, cat. 29; Genoa 1992, cat. 29, p. 53.

State Historical Museum, Moscow (Inv. 81812/ok 13889)

209

CAVIAR BOWL SHAPED AS A STURGEON

Silver

L: 60 cm

Marks: Fabergé's Imperial Warrant, assay mark of Moscow, 1896, initials of assay master LO, inv. 6549

Naturalistically cast and chased as a swimming fish with detailed modelling of body structure, teeth, fins, and scales.

Gerald M. Sylvar

210***

SILVER SPIRIT LAMP SHAPED AS A BABOON

Silver

H: 11.5 cm

Marks: Fabergé's Imperial Warrant, initials of workmaster Julius Rappoport, assay mark of St. Petersburg 1899–1908, initials of assay master Iakov Liapunov, 88 (*zolotnik*)

Naturalistically chased and partially gilt baboon turning backwards, with hinged head and drilled tail for the wick.

Provenance: State Repository of Valuables of the USSR.
Literature: Kovarskaia 1984, ill. p. 160.
Exhibitions: Kremlin 1992, cat. 227.

The Kremlin Armoury, Moscow
(State Historical Cultural Reserve, Inv. MR 5667)

211

BELL-PUSH SHAPED AS A CAT
Silver, green glass
H: 7 cm
Marks: Fabergé, assay mark of St. Petersburg 1908–1917,
88 (*zolotnik*)

Cat portrayed naturalistically, grooming itself, with green glass
eyes as pushpieces. Inscribed under tail in Russian: 'To dear P.G.
Kartsev from the Cavalry Brigade 1912–1913. Prince D. Kildishev'.

Prince Dmitri Pavlovich Kildishev was a Cavalry Guard of the
Empress Maria Feodorovna Regiment. Pavel Georgievich Kartsev
was an officer of the same regiment.

Provenance: Acquired from the family of the jeweller
Blagoslavenski, 1987.
Exhibitions: Elagin Palace 1989, cat. 96.

'Peterhof' State Museum-Reserve (Inv. PDMP 663)

212

LOUIS XVI-STYLE WINE COOLER AND COVER
Silver, gilded interior
H: 43.5 cm
Marks: Fabergé's Imperial Warrant,
assay mark of Moscow 1908–1917,
88 (*zolotnik*)

Vase-shaped wine cooler with lion head
and ring handles, chased with draperies,
with laurel leaf rim, and bead-and-wave
borders; stands on a square base with
fluted and reed-and-tie foot; domed cover
with artichoke finial.

This is probably a Fabergé piece made
to complete an existing Louis XVI service.
For a similar drawing by Fabergé see cat.
306.

Provenance: Diamond Room of the Winter
Palace.
Literature: State Hermitage 1979, no. 174.
Exhibitions: Helsinki 1989, cat. 91.

The State Hermitage, St. Petersburg
(Inv. ERO – 5000)

The Moscow Workshops

The Moscow workshops catered principally to the rich Boyar and bourgeois families who preferred things more typically Russian. These included *cloisonné* enamel objects made in the factory of Feodor Rückert, silver objects and services, and lesser objects of vertu (see Odom, 'The Moscow Workshops').

213

RECTANGULAR CLOISONNE ENAMEL BOX
Silver gilt, enamel
H: 2.7 W: 6.5 L: 8.4 cm
Marks: Fabergé's Imperial Warrant, assay mark of Moscow 1908–1917, inv. 391831

Cover painted *en plein* with *The Boyar* after Konstantin Makovski; rest with filigree enamel Neo-Russian ornament, leaf and vine design, and pineapples in dark blue, brown, grey, and orange.

Provenance: Johann Georg, Prinz von Hohenzollern.

Hillwood Museum, Washington, D.C. (15.209)

214

CLOISONNE ENAMEL BOX
Silver, enamel
L: 8.4 cm W: 6.4 cm H: 3.9 cm
Marks: Fabergé's Imperial Warrant overstriking initials of
workmaster Feodor Rückert, assay mark of Moscow 1908–1917,
88 (*zolotnik*)

Cover with *en plein* matte enamel painting of *Blind Man's Bluff*
after Konstantin Makovski (*c.* 1905); decorated in the Neo-Russian
style with elaborate filigree decoration, with the front imitating a
clasp.

Private collection, United States

215

ENAMEL BOX
Silver, enamel, Siberian stones
L: 12.7 cm W: 9.8 cm H: 4.6 cm
Marks: Fabergé's Imperial Warrant, assay mark of Moscow
1908–1917, 88 (*zolotnik*), inv. 38445

Shaped as a casket, with winged lion feet; cover with *en plein*
enamel painting of *The Prophecy of Oleg* signed by A. Borozdin,
after Viktor Vasnetsov (1899); cabochon Siberian stones under
foliate arches to the sides.

Private collection, United States

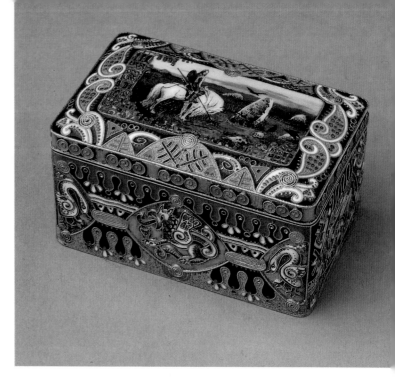

216

ENAMEL KOVSH
Silver, enamel, river pearls
L: 11.5 cm H: 7 cm
Marks: Fabergé's Imperial Warrant, initials 'CF' in Latin letters,
assay mark of Moscow 1908–1917, 91 (*zolotnik*), London import
marks for 1911

Of traditional shape; a band of wine matte enamel circles the
upper part, with irregular scrolls of tiny river pearls affixed to
enamel; a stylised ram is incorporated into the angular handle.

Private collection, United States

217

CLOISONNE ENAMEL BOX

Silver, enamel

L: 7.6 cm W: 7.3 cm H: 5 cm

Marks: Fabergé's Imperial Warrant, assay mark of Moscow 1908–1917, 88 (*zolotnik*)

Cover with *en plein* glossy enamel painting of *The Bogatyr at the Crossroads* after Viktor Vasnetsov (1882); sides with swans, birds, and dragons in light brown and blue-grey colours.

Private collection, United States

218

CLOISONNE ENAMEL KOVSH

Silver, enamel

L: 10.9 cm H: 8.1 cm

Marks: Fabergé's Imperial Warrant overstriking workmaster's initials of Feodor Rückert, assay mark of Moscow 1908–1917, inv. 26212, French import mark

With *en plein* enamel miniature of *Evening Walk* after a watercolour by Sergei Solomo (1908); sides with scrolls in dark green and dark blue enamel with lighter highlights; cockerel handle.

Private collection, United States

219

COMMEMORATIVE CLOISONNE ENAMEL BEAKER
Silver gilt, enamel
H: 12 cm
Marks: Initials of workmaster Feodor Rückert

Of tapering shape; painted *en plein* with a view of Fabergé's shop
in Moscow on front, reverse with green enamel cartouche that
bears a gilded inscription in Russian: 'XXV To the Highly
esteemed Carl Gustavovich in Gratitude. F.I. Rückert 1912';
surrounded by geometric ornamentation and stylised foliage on
pale grey and blue ground.

    This beaker is proof of Rückert's collaboration with Fabergé as
of 1887, the date of the opening of the Moscow branch.

Provenance: Presented by F.I. Rückert to Carl Fabergé, 1912.
Exhibitions: V&A 1977, cat. S 5; ALVR 1983, cat. 55.

Courtesy of A La Vieille Russie

220

LARGE CLOISONNE ENAMEL KOVSH
Silver gilt, enamel, amethysts
L: 38 cm
Marks: Fabergé's Imperial Warrant, initials of workmaster
Feodor Rückert, assay mark of Moscow 1899–1908, 91 (*zolotnik*),
inv. 212714
Original fitted case stamped with Fabergé's Imperial Warrant, St.
Petersburg, Moscow; applied with a silver plaque bearing facsimile
signatures and a dedication inscription.

Of Art Nouveau design; elaborately decorated in shaded enamels
with foliate scrolls, Neo-Russian ornament, and monogram 'LO';
set with cabochon amethysts.

Provenance: Presented by the workmen of the Nobel Factory to
Ludwig Olsen, Director of the company and son-in-law of Ludwig
Nobel.
Literature: Habsburg 1987, ill. p. 136.
Exhibitions: ALVR 1983, cat. 5; Munich 1986/87, cat. 85.

Courtesy of A La Vieille Russie

221***
CLOISONNE ENAMEL KOVSH
Silver, enamel
L: 15.5 cm
Marks: Fabergé's Imperial Warrant,
assay mark of Moscow 1908–1917, 88 (*zolotnik*), inv. 39179

In the Russian Art Nouveau style; partially gilt silver decorated with gilt scrolls and polychrome enamels, and painted *en plein* with a scene from Russian history.

Provenance: Investigation Department of the KGB of the USSR.
Exhibitions: Kremlin 1992, cat. 158.

The Kremlin Armoury, Moscow
(State Historical Cultural Reserve,
Inv. MR 11521)

222
PUNCH-BOWL AND LADLE
Silver, enamel, moonstones, garnets
H: 30.3 cm L: (ladle) 26.6 cm
Marks: Fabergé's Imperial Warrant,
assay mark of Moscow 1908–1917, 84
(*zolotnik*), inv. (2)4411 (on the ladle)

Partially gilt silver circular bowl on three ball feet; rim chased with Old Russian motifs and set with alternating cabochon moonstones and garnets, inscribed in Russian beneath: 'To the Highly Respected Vladimir Gerasimovich Mukhin in Memory of the 10th Anniversary of his Work in the Iron Ore Mines of the Briansk Works. 1906 27 IV 1916', followed by fifty signatures. Handle with circular grisaille enamel painting of the Aleksandrovski and Sukhaia Balka Mines.

Provenance: Acquired in 1988 from N.V. Mukhina, daughter of Vladimir Gerasimovich Mukhin, a mining engineer who worked in the iron ore mines of the Briansk Works since 1906.
Exhibitions: Elagin Palace 1989, cat. 161.

'Peterhof' State Museum-Reserve
(Inv. PDMP 783, 784)

223
DUCK-SHAPED KOVSH
Hardwood, silver, rubies, emeralds
L: 14.5 cm
Marks: Fabergé's Imperial Warrant, assay mark of Moscow
1908–1917

Of traditional Russian shape and design, applied with openwork
mounts chased with stylised feathers, with cabochon ruby eyes and
two suspended emerald drops.

Provenance: Grand Duchess Maria Pavlovna.

Madame Josiane Woolf, France

224
SILVER-GILT CREAM JUG
Silver
H: 6.5 cm
Marks: Fabergé's Imperial Warrant, assay mark of Moscow before
1899

Heavily gilded silver container of triangular section and tapering
shape, with three lobes to the rim; twisted tendril handle.

Literature: Habsburg/Solodkoff 1979, ill. p. 36; Snowman 1979,
p. 57; Habsburg 1987, ill. p. 155.
Exhibitions: Munich 1986/87, cat. 168; Zurich 1989, cat. 55.

Madame Josiane Woolf, France

225

SIREN VASE
Silver, tourmalines, copper
H: 22.5 cm
Marks: Fabergé, assay mark of Moscow
1908–1917

Copper-oxidised vase with a siren perched
on rim in the form of a half-naked female
figure wearing a *kokoshnik* and with
spread wings set with tourmalines.
  The vase was designed by S. Vashkov.

Exhibitions: Mikimoto 1991, cat. 57;
Genoa 1992, cat. 153, p. 129.

State Historical Museum, Moscow
(Inv. 107722/ok 23454)

226
LILY PAD DISH
Silver
L: 20.5 cm
Marks: Fabergé, assay mark of Moscow 1893

Naturalistically shaped as a water lily leaf, with curved handle,
three ball feet, and water lily blossom to the side.

Provenance: Acquired from the State Museum Fund in the 1940s.
Exhibitions: Mikimoto 1991, cat. 47.

State Historical Museum, Moscow (Inv. 58954/ok 5786)

227
SILVER ALBUM COVER
Silver
H: 37.5 cm L: 45.5 cm
Marks: Fabergé's Imperial Warrant,
assay mark of Moscow 1908–1917, 88 (*zolotnik*)

Rectangular cover engraved with four St. Petersburg buildings: the
Ministry of Trade and Industry on Tuchkov Embankment (above),
the Senate building (left), the Trade Ministry with the General
Staff Arch on the Palace Square (right), and the State Bank as
seen from the Ekaterinski Canal (below). Octagonal frame in
middle with Russian inscription: 'To dear Sergei Ivanovich
Timashev in memory of the 35th year of service, from his
colleagues'; below it are dates: '1878 16 December 1913'. Applied
with two sphinxes and laurel swags; border chased with palmettes,
the corners with rosettes.

Sergei Ivanovich Timashev (1858–1926), a high-ranking official
who served in the Senate and in the Ministry of Finances, was
Bank Manager and, since 1910, Minister of Trade and Industry.

Provenance: From the Leningrad branch of the State Central Book
Chamber, 1931.

The State Hermitage, St. Petersburg (Inv. ERO – 7048)

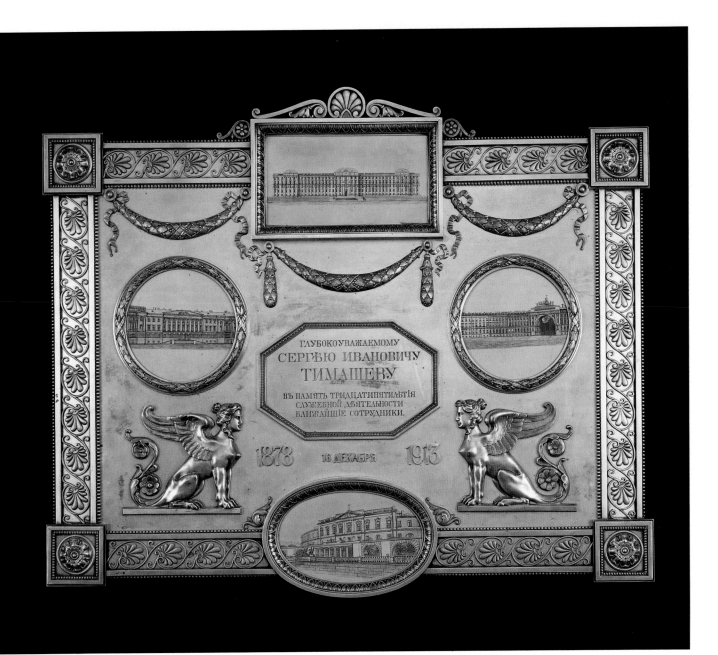

ГЛУБОКОУВАЖАЕМОМУ
СЕРГѢЮ ИВАНОВИЧУ
ТИМАШЕВУ
ВЪ ПАМЯТЬ ТРИДЦАТИПЯТИЛѢТІЯ
СЛУЖЕБНОЙ ДѢЯТЕЛЬНОСТИ
БЛИЖАЙШІЕ СОТРУДНИКИ.

1878   16 ДЕКАБРЯ   1913

228

SILVER SALT-CELLAR AND COVER
Silver
H: 14.5 cm
Marks: Fabergé's Imperial Warrant, assay mark of Moscow before 1899, 84 (*zolotnik*)

Circular salt-cellar standing on three dolphin feet and round base, lip with *entrelac* border; cover surmounted by an Imperial crown; gilded interior.

This was possibly presented to Tsar Nicholas II and Alexandra Feodorovna during the Coronation festivities in 1896.

Provenance: Storage rooms of the Winter Palace.

The State Hermitage, St. Petersburg (Inv. ERO – 3894)

229

SILVER SALT-CELLAR
Silver
Diam: 7 cm
Marks: Fabergé's Imperial Warrant, initials of assay master Ivan Lebedkin, assay mark of Moscow 1899–1908, 84 (*zolotnik*)

Circular salt-cellar applied with laurel swags, with bead and laurel leaf borders, two-colour gilding, inscribed in Russian: 'TO THEIR IMPERIAL MAJESTIES FROM THE LOYAL KIRGHIZES OF BUKEIEV HORDE'.

Provenance: Diamond Room of the Winter Palace.

The State Hermitage, St. Petersburg (Inv. ERO – 3896)

230

ART NOUVEAU JUG
Rock crystal, silver gilt
H: 22.5 cm L: 16.5 cm
Marks: Fabergé's Imperial Warrant, assay
mark of Moscow 1899–1908, initials of
assay master Ivan Lebedkin, 84 (*zolotnik*),
inv. 12672

Pear-shaped body carved with scrolling
foliage and birds, silver mounts with
trailing wild roses.

Exhibitions: Leningrad 1985, cat. 159;
Elagin Palace 1989, cat. 104, ill. p. 100.

'Peterhof' State Museum-Reserve
(Inv. PDMP 693)

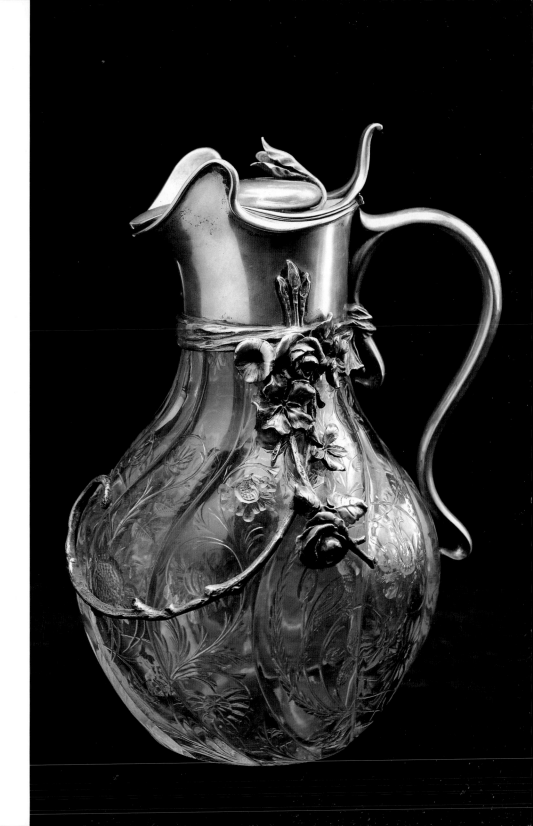

231

BOWE PRESENTATION TRAY
Silver, enamel
L: 66 cm
Marks: Fabergé's Imperial Warrant, assay mark of Moscow, 1895

Of shaped oval outline, cast and chased with vigorous rocaille scrolls and flowers; rim with dates '1890' and '1895', enamelled photographic portrait of Allan Bowe, and Roman numeral 'V'; centre with presentation inscription in Russian: 'To the much respected Allan Andreevich from sincerely grateful employees'. Reverse engraved with names of employees of the Moscow branch.

The Moscow branch was opened in Moscow at 4 Kuznetski Most in 1887 by Fabergé in partnership with the Englishman Allan Bowe. The partnership was dissolved in 1906. With only a few exceptions, Moscow objects are all marked with the Imperial Warrant and bear no workmaster's initials because, unlike in St. Petersburg, they were employed by Fabergé himself. Moscow produced mainly silver, under manager Mikhail Tchepournov, and *cloisonné* enamel (cf. Odom, 'The Moscow Workshops'). Objects of vertu from Moscow include such exceptional items as the Cléo de Mérode miniature frame (cat. 188) and the Art Nouveau cigarette case formerly owned by Mrs George Keppel (cat. 165).

Provenance: Presented by the employees of Fabergé's Moscow branch to their manager, Henry Allan Talbot Bowe, 1895.
Exhibitions: London 1991, cat. 40.

The FORBES Magazine Collection, New York (FAB88003)

MONUMENTAL BOGATYR KOVSH
Silver, silver gilt, semiprecious stones
L: 58.2 cm
Marks: Fabergé's Imperial Warrant,
assay mark of Moscow 1899–1908, initials
of assay master Ivan Lebedkin, inv. 21843

Of massive, almost spherical form,
surmounted by a handle cast with roughly
hewn *bogatyrs* gazing threateningly under
an unfurling flag; bowl chased with Neo-
Russian cloud ornaments, set with
cabochon moonstones.

Bogatyrs, the legendary warriors of
medieval Russia, decorate this kovsh. The
designer may have been inspired by the
late twelfth-century epic poem, 'The Tale
of the Armament of Igor,' which recounts
the defeat of a young Christian Prince of
Kiev at the hands of pagan warriors. This
piece is a highly stylised example of a
kovsh, a traditional Russian drinking cup,
originally carved out of wood in the form
of a bird.

For a design of this *kovsh* cf. cat. 338.

Literature: Solodkoff 1984/89, p. 173; Kelly
1985, p. 12; Hill 1989, p. 223, pl. 193;
Kirichenko 1991, p. 194, ill. p. 195 and
opp. title page.
Exhibition: Virginia/Minneapolis/Chicago
1983, cat. 63; Fort Worth 1983, cat. 63;
Detroit 1984, cat. 32; Lugano 1987, cat. 1,
pp. 23–24, 26–28, 32, 39; Paris 1987, cat. 1,
pp. 19–20, 22–24, 28, 35; London 1991, cat.
14, pp. 3, 24, ill. pp. 24–25 and on
catalogue cover; Vienna 1991, cat. 75.

The FORBES Magazine Collection,
New York (FAB81001)

KITE-SHAPED FRAME

Moss agate, gold, diamonds, ivory

H: 10.3 cm W: 7.8 cm

Marks: Fabergé's Imperial Warrant, initials 'KF', assay mark of
Moscow before 1899, 56 (*zolotnik*)

Original fitted case stamped with Fabergé's Imperial Warrant,
Moscow, St. Petersburg

Of green variegated transparent stone, oval bezel with three-colour
gold flower garlands, borders of crossed staffs and interlacing
laurel branches. Ivory back and silver-gilt strut.

Exhibitions: Zurich 1989, cat. 87.

Madame Josiane Woolf, France

234

EASEL-SHAPED FRAME
Gold, enamel, diamonds, ivory
H: 14.7 cm W: 6 cm
Marks: Fabergé's initials, assay mark of Moscow 1899–1908,
56 (*zolotnik*), inv. 23403
Original fitted case stamped with Fabergé's Imperial Warrant,
St. Petersburg, Moscow, Odessa

Rectangular frame of white *guilloché* enamel, bezel set with rose-cut diamonds, flanked by applied laurel sprays; easel on three yellow gold reeded legs with red gold bow above. Ivory back plate.

Literature: Habsburg 1987, ill. p. 245.
Exhibitions: V&A 1977, cat. O 19; Munich 1986/87, cat. 491; Zurich 1989, cat. 99.

Madame Josiane Woolf, France

235

CIRCULAR MINIATURE FRAME
Gold, enamel, ivory
Diam: 3.9 cm
Marks: Fabergé's initials 1899–1908, inv. 18166

Of yellow translucent enamel painted with tendrils of red flowers with green leaves; four hinged mauve enamel covers conceal photographs. With gold ribbon cresting, ivory back, and gold strut.

Madame Josiane Woolf, France

236

PHOTOGRAPH FRAME
Silver gilt, sapphire
W: 6.2 cm
Marks: Fabergé's Imperial Warrant, assay mark of Moscow 1899–1908, inv. 15307

Naturalistically shaped as a water lily leaf, reeded stem with cabochon sapphire finial. Contains a photograph of Tsarevich Alexei as a baby.

Provenance: From the Leningrad Regional Department Museum of Public Education, 1926, in Count Sheremetev's House, in the Fountain House.

The State Hermitage, St. Petersburg (Inv. ERO – 6750)

Jewels

Despite his wide-ranging success, Fabergé considered himself primarily a jeweller. A large percentage of his turnover must have originated from this specialty. Of the lavish pearl and diamond necklaces mentioned in accounts, contemporary sources, and sales ledgers, none seems to have survived the decimation of war. The best source for the thousands of smaller jewels produced in the Holmström, Hollming, Thielemann, and Pihl workshops are the sketch-books of the workshop (cat. 348–354) and the inventory books of Albert Holmström's workshop dating from 1907 to 1917 (see A.K. Snowman, 'Two Books of Revelations', in Habsburg 1987, pp. 45–61).

237

AQUAMARINE BROOCH

Gold, silver, aquamarine, diamonds
L: 3.7 cm W: 3.2 cm
Marks: Fabergé, assay mark of St. Petersburg 1908–1917

Emerald-cut aquamarine in a narrow gold mount set with rose diamonds, with three diamond-set leaves at each corner.

Exhibitions: Mikimoto 1991, cat. 38; Genoa 1992, cat. 32.

State Historical Museum, Moscow (Inv. 102157/ok 17233)

238

ART NOUVEAU PENDANT

Gold, diamonds, enamel
L: 5.2 cm W: 3.8 cm
Marks: Fabergé, assay mark of St. Petersburg 1899–1908
Original fitted case

Shaped as a branch with three leaves covered in gold-green translucent enamel, with three circular diamonds suspended on stalks.

Exhibitions: Mikimoto 1991, cat. 40.

State Historical Museum, Moscow (Inv. 107584/ok 23285)

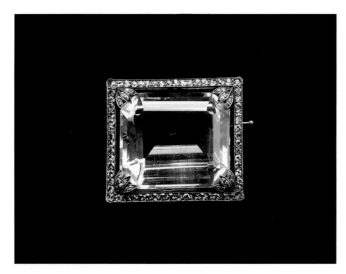

239

PENDANT

Gold, diamonds, silver

L: 4 cm

Marks: KF (in Cyrillic), assay mark of Moscow 1908–1917

Of ogival shape, chased with two horse heads and foliage above, set with a navette-shaped diamond in a silver setting.

State Historical Museum, Moscow (Inv. 108076/ok 23454)

240***

OVAL JEWELLED PENDANT/BROOCH

Platinum, gold, diamonds, pearls

H: 5.2 cm W: 3.3 cm

Inv. 95699

Centrally set with a pendant baroque pearl; an openwork garland surrounds rosette-shaped clusters of rose diamonds.

Provenance: From the treasure found at 13 Solianka Street (see Muntian, 'A Treasure Found in Solianka Street').

Exhibitions: Kremlin 1992, cat. 65.

The Kremlin Armoury, Moscow

(State Historical Cultural Reserve, Inv. MR 11567)

241***

OVAL DIAMOND-SET PENDANT

Silver, diamonds

H: 5 cm W: 3.1 cm

Inv. 99724

Three concentric ovals set with rose diamonds, with a suspended pear-shaped diamond at the centre.

Provenance: From the treasure found at 13 Solianka Street (see Muntian, 'A Treasure Found in Solianka Street').

Exhibitions: Kremlin 1992, cat. 69.

The Kremlin Armoury, Moscow

(State Historical Cultural Reserve, Inv. MR 11557)

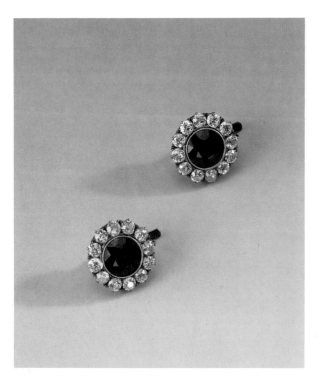

242***
PAIR OF JEWELLED EARRINGS
Gold, silver, emeralds, diamonds
H: 2 cm Diam: 1 cm
Marks: K. Fabergé, assay mark of Moscow 1899–1908,
initials of assay master Ivan Lebedkin, 56 (*zolotnik*), inv. 32484

Oval, each with a central cabochon emerald set within a border of
circular diamonds, in gold and silver mounts.

Provenance: From the treasure found at 13 Solianka Street
(see Muntian, 'A Treasure Found in Solianka Street').
Exhibitions: Kremlin 1992, cat. 73.

The Kremlin Armoury, Moscow
(State Historical Cultural Reserve, Inv. MR 11562/1–2)

243***
JEWELLED RING
Gold, silver, diamonds, pearl
H: 2.5 cm W: 2 cm
Marks: K. Fabergé, 56 (*zolotnik*), inv. 27568

Bezel set with a grey pearl in a rose diamond surround flanked by
two circular diamonds.

Provenance: From the treasure found at 13 Solianka Street (see
Muntian, 'A Treasure Found in Solianka Street').
Exhibitions: Kremlin 1992, cat. 74.

The Kremlin Armoury, Moscow
(State Historical Cultural Reserve, Inv. MR 5667)

Workmasters

Fabergé's workmasters each specialised in a given and restricted field. Consequently, their styles differ and can be readily identified. Erik Kollin (head workmaster 1872–1886), Mikhail Perkhin (1886–1903), and Henrik Wigström (1903–1917) supervised the entire production of the St. Petersburg workshops.

Erik Kollin

Erik Kollin worked mainly in gold and specialised in antiquarian jewellery.

244
HELMET TCHARKA
Silver gilt, enamel
H: 9.5 cm
Marks: Fabergé, initials of workmaster Erik Kollin, assay mark of St. Petersburg 1899–1908

Shaped as a cavalry helmet surmounted by a double-headed eagle, applied at front with an enamelled Star of the Order of St. Andrew. Interior inscribed: 'To Prince Nikolai Nikolaievich Odoievski-Maslov from fellow officers of the First Guard Division.'
   Prince Vladimir Feodorovich Odoievski died without descendants in 1869. His name and title were bestowed in 1878 upon Nikolai Nikolaievich Maslov, Life Guard Cavalry Regiment Commander.

Provenance: Odoievski-Maslov family collection; acquired from the State Museum Fund, 1921.

State Historical Museum, Moscow (Inv. 53030/ok 1489)

Mikhail Perkhin

Mikhail Perkhin's art represents the finest of the firm's creations, both technically and stylistically. His characteristic styles were Louis XV and Art Nouveau.

245
MINIATURE SHOE
Heliotrope, gold, rose diamonds, silver
W: 8.9 cm H: 7.1 cm
Marks: Inv. 49194

Rococo-style lady's shoe applied with chased gold rococo scrolls, buckle of rose diamonds set in silver.

Literature: Hawley 1967, no. 2.
Exhibitions: ALVR 1961, cat. 276;
San Francisco 1964, cat. 132.

The Cleveland Museum of Art (The India Early Minshall Collection, 66.482)

246
MINIATURE TEAPOT
Jade, gold
H: 5.7 cm W: 10.9 cm
Marks: Fabergé, initials of workmaster Mikhail Perkhin, assay mark of St. Petersburg before 1899, inv. 47274

Pale green jade teapot with elongated spout and C-shaped handle applied with chased gold rococo scrolls; cover with flame finial.

Literature: Hawley 1967, no. 1.
Exhibitions: ALVR 1961, cat. 275;
San Francisco 1964, cat. 131.

The Cleveland Museum of Art (The India Early Minshall Collection, 66.479)

247

HIPPOPOTAMUS SNUFF-BOX

Heliotrope, gold, ruby, diamond

L: 9 cm

Marks: Fabergé, initials of workmaster Mikhail Perkhin, assay mark of St. Petersburg before 1899, 56 (*zolotnik*)

Humorous carving of a hippo's head of dark green heliotrope (bloodstone) speckled with red; waved gold mounts with ruby and rose diamond thumbpiece.

Provenance: Countess Zoubov, Geneva.
Literature: Habsburg/Solodkoff 1979, ill. p. 77; Habsburg 1987, ill. p. 178.
Exhibitions: ALVR 1983, cat. 452; Munich 1986/87, cat. 266.

Courtesy of A La Vieille Russie

248

CIRCULAR MINIATURE FRAME

Gold, enamel, diamonds, gilded silver, ivory

Diam: 4.3 cm

Marks: Fabergé, initials of workmaster Mikhail Perkhin, assay mark of St. Petersburg 1908–1917

Of apple green *guilloché* enamel over radiating sunray pattern, white enamel bezel, surrounded by three tied bows each set with a rose-cut diamond. Ivory back and silver-gilt strut.

Madame Josiane Woolf, France

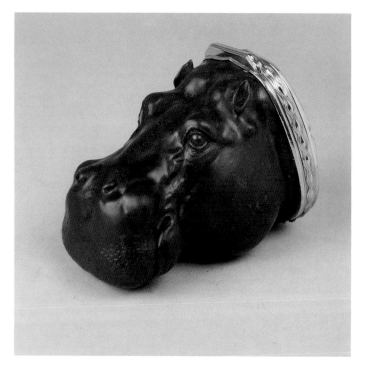

249

FEMALE BUST ON COLUMN

Bowenite, smoky quartz, gold, diamonds, rubies

H: 11.5 cm

Marks: Fabergé, initials of workmaster Mikhail Perkhin,
assay mark of St. Petersburg before 1899

Smoky quartz bust of a lady in the Renaissance style on a tapering
fluted golden base with laurel leaf and ruby-and-diamond rings.
Fluted pale green bowenite column applied with husks; laurel leaf
ring at base.

Provenance: S. Bulgari Collection, Rome.
Literature: Habsburg 1987, ill. p. 171.
Exhibitions: Munich 1986/87, cat. 242; Zurich 1989, cat. 63.

Madame Josiane Woolf, France

250

GUMPOT

Bowenite, gold, rubies, moonstone, diamonds

H: 5.6 cm Diam: 5.5 cm

Marks: Initials of workmaster Mikhail Perkhin,
assay mark of St. Petersburg before 1899

Conical gumpot with domed cover; applied with four-colour gold
flower swags suspended from cabochon rubies, *entrelac*, husk-and-
bead borders, and pilasters with Greek key pattern terminals.
Cover with cabochon moonstone finial in rose-cut diamond setting.

Literature: Habsburg 1987, ill. p. 171.
Exhibitions: Munich 1986/87, cat. 244; Zurich 1989, cat. 68.

Madame Josiane Woolf, France

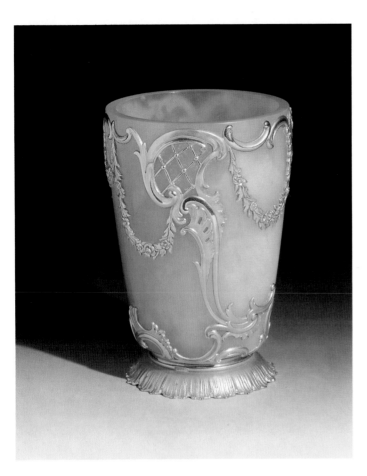

251

ROCOCO BEAKER
Bowenite, gold
H: 8.1 cm Diam: 5.6 cm
Marks: Initials of workmaster Mikhail Perkhin,
assay mark of St. Petersburg before 1899

Conical beaker applied with yellow gold scrolls, cartouches, and
flower swags; shaped golden foot.

Literature: Habsburg 1987, ill. p. 171.
Exhibitions: Helsinki 1980, cat. A 48; Munich 1986/87, cat. 243;
Zurich 1989, cat. 42.

Madame Josiane Woolf, France

252

EGG-SHAPED BONBONNIERE
Jasper, gold, enamel, emerald, diamonds
H: 7 cm
Marks: Fabergé, initials of workmaster Mikhail Perkhin,
assay mark of St. Petersburg before 1899, inv. 53584
Original fitted case stamped with Fabergé's Imperial Warrant,
St. Petersburg, Moscow

Banded red-brown hardstone shell, gold mounts with opaque
white enamel bands tied with green enamel foliage. Pushpiece
with emerald in collet mount and foliage set in rose-cut diamonds.

Literature: Habsburg 1987, ill. p. 167.
Exhibitions: Munich 1986/87, cat. 229.

Madame Josiane Woolf, France

253

MINIATURE SEDAN CHAIR
Gold, enamel, rock crystal, mother-of-pearl
H: 9.1 cm
Marks: Fabergé, initials of workmaster Mikhail Perkhin,
assay mark of St. Petersburg 1899–1908, 72 (*zolotnik*), inv. 2707

Of Louis XVI design, with pink translucent enamel panels over
engine-turned sunbursts, decorated underglaze in gold leaf and
coloured enamels with trophies of Love, Gardening, and the Arts
within opaque white enamel borders and white enamel rosettes at
each corner; rock crystal windows engraved with simulated
curtains; opening at front to reveal mother-of-pearl lining.

This is one of a group of such miniature toys, the closest of
which is a sedan chair in the FORBES Magazine Collection.

Private collection, Finland

254

BONBONNIERE
Gold, enamel, rubies, emeralds, diamonds, pearls
H: 3.4 cm
Marks: Fabergé, assay mark of St. Petersburg 1899–1908, inv. 6659

Shaped as a Doge's hat, enamelled in translucent yellow over
engraved swirling foliage; two opaque white bands set with rubies,
emeralds, rose-cut diamonds, and pearls.

Literature: Habsburg 1987, ill. p. 245.
Exhibitions: Munich 1986/87, cat. 489; Zurich 1989, cat. 15.

Madame Josiane Woolf, France

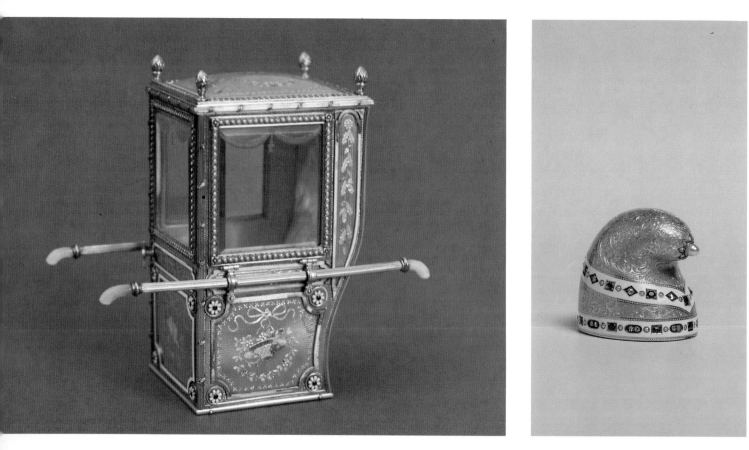

Henrik Wigström

Henrik Wigström's period saw the prevalence of Louis XVI, Marie Antoinette, and Empire styles. (For the discovery of his design books see Tillander-Godenhielm, 'New Light on the Workshop of Henrik Wigström'.)

255

BELT BUCKLE

Silver, gold, rubies, enamel

H: 6.8 cm W: 6.3 cm

Marks: Fabergé, initials of workmaster Henrik Wigström, assay mark of St. Petersburg 1899–1908; initials of assay master A. Richter, 56 and 88 (*zolotnik*), inv. 13529

Shaped as a rhombus, of white *guilloché* enamel, applied with two green gold laurel crowns tied with red gold ribbons and set with two cabochon rubies.

Exhibitions: Elagin Palace 1989, cat. 18.

'Peterhof' State Museum-Reserve (Inv. PDMP 660)

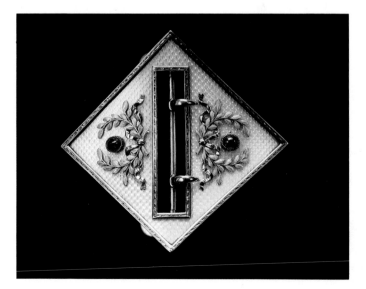

256

MINIATURE FRAME
Gold, diamonds, enamel, bone, wood
H: 12.5 cm W: 13.5.
Marks: Fabergé, initials of workmaster Henrik Wigström,
assay mark of St. Petersburg 1899–1908,
initials of assay master A. Richter

Rectangular frame with rounded top, of white *guilloché* enamel;
applied above with monogram 'MO' set with rose diamonds, dates
'1894' and '1906', and inscription in Russian: 'To Mikhail
Aleksandrovich Ostrogradski in good memory'. Contains a
watercolour view of the Chernyshev Bridge and the building of
the Ministry of the Interior and Finances. On the reverse are
names of the donors.
   Mikhail Aleksandrovich Ostrogradski was a high-ranking
official, the Insurance Manager of a department at the Ministry of
the Interior from 1894 to 1906.

Provenance: From the Art Section of the State Russian Museum,
1919.
Literature: Leningrad 1987, no. 148.
Exhibitions: Leningrad 1981b, cat. 186.

The State Hermitage, St. Petersburg (Inv. ERO – 6137)

257*

CHINESE SCENT FLASK
Gold, jade, diamonds, pearl
H: 7 cm
Marks: Fabergé, initials of workmaster Henrik Wigström,
assay mark of St. Petersburg 1908–1917
Original fitted case stamped with Fabergé's Imperial Warrant,
St. Petersburg, Moscow, London

Carved as a bearded Chinese head; cover forms a hat with rose
diamond border and pearl and rose diamond finial.
   For another, almost identical flask in the FORBES Magazine
Collection, see Habsburg 1987, p. 178.

Literature: Snowman 1953, pls. 60, 61; Fagaly 1972, cat. 28.

The Matilda Geddings Gray Foundation Collection, New Orleans
Museum of Art

258*

BRITISH BOBBY AND JOHN BULL BOX

Gold, enamel, ivory, glass

Diam: 7.3 cm

Marks: Fabergé, initials of workmaster Henrik Wigström, assay mark of St. Petersburg 1908–1917

Circular *bonbonnière* of ruby red *guilloché* enamel with green gold laurel borders; cover applied with articulated painted ivory figures of a British bobby and John Bull, on an ivory background.

One of a series of such boxes with articulated figures, which includes two examples in private collections (see Snowman 1964, pls. LVII and LX/LXI).

Literature: Fagaly 1972, cat. 34.

The Matilda Geddings Gray Foundation Collection, New Orleans Museum of Art

259

CLOCK

Nephrite, gold, enamel, diamonds

H: 7.7 cm

Marks: Fabergé, initials of workmaster Henrik Wigström (both in Latin letters), assay mark of St. Petersburg 1899–1908, 72 (*zolotnik*), inv. 22681. Destined for export, probably to London.

Block of spinach green nephrite hollowed to hold the clock's movement; dial with pink roses instead of numerals, rose diamond-set hands, with sets of Roman 'III' to front and sides.

Provenance: Probably a third anniversary gift.
Literature: Snowman 1962, pl. XXVIII; Hawley 1967, no. 14.
Exhibitions: Hammer 1951, cat. 332; ALVR 1961, cat. 178; San Francisco 1964, cat. 90.

The Cleveland Museum of Art (The India Early Minshall Collection, 66.475)

260

MINIATURE BIDET

Gold, enamel, nephrite, seed pearls
H: 8.2 cm
Marks: Fabergé (in Latin letters), initials of workmaster Henrik
Wigström, assay mark of St. Petersburg 1908–1917, 72 (*zolotnik*),
inv. 25256

Salt-cellar shaped as a Louis XVI bidet; stands on three tapering
legs, with nephrite bowl; seat and back with trophies of Music
painted in sepia on oyster *guilloché* enamel; back with seed pearl
border.

Illustrated in Henrik Wigström's design book with date (see
Tillander-Godenhielm, 'New Light on the Workshop of Henrik
Wigström', fig. 12).

Literature: Bainbridge 1949, pl. 38; Snowman 1962, pl. LII;
Bainbridge 1968, pl. 53.
Exhibitions: ALVR 1961, cat. 272; San Francisco 1964, cat. 129.

The Cleveland Museum of Art (The India Early Minshall
Collection, Inv. 66455)

261

BOX WITH VIEWS OF THE FORTRESS OF ST. PETER AND ST. PAUL

Gold, enamel, pearls
L: 5.7 cm
Marks: Fabergé, initials of workmaster Henrik Wigström,
assay mark of St. Petersburg 1899–1908, 72 (*zolotnik*)

With cut corners, painted in *camaieu rose* with views of the
Fortress of St. Peter and St. Paul, St. Petersburg; cover with split
pearl border, corners with green enamel foliage.

Views painted in sepia on oyster rose ground became popular
around 1908–1910. Objects with views of Sandringham (cat. 83)
and Windsor, as well as Siamese palaces and temples are known.
A similar box painted with views of Chatsworth is in the collection
of the Duke of Devonshire. The shape and decoration of both
boxes were inspired by eighteenth-century snuff-boxes in the
manner of Joseph-Etienne Blerzy.

Provenance: Miss Yznaga della Valle, Paris and London.
Literature: John Herbert, ed., *Christie's Review of the Season 1982*,
ill. p. 305; Solodkoff 1984, pp. 25, 27, 174, ill. pp. 137, 174;
Habsburg 1987, ill. p. 238.
Exhibitions: London 1935, cat. 588 DD; Virginia/Minneapolis/
Chicago 1983, cat. 14, p. 12; Fort Worth 1983, cat. 36; Detroit
1984, cat. 48; Munich 1986/87, cat. 470, ill. p. 238; Lugano 1987,
cat. 112, ill. p. 103; Paris 1987, cat. 112, ill. p. 99.

The FORBES Magazine Collection, New York (FAB82006)

262

FIRE-SCREEN FRAME
Varicoloured gold, enamel, pearls
H: 18 cm
Marks: Fabergé, initials of workmaster Henrik Wigström,
assay mark of St. Petersburg 1908–1917, 72 (*zolotnik*)
Original fitted case stamped with Fabergé's Imperial Warrant,
Petrograd, Moscow, Odessa (1914–1917)

Shaped as a two-sided Louis XVI-style fire-screen, with opalescent
white translucent enamel panels over *guilloché moiré* ground;
applied with varicoloured gold husks and four-colour gold flower
swags, oval apertures with split pearl borders, reeded gold and
opaque white enamel columns with pearl finials, laurel leaf and
flower wreath cresting. Photographs of Tsar Nicholas and Tsarina
Alexandra Feodorovna of later date.

Provenance: Maurice Sandoz, Switzerland; Lansdell K. Christie,
Long Island, New York.
Literature: Snowman 1962, p. 147, pl. XXVII; Waterfield/Forbes
1978, pp. 62, 63; Kelly 1983, ill. p. 5, fig. 4; Solodkoff 1984,
ill. p. 170; Forbes 1986, ill. p. 55; Habsburg 1987, ill. p. 245.
Exhibitions: ALVR 1961, cat. 183, ill. p. 68; Corcoran 1961, cat. 6,
ill. p. 27; ALVR 1968, cat. 365, ill. p. 137; V&A 1977, cat. L 1, p.
71; Virginia/Minneapolis/Chicago 1983, cat. 17, ill. p. 6; Fort
Worth 1983, cat. 5; Detroit 1984, cat. 52; Munich 1986/87, cat.
493; Lugano 1987, cat. 29, ill. p. 56; Paris 1987, cat. 29, ill. p. 52.

The FORBES Magazine Collection, New York (FAB73005)

263

TABLE BOX

Silver gilt, enamel

L: 14.2 cm W: 10.5 cm

Marks: Fabergé (in Latin letters), initials of workmaster Henrik Wigström, assay mark of St. Petersburg 1908–1917, 88 (*zolotnik*), inv. 22683. London import marks for 1912–1913.

Silver gilt and waved red *guilloché* enamel table box of waisted shape with *D*-shaped handle; two lidded compartments; upper reed-and-tie border, lower laurel leaf border; handle chased with laurel leaves.

This box appears in Wigström's design books as no. 13175 with the date '25 IX 1912' (old Russian style) or 12 October 1912 (new style) (see Tillander-Godenhielm, 'New Light on the Workshop of Henrik Wigström', fig. 3).

Provenance: Sold at Fabergé's, London to R. Young Esq.
(14 October 1912, 'Box, red enamel [no.] 22683 [price] £ 60 [cost] R. 358).

Courtesy of A La Vieille Russie

264

COMPOSITE NEPHRITE DESK SET
Nephrite, gold, silver, enamel
H: (clock) 20.5 cm L: (tray) 21.5 cm
Marks: Fabergé, initials of workmaster Henrik Wigström,
assay mark of St. Petersburg 1899–1908,
initials of assay master A. Richter

In the Louis XVI style; objects carved with fluting, applied with
gold fluting, husks, laurel swags, and reed-and-tie and laurel-and-
tie borders. Desk set consists of:

1. an upright table clock	7. pen
2. inkpot	8. pencil
3. matchbox	9. another matching table clock
4. bell-push	10. pair of candlesticks
5. blotter	11. gumpot
6. pentray	

Provenance: Nos. 1–8, King Farouk of Egypt; Sir Bernard Eckstein;
nos. 9–11, Dr James Hasson.
Literature: Bainbridge 1966, pl. 41 (nos. 9–11); Thyssen 1984,
no. 125, ill. p. 343; Habsburg 1987, ill. p. 170.
Exhibitions: Munich 1986/87, cat. 241; Zurich 1989, cat. 67,
ill. pp. 91, 92.

Thyssen-Bornemisza Collection

265

LOUIS XVI-STYLE CLOCK
Silver, gold, rubies, enamel
H: 20 cm L: 9.5 cm
Marks: Fabergé, initials of workmaster Henrik Wigström,
assay mark of St. Petersburg 1899–1908,
initials of assay master A. Richter, 88 (*zolotnik*), inv. 13891

Opaque pale blue enamel circular clock case with laurel leaf bezel,
white enamel dial, Arabic numerals, and gold hands; surmounted
by ribbon cresting. Stands on a fluted column applied with gold
husks, reed-and-tie border, laurel swags, and band.

Provenance: Acquired 1981.
Exhibitions: Leningrad 1985, cat. 158; Elagin Palace 1989, cat. 23.

'Peterhof' State Museum-Reserve (Inv. PDMP 334)

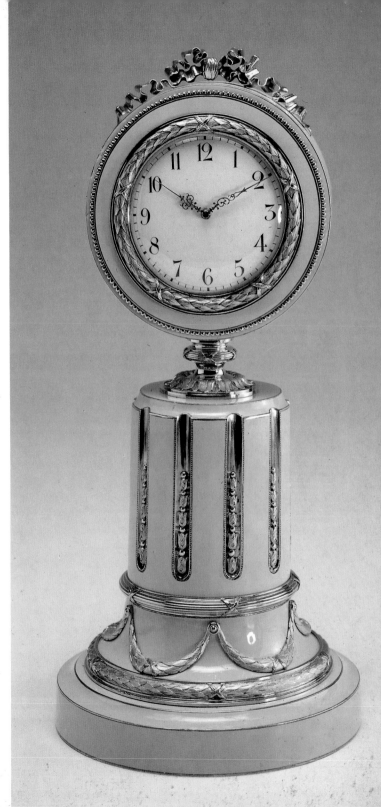

Victor Aarne

266

CANE HANDLE
Bowenite, gold, rubies, emeralds
H: 9.5 cm W: 9.5 cm
Marks: Fabergé, initials of workmaster Victor Aarne,
assay mark of St. Petersburg 1899–1908

L-shaped bowenite cane handle applied with gold foliage and
blossoms, set with cabochon rubies and emeralds.

State Historical Museum, Moscow (Inv. 108073/ok 23506)

267

HEART-SHAPED FRAME
Gilded silver, gold, enamel, ivory
H: 8.3 cm W: 6.8 cm
Marks: Fabergé, initials of workmaster Victor Aarne,
assay mark of St. Petersburg 1899–1908, 88 (*zolotnik*), inv. 3383

Opalescent white *guilloché* enamel, with beaded gold border, oval
bezel with laurel leaf border; applied three-colour gold laurel
swags and flower sprays. Ivory back and silver-gilt strut.

Literature: Habsburg 1987, ill. p. 245.
Exhibitions: Munich 1986/87, cat. 490; Zurich 1989, cat. 95.

Madame Josiane Woolf, France

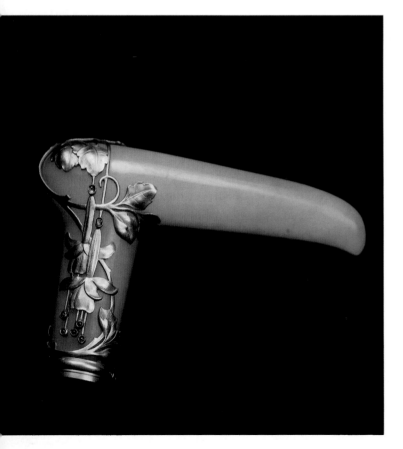

Hjalmar Armfelt

268

'THE WEDDING GIFT', TWO SILVER SLEDGES ON HARDSTONE BLOCK
Silver, quartz
L: 33.5 cm
Marks: Initials of workmaster Hjalmar Armfelt, assay mark of
St. Petersburg 1908–1917

Model of two silver sledges drawn by horses, one with a driver and
passenger, the other with driver only, on yellowish white quartz
base simulating snow; base applied with plaque inscribed in
Russian: 'SCHMUL JANKELOWITSCH MORDOWSKI EN ROUTE 1915'.

This group commemorates an actual event and portrays Mr
Mordowski travelling to a wedding, laden with a large silver tea-
and coffee-service from Fabergé, complete with table, as wedding
gifts.

Exhibitions: Helsinki 1980, ill. 94, pp. 96, 97. The event is
described in detail based on the memoirs of an old gentleman,
1965.

Private collection, Finland

269

OVAL DOUBLE BELL-PUSH
Birchwood, silver gilt, enamel, pearls, mecca stones
L: 10 cm
Marks: Fabergé, initials of workmaster Hjalmar Armfelt,
assay mark of St. Petersburg 1899–1908, initials of assay master
Iakov Liapunov, 88 (*zolotnik*)

Of birchwood; pushpieces of pink and grey cabochon mecca stones
in opaque white enamel mounts, applied with acanthus scrolls and
a trophy of Music; stands on four stud feet.

'Peterhof' State Museum-Reserve (Inv. PDMP 778)

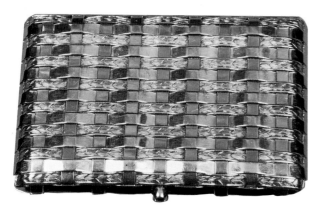

August Hollming

270

'TULIP' BROOCH
Gold, diamonds, aquamarine
L: 5 cm
Marks: Initials of workmaster August Hollming

Of floral shape; stem, three leaves, and petals set with brilliants and rose diamonds, flower set with a single faceted aquamarine.

Based on mid-eighteenth-century brooches amongst the Russian Crown Jewels.

Exhibitions: ALVR 1983, cat. 355.

Courtesy of A La Vieille Russie

271

WOVEN GOLD AND PLATINUM CIGARETTE CASE
Gold, platinum, diamond
L: 8.1 cm
Marks: Fabergé, initials of workmaster August Hollming, 1899–1908, 72 (*zolotnik*)

Basket weave design with burnished interlacing bands of platinum and red gold, with green gold bands chased with laurel leaves; circular-cut diamond pushpiece.

Literature: Snowman 1979, ill. p. 54; Habsburg 1987, ill. p. 153.
Exhibitions: V&A 1977, cat. R 17; Munich 1986/87, cat. 162.

Mrs A. Kenneth Snowman, London

272

AGATE BROOCH
Gold, silver, agate, diamonds, ruby
W: 3.4 cm
Marks: Initials of workmaster August Hollming(?), assay mark of St. Petersburg before 1899

A rectangular dendritic agate plaque, encased in a frame of rose diamonds with a ruby in the centre.

Provenance: P. Schukin Collection.
Exhibitions: Mikimoto 1991, cat. 39.

State Historical Museum, Moscow (Inv. 14714/ok 2142)

August Holmström

273
GRISAILLE PIN
Gold, enamel, diamonds
W: 3.8 cm
Marks: Fabergé (engraved), initials of workmaster August Holmström

Camaieu rose painting of a seated cupid, allegorical of winter, after François Boucher, in a frame of grey *guilloché* enamel between two bands of rose diamonds, surmounted by a diamond-set flower spray.

This image is almost identical to one of a series of eight grisaille enamels painted by Vasilii Zuiev which decorate the egg presented to Dowager Empress Maria Feodorovna, Easter 1914 (cat. 9).

Provenance: Ruth E. Gould, New York.
Literature: Solodkoff 1984, p. 100; Forbes 1986, ill. p. 55; Habsburg 1987, ill. p. 141.
Exhibitions: Fort Worth 1983, cat. 72; Baltimore 1984, cat. 24; Detroit 1984, cat. 73; Munich 1986/87, cat. 105; Lugano 1987, cat. 90, ill. p. 90; Paris 1987, cat. 90, ill. p. 86.

The FORBES Magazine Collection, New York (FAB83006)

Anders Nevalainen

274
SPIRIT LAMP SHAPED AS A LIGHTHOUSE
Silver
H: 11.5 cm
Marks: Fabergé, initials of workmaster Anders Nevalainen, assay mark of St. Petersburg 1899–1908, initials of assay master A. Richter

Of tapering shape; chased with stiff leaf border at base, two bands of rosettes, and gadrooned top.

The State Hermitage, St. Petersburg (Inv. ERO – 4318)

Julius Rappoport

275

A PAIR OF CANDLESTICKS
Nephrite, silver
H: 13 cm
Marks: Fabergé, initials of workmaster Julius Rappoport,
assay mark of St. Petersburg, 88 (*zolotnik*), inv. 2026

Pair of nephrite and silver candlesticks, standing on silver bases
with three winged griffin feet, fluted hemispherical nephrite parts,
fluted and gadrooned nozzles.

Provenance: From the Leningrad Regional Department Museum
of Public Education, 1926, Count Sheremetev's House, in the
Fountain House.
Literature: Berniakovich 1977, cat. 190.
Exhibitions: Leningrad 1975, cat. 256; Sofia 1984, cat. 46, 47.

The State Hermitage, St. Petersburg (Inv. ERO – 4922, 4923)

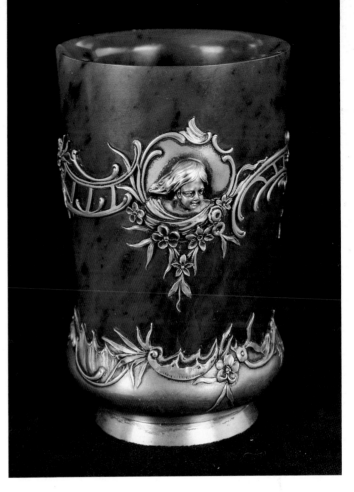

276

NEPHRITE BEAKER
Nephrite, silver
H: 11 cm
Marks: Fabergé, initials of workmaster Julius Rappoport,
assay mark of St. Petersburg before 1899, 88 (*zolotnik*),
initials of assay master Alexander Sewjer

Slightly tapering beaker applied with rococo scrolls and flowers
and with a child's head in a cartouche, on similar base.

Provenance: Diamond Room of the Winter Palace.
Literature: Berniakovich 1977, no. 190.

The State Hermitage, St. Petersburg (Inv. ERO – 4911)

Gabriel Niukkanen

277

CIGARETTE CASE

Gold, sapphire, cotton

L: 9.6 cm

Marks: Initials of workmaster Gabriel Niukkanen,
assay mark of St. Petersburg before 1899

Red gold case chased with fan-shaped concentric circle segments;
with cabochon sapphire thumbpiece, match compartment, and
gold-tipped tindercord.

Literature: Bainbridge 1968, pl. 106; Snowman 1979, p. 48.

Courtesy of Wartski, London

Eduard Schramm

278

ART NOUVEAU JEWELLED GOLD DISH
Gold, rubies, sapphires, diamonds
Diam: 10.8 cm
Marks: Initials of workmaster Eduard Schramm, 72 (*zolotnik*),
inv. 24870

Of shaped circular form of yellow gold, chased with swirling
rocaille, acanthus foliage, and flower heads set with cabochon
stones; centre with flower spray set with rose-cut diamonds.

Literature: Habsburg 1987, ill. p. 155.
Exhibitions: V&A 1977, cat. O 17; Munich 1986/87, cat. 167;
Zurich 1989, cat. 30.

Madame Josiane Woolf, France

Cigarette Cases from the
Luzarche d'Azay Estate

Charles Antoine Roger Luzachre d'Azay (1872–1961) played an elusive role in the French army and is suspected to have been in the *Renseignements*. Unmarried, wealthy, and fluent in both English and German, he was registered as *Maréchal de Logis* between 1893 and 1914 and served in the cavalry in the 32d, 23d, and 22d *Régiment de Dragons* from 1914 to 1918. His participation in various campaigns is proudly cited in the series of Fabergé and Cartier cigarette cases left to the Musée des Arts Décoratifs. The following eighteen cases by Fabergé and a number of cases by Cartier bear the dates of 31 December or 1 January and must have been New Year presents. The Arabic inscription that recurs on a number of the cases remains to be explained, as does the role he played in connection with Russia. His name appears once in Fabergé's London sales ledgers. The remainder of his commissions must have been made directly in St. Petersburg and Moscow.

279

RECTANGULAR ENAMELLED GOLD CIGARETTE CASE AND
VESTA CASE
Gold, enamel, moonstones
Cigarette case L: 8.2 cm W: 5.3 cm; vesta case L: 5.9 cm W: 3.8 cm
Marks: Fabergé, initials of workmaster Mikhail Perkhin, assay mark of St. Petersburg 1899–1908, initials of assay master Iakov Liapunov, 56 (*zolotnik*)

Primrose yellow enamel over engine-turned ground, black sunray pattern issuing from cabochon moonstone thumbpiece, panels painted with entwined *camaieu brun* foliage swags.

Musée des Arts Décoratifs, Paris (Inv. 39438 A/B), Estate Luzarche d'Azay, 1962

280

RECTANGULAR GOLD CIGARETTE CASE

Gold, lacquer, diamonds, cotton

L: 10 cm W: 6.4 cm

Marks: Fabergé (in Latin letters for export), initials of workmaster
Henrik Wigström, assay mark of St. Petersburg 1908–1917,
inv. 22913, 72 (*zolotnik*)

Vertically engine-turned reeded body of yellow gold with two
horizontal black enamel stripes, with rose-cut diamond
thumbpiece; interior inscribed in French: *'1 janvier 1913'*.
With match compartment and purple tindercord.

Exhibitions: MAD 1966, cat. 826; Amersfoort 1972, cat. 99;
Tokyo 1975, cat. 128.

Musée des Arts Décoratifs, Paris (Inv. 39444),
Estate Luzarche d'Azay, 1962

281

RECTANGULAR GOLD CIGARETTE CASE

Gold, sapphire, cotton

L: 9.4 cm W: 6 cm

Marks: Fabergé, initials of workmaster Henrik Wigström,
assay mark of St. Petersburg 1899–1908, initials of assay master
Iakov Liapunov, 72 (*zolotnik*)

Boldly chased with fan-shaped motifs in pink and yellow gold,
with cabochon sapphire thumbpiece; interior engraved with
monogram and date *'31 decembre 1901'*. Match compartment and
yellow/black tindercord.

Musée des Arts Décoratifs, Paris (Inv. 38339),
Estate Luzarche d'Azay, 1960

282

RECTANGULAR GOLD CIGARETTE CASE

Gold, enamel, cotton

L: 9.7 cm W: 6.9 cm

Marks: Fabergé, initials of workmaster Henrik Wigström,
assay mark of St. Petersburg 1899–1908,
initials of assay master A. Richter, 56 (*zolotnik*)

Of oval section, burnished gold cover applied with central
medallion containing monogram, blue Arabic lettering on white
ground; cover inscribed in French: *'4e Houzard, 1er Chasseurs
d'Afrique, 1er Senegalais, 32e Dragons, 10 Dsion. d'Inf.ie'*. Reverse
inscribed in French: *'22e Dragons/1894/Afrique/1895/Madagascar/
1908/Maroc/1914–1918/Argonne/Vauquois/Verdun/Avocourt/La
Somme/Bouchavesnes/St. Pierre Vast/L'Aisne/Roucy/Craonne/Route
44/Italie/Mourmansk/SPA'*. Central medallion bears an enamelled
Arabic inscription: 'To the most Holy One'. Interior inscribed: *'1er
janvier 1905'*. Match compartment and blue/white/red tindercord.

Musée des Arts Décoratifs, Paris (Inv. 39447),
Estate Luzarche d'Azay, 1962

283

RECTANGULAR GOLD CIGARETTE CASE

Gold, diamonds, rubies, emeralds, sapphires, cotton

L: 11.4 cm W: 7 cm

Marks: Fabergé, initials of workmaster Henrik Wigström,
assay mark of St. Petersburg 1899–1908,
initials of assay master Iakov Liapunov, 72 (*zolotnik*)

Of yellow, white, and red gold; inlaid on both sides with an Arabic
inscription: 'To the most Holy One'; also inlaid with map of the
Valley of the Nile, with towns inset in precious stones. Interior
dated '1904'. Match compartment and red tindercord with
crescent-shaped finial.

Exhibitions: MAD 1961/62, cat. 1393.

Musée des Arts Décoratifs, Paris (Inv. 38340),
Estate Luzarche d'Azay, 1960

284

OBLONG SAMORODOK GOLD CIGARETTE CASE
Gold, diamonds, morocco leather
L: 7.9 cm W: 5.1 cm
Marks: Fabergé's Imperial Warrant,
assay mark of Moscow before 1899, 56 (*zolotnik*)

Of yellow gold chased with horse-drawn carriage, coachman, and
two figures promenading in wooded landscape; reverse inset with
rose-cut diamond moon crescent and stars. Interior with
monogram and date: '*21 mai 1901*'. Leather etui.

Musée des Arts Décoratifs, Paris (Inv. 39440),
Estate Luzarche d'Azay, 1962

285

RECTANGULAR GOLD CIGARETTE CASE

Gold, cotton

L: 10.4 cm W: 6.7 cm

Marks: Fabergé, initials of workmaster Henrik Wigström,
assay mark of St. Petersburg 1908–1917, 72 (*zolotnik*)

Of yellow gold chased, burnished, and applied with a head of a
cobra, inlaid above with white gold Arabic inscription: 'To the
most Holy One'. Interior inscribed with date: '*1er janvier 1909*'.
Match compartment and blue/white/red tindercord.

Musée des Arts Décoratifs, Paris (Inv. 38342),
Estate Luzarche d'Azay, 1960

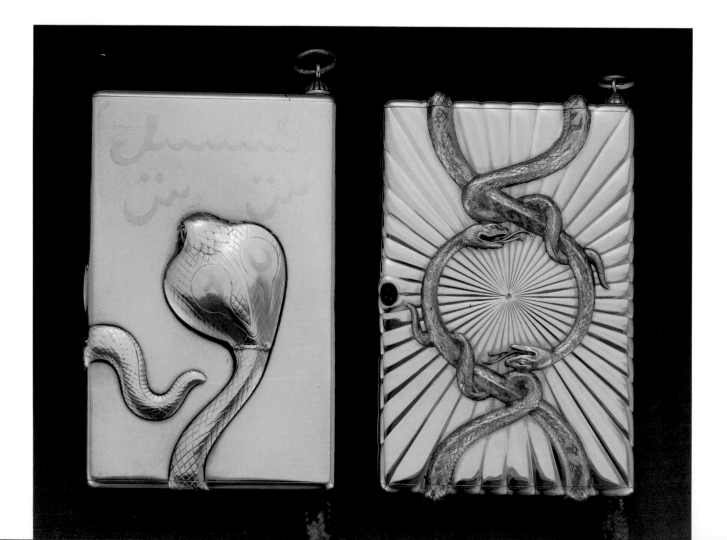

287

RECTANGULAR GOLD CIGARETTE CASE

Gold, enamel, diamonds, cotton

L: 6.4 cm W: 9.7 cm

Marks: Fabergé, initials of workmaster Henrik Wigström,
assay mark of St. Petersburg 1899–1908,
initials of assay master Iakov Liapunov, 72 (*zolotnik*)

Of burnished yellow gold. Arabic inscription applied in red *plique-a-jour* enamel: 'To the most Holy One'. With rose-cut diamond thumbpiece. Interior set with medallion of lady in profile dated: '*XXXI juillet MCMIV*' and inscription with date: '*1er janvier 1908*'. Match compartment and blue tindercord.

Musée des Art Décoratifs, Paris (Inv. 38341),
Estate Luzarche d'Azay, 1960

286

RECTANGULAR GOLD CIGARETTE CASE

Gold, ruby, cotton

L: 10.2 cm W: 6.8 cm

Marks: Fabergé, initials of workmaster Henrik Wigström,
assay mark of St. Petersburg 1908–1917, 72 (*zolotnik*)

Pink gold engine-turned with sunray fluting, applied with two chased entwined serpents in yellow and white gold. With cabochon ruby thumbpiece, match compartment, and black/grey/yellow tindercord.

A design for this case exists in Henrik Wigström's ledger ('Inv. 12646, 1/XII/1911') (see Tillander-Godenhielm, 'New Light on the Workshop of Henrik Wigström', fig. 25).

Exhibitions: MAD 1961/62, cat. 1394.

Musée des Arts Décoratifs, Paris (Inv. 38344);
Estate Luzarche d'Azay, 1960

RECTANGULAR GOLD CIGARETTE CASE

Gold, enamel, ruby, diamond, cotton

L: 9.7 cm W: 6.3 cm

Marks: Fabergé, initials of workmaster Henrik Wigström,
assay mark of St. Petersburg 1899–1908,
initials of assay master Iakov Liapunov, 72 (*zolotnik*)

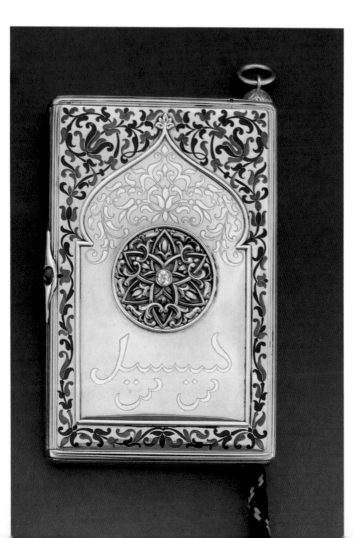

Cover burnished, chased, and inlaid in red, blue, and white
champlevé enamel with scrolling foliage, a *Mihrab*, a rosette
centring on a rose-cut diamond, with an Arabic inscription
beneath: 'To the most Holy One'. Reverse with enamel rosette.
Interior with dated inscription: '*1 janvier 1907*'. With cabochon
ruby thumbpiece. Match compartment and black/yellow
tindercord.

Musée des Arts Décoratifs, Paris (Inv. 39452),
Estate Luzarche d'Azay, 1962

289

RECTANGULAR IMPERIAL PRESENTATION GOLD CIGARETTE CASE

Gold, silver, enamel, diamonds

L: 10.2 cm W: 6.7 cm

Marks: Fabergé, initials of workmaster Henrik Wigström, assay mark of St. Petersburg 1908–1917, 72 (*zolotnik*)

Engine-turned reeded sides, cover applied with eagle, silver moon crescent, and '*Ich Dien*' in red enamel. Inlaid with Arabic inscription: 'To the most Holy One'. With rose-cut diamond thumbpiece. Interior with engraved date: '*31 decembre 1909*'.

Musée des Arts Décoratifs, Paris (Inv. 39454), Estate Luzarche d'Azay, 1962

290

OVAL GOLD CIGARETTE CASE

Gold, silver, diamonds

L: 9.3 cm W: 7.5 cm

Marks: Fabergé (in Latin letters for export), initials of workmaster Henrik Wigström, assay mark of St. Petersburg 1908–1917, 72 (*zolotnik*)

Vertically engine-turned reeded yellow gold body, cover inlaid with silver moon; reverse with inlaid silver Arabic inscription: 'To the most Holy One'. With rose-cut diamond thumbpiece. Interior inscribed: '*1 janvier 1914*'.

Musée des Arts Décoratifs, Paris (Inv. 39445), Estate Luzarche d'Azay, 1962

291

RECTANGULAR GOLD CIGARETTE CASE
Gold, ruby, cotton
L: 9.7 cm W: 6.2 cm
Marks: Fabergé, initials of workmaster August Holmström,
assay mark of St. Petersburg 1899–1908, 56 (*zolotnik*)

Chased with elongated fluted triangles in pink and yellow gold.
Interior inscribed with date: '*1 janvier 1901*'. With cabochon ruby
thumbpiece. Match compartment and black/yellow/grey
tindercord.

Exhibitions: MAD 1962, cat. 1392.

Musée des Arts Décoratifs, Paris (Inv. 38338),
Estate Luzarche d'Azay, 1960

292

RECTANGULAR GOLD CIGARETTE CASE
Gold, sapphire, cotton
L: 9.7 cm W: 6.2 cm
Marks: Fabergé, initials of workmaster August Hollming,
assay mark of St. Petersburg 1899–1908,
initials of assay master Iakov Liapunov, 56 (*zolotnik*)

Engine-turned yellow and red gold reeded body. Interior inscribed:
'*31 decembre 1920*', '*Amiens*', and '*Evian*'. With cabochon sapphire
thumbpiece. Match compartment and blue/red/white tindercord.

Exhibitions: MAD 1966.

Musée des Arts Décoratifs, Paris (Inv. 39443),
Estate Luzarche d'Azay, 1962

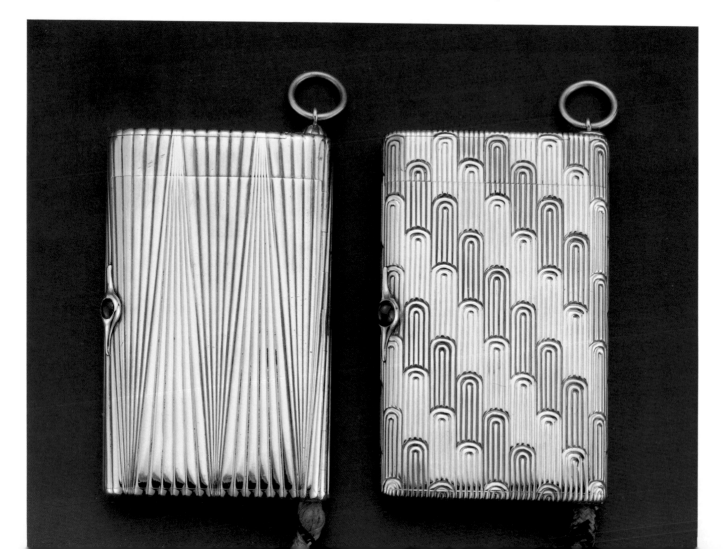

293

RECTANGULAR GOLD CIGARETTE CASE
Gold, enamel, silver
L: 9.8 cm W: 6.4 cm
Marks: Fabergé, initials of workmaster Henrik Wigström,
assay mark of St. Petersburg 1908–1917, 72 (*zolotnik*)

Of oval section; burnished gold cover inlaid in silver with Arabic
inscription: 'To the most Holy One'. Reverse engraved with map,
with silver moon crescent and applied green enamel inscription:
'*NIERI-KO 1914*'. Interior inscribed: '*1 janvier 1915*' and
'*Roquencourt-Versailles*'. Match compartment.

Musée des Arts Décoratifs, Paris (Inv. 39451),
Estate Luzarche d'Azay, 1962

294

RECTANGULAR GOLD CIGARETTE CASE

Gold, sapphire, cotton

L: 8.7 cm W: 7.5 cm

Marks: Fabergé, initials of workmaster August Hollming,
assay mark of St. Petersburg 1899–1908, 56 (*zolotnik*)

Burnished pink gold cover inlaid with yellow gold Arabic
inscription: 'To the most Holy One'; reverse inscribed in French in
capitals: '*Alors qu' on engage une bataille dont depend le salut du
pays, il importe de rappeler a tous que le moment n' est plus de
regarder en arrière, tous les efforts doivent etre employés à attaquer
et à refouler l' ennemi, une troupe qui ne peut plus avancer devra
coute que coute garder le terrain conquis et se faire tuer sur place
plutôt que de reculer, dans les circonstances actuelles aucune
défaillance ne peut etre tolerée*'. Interior inscribed: '*31 décembre
1902*'. With cabochon sapphire thumbpiece. Match compartment
and orange tindercord.

Musée des Arts Décoratifs, Paris (Inv. 39448),
Estate Luzarche d'Azay, 1962

295

RECTANGULAR SAMORODOK GOLD CIGARETTE CASE

Gold, diamonds, cabochon sapphire, silver, cotton

L: 9.8 cm W: 6.4 cm

Marks: Fabergé, initials of workmaster Henrik Wigström, assay mark of St. Petersburg 1899–1908, 82 (*zolotnik*)

Of oval section, cover centrally set with hinged red gold circular section and rose-cut diamond crescent moon; lifts to reveal silver medallion with female profile with date: *'XXXI juillet MCMIV'.* Interior inscribed '1906'. With cabochon sapphire thumbpiece.

Musée des Arts Décoratifs, Paris (Inv. 39449), Estate Luzarche d'Azay, 1962

296

RECTANGULAR GOLD CIGARETTE CASE

Gold, diamonds, platinum, enamel, cotton

L: 10 cm W: 6.2 cm

Marks: Fabergé, initials of workmaster Henrik Wigström, assay mark of St. Petersburg 1908–1917, 72 (*zolotnik*)

Cover chased with frontal elephant. A moon segment set with diamonds encircling hinged cover reveals a silver medallion chased with a female profile, inscribed: *'XXXI juillet MCMIV'.* Reverse inlaid in platinum with Arabic inscription: 'To the most Holy One', applied *'Moise'* in red enamel, and red enamel escutcheon with white cross. Interior inscribed: *'1 janvier 1911'.* With rose-cut diamond thumbpiece. Match compartment and green tindercord.

Musée des Arts Décoratifs, Paris (Inv. 38343), Estate Luzarche d'Azay, 1960

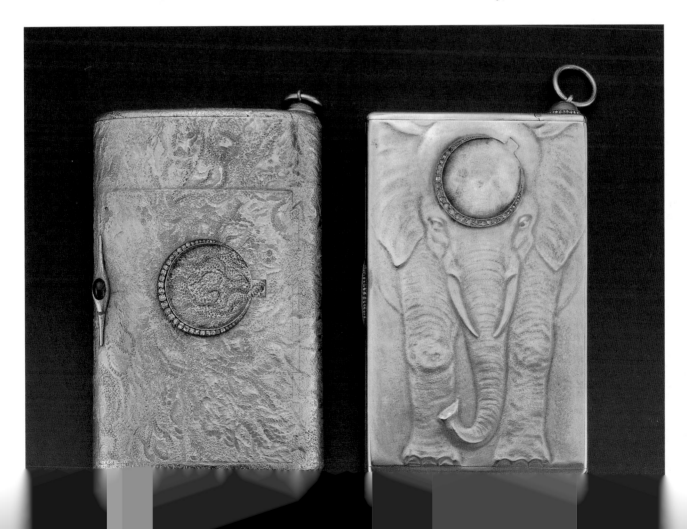

Forgeries

Following the death of Carl Fabergé in 1920, the forging of his creations began, where once it had been a rare occurrence. More recently, tens of thousands of fakes have been produced, mainly in the United States and in Russia, as seen in this selection of works by Russian forgers (also see Habsburg, 'Fauxbergé').

297

THE FIGURE OF A MERCHANT'S WIFE
Corundum, ceramics, chalcedony, agate, amazonite(?), jasper, rhodochrosite, lapis lazuli
H: 15.7 cm W: 9.4 cm Diam: 6.8 cm
By A. Konovalenko, Moscow, 1970s

Woman's figure in full height, with arms folded on her chest. Dressed in chalcedony jacket and cap, with wide amazonite skirt; over her shoulders she wears a large green jasper scarf ornamented with rhodochrosite and lapis lazuli stripes and held at the collar with an agate brooch. Face and hands made of ceramics, eyes of corundum.

State Historical Museum, Moscow (Inv. 102175/ok 17286)

298

'FABERGÉ' PERCHERON STALLION
Obsidian, gold, rubies, diamonds, phiantites, enamel
H: 13.5 cm
Spurious marks: K. Fabergé, initials of workmaster Mikhail
Perkhin, assay mark of St. Petersburg before 1899, 72 (*zolotnik*)

Obsidian horse with cabochon ruby eyes on white enamel ground,
bridle and reins of black enamel and gold, and gold horseshoes set
with phianites.

    An imitation by a Russian forger, almost identical in size to
an original figure in a private collection in the United States
(cf. Snowman 1964, pl. XXXV), but with the addition of white
enamel eye whites and jewelled hoofs.

Provenance: Moscow Customs, 1982.
Literature: Kovarskaia 1987, p. 155, ill. p. 128.

The Kremlin Armoury, Moscow
(State Historical Cultural Reserve, Inv. MR 10212)

299

'IMPERIAL EASTER EGG'
Porphyry, silver, metal, synthetic rubies
H: 35 cm
Spurious Fabergé marks

Spotted dark green porphyry egg with detachable cover, on three
silver-gilt double-headed eagles standing on ball feet, applied with
crowned initials 'N' and 'A'; domed cover applied with laurel
swags and surmounted by a double-headed eagle with spread
wings.

   This is a typical example of a recent Russian forgery.

Provenance: Moscow Customs, 1982.

The Kremlin Armoury, Moscow
(State Historical Cultural Reserve, Inv. MR 5653)

300

SEATED CHIMPANZEE

Bowenite, chalcedony, rubies, gold

H: 10.4 cm

Forged marks: Fabergé's Imperial Warrant, initials of workmaster Mikhail Perkhin, 96 (*zolotnik*)

Chimpanzee seated on its hind quarters, with crossed arms, cabochon ruby eyes; hardstone base, gold mount chased with laurel leaf border.

This copy of a Fabergé model was made in 1981 or 1982 by a group of forgers working in Leningrad: Yu. Zolotov, senior restoration master at the Miklukho-Maklai Ethnographic Institute (figure); N. Klochkov, jeweller, a member of the Artists' Union, from the Decorative and Applied art workshops (set and mounted rubies); A. Ivanov of the Restoration workshops (gold rim to the base); and V. Iakovlev, stonecarver (base).

Provenance: From the KGB Investigation Department, 1984.

'Peterhof' State Museum-Reserve (Inv. PDMP 533)

301

TOPER WITH A BEER TANKARD

Aventurine quartz, rhodonite, lapis lazuli, quarzite, jasper,
nephrite, obsidian, moss agate, flint, gold, silver, enamel,
diamonds, sapphires

H: 16.7 cm

Forged marks: *kokoshnik*, assay mark of St. Petersburg, 72
(*zolotnik*)

Inscribed in Russian: 'Fabergé, St. Pb. Morskaia 24'

Toper in early nineteenth-century attire seated on a stool, toasting
with a tankard.

   An interesting forgery made around 1981 or 1982 by the same
workshop as cat. 300 above: A. Korenkov, stonecarver at the
'Yuvelirprom' Institute (figure); Yu. Zolotov (face and hands); and
N. Klochkov (cut, set, and mounted precious stones).

Provenance: From the KGB Investigation Department, 1984.

'Peterhof' State Museum-Reserve (Inv. PDMP 532)

Drawings

A selection of forty-five Fabergé drawings from the
extensive collection of the State Hermitage in St. Petersburg
follows. Illustrated here are numerous projects submitted
to the Imperial Cabinet, many of which were rejected.
These drawings also demonstrate the close collaboration
that existed between Fabergé and the Imperial Cabinet.
A hitherto unknown aspect shown here is the series of
Imperial *cloisonné* enamel frames in the Neo-Russian style
that were designed in St. Petersburg, not Moscow.

302
Design for a silver box, optionally
decorated with pearls or turquoises,
and a monogram
Cardboard, pencil, ink, gouache
47.8 × 62.7 cm
Signed in Russian:
'Court Jeweller C. Fabergé'

The State Hermitage, St. Petersburg
(Inv. ERO III – 1493)

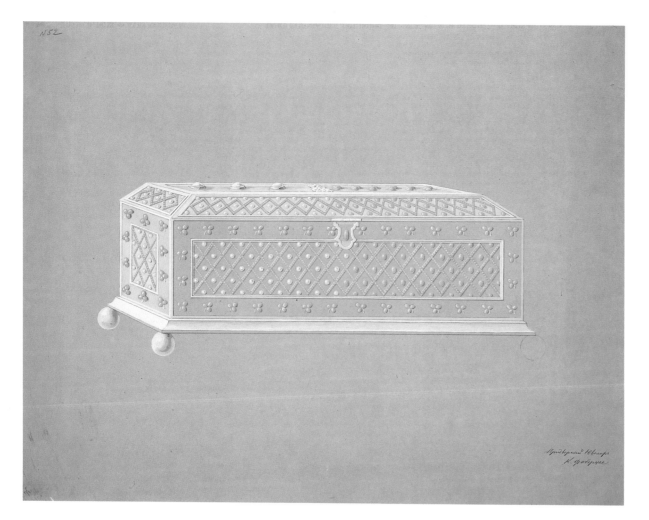

303
Design for a circular nephrite tray with
pink enamelled handles and diamond-set
crowned monograms 'N II' (in Russian)
and 'AW'.
Paper, watercolour, gouache
47.2 × 65.3 cm
Signed: 'C. Fabergé'

Presumably the finished work was
intended for presentation by Tsar Nicholas
II to Kaiser Wilhelm II and his wife
Augusta at the occasion of one of their
visits.

A virtually identical tray in the FORBES
Magazine Collection, New York, with
crowned Russian cyphers 'N II' and 'A'
was presented to the Imperial couple at
the Coronation in 1896 by Dignitaries of
the City of St. Petersburg (cf. Solodkoff
1984, p. 47). Another tray, with differing
handles, is in the collection of Lady Myra
Butter and Lady Georgina Kennard
(cat. 169).

The State Hermitage, St. Petersburg
(Inv. ERO III – 1596)

304

Design for a hardstone (Kalgan jasper?) vase on a stand, with entwined crowned initials 'N' (in diamonds) and 'A' (in rubies). Flanked by designs for crowned monogram 'W II A' and the State Emblems of Russia and Germany
Paper, watercolour, pencil
66.7 × 47.8 cm
Stamped in French:
'C. Fabergé, Joallier de la Cour. St. Petersbourg'
Inscribed in Russian: '4 monograms – 3200, 4 eagles – 600 – 3800 – 4200 rbls'.

Another design for a presentation piece from the Russian Imperial couple to the German Kaiser Wilhelm II and his wife Augusta, possibly for the occasion of their Silver Wedding Anniversary, 1906.

The State Hermitage, St. Petersburg (Inv. ERO III – 1613)

305

Design for a silver and purpurine(?) table clock shaped as a double-headed eagle
Paper, watercolour, pencil
38.8 × 27.5 cm
Stamped: Fabergé's Imperial Warrant, 'Court Jeweller. St. Petersburg'
Inscribed in Russian: '½ of natural height/750 rbls'.

An interesting adaptation to a table clock of the celebrated *Aigle de Suger* from the Abbaye de St. Denis (Musée du Louvre, Galerie d'Apollon, Paris), which Fabergé had copied elsewhere, but here he modified it into a Romanov double-headed eagle.

The State Hermitage, St. Petersburg (Inv. ERO III – 1592)

306
Design for a Louis XVI-style silver wine cooler and cover
Paper, watercolour, pencil
69 × 46 cm
Stamped: Fabergé's Imperial Warrant,
'Court Jeweller. St. Petersburg'

With lion head and ring handles, surmounted by a crowned
double-headed eagle and anchor.
   A wine cooler with an identical body but with a finial shaped as
an artichoke is in the Hermitage Collection (cat. 212), dated:
'18.V.1910'.

The State Hermitage, St. Petersburg (Inv. ERO III – 1619)

307
Design for a silver racing trophy applied with three double-headed
eagles, surmounted by an Imperial Crown
Paper, watercolour, pencil
35.7 × 25.2 cm
Stamped: Fabergé's Imperial Warrant,
'Court Jeweller. St. Petersburg'
Inscribed in Russian: '$\frac{1}{2}$ of natural height/900 rbls.'

One of numerous horse racing or sailing trophies that were
presented yearly by the Tsar (for another version cf. Habsburg
1987, cat. 31).

The State Hermitage, St. Petersburg (Inv. ERO III – 1593)

308–316
Nine designs for a silver toilet set in the
Louis XVI style, decorated with fluting
and laurel swags
Cardboard, watercolour, gouache
47.8 × 30.2 cm (cat. 308, 310)
30.2 × 47.8 cm (cat. 309, 311–316)
Inscriptions in Russian

The State Hermitage, St. Petersburg
(Inv. ERO III – 1698–1706)

308. Two-light candlestick. Stamped with
Fabergé's Imperial Warrant and 'Court
Jeweller. St. Petersburg'.
Inscribed: '½ natural height'.

309. Candlestick.

310. Three-fold mirror. Inscribed: '$\frac{1}{3}$ of natural height'.

311. Hand mirror.

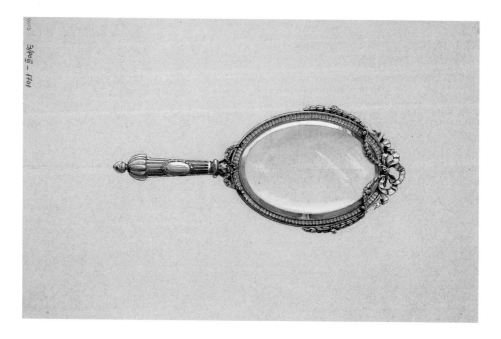

312. Ewer and basin. Inscribed: '$\frac{1}{2}$ of natural height'.

313. Two toilet boxes and two flacons. Inscribed: 'For hairpins', 'Large scent bottle', 'Tooth-powder', 'Small scent bottle'.

314. Two toilet boxes, a tooth glass and basin, and a pincushion, each item accordingly inscribed.

315. Large toilet box.

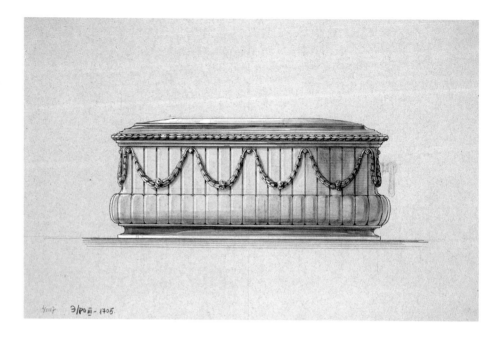

316. Glove box and boxes for toothbrushes and haircombs. Inscribed: 'For gloves', 'For toothbrushes', 'For haircombs'.

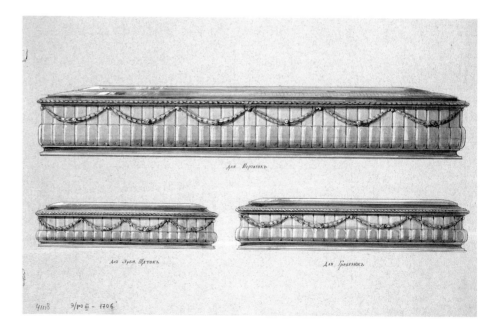

317–325
Nine designs for a silver toilet set in the
Empire style; some items with crowned
monogram 'M'
Cardboard, ink, gouache, watercolour
47.5 × 31.5 cm (cat. 317)
31.5 × 47.5 cm (cat. 315–318)
Stamped: On reverse with Fabergé's
Imperial Warrant and 'St. Petersburg'.
Inscriptions in Russian

The State Hermitage,
St. Petersburg (Inv. ERO III – 1707–1715)

317. Five-light candlestick shaped as a
female figure with a cornucopia. Inscribed:
'½ of natural height'. Stamped with
Fabergé's Imperial Warrant and 'St.
Petersburg'.

318. Three-fold mirror. Inscribed: '⅓ of natural height'.

319. Circular hand mirror.

320. Ewer and basin, with handle of jar shaped as a female figure. Inscribed: '½ of natural height'.

321. Two scent bottles and a waste bowl with tooth glass. Inscribed: 'Large scent bottle', 'Rinse cup with a glass', 'Small scent bottle'.

322. Toilet box. Inscribed: *Vide poches.*

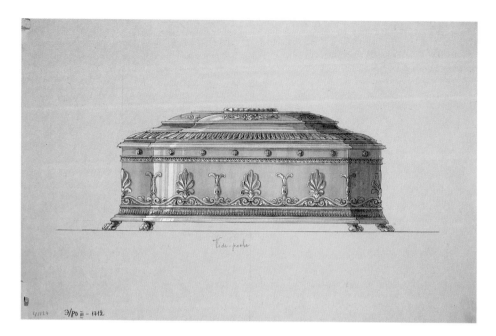

323. Four toilet boxes. Inscribed: 'For hairpins', 'For powder', 'Tooth-powder', 'For soap'.

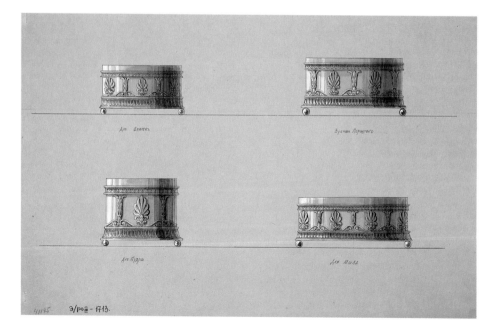

324. Pincushion and chamber candlestick, both with crowned monogram 'M'. Inscribed: 'A pillow for needles and pins'.

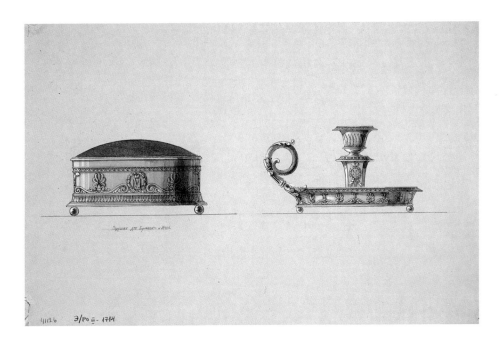

325. Three toilet boxes. Inscribed: 'For gloves', 'For toothbrushes', 'For haircombs'.

326–328
Three designs for a silver *surtout de table*
in the Empire style.
Cardboard, pencil, watercolour
27 × 36.4 cm each

The State Hermitage,
St. Petersburg (Inv. ERO III – 1722, 1724,
1725)

326. Centre-piece with female figures,
sphinxes, and swans. Inscribed in English:
'Empire'. Stamped with Fabergé's Imperial
Warrant and 'St. Petersburg'.

327. Tazza *en suite*. Stamped with Fabergé's Imperial Warrant and 'St. Petersburg'.

328. Silver and crystal *épergne* flanked by two similar sweetmeat dishes. Stamped with Fabergé's Imperial Warrant and 'St. Petersburg'.

329–332

Four designs of a silver *surtout de table* for the *trousseau de mariage* of Grand Duchess Olga Aleksandrovna, in the Neo-Baroque manner with crowned monogram 'AO'
Cardboard, pencil, ink, gouache
31 × 44.4 cm each
Signatures and inscriptions in Russian

These drawings for a Neo-Baroque service were submitted by Fabergé for the wedding of Grand Duchess Olga Aleksandrovna in 1901 to Peter, Duke of Oldenburg. They were apparently not executed.

The State Hermitage,
St. Petersburg (Inv. ERO III – 1718–1721)

329. Centre-piece for flowers, with two putti flanking the crowned monogram and two nymphs. Signed: 'C. Fabergé'.

330. Three fruit bowls, the central one with figures of a nymph and a putto, flanked by glass bowls on silver stands with figures of putti. Signed: 'C. Fabergé'.

331. Seven-light candelabra with figures of putti, flanked by two wine coolers. Inscribed above: '15 candles'. Signed: 'C. Fabergé'.

332. Fruit stand, front and back. Signed: 'C. Fabergé'.

333–334
Two designs of a silver *surtout de table* in
Louis XVI style for the *trousseau de
mariage* of Grand Duchess Olga
Aleksandrovna, with crowned monogram
'AO'
Cardboard, pencil, watercolour, gouache
30 × 41.7 cm each

The State Hermitage,
St. Petersburg (Inv. ERO III – 1695, 1697)

333. Centre-piece with five flower stands.
Inscribed in pencil in English: 'Louis XVI'.
Signed: 'C. Fabergé'.

334. Fruit stand with crystal bowl, flanked
by two two-tiered fruit stands *en suite*.
Signed: 'C. Fabergé'.

335
Design for a silver punch-bowl, cover, stand, and ladle
in the Old Russian style, set with cabochon stones surmounted
by a crowned double-headed eagle
Paper, watercolour, ink
61 × 46.3 cm
Stamped: 'K. Fabergé. St. Petersburg. 27 April 1911'
Inscribed in Russian: 'circular in plan/no plateau'

The State Hermitage, St. Petersburg (Inv. ERO III – 1606)

336
Design for a silver parcel-gilt cup and cover in the shape of the
Monomakh Crown, with stem shaped as a double-headed eagle;
dated 1913
Paper, watercolour, pencil
68.0 × 60.3 cm
Stamped: Fabergé's Imperial Warrant and
'Court Jeweller. St. Petersburg'
Inscribed: '600 rbls.'

Designed in the Old Russian style, this cup and cover were
intended for the Romanov Tercentenary in 1913.

The State Hermitage, St. Petersburg (Inv. ERO III – 1618)

337
Design for a chased parcel-gilt silver *kovsh* in the seventeenth-
century manner
Paper, watercolour
49.5 × 67.8 cm
Stamped: Faberge's Imperial Warrant and
'Court Jeweller. St. Petersburg'
Inscribed: '650 rbls.'

Decorated with the Romanov double-headed eagle, Monomakh
Crown, and the dates '1613' and 1913', this *kovsh* was intended for
the Romanov Tercentenary.

The State Hermitage, St. Petersburg (Inv. ERO III – 1617)

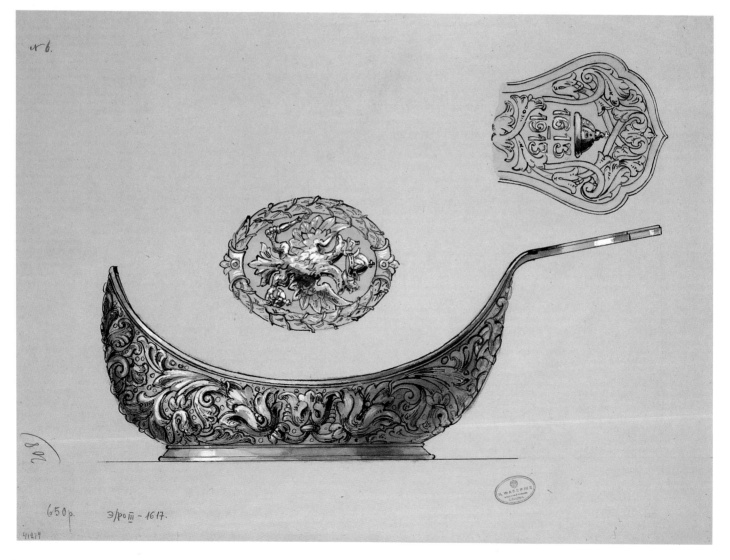

338

Design for a silver *kovsh* with figures of Old Russian warriors
Paper, watercolour, pencil
40.5 × 32.8 cm
Stamped: Fabergé's Imperial Warrant and
'Court Jeweller. St. Petersburg'
Inscribed in Russian: '½ of natural height/2000 rbls.'

While this is an almost exact design for the Forbes 'Monumental
Bogatyr Kovsh' (cat. 232), the main differences lie in the
decoration of the bowl and in the shape of the 'prow'.

The State Hermitage, St. Petersburg (Inv. ERO III – 1591)

339

Design for an enamelled silver charger and salt-cellar
in the Old Russian style
Paper, watercolour, pencil
54.2 × 46.3 cm
Signed: 'C. Fabergé'
Inscribed in Russian: 'Highest approval. Baron Frederiechs.
26 June 1902. St. Petersburg'

On top and at the bottom of the tray are State Emblems, to the
right and to the left are dates: '20 July' and '1902'.

These objects were intended for a state visit of a member of the
Swedish(?) Royal Family. Such items were traditionally given as
mementoes to visiting Heads of State or Kings (cf. Habsburg 1987,
cat. 557, 558).

The State Hermitage, St. Petersburg (Inv. ERO III – 1597)

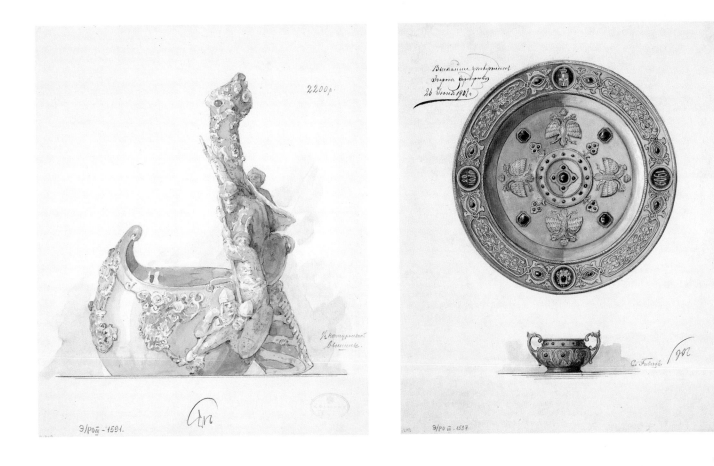

340

Design for a silver *kovsh* in the Old
Russian style, with figures of three
warriors
Paper, watercolour
34.1 × 47.5 cm
Stamped: 'K. Fabergé. St. Petersburg.
27 October 1910'
Inscribed in Russian: 'Three Warriors'

Based on V.V. Vasnetsov's painting
Three Warriors.

The State Hermitage, St. Petersburg
(Inv. ERO III – 1602)

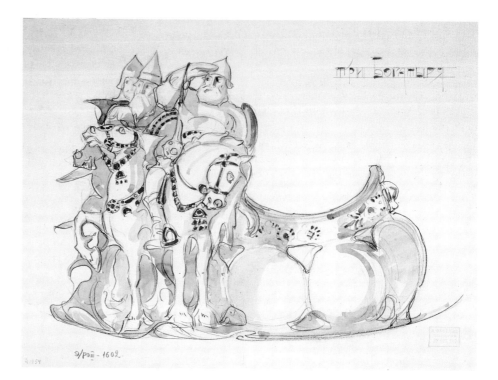

341

Studies for a silver 'Peter the Great' *kovsh*
Paper, watercolour, ink
41 × 65 cm
Stamped: 'K. Fabergé. St. Petersburg.
27 April 1911'
Inscribed in Russian: 'Kovsh of the time of
Peter the Great'

Details of front, interior, and handle of the
kovsh are shown and described.

The State Hermitage, St. Petersburg
(Inv. ERO III – 1608)

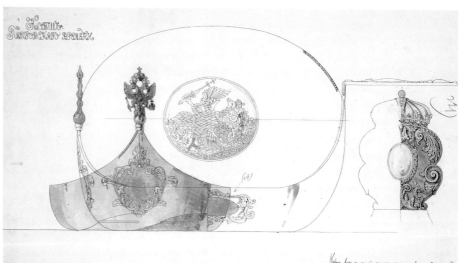

342

Study for a photograph frame in the Neo-Russian style crowned
with the Russian State Emblem, with options for decoration
Paper, watercolour, pencil
65.5 × 46.9 cm
Stamped: 'K. Fabergé. St. Petersburg. 13 March 1909'
Inscribed in Russian: 'No enamel/this side/old style eagle in the
frame/no legs'

The State Hermitage, St. Petersburg (Inv. ERO III – 1489)

343

Design for an Imperial frame in Neo-Russian style, with blue
cloisonné enamel decoration and cypher 'N II', surmounted by a
crowned double-headed eagle
Paper, watercolour, pencil
47.3 × 66 cm
Stamped: 'K. Fabergé. St. Petersburg. 13 March 1909'
Inscribed in Russian: 'light wood'

The State Hermitage, St. Petersburg (Inv. ERO III – 1488)

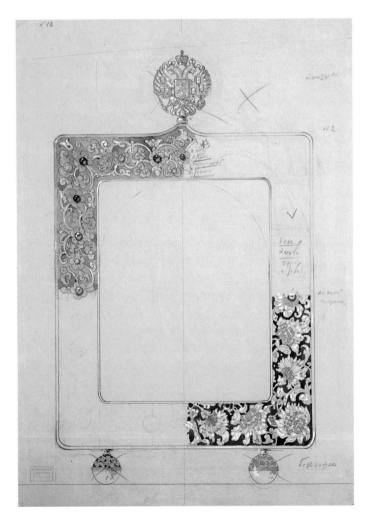

344
Design for a rectangular enamel frame with geometrical
ornament, surmounted by an Imperial Crown
Paper, watercolour, pencil
46.9 × 65.4 cm
Stamped: 'K. Fabergé. St. Petersburg. 13 March 1909'

The State Hermitage, St. Petersburg (Inv. ERO III – 1470)

345
Design for an Imperial frame in the Neo-Russian style,
with cypher 'N II', surmounted by a double-headed eagle
Paper, watercolour, pencil
46.9 × 65.6 cm
Stamped: 'K. Fabergé. St. Petersburg. 13 March 1909'
Inscribed in Russian: 'Edge, no enamel, no stones'

The State Hermitage, St. Petersburg (Inv. ERO III – 1488)

346
Design for a wooden photograph frame in the Neoclassical style, decorated with applied garlands
Paper, watercolour, pencil
69 × 45.7 cm
Stamped: Fabergé's Imperial Warrant and
'Court Jeweller. St. Petersburg, 1909'

The State Hermitage, St. Petersburg (Inv. ERO III – 1465)

347
Design for an Imperial wooden frame with gilded applications in the Neoclassical style
Paper, watercolour, pencil
46.0 × 69.2 cm
Stamped: Fabergé's Imperial Warrant and
'Court Jeweller. St. Petersburg'

The State Hermitage, St. Petersburg (Inv. ERO III – 1479)

Album of Jewellery Designs from the Fabergé Workshops

This album, which measures 50 × 60 cm, contains fifty-seven cardboard sheets, with gouache, pencil, and watercolour drawings applied to both sides of the cardboard. The album itself is bound in thick cardboard that has been covered with dark green fabric to imitate leather.

The drawings cover much of the early years of Fabergé's production, but numerous designs also stem from his mature period. The earliest of the dated drawings is 1876, while the later ones are marked with the stamps of the workshops of Wigström and Holmström. It can safely be assumed that the hibiscus flower brooches, sprigs of wheat, and bouquets of lilies-of-the-valley, which are consistent with jewellery production in France in the 1860s, span Fabergé's output during the first decades of the firm's existence. More sophisticated drawings, some of them signed A. Fabergé, show the input of the more adventurous spirit of Carl's brother Agathon between 1882 and 1895. A group of drawings of parasol handles and hand mirrors, dated 1905 and 1908, are signed by Henrik Wigström.

348
Emerald and diamond *résille* necklace
(no. 402)
Agathon Fabergé
Tinted cardboard, pencil, gouache
28 × 38 cm
Signed: 'A. Fabergé'
Ink stamp in lower right-hand corner:
'K. Fabergé. 18 B. Morskaya, St. Petersburg'

349
Emerald and diamond *résille* necklace
(no. 2)
Tinted cardboard, pencil, gouache
28 × 38.6 cm

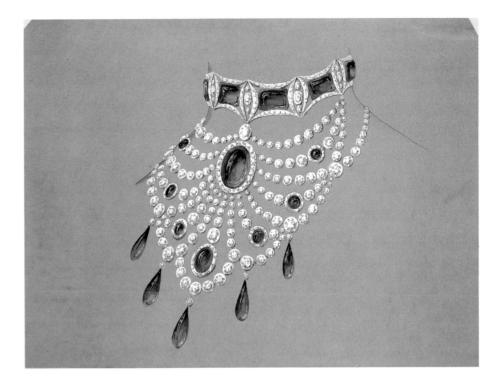

350
Emerald and diamond *résille* necklace
(no. 1)
Signed: 'A. Fabergé'
Tinted cardboard, pencil, gouache
26.2 × 38.5 cm

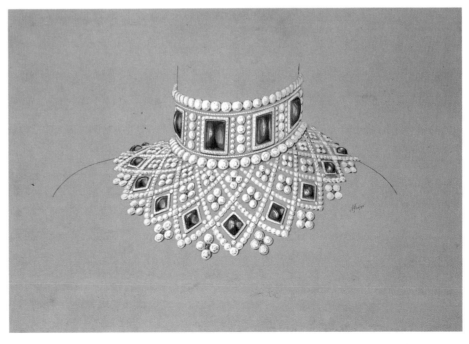

351
Designs for parasols and cane handles, belt
buckles, bracelets, and magnifying glasses
(nos. 325–335)
Paper, pencil, watercolour
6.7 – 21.3 cm × 4.5 – 19 cm
One design stamped 'K. Fabergé.
St. Petersburg. 16 May 1905' and another
stamped 'H. Wigström 15 March 1905'

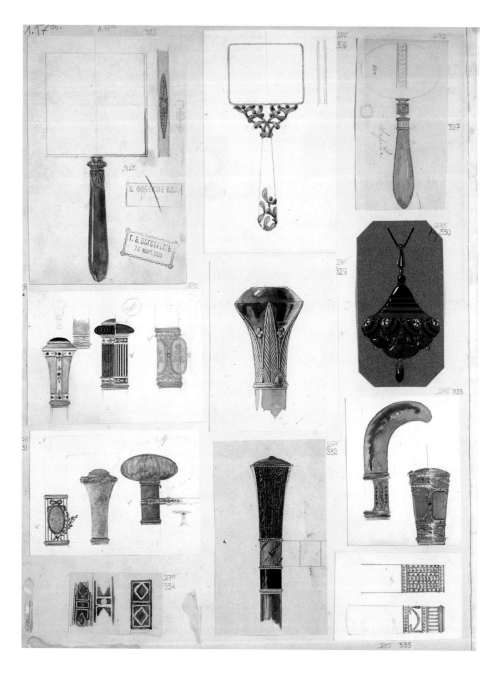

352
Detail of a diadem (no. 3)
Tinted paper, pencil, gouache
11.2 × 12 cm

Detail of a diadem (no. 4)
Paper, pencil, gouache
13.1 × 19.5 cm

Diadem (no. 5)
Tinted paper, pencil, gouache
8.3 × 25.8 cm

Diadem (no. 6)
Tinted paper, pencil, gouache
10 × 20.7 cm

Diadem (no. 7)
Paper, pencil, gouache
11.3 × 26.2 cm

353
Diamond chatelaine (no. 898)
Black paper, white gouache
33.2 × 16.5 cm
Signed: 'K. Fabergé'

Diamond *esclavage* (no. 899)
Black paper, white gouache
21.6 × 14.7 cm
Signed: 'K. Fabergé'

Diamond corsage brooch (no. 900)
Black paper, white gouache
12.4 × 10 cm

Diamond *esclavage* (no. 901)
Black paper, white gouache
17.7 × 10.8 cm
Signed: 'K. Fabergé'

Diamond *esclavage* (no. 902)
Black paper, white gouache
18.4 × 8.9 cm
Signature cut off

354

Diamond *sautoir* with tassels (no. 903)
Black paper, white gouache
28.2 × 21.3 cm
Signed: 'K. Fabergé'

Diamond and sapphire necklace (no. 904)
Black paper, white gouache
18.6 × 18.8 cm
Signed: 'K. Fabergé'
Inscribed in Russian: 'of 2200–18
November 04. 2300–2500'

Diamond and sapphire necklace (no. 905)
Black paper, white gouache
14.4 × 15.4 cm

Diamond and sapphire necklace (no. 906)
Black paper, white gouache
16 × 19.2 cm

Caricatures from an Album (Historic Journal since 1907)

Cardboard album, cloth, paper, pencil, watercolour ink
H: 22.5 cm W: 36 cm
By Evgeni Jakobson

This album contains thirty-two pages with fifty-four caricature drawings in pencil, watercolour, and ink. Dating between 1907 and 1914, these scenes were drawn by one of Fabergé's designers and depict various obscure comic incidents or situations in Fabergé's firm.

Provenance: Presented by V. N. Gonseva, granddaughter of the designer, 1990.

Elagin Palace Museum, St. Petersburg

355
'Eating the Boss's Food'
Paper, pencil, watercolour
11.3 × 14.7 cm

A group of Fabergé's employees are assembled for a meal. Fabergé presides to the left, to the right is Gurje.

356
'Winners of the Horse Race'
Paper, pencil, watercolour
16.6 × 23.1 cm

A scene at a stable with rear views of horses and three prizes displayed on wooden crates with a name-plate inscribed: 'K. Fabergé'.

357
'Incident on 16 July 1908;
Borisov and Gurje as protagonists'
Paper, pencil, watercolour
29.0 × 21.4 cm

A scandal at Fabergé's shop in
Bolshaya Morskaya Street involved
an elegant lady client.

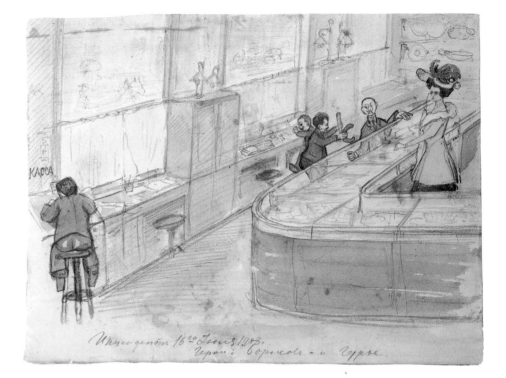

358
Caricature of Agathon Fabergé, 1912
Paper, pencil
18.7 × 22.6 cm

Inscribed: 'AF 4.IV.12'

Photographs of the
Alexander Palace Apartments

359
Tsarina Alexandra Feodorovna's Mauve Room
at the Alexander Palace, Tsarskoe Selo.

360
Tsarina Alexandra Feodorovna's Palisander Drawing-Room
at the Alexander Palace, Tsarskoe Selo.

Cat. 32, 37, 38, are visible on this photograph.

Photographs from the 1902 Album

Folder with ten photographs (each measuring 18 × 24 cm) of *A Charity Exhibition of Fabergé Artistic Objects, Old Miniatures, and Snuff-Boxes*, which was held in March 1902 at the von Dervise House on the English Embankment in St. Petersburg. The folder's cover is applied with the monogram of Empress Alexandra Feodorovna. (For two additional photographs see Lopato, 'New Insights into Fabergé from Russian Documents', figs. 2, 3).

The State Hermitage, St. Petersburg

361. Objects belonging to Her Imperial Majesty Empress Maria Feodorovna

365. Showcase with objects belonging to Grand Duchess Maria Georgievna and Maria Pavlovna

366. Showcase with objects belonging to Empress Alexandra Feodorovna

367. Console and mantelpiece with objects belonging to
Her Imperial Highness Grand Duchess Xenia Aleksandrovna
and to Empress Maria Feodorovna

368. Showcases with Easter eggs belonging to the Empresses

The Hermitage 1793 Carriage

Vladimir Chernyshev

For the Easter of 1897, Nicholas II presented his wife, Tsarina Alexandra Feodorovna, with a magnificent Easter egg by the celebrated Fabergé (cat. 110). The egg, made by jewellers Mikhail Perkhin and Henrik Wigström, contained a surprise: a miniature replica of the coach which, by tradition, drove the Empress to the Coronation in 1896.

The maker of the original carriage (fig. 1), Johann Konrad Buckendal (1725–1795), originated from Hannover and was the main supplier of carriages to the Court of St. Petersburg. Although German by birth, Buckendal is rightly considered a Russian artist. He spent most of his life – from 1756 to 1795 – in Russia. His main claim to fame is the carriage made for Catherine the Great in 1793. Buckendal trained a number of Russian artists who worked under his guidance and carried out his designs. These included apprentices Morozov, Surkov, Chubokov, and Polygalov, who later became masters in their own right.

The Hermitage coach is very characteristic of Buckendal's work. It is distinguished by the master's ability to combine elaborate decoration with exquisite form and lightness of structure. Buckendal's work was a blend of the best qualities of German, French, and Russian art.

The first alterations to the carriage probably did not occur until 1826 when the coach was restored for use by Empress Alexandra Feodorovna for the coronation of Tsar Nicholas I in Moscow. At that time were added the bronze Doric capitals and caryatids, rosettes and garlands, double-headed eagles, Nicholas I's monogram, and the Russian State Emblems on the doors of the carriage. It was probably then that the copper-gilt, aquamarine-set crown was placed on the roof.

For the coronation of Tsar Alexander II in 1856, the coach was restored again at the Court Carriage Department, upholstered with new Lyonnaise velvet, and re-gilt. The wheel stoppers were capped with metal gilded hubcaps, and some new embroidery was added.

In 1894 the crown on the top was renovated. The coach might have been used for Nicholas II and Alexandra Feodorovna's wedding cortège. Two years later it was renovated again for Nicholas II's coronation. The restorers, headed by coach master I. Breitigam, were paid 16,512 roubles for the work.

A contemporary photograph (fig. 2) shows the carriage as used by Alexandra Feodorovna in her ceremonial procession into Moscow before the coronation. In his book *Ocherki Deiatelnosti Ministerstva Imperatorskogo Dvora po Prigotovleniiu i Ustroistvu Torzhestv Sviaschennogo Koronovaniia v 1896 godu* (Activities of the Imperial Court Ministry for the Preparation of the ceremony of the 1896 Coronation) (vol. 3, St. Petersburg, 1896, p. 317), V. Pogozhev describes the Empress's carriage. His description is almost identical with the carriage with inventory no. 683 from the State Hermitage collection, except for some divergences in dimensions.

In 1917 the coach, along with other carriages from the Stable Museum, was evacuated to Moscow and not returned until 1929, when it was transferred from the Toy Museum, Moscow, to the Hermitage. (The Stable Museum had by that time been closed.) The velvet at the back of the coach had been lost, the aquamarine-set crown and the State Emblems on the door had disappeared, and some braids had been ripped off. During World War II the coach remained at the Hermitage. Further damages included a broken glass pane, and torn tassels and embroidery on the ceiling.

This remarkably well-preserved carriage was faithfully copied by Fabergé's craftsmen, including George Stein, who visited the Stable Museum numerous times. Work on the replica took fifteen months. Its inclusion in the Easter egg for 1897 was meant as a lasting souvenir to Tsarina Alexandra Feodorovna of her own accession to the Russian Imperial throne.

The carriage has been restored for this exhibition thanks to a generous grant from Ford Motor Company. Special assistance from Margaret Kelly, Curator of The FORBES Magazine Collection who provided photographs of the Fabergé miniature coach, made it possible to identify certain details needed for the precise restoration of the original carriage. Additional thanks are extended to Sepp Leaf Products, Inc., of New York City for its contribution of gold leaf.

369

COUPE COACH

Oak, ash, birch, lime, iron, steel, copper, brass, bronze, silver, gold, canvas, velvet, silk, horsehair, leather, glass
L: 512 cm W: 207 cm H: 270 cm
By Johann K. Buckendal, Imperial Court Stable Workshops, St. Petersburg, 1793
Renovated 1826, 1856, 1894, and 1896 (J. Breitigam)
Restored 1992–1993 in the Hermitage by the masters of the Specialised Restoration Workshops

The State Hermitage, St. Petersburg (Inv. 683)

Figure 1. Carriage made by Johann Konrad Buckendal for Catherine the Great in 1793. Photograph on *passe-partout*, 30 × 19.5 cm, by S.L. Levitski's studio, 1860s. Photo: Hermitage Library (Inv. 99761).

Coupé coach with two poles connecting the front and rear, a turning wheel, rear steps for the footmen, and seats for the coachman and pages. Carriage body suspended on four *C*-shaped transverse springs and also on longitudinal and transverse large and small straps. Windows with mirrored faceted glass. Folding steps attached to floor of carriage.

Most of the coach is covered with ornaments. Carved oak, laurel, and acanthus foliage, flower garlands, and similar motifs decorate the base. Two wooden carved putti with garlands in their hands are in the rear issuing from acanthus foliage. The outside of the carriage is upholstered with dark red (purple?) velvet, decorated with sequins, artificial diamonds, tassels, and golden embroidery of trelliswork, flowers, and foliage. Similar decoration is found on the roof of the coachman's seat. A copper-gilt crown set with artificial diamonds (originally with aquamarines) tops the roof of the carriage. Golden galloons with tassels are attached to the front and the rear. The cornice is set with bronze double-headed eagles with the monogram 'N I' and garlands with rosettes between them. At the corners of the body are gilded bronzes cast as Atlas supporting columns with capitals and bases. The doors are applied with (replacement) gilded brass Russian State Emblems. The carriage's interior is upholstered with velvet and embroidery on the ceiling.

Figure 2. Alexandra Feodorovna enters Moscow in Buckendal's carriage before her Coronation cortège, 1896.

Hallmarks

Géza von Habsburg

Head Workmasters

From 1872 to 1917, the Fabergé workshops in St. Petersburg operated under the direction of three Head Workmasters.

ERIK AUGUST KOLLIN
(28 December 1836 – St. Petersburg, 16 July 1901)
Apprenticed to goldsmith Alexander Palmen in Tammisaari, Finland, in 1852. Registered as a goldworker in St. Petersburg in 1858. Employed by August Holmström at Gustav Fabergé's workshop at Bolshaya Morskaya Street. Qualified as a Master in 1868 and opened his own workshop at 9 Kazanskaya Street. Served as Carl Fabergé's head workmaster from 1872 to 1886. Later worked independently and produced objects retailed by Fabergé. Specialised in Revivalist gold objects.

MIKHAIL EVLAMPIEVICH PERKHIN
(Olonetsk District, 1860 – St. Petersburg, 28 August 1903)
A self-taught goldsmith who learned his trade from rural craftsmen. Qualified as a Master and with Fabergé in 1884; head workmaster in 1886. Had workshops situated at 11 Bolshaya Morskaya Street, and from 1900 to 1903 at 24 Bolshaya Morskaya Street. Together with the brothers Carl and Agathon Fabergé introduced new techniques and inventions, including transparent enamels and varicoloured gold, the Imperial Easter eggs, and hardstone animals and flowers.

HENRIK EMANUEL WIGSTRÖM
(Tammisaari, 2 October 1862 – Kivennapa, 14 March 1923)
Registered as a goldworker in St. Petersburg in 1878. Became a journeyman under Mikhail Perkhin in 1884 and later his assistant. From 1903 served as Fabergé's head workmaster. Taught his son, *Henrik Wilhelm Wigström (1889–1934)*, who worked with him until 1917 and returned to Finland after the Revolution. Specialist in objects of art in Louis XVI style. In charge of production of Imperial Easter eggs from 1903 to 1917. Majority of Fabergé hardstone animals, flowers, and figures carry his hallmarks.

Workmasters

JOHANN VICTOR AARNE
(Tampere, 6 May 1863 – Viipuri, 30 June 1934)
Apprenticed to Johan Erik Hellstein in Tampere, Finland. Worked for Fabergé from 1880 to 1890, and from 1891 to 1904 at 58 Demidov Cross Street. Sold his workshop to Hjalmar Armfelt and returned to Finland in 1904.

FEODOR AFANASSIEV
Specialist in small work, including miniature Easter eggs, picture frames, and objects in gold, silver, and enamel.

KARL GUSTAV HJALMAR ARMFELT
(Artjarvi, 6 April 1873 – Helsinki, 22 July 1959)
In St. Petersburg from 1886 and apprenticed to silversmith Paul Sohlman.
Became a journeyman in 1891. Served as workmaster under Anders
Nevalainen from 1895 to 1904. Qualified as a Master in 1904 and acquired
Aarne's workshop at Ekaterinski Canal. Produced high-quality objects of
art in gold and silver and miniature frames until 1916.

ANDREI GORIANOV
Worked independently, supplying Fabergé with gold cigarette cases. Took
over Wilhelm Reimer's workshop in 1898. Items with his initials never
bear Fabergé's mark.

AUGUST FREDERIK HOLLMING
(Loppi, 3 December 1854 – Helsinki, 4 March 1913)
Apprenticed to Fridhoff Ekholm in Helsinki in 1870, becoming a
goldworker in St. Petersburg in 1876 and a Master in 1880. Worked at
35 Kazanskaya Street until 1900, then moved to the Fabergé house at
24 Bolshaya Morskaya Street. Son *Vaino Hollming (1885–1934)* and Otto
Hanhinen took over workshop (1913–1917). Specialist in fine enamelled
gold boxes and jewellery.

AUGUST WILHELM HOLMSTRÖM
(Helsinki, 2 October 1829 – St. Petersburg 1903)
Apprenticed to jeweller Herold in St. Petersburg, becoming a journeyman
in 1850 and a Master in 1857. Acquired workshop of goldsmith
Hammarström in 1857 and joined Gustav Fabergé as principal jeweller.
Remained Carl Fabergé's jeweller until 1903, when his son *Albert
Holmström (1876–1925)* and Lauri Ryynanen took over workshop.
August's superb-quality work includes the Lilies-of-the-Valley Basket and
the Miniature Replica of the Imperial Regalia (cat. 113). Albert's output
includes the Mosaic egg (cat. 29) and the 1913 Winter egg.

ГЛ

KARL GUSTAV JOHANSSON LUNDELL
(Loppi, 26 September 1833 – St. Petersburg, 29 May 1906)
Principal workmaster in Odessa. Initials found on some cigarette cases
retailed by Fabergé. Seems not to have qualified as a Master.

ANDERS MICKELSON
(Pyhtaa, 8 January 1839 – St. Petersburg, 8 November 1913)
In St. Petersburg by 1855. Master with his own workshop by 1867.
Possibly worked with Vladimir Soloviev in Philipp Theodor Ringe's
workshop. Produced cigarette cases and small enamelled objects.

ANDERS JOHANSSON NEVALAINEN
(Pielisjarvi, 1 January 1858 – Treijoki, 15 April 1933)
In St. Petersburg by 1874. Became a goldworker in 1875 and a Master in
1885. Worked in August Holmström's workshop, and later became an
independent workmaster, exclusively active for Fabergé. Produced mainly
enamelled objects and frames, silver-mounted ceramics, and wooden
items.

GABRIEL ZACHARIASSON NIUKKANEN
Master goldsmith with own workshop at 39 Kazanskaya Street from 1898 to 1912, where gold and silver cigarette cases were produced. For a time he managed the Odessa workshop.

 KNUT OSKAR PIHL
(Pohja, 13 April 1860 – Moscow, 22 August 1897)
Apprenticed to August Holmström. Became a Master in 1887. Served as head of the jewellery workshop at 4 Bolshoi Kiselny Street in Moscow from 1887 to 1897. Produced mainly small jewellery items. Family included daughter *Alma Theresia Pihl (1888–1976)*, who also designed for Fabergé.

 JULIUS ALEKSANDROVICH RAPPOPORT
(1864–1916)
Apprenticed to silversmith Scheff in Berlin. Resided in St. Petersburg by 1883. Head of Fabergé's silver factory at 65 Ekaterinski Canal. Production included large silver objects, animal figures, and silver-mounted objects.

 WILHELM REIMER
Manufactured small objects of gold and enamel.

 PHILIPP THEODOR RINGE
Independent workmaster from 1893. Occasionally made objects for Fabergé in gold, silver, and enamel.

 FEODOR RÜCKERT
Worked for Fabergé from 1877, producing objects in *cloisonné* enamel for the Moscow workshop. Worked independently for himself and for other retailers.

 EDUARD WILHELM SCHRAMM
Occasional supplier to Fabergé of gold cigarette cases and small gold objects, most with hammered surfaces.

 VLADIMIR SOLOVIEV
Minor silversmith and enameller who took over Theodor Ringe's workshop after Ringe's death. Specialised in pencils and other small objects.

 ALFRED THIELEMANN
Master in St. Petersburg from 1858. Head of Fabergé's second jewellery workshop from 1880. Specialised in small jewels, trinkets, and decorations.

 STEPHAN WÄKEVA
(Sakkijarvi, 4 November 1833 – St. Petersburg, 17 June 1910)
Apprentice silversmith in St. Petersburg by 1843. Became a journeyman in 1847 and a master in 1856. Workshop located at 5 Rozhdestvenskaya
 Street. Supplied Fabergé with silver articles, tea and coffee services, and table silver. Son *Aleksandr Wäkeva (1870–1957)* headed workshop between 1910 and 1917.

Hallmarks of the House of Fabergé

St. Petersburg

Firm's Marks

As a rule all items produced in St. Petersburg, whether in Fabergé's own workshops or under contract in other workshops, are marked with Fabergé's name, without an initial, in Cyrillic letters whenever possible. Small objects are sometimes marked with only the initials 'KF' in Cyrillic. Some silver objects made by Nevalainen or Rappoport have Fabergé's name, including the initial 'K' and a double-headed eagle in a round punch.

Workmaster's Marks

In general all Fabergé items in St. Petersburg, whether produced in Fabergé's workshops or retailed by the firm, carry the firm's mark in combination with the initials in Cyrillic of the head workmaster, the head of workshop, or the maker. Small items sometimes supplied by outworkers such as Gorianov, Niukkanen, Lundell, or Schramm, and after 1896, Kollin, often carry only the maker's initials.

Moscow

As a rule all objects made in Moscow bear the firm's mark, Fabergé's Imperial Warrant (a double-headed eagle above the full name 'K. Fabergé' in Cyrillic letters) and no workmaster's initials. Small objects are marked only 'KF' in Cyrillic letters. As opposed to St. Petersburg, where workmasters held individual contracts with Fabergé, Moscow was a partnership. Hence, with few exceptions workmasters did not apply their initials on Moscow products. The exceptions are silversmiths Nevalainen, Rappoport (and the First Silver Artel, which took over his workshop) and Wäkeva, who were all resident silversmiths in St. Petersburg.

London

Articles produced for export to Europe, and in particular to London, were hallmarked with Fabergé's name or with the initials 'CF' in Latin letters, together with the workmaster's initials. Most items sent to London for sale came from the workshop of Henrik Wigström. On smaller items the initials of Vladimir Soloviev are occasionally found beneath the translucent enamel.

The fitted cases

Several dozen makers of fitted cases were employed by Fabergé at each production centre. The linings of these cases – which are made of ivory-coloured holly wood, sycamore, or maple, or for larger items, oak – carry the names of the firm's locations under Fabergé's Imperial Warrant, which he obtained in 1885. The contents of the cases can often be dated by these stamps. Boxes that mention 'St. Petersburg' only under the Imperial Warrant generally date from before 1887. 'St. Petersburg, Moscow' indicate a date from 1887 until 1890, while 'St. Petersburg, Moscow, Odessa' point to an origination between 1890 and 1903. The addition of 'London' places the time of manufacture between 1903 and 1915. 'Odessa, Kiev' denotes a date between 1905 and 1910, and 'Petrograd' points to a date between 1914 and 1917.

Russian Hallmarks

Russian State Hallmarks

Until 1896[1]

 St. Petersburg
City coat of arms of crossed anchors and sceptre, combined with metal standard in *zolotniki*, and/or with initials of assay master and date.

 Moscow
City coat of arms of St. George and the Dragon, combined with metal standard in *zolotniki*, and/or with initials of assay master and date.

1896–1908

 St. Petersburg
Kokoshnik (female profile turned left), with metal standard to left and initials of assay master Iakov Liapunov or A. Richter to right.

 Moscow
Kokoshnik turned left, with metal standard to left and initials of assay master Ivan Lebedkin to right.

1908–1917

 St. Petersburg
Kokoshnik turned right, with small Greek letter *alpha* to left and metal standard to right.

 Moscow
Kokoshnik turned right, with small Greek letter *delta* to left and metal standard to right.

Precious metal standards
These are expressed in *zolotniki*, with one *zolotnik* corresponding to 4.25 grams and 96 *zolotnik* being pure gold or silver. Habitual standards are 56 (14kt) or 72 (18kt) for gold, and 84 (875), 88 (916), or 91 (947) for silver. Fabergé used metals only on the basis of their technical utility, not their material value. Thus enamelling was normally done on 84, rather than 91, standard silver, with the quality of the finished product being considered superior. The lawsuit with the Worshipful Company of Goldsmiths in London obliged him to use only the highest metal standard (91) for silver that was to be imported to Britain.

Note
1. On the opposite page Anne Odom provides a useful note on the controversy concerning the introduction of the *kokoshnik* mark.

The *Kokoshnik* Faces Left: 1896–1908

Anne Odom

There has long been discussion among Fabergé specialists about the date when the assay mark (e.g., the St. George for Moscow, the crossed anchors for St. Petersburg, etc.) on Russian silver changed to a national mark of the *kokoshnik* facing left. Kenneth Snowman, Marvin Ross, and the 1967 edition of Tamara Goldberg's monumental dictionary of Russian marks, *Russkoe zolotoe i serebriannoe delo, XV–XX vekov* (Russian Gold and Silversmith Work, XV–XX Centuries) all use 1896. Then in 1983 Marina Postnikova-Loseva came out with a new edition of this volume, in which she stated (p. 128) that a decree had been passed in 1896 announcing the change in marks and giving silversmiths three years to comply. The specialists all switched to 1899, as did Postnikova-Loseva herself.

Kenneth Snowman, however, was absolutely right when he noted in 1953 (p. 109) that there were no crossed anchors or St. Georges between 1896 and 1899. Before the *kokoshnik* was used, the assayers' mark in Moscow was usually stamped with the date, and no one has found any objects dated 1897, 1898, or 1899.

If the mark was not changed until 1899, what did the assayers use as a mark until 1899? If the 1899 mark was used for three years, this would mean an inordinately large number of objects with the dates of 1896 – a bubble in the production. This is not the case. It suggests, therefore, that the mark was changed immediately after the decree was issued in 1896.

Occasional instances occur when an object, such as the Lilies-of-the-Valley egg (cat. 23), which was presented in 1898, has the crossed anchors of St. Petersburg. (The miniatures are dated on the back 5 April 1898, but they would have been one of the last things applied.) The preparation time for the Imperial eggs is known to have been at least a year, sometimes longer, and marking the gold or silver base would have been the first step before any other decoration had been applied. There are also cases of inscriptions in 1897 or 1898 on objects with the old assay marks. Inscriptions are unreliable for dating because they were often added later.

It is the purpose of these comments to propose that all specialists consider returning to 1896 as the date when the assayers actually initiated the mark of the *kokoshnik* facing left.

Birbaum Memoirs

Translated by Felicity Cave

Introduction

A few years ago Valentin Skurlov discovered the memoirs of François (Franz) Petrovich Birbaum (fig. 1), one of the prominent employees of Carl Fabergé, among the papers of the renowned mineralogist A. E. Fersman. When speaking of the jewellers of the old school who were equally successful in the craft of jewellery, stonecarving, gem-cutting, and sculpting, A. E. Fersman said that 'the brightest figure was F. P. Birbaum, a Swiss by his origin, but a Russian by his life and love of Russia'.

After joining Fabergé in 1893, Birbaum soon became the firm's head workmaster. He was considered a 'trend-setter', especially in enamels. An excellent graphic artist, he initiated many interesting ideas and was responsible for some of the firm's most creative projects.

In the early 1900s Birbaum became a member and later Secretary of the Russian Society of Art and Industry, which was dedicated to 'disseminating art education amongst craftsmen' and which also 'set it as an honourable task for itself to support original creativity'.

'An initiative very useful for this purpose was undertaken by a member of the Society F. P. Birbaum who delivered a few lectures on enamel production with practical studies on making various sorts of enamels. These were preceded by an historic outline of enamel production since very old days' (*Prikladnoie Iskusstvo* magazine, 1905). A number of articles which Birbaum wrote for *Yuvelir, Iskusstvo i Zhizn, Iskusstvo i Khudozhestvennaia Promyshlennost, Vestnik Uchitelei Risovaniia* prove that he was not only a knowledgeable educator in jewellery and stonecarving but also a thoughtful theoretician.

In 1917–1918 Birbaum was actively involved in the Union of Arts. After the Revolution he worked for two years at the hardstone-cutting factory in Peterhof. In 1920 he left for Switzerland, from where he wrote letters offering his advice and services to the new Russia.

The memoirs of Birbaum published here have been previously edited so a few fragments of the original text are missing. The continuity of the text is not assured, and the original sequence of the chapters may be incorrect. The spelling of the proper names as well as the style of the original text have been kept intact.

Marina Lopato
October 1992

1. Franz Birbaum.

The founding of the Firm and a Survey of Production[1]

Fabergé's jewellery business was founded in Petrograd in 1885 by Gustav Fabergé.[2] The first workshop was modest, and the work produced was correspondingly so: somewhat clumsy gold bracelets, which were fashionable at the time, brooches and medallions in the form of straps with clasps, all made with varying degrees of skill. They were decorated with stones or enamels, and samples can still be seen in the old drawings of the firm. There were many similar workshops and, with the arrival in the business of two sons, Carl and Agathon Gustavovich, the workshop expanded and the artistic aspect of production became particularly important. Both brothers had received their artistic education abroad and were not slow in putting what they had learnt into practice. Carl Gustavovich was a convinced admirer of classical styles (which he has remained to this day) and devoted all his attention to these styles. Agathon Gustavovich, by nature more lively and impressionable, sought his inspiration everywhere – in ancient works of art, in Eastern styles which had been little studied at that time, and in nature. His extant drawings are evidence of constant work and ceaseless questing. Ten or more variations on one theme can often be found. However simple the object planned, he examined it from all points of view and started making it only when he had exhausted all possibilities and calculated all the effects. Suffice it to say that in his jewellery designing he was rarely satisfied with a drawing, so he made a wax model and set out all the stones in it, taking care to make the most of the beauty of each and every one. The design of a setting for large stones took weeks. Each stone had to be used to its best advantage and attention paid to whether the stone was to be in a brooch, a ring or a diadem; on one article it could pass unnoticed, on another just the opposite – all the qualities would stand out. Then the problem of the 'entourage', i.e., what should surround it, had to be decided. The 'entourage' should not diminish its qualities, but enhance them, while at the same time concealing any possible defects. Finally, the stone had to be positioned in such a way that it radiated the maximum quantity of rays. This is how Agathon Gustavovich worked, and I was fortunate to have been able to work with him for several years. It goes without saying that just as much attention was paid to the execution – an object was often rejected for an insignificant fault and put in the crucible, i.e., the melting pot. Some of the works that first made the brothers Fabergé famous were copies of Kerch ornaments (commissioned by the German Emperor Wilhelm II). The copy of the famous necklace with pendants in the shape of amphorae attracted the attention of specialists and of the Court circles. The execution of this work required not only considerable exactitude but also the reintroduction of some long-forgotten methods of working. The brothers Fabergé overcame all the obstacles brilliantly and subsequently received orders for a whole series of copies of Kerch antiquities. The Hermitage and its jewellery gallery became the school for the Fabergé jewellers. After the Kerch collection they studied all the ages that are represented there, especially the age of Elizabeth and Catherine II. Many of the gold and jewellery exhibits were copied precisely and then used as models for new compositions. Foreign antique dealers frequently suggested making series of objects without hall-marks or the name of the firm. This is one of the best proofs of the perfection of these works, but the proposals were, of course, rejected.

The compositions preserved the style of past centuries, but the objects were contemporary. There were cigarette cases and necessaires instead of snuff-boxes and desk clocks; inkpots, ash-trays, and electric bell-pushes instead of objects of fantasy with no particular purpose. Production increased daily, and it became necessary to assign goldwork to one workshop and subsequently silverwork to another. The brothers Fabergé had too much work and were unable to run the workshops properly, so they decided to establish autonomous workshops, whose owners would undertake to work only on the sketches and models of the firm and exclusively for it. This was how the jewellery workshops of Holmström and Thielemann were set up, as were the Reimer, Kollin, and Perkhin gold workshops and the silver workshops of Rappoport, Aarne, Wäkeva, and others. Each was allocated a specific form of production, and their apprentices specialised in different forms of work. All objects produced by these workshops bear the mark of the craftsman and, when space permits, the mark of the firm as well. Chronologically, the jewellery workshops of Reimer, Kollin, and Holmström came first. Reimer's was in the time of Gustav Fabergé, and I have already mentioned the nature of the work done there. In Kollin's workshops, copies of the Kerch antiquities were made and all the other work was of this kind. At that time settings of large engraved carnelians and other kinds of agate in the form of brooches, necklaces, etc. were very popular. These settings were made of high-quality matte gold in the form of hoops of fine beads, or laces, interlaced with carved or filigree ornamentation. The third workshop, which was exclusively devoted to jewellery, was managed by Holmström senior and, on his death, by his son. The workshop produced work of extreme precision and impeccable technique. The stones are perfectly fixed, in a way not seen even in the best Parisian work. On the whole, Parisian work is sometimes artistically superior, but from the technical point of view, the durability and finish of Holmström's work is always better. The workshop functioned for more than fifty years, and the nature of the jewellery work changed considerably. At the beginning, in the 1860s, diamonds and precious stones merely supplemented the gold, but then the traditions of the eighteenth and early nineteenth centuries were revived and the work was exclusively diamonds set in silver. The settings were calculated mainly for effect, and the chatons were highly polished, sloping in such a way that the stone seemed large. Soon this deceit palled, particularly because the silver tarnished and the eye was no longer deceived as to the size of the stones. Then the settings became as inconspicuous as possible, leaving only the barest essential thickness of metal. Favourite motifs were branches of blossoms, ears of wheat, and artfully tied ribbons; the modelling of the petals and the leaves were realised by welding and by the setting of the diamonds. They were carefully selected, their outline perfecting the details of the modelling. This was the best period for diamond work. The works of this period are characterised by a rich design, visible even at a distance. The fashion was for large diadems, small egret-plumes, necklaces in the shape of collars, breastplates for the corsage, clasps, and large ribbons. The following period was influenced by the 'Empire' style and was distinguished by a certain dryness. The severe lines of the meanders and volutes did not permit the use of reliefs; the diamonds were set flat and lost part of their effect, destroying each other with their brilliance. The 'Modern' style, which

appeared at the end of the nineteenth century, was not very widely reflected in the firm's jewellery: the artists were used to a certain artistic discipline and were not attracted by the undisciplined forms and the unbridled fantasy that often came close to the absurd. While we recognised the artistic merit of an individual artist's work, such as Lalique, we nevertheless considered it would be pointless to imitate him, and we were right. Imitators have left nothing that equals his work, but simply lost their own identity. With very few exceptions, which were special commissions, the firm did not produce any significant work in this genre. In a short time enthusiasm for the modernist style, with the vulgarity of its endless repetitions and the absence of content, began to wane. The new fashion was for detailed ornamentation, set with such small diamonds, both cut and uncut, that the works give the impression of a grey compact mass, even when seen from quite close. This kind of work is only suitable for some kinds of objects: rings, bracelets, brooches, and pendants, where the eye can distinguish and assess the richness of the design and the detailed finish. Most of this work was in platinum, pure or alloyed with silver. The use of platinum can be regarded as progress, as it does not tarnish and the beautiful grey shades emphasise the whiteness of the diamond. The abundance of straight parallel lines and concentric circles gives these works a dryness that no richness of detail can redeem.

A successful novelty of the work of this time was the use of single-faced, rectangular coloured stones. These stones are fixed in a narrow, even band, leaving no metal in the intervals between them. If the stones chosen are even, these coloured strips between the diamonds create a marvellous impression. Using too many small diamonds is a clumsy mistake in all respects, as the objects lose their playfulness, which is the chief advantage of a diamond. A superabundance of small stones lessens the material value of the work, while at the same time it considerably increases the cost of production. One can be sure that this fashion will be short-lived and that the art of the jeweller will once more return to healthier traditions.

Gold objects
There is no very clear dividing line between objects of jewellery i.e., those that are exclusively precious stones, and gold objects. A diamond, of

course, fits ill with gold as the contrast is too great, but precious stones are the perfect complement. Nevertheless, with the exception of simple brooches, rings, chains, and bracelets, gold was rarely used for women's jewellery. Its main use was in small objects of function: pocket necessaires, flacons for scent or salt, various non-table objects of fantasy and in objects for men: cigarette cases, cigarette holders, canes, seals, etc. Gold was worked in many different ways. It was cut, chased (*repoussé*), engraved and polished, covered with enamel and decorated with stones. As jewellery fashions changed there were periods when various styles of chased work were more dominant. Louis XIV, XV, XVI styles were fashionable for some time, to be followed by the Empire styles. Chasing (*repoussé*) was rarely used in the Empire styles, as the detailing was too dry: carved chasing and engraving were preferred. The last chronological period was distinguished by the extensive use of enamel. These had been used with gold from ancient times, but as *cloisonné* (sectioned) or *champlevé* (raised). The eighteenth-century works of art in the Hermitage inspired the use of transparent enamel on engraved and guilloched gold and silver. In these works, where fairly significant areas, sometimes the whole object, are covered with enamel, the firm's works were unsurpassed, even abroad. At the 1900 World Exhibition their richness of tone and perfect technique made them very successful. The works that were exhibited were all sold and attracted many orders and clients.

The manufacture of gold objects was distributed among several workshops. Kollin's workshop produced copies of the Kerch antiquities and other works of this kind. Perkhin's workshop produced chased and engraved works, settings in nephrite and other Siberian stones. This was important work; his workshop produced the best gold works. Perkhin, its owner, deserves a few words. He was born in the Olonetsk region and came to Petersburg as a boy, with no education at all, probably unable even to read and write. Hard work and natural quickness enabled him to progress from apprentice to workmaster and, with the help of the firm, to organise a workshop and attract able workers in all specialised areas of production. He combined an enormous capacity for work, knowledge of his subject and persistence in the pursuit of certain technical aims. He was highly esteemed by the firm and had a rare authority among the apprentices. He made a comfortable fortune in a relatively short time, but was unable to enjoy it as he died in a hospital for the mentally ill in [1903]. On his death the workshop passed to his senior apprentice and friend, with whom he had studied, A.G. Wigström.

A special workshop was designated for enamelling. It was run by N.A. Petrov and the fame of the firm's enamel works is mainly due to him. He was the son of the enameller A.F. Petrov. Since he was a child he had been familiar with the complicated process where there are so many failures, the reason usually being in the metal, the burning, or the enamel itself. He knew all the finer points of the technique and was successful in tasks which had defeated even very famous foreign enamellers. Had he had any artistic training he would without doubt have surpassed many of them. He was in his element when working – unlike other workmasters he himself worked on every job and often sat far into the night over a problem that interested him. If a commission was particularly important the firm often commissioned the same work both from him and from someone abroad but the foreign work was rarely superior. When the workshop was closed down, he was invited to the Mint to make enamel badges for the Red Army. This he did, to earn himself a living, though the work was of no interest to him, but he gave himself unstintingly to the job. Bad food and nervous exhaustion brought him down: the best enameller in Petrograd, perhaps in Russia, is no more. Both as a person and as a worker he was a kind, honest man.

The third workshop, Thielemann's, produced almost exclusively badges and medals, Jubilee and other kinds. This was to a certain extent imposed on them, as many of the firm's clients were dissatisfied with the official medals and badges, which were extremely clumsily made, and asked the firm to produce similar badges, but more artistically made. The workshop was mainly engaged in producing these private commissions and, sometimes, in the mass production of medals. On the death of the owner the workshop was taken over by the firm itself and managed by the workmaster V.G. Nikolaev.

Silver objects
Production started gradually and was at first of small articles, where the work was not very different from gold works and was executed by the workmasters described above. Demand soon necessitated the opening of special workshops. The first, under the workmaster Rappoport, produced very varied works, from small objects for the writing desk to vases, candelabras and whole sets, such as the ceremonial set of dinner table decorations (*surtout de table*). The largest object produced by this workshop was the *surtout de table* commissioned by Alexander III for the dowry of his daughter, the Grand Duchess Xenia Aleksandrovna. Sketches for this work were done by the architect . . ., but so badly that when the working drawings were done, in spite of all the alterations, the style and proportions[3] of these huge and valuable objects left a great deal to be desired. As the outline had been agreed by the Emperor, drastic alterations were out of the question and all that was possible was a certain amount of correction of detail. This shows yet again that drawing up plans for the production of works of art demands specialist knowledge of the production process from the artist. In the end Rappoport's workshop served as an interesting experiment. In 190 . . the owner decided to retire and, as a way of rewarding his workers, he left them the workshop and all the contents. The first Artel (cooperative) producing silver articles was formed, and the firm welcomed this experiment, giving the Artel the necessary credit and making sure it had orders. No more than twenty people were involved in this small business which reflected all the disadvantages inherent in all social organisations of the time: absence of solidarity, discipline, and lack of any understanding of common interests. After two or three years of internal strife the costs of production were increasing and quality was decreasing, so the Artel closed down. Its place in the firm's production was taken by Armfelt's workshop.

Silverware such as samovars, tea services, etc. was the specialty of Wäkeva's workshop. As the Moscow Fabergé factory produced table silver and silver dishes on a large scale, this workshop was only a subsidiary. The Petersburg workshops employed some 200 or 300 people before 1914. They were scattered all over the city until the firm built special premises in Morskaya street. Afterwards the chief workshops were accommodated in the outbuildings in the courtyard but for reasons of lack of space some of them remained outside the main building.

The Moscow Factory
As well as the Petersburg workshops there was the Moscow factory, founded in 1887. The factory combined all the specialties which in Petersburg were distributed among the various workshops. Some branches, for example, jewellery, gold and enamel works, were inferior, both in quality and quantity to those in Petersburg, but silverwork was more extensive and better organised. From 1900 all large silver orders were made by the Moscow factory. The jewellery and goldwork can be passed over as they were, on the whole, inferior editions of the Petersburg work, but silverwork deserves a special mention both for its artistic merits and for the organisation of production. The largest silverworks were concentrated in Moscow, which has always been the centre of silver production. I explain this phenomenon to myself in two ways: firstly an enterprise, like a plant, spreads seeds around (the workmasters) and these give rise to new plants (new businesses) and secondly, salaries in Moscow were always lower than in Petersburg and therefore the workforce was cheaper.

The first thing that distinguishes work produced by the Moscow firm is the predominance of the Russian folk style. One can disagree with many of its special characteristics, with the lack of purpose in its structure, the archaic, intentionally crude execution, but all these temporary defects are redeemed by the freshness of the design and the cliché-free composition. I shall indicate the main works of this genre in a special list. In most cases they are *bratini*, jugs, *kovshi*, caskets, and decorative vases, etc. Figures of heroes, folk poems and tales, historical events or people all served as subjects – as separate figures of groups, or in bas relief on the objects themselves. The works are mainly cast from wax models and one object only was produced from each model.

The Moscow factory also produced a great deal of table silver, which is qualitatively superior to foreign work. Works of rare perfection were produced at low cost, owing to a rich selection of dies and strong presses specially made for this purpose. The factory had at its disposal several thousand dies, whole or in parts.

A large part of the production was church silver and icons. The artistic qualities of many of these works found them a market abroad and brought in orders.

The administration: The factory building was

in Kiselny Lane. It occupied the building of the former St. Galli factory and was divided into two sections: jewellery, and gold and silver. At the head of each section was a workmaster, a manager and his assistant. The accounts for the whole factory were managed by one department, and the workforce varied from 200 to 300.

Some conclusions

Every business depends directly on the materials it uses and consequently on the industry that produces them. Thus, jewellery production depends on the mining and cutting of precious stones, gold and silver production on the quantity and quality of precious metals on the market. In this respect the businesses under discussion were working in particularly unfavourable conditions. The mining of precious and semi-precious stones in the Urals and Eastern Siberia was in a chaotic state: deposits were not mined but plundered; the methods of extraction were so primitive and badly organised that what was extracted was almost by chance, and only where no particular effort was required. The correct methods of extraction were not applied. The cutting of precious stones was so amateurish and imperfect that good stones were sent abroad for cutting and were lost in the markets there. In this way any even slightly exceptional stone found its way to Russian jewellers abroad, although some of them may first have seen the light of day in Siberia. Foreign lapidaries and dealers paid considerably over the odds in these deals.

Large quantities of semi-precious stones, azurites from Bukhara and Siberia, nephrites and others are taken to Germany and come back to us already cut. This is exactly what happened with the dressing of furs and leather, the processing of which has moved almost entirely to Germany.

The situation with precious metals is not much better. The processes of cleaning, smelting, and conversion into sheets were extremely imperfect. For fine work we had to order English silver. The acquisition of gold is complicated by all kinds of obstacles and prohibitions, and this means that small producers find it advantageous to melt down gold coins, in spite of the law.

Many faults in the treatment stem from imperfect equipment, but many also from carelessness in the process itself. I have been able to compare the process of rolling (converting bars of silver into sheets) both here and abroad. Abroad

this work is carried out with special care, in conditions of ideal cleanliness. In Russia the bars and sheets lay on the dirty floor, sometimes an earth floor. Substances stick to the metal and impress themselves on it as it passes through the rollers. It is not difficult to imagine the unexpected things that might happen when working with such metal. The extraneous admixtures come to the surface when the metal is being burnished, or they fall off, leaving all kinds of marks or pores.

Generally speaking, even in the big firms production is not organised rationally, and this leads to large-scale losses of material and of time. In foreign workshops dirty water passes through six or seven filters, leaving a deposit of the precious metal each time. In Russia we make do with one or two filters and for this reason the loss percentage of gold or silver is significantly higher. In a large firm this adds up to considerable sums of money. The sweepings containing metal are not purified in Russia: they are sent in barrels to Hamburg where they are burnt, and the requisite sum of money for the gold and silver recovered is paid to the sender. Attempts have been made to carry out the purifying in Russia, but the money paid over was always lower than the sum from abroad. This in all probability can be ascribed to the unsatisfactory methods of cleansing sweepings here and extracting precious metals from them.

If we look at the trade itself, then the main obstacle to its development must be the workmasters' lack of artistic and technical knowledge, the lack of specialist schools and technical or artistic literature. The existing artistic-industrial schools are not fulfilling their main task – the artistic and technical education of craftsmen – they only produce artists or drawing teachers. What production needs more than anything else is trained workmasters and craftsmen.

In other countries, as well as the numerous specialised schools and courses for craftsmen, there is extensive artistic and technical literature, and individual branches of the trade have their own periodicals. In Russia, not only are there no original works on these subjects, there are not even any translations of foreign publications. In conditions such as this it is hardly surprising that our firms lag far behind. What is surprising is that they still manage to compete with foreign firms. If they are sometimes successful in this struggle, it

is entirely due to the work of individual workmasters.

The Craftsman's world, Workmasters, Owners and Apprentices

There are some talented workmasters, but there is no regular supply, no army of good craftsmen to maintain production. The first and main condition for developing production and our guarantee of success in the struggle against foreign competition is the establishment of a regular supply of trained craftsmen.

I have worked for more than twenty-five years with the Russian craftsman and I should like to dwell briefly on the type. He is certainly more able than his European colleague, but he lacks the conscientiousness that comes from training and general education. The craftsman who loves his craft and is proud of it is a rare phenomenon in our country, and this gives rise to negligence and a careless attitude to work, a lack of stamina and diligence. I have seen workmasters who are capable of working sixty hours over three days in exceptional circumstances, but when there is no such need or no chance of extra earnings they rarely work eight hours a day. Lack of system in the work process also severely decreases the productivity of Russian craftsmen. While a Western craftsman is methodical at every stage of his work, managing thus to avoid many surprises and faults, the Russian craftsman is disorganised and inconsistent, wasting a great deal of time.

Families of craftsmen are still a rare phenomenon in Russia: most craftsmen take up the job by chance. They usually come from the country, with a minimum of education, if any at all. They settle in the city and their children receive some kind of education, but they never carry on the trade of their father, preferring to find more lucrative and honourable occupations. It is thus impossible to develop a supply of traditional craftsmen, and as traditions play an important cultural part in the development of such trades, the lack of tradition lowers the general artistic level of work.

The experience of the Revolution should completely alter this situation: the intelligentsia and the semi-intelligentsia discovered at this time that the knowledge of some kind of trade gives better security than an office career, or a career of any other kind. It is capital that cannot be confiscated or annulled. The product of a craftsman's labour will always be needed and this is true even of trades producing luxury objects such as a jeweller. Even now, if conditions were right and the necessary materials available, jewellery and gold objects would be selling better than ever before.

I have observed a Russian and an Austrian craftsman working at similar machines: the latter, being methodical in his work and diligent, produced three times more than the Russian during the same time. If we take working hours, it becomes apparent that an Austrian craftsman can work a three-hour day with no fear of competition from us. I have always said that the working day could be eight hours, or even six, if these six hours were really worked intensively. To bear this out I can give examples where the productivity of one ten-hour working day on piecework was equal to the productivity of three days of day-work. Such intensity of work is possibly harmful and cannot be repeated day in, day out, but if we reduce it by even a half, then the result is a six-hour working day. The world of the craftsman lacks the knowledge and culture that bring in their wake conscientiousness and moral discipline.

There are two trends in contemporary jewellery and gold and silver production. One is towards mass production and the other to single works of art. It would, however, be erroneous to infer from this that the first trend precludes the creation of works of art. On the contrary, mass production should be regarded as a means of multiplying works of art with the aim of making them accessible to a large number of people. Let me explain with an example: a Roti plaquet or medal is without doubt a high-quality work of art, although it is manufactured by pressing, i.e., by means of mass production. It all depends on the merits of the original and on the model that is being reproduced.

The two trends were combined in the work of the firm. As well as the unique, handmade works of art there were the methods of mechanical reproduction that were used mainly for mass objects, such as table silver, or in the repeated ornaments of frieze garlands, etc. Recently I have carried out experiments to combine both methods of working in one object. The original was executed by hand by the best workmasters and then reproduced in great numbers by mechanical means. In this way the object became more than

100 percent cheaper, but remained true to the original in appearance. The often-expressed fears that mechanical production would kill the craft were severely exaggerated. The method of production I have just described (and this is the only correct one) means that the craftsman will always be essential for the execution of the original and his work will be much better paid, because the cost is subsequently divided among many hundreds of reproductions and is not a significant part of the object's final price. Lastly, however mass production develops, there will always be artistic work that needs to be handmade and cannot be produced by mechanical methods. It is true the number of craftsmen is decreasing, but the artistic qualities of those remaining will increase as the most capable will be able to produce artistic originals.

As I have already said, the workmaster-owners of the workshops managed them autonomously and the firm very rarely interfered in the relations between workmasters and apprentices. Typically, a workmaster who owned a workshop would exploit his workers, but there were exceptions, for example . . ., Petrov, ...[4] Characteristically these three workmasters were the best workers in their own workshops, that is to say, they themselves worked at the joiner's bench and loved their trade; they had artistic natures. But we have seen that nervous exhaustion forced the first to give up the workshop, the second died of the same exhaustion, and none of the three was able to make a living, while the workmasters of the other kind were making themselves nice little fortunes. The attitude of the workmasters to their workers and to the firm was made especially clear when the Revolution and the Decree on the 36th standard made it necessary to start closing down the workshops. All the expenses connected with satisfying the claims of the apprentices, the three-month salary, etc., were pushed by the workmasters on to the firm, with no consideration of the fact that they themselves were receiving a handsome income from the labour of the workforce. As most of the workers worked for the firms, if only indirectly, the firm met their demands for a long time, and the workshops were closed with the consent of the workers and without incident. Where earnings were concerned, workmaster-owners were inert, disorganised and completely lacking in solidarity, even when protecting their own interests. The existing

Society of Jewellers did little towards achieving any unity. When a workmaster was faced with demands from his apprentices, the rules of the Society were not observed, and whether he acceded to their demands or refused to do so depended entirely on his own personal interests. Ideas of social enlightenment were not supported or sympathised with by the majority; the magazine *The Jeweller*, founded by a small group of jewellers, mainly dealers, was to cease functioning, as did the Society for Artistic and Technical Education.[5] This was the situation in the world of production before 1914. The war created panic. Even the large workshops and firms ceased production, assuming, not without foundation, that there would be no demand for objects of luxury such as the jewellery and gold. Nevertheless, the experienced old dealers, who had already lived through times of war, pointed out that on the contrary, at times of war, when state orders create an abundance of money, purchases of gold and silver represent an opportunity for owners to realise the money. Speculation and playing the stock market throw up new rich men who are in a hurry to acquire all kinds of objects of luxury. The old men were right, and this phenomenon continues to this day. The stagnation in the jewellery trade lasted only for the first year of the war. At this time Fabergé decided to turn his production over to the needs of wartime and applied to the War Department with a definite proposal to this end. The firm waited a whole year for a reply, but the workforce meanwhile had to be occupied. Various palliatives were tried: they started producing copper items – sets of dishes with covers, plates, mugs, tobacco cases, etc.

The only purpose for this kind of production was to guarantee work for several hundred apprentices. There was, of course, no question of profit. There were losses, but these were insignificant. If the directors of the firm had been less patriotically inclined at that time and taken account of the confusion that surrounded supplies and munitions orders, they would have laid up stores of goods during this year of stagnation in the trade and then realised them with a large profit in the ensuing years.

It was only in the second year of the war that the firm was accorded the munitions order. The Moscow silver works were re-equipped and another workshop was opened in Petersburg. At the same time one of the workmasters, the jeweller Holmström, opened a workshop that produced Pravatsa syringes.

Work on the munitions order was carried out by the remaining jewellers and silversmiths and by workers who had been recently taken on. The works and workshops functioned right up to the Revolution. Instantaneous and distant fuses were made, as well as grenades and parts for equipment. At the beginning the production was difficult to organise, but it soon became exemplary, both in its precision and meticulousness of execution.

I have quoted this only as an example of the firm's activities. Now I shall return to the basic production, to say a few words about the organisation of the workshops.

Each workshop employed forty to sixty apprentices: about twenty or thirty setters, five engravers, five chasers, five fixers, five burnishers, one or two guilloché workers and one joiner.

The specialisation of work went even further: the setters were sub-divided into cigarette-case makers, that is, specialists making boxes, snuff-boxes, cigarette cases, ladies' necessaires, that is, objects where hinges and clasps require special attention. Foreign craftsmen were always surprised at the perfection of these works of ours. The fastenings were so compact that it was difficult to see at once on the polished surface of the cigarette case the line that divided the lid from the body of the box, and all the boxes and similar objects closed absolutely noiselessly. Other setters specialised in purely jewellery work: brooches, necklaces, diadems, ... for fixing on the settings of works made of semi-precious stones – nephrite, rock crystal, azurite, etc. This kind of specialisation perfects the technique, but rather spoils the artistic image of the object. It passes through so many hands that evidence of the workmaster's individuality is eroded; and in addition to this, as each specialist is only concerned with the perfection of his own part of the work he is inclined, where necessary, to sacrifice the work of another specialist, for example, a chaser, engraver, or enameller.

The engraver's work is also subdivided into two special areas: hatch engraving, typefaces, ornamentation, pictures and carved relief engraving, and . . . for medals.

Chasing in its turn subdivides into chasing of cast works and chasing on brass. . . .

Silverwork setters are divided into two categories: those that make services, samovars, and other dishes, and those that are mainly occupied with special cast works: candelabras, statues, and clocks.

As practically all types of work include several specialties, objects passed through several hands and then the parts were assembled by a special assembler.

Enamelling and gilding were carried out in special workshops.

List of Designers working for Fabergé firm in Petrograd

Full-time artists and designers

K. Fabergé	1919
A.G. Fabergé	1896
V.A. Kritski	1888–1894
F.P. Birbaum	1893–1919
A.I. Ivashov	1895–1919
I.I. Liberg	1898–1919
E.E. Iakobson	19 . .-1919
O.O. Mai	1900–1914
L.I. Mattei	1896–1898
G.G. Eber	
M.D. Rakov	1915–1919
M.I. Ivanov	1916–1918
G.Yu. Kurtz	1900–1919
I.E. Komalenkov	1908–1919

Part-time (artists) for individual commissions

I.A. Galbinek [Galnbeck], Architect
Shekhter [probably Shekhtel], Architect
Mashner [probably Marshner], Architect
G.K. Savitski, Artist

Miniaturists

V.I. Zuiev
S.S. Solomko
A.I. Timofeev (enamel)
K.I. Tseidler (enamel)
M.V. Muselius (enamel)
E.E. Iakobson (enamel)
F.P. Birbaum (enamel)
Rudnaltsev (engraving)

Sculptors

A.A. Timus	Ilyina
Grachov	L.L. Strikh
B.O. Fredman-Klyuzel	G.K. Savitski
E.I. Malyshev	M.I. Ivanov
Aubert	
Bach	
Skilter	

Specialist chasers

Sergeev 1890–1907
K. Mattei 1900–1903
Struev 1900–1917
M.N. Zakhudalin 1890–1895
M.Kh. Bogdanov 1912–1917
Epifanov 1890–1905
E.I. Komalenkov 1890–1902
Jacquard 1890–1917
Kostylov 1910–1917

Engravers

D.M. Zakhudalin 1890–1914
Vasilyev 1907–1917

Enamellers

Killender 1870–1885
V.V. Boitsov 1890–1905
A.F. Petrov 1895–1904
N.A. Petrov 1895–1917

Sculptors-stonemasons

Pestu 1880–1914
Kremlyov 1910–1917
Derbyshev 1910–1914

Workmasters owning workshops

Reimer, Kollin, Solovyov, M.E. Perkhin, Nevalainen, Holmström, Hollming, Aarne, Armfelt, Wäkeva, Thielemann, Rappoport, 1st Silver Artel

MOSCOW

Artists

Ivanov	Lozhkin
Klodt 1	Sheverdyaev
Klodt 2	Liberg
Balashov	Obradushkin
Borisov	Andrianov
Pets	

Sculptors

Sokolov	Cheshuin
Buttsi	Chaser
Sokolovski	Kulesha
Shishkina	

Engraver

Konstantinov

Workmasters managing the factory

Sazikov
Chepurnov

The Court and its Orders

For a long time the main clients of the firm were members of the Imperial household and court circles. They were joined by the aristocracy of the financial and commercial worlds only in the 1890s. There was one characteristic feature common to all the clients up to very recent times and that is a blind admiration for everything foreign. They did not hesitate to pay fantastic sums for works that were often inferior to Russian works. This was easy enough to prove as hardly a day passed without someone bringing in a masterpiece to be repaired. The exception was Alexander III, who on principle preferred and encouraged everything Russian.

Unfortunately, at the time Russian decorative art was going through a period of unprecedented decline. The dominant style was the so-called Cockerel, with its flat, monotonous ornamentation. Imperial commissions were always very urgent; everything had to be done as if by the waving of a magic wand. Often only a few hours were given for the execution of a commission, and these were at night. This was because the orders came to us through various court departments, and we had to work so hard to rescue them from the results of their carelessness. Orders came to us by two routes: from the Cabinet of His Majesty or, bypassing this, directly from the Emperor or the Empress – these were for personal and family presents. The Easter egg presented every year by the Emperor to his wife is of particular interest. It was Alexander III who started this tradition, and it was continued by Nicholas II, who presented them to both Empresses. The designs for these eggs did not have to be approved. Fabergé was given a completely free hand in the choice of theme and in the execution itself. About fifty or sixty of these eggs were made, and I composed more than half of them myself. It was not easy work as there could be no repetition of theme and the ovoid shape was compulsory. We tried to make use of family and other events in the Imperial household to give some meaning to the gift, but political events were, of course, avoided. The eggs could almost always be opened and there would be a surprise inside. For the most part, work on these eggs was very complicated. To avoid repetition we had to vary the materials, the exterior, and the content of the egg. I shall try and describe some of them to give an idea of what kind of work this was.

1. A rock crystal egg horizontally fixed on a *plique à jour* base, style Louis XV. Within the egg a golden tree with blossoms made of small diamonds and rubies; a gold mechanical peacock sits on one of the branches. When the egg is opened, the peacock can be taken out and wound up: he then walks in a typical manner, spreading and closing his tail. The size of the peacock from head to tail is no more than 12 cm.[7]

2. The egg made for the year of the opening of the Great Trans-Siberian Railway. An egg of green enamel with a silver band depicting the map of the Siberian Railway stands on a base of white onyx, decorated with the three griffins of the Romanovs. Within the egg a miniature gold-and-platinum model of the Imperial train. The train is moved by a mechanism in the engine the size of which is no more than 3 cm. long. The egg is decorated in Russian style.[8]

3. A clock egg of green, grape-colour ophite and pink enamel. The enamel egg is encircled by a horizontal rotary clock face with numbers made of rose diamonds. The egg is supported by four ophite columns entwined with floral swags of varicoloured gold. The columns are fixed on a base of the same stone. Golden figures of four girls (the Emperor's four daughters) sit on the steps of the base. On the upper part of the egg is the figure of a boy (the Heir), who is indicating the hour with a twig. In appearance, the egg is reminiscent of a large summer house with a colonnade under the egg; between the columns there is a group of white silver kissing doves.[9]

4. The egg for the Bicentenary of Petersburg. The egg is of chased gold in the style of Peter I, with views of Petersburg old and new (Peter the Great's hut and the Winter Palace), and portraits of Peter the Great and Nicholas II. Within the egg is a miniature reproduction of Falconet's monument of Peter. The granite block is made of carved emerald. The statue of the horse is 3 cm. long and 2 cm. high.[10]

5. The egg for the Tercentenary of the House of Romanov. The chased gold egg is supported by the two-headed eagle. On the egg's surface are portraits of the Tsars and Emperors of the House of Romanov. Within the egg is a blue steel globe set on an axis with maps of the Russian Empire

inset in gold on both halves of the globe: a) when the Romanovs came to the throne, and b) during the reign of Nicholas II.[11]

Sometimes the appearance and content of the eggs reflected family events. For example, in the year of the Tsarevich's birth, the egg was like a cradle, decorated with floral swags. Within, the first portrait of the Heir in a medallion surrounded with diamonds.[12] During the war years eggs were either not made at all or were very modest and inexpensive as, for example, the 1915 eggs. For the widowed Maria Feodorovna there was an egg of polished steel, set on three steel artillery shells. Inside is a miniature showing the Emperor visiting the Front.[13] For the Tsarina Alexandra Feodorovna there was an egg of white enamel with the Red Cross and portraits of two of her daughters as Sisters of Mercy.[14] The eggs made for Easter 1917 were unfinished: there was a proposal from a person unknown to me that the eggs should be completed and sold to him, but the proposal was rejected by the firm.

Many of these works are of artistic interest both for their composition and for the perfection of the jewellery work. They could well take their places in the Hermitage Gallery of Treasures.

The process of making these eggs usually took about one year. Work started soon after Easter, and they were only just ready for Holy Week of the following year. They were usually presented to the Emperor himself by the head of the firm on Good Friday. The last days were anxious for everyone: nothing could be allowed to happen to these fragile works of art. In case anything unexpected happened, the craftsmen remained at their places of work until Fabergé returned from Tsarskoe Selo. Other private commissions were not very important and of no particular artistic interest. The jewellery part of a dowry was entrusted to the jeweller Bolin,[15] and the table silver to us. These ceremonial table decorations consisted of a central vase for flowers (jardiniere), several pairs of vases for fruit of various sizes, candelabras, champagne coolers and other objects, usually about twenty. Three such dowries were commissioned from us: for the Grand Duchess Xenia Aleksandrovna, the Emperor Nicholas II, and the Grand Duchess Olga Aleksandrovna. I have already mentioned the first, but it was the last that was the most successful. The central part was a colonnade with a cupola

crowned with a two-headed eagle. The colonnade rested on a base of several steps, and the whole construction stood on a mirrored tray surrounded by a balustrade. On the steps stands a group of cupids holding a shield with a monogram. The base is surrounded by flowers. At the ends of the mirror tray stand two fruit vases similar in character to the central part. All these decorations were executed in the style of Louis XVI. The whole order weighed . . . and cost . . . roubles.[16]

With occasional exceptions, the numerous presents of the Emperors and Empresses were selected from objects already made – the firm sent a series of objects to the Court for selection. Official presents were ordered through His Majesty's Cabinet. These were snuff-boxes, cigarette cases, rings, panagias and crosses, brooches, cuff-links, and tie-pins. The prices were specially set according to the category of the object.

The portraits had the portrait of the Emperor painted on ivory, surrounded with diamonds, and the portrait was surmounted with a diamond crown. The body of the snuff-box was made of gold and decorated with chasing, varicoloured gold, enamels, and diamonds. Sometimes the snuff-boxes were made of nephrite. The cigarette cases were similar in character, but the portrait was replaced by a monogram. Some panagias and crosses were of artistic interest. They were most frequently Russian and Byzantine in style and were richly decorated with gold or coloured stones. The central image was executed in Byzantine *cloisonné* enamel, chasing on gold or engraved stone (cameo). Smaller presents were decorated with the two-headed eagle of the Imperial crown.

Gifts presented to Emperors and Empresses were of considerably greater artistic interest. I list here some of them that I can still remember: a silver chimney clock presented to Alexander III by the members of his household on the occasion of his Silver Wedding.[17] Around the clock face there is a group of about twenty-five flying cupids. The composition included the griffins of the Romanov coat of arms and the coat of arms itself. The wax model was made by the sculptor Ober and is one arshin in height. Of the numerous dishes presented on the occasion of Nicholas II's Coronation, particularly noteworthy are the nephrite dish that is twelve *vershki* in diameter and set in Baroque style silver, and the dish of engraved rock crystal,[18] mounted in Renaissance

style with enamel and precious stones. The basket of snowdrops presented by the merchants of Nizhni Novgorod to Alexandra Feodorovna was woven of golden branches and filled with moss made of various shades of gold, the leaves of the snowdrop were nephrite, the flowers were whole pearls, and the projections of the petals were made of rose diamonds. The size of the basket was 22 cm.[19]

Nicholas II's taste was not particularly sophisticated and he laid no claims to sophistication. His wife, Alexandra Feodorovna, was, however, different. Her grasp of artistic concepts was meagre, her meanness was not in keeping with her royal status and often placed Fabergé in tragicomic situations. Her commissions were accompanied by sketches and pre-determined ideas of cost. It was technically and artistically impossible to follow the drawings, so various cunning devices were used to explain changes that had been made – the craftsman had not properly understood, the drawing had been lost, etc. Where price was concerned, the works of art were delivered at the price she had stipulated, so as to avoid incurring her displeasure. As the cost of the orders was relatively insignificant, we regarded her favour when the order was a more serious one than compensation. The Grand Dukes and Duchesses came with pleasure to the shop and spent a long time choosing their purchases. Every day from four to five all the Petersburg aristocracy could be seen there: the titled, the civil service, and the commercial. In Holy Week these rendezvous were particularly crowded as everyone hurried to buy the traditional Easter eggs and, at the same, to glance at the egg made for the Emperor.

This reminds me of an incident that was not without piquancy. One of our lady clients from the highest aristocracy, who was not particularly clever, had several weeks before Easter started pressing old Mr. Fabergé to say whether anything novel could be expected in the Easter eggs. It must be said that novelty was achieved with great difficulty, and everyone had had more than enough of trying. When roused, old Mr. Fabergé was not noticeably restrained. He innocently declared to the lady that in two weeks' time he would be finishing work on square eggs. Some of the people standing around smiled, others were discomfited, but the lady did not grasp the point. As if that were not enough, she actually came to the shop in two weeks' time to buy these eggs. The old man explained to her quite seriously that he had hoped to produce them but had been unsuccessful.

Among the members of the Imperial Family, the Grand Duke Aleksei Aleksandrovich was the greatest connoisseur and judge.[20] He could be relied on to buy anything interesting. He collected not only antiques but everything that had any artistic merit, whatever period it belonged to. He never required things to be sent to him, but preferred, and not without good reason, to examine personally what was on sale, what was new. When he appeared in the shop everything new was shown to him, unfinished works were often brought from the workshops, and he bought them all if he liked the design. Every year he went to France, taking with him as presents a good quantity of our works, and he created a very good reputation for us by distributing them in high society. He was, incidentally, one of the first to encourage Lalique by ordering and buying from him and, just as he took our work to France, he brought French work back to Russia. It was on his commission that Lalique made the large *bratina* that was presented to the Moscow Regiment. Aleksei Aleksandrovich's collection was inherited by his brother Vladimir. On his death it was presented to the Hermitage.[21]

His Majesty's Cabinet and its Orders[22]
The Cabinet was always run by military or civil generals who knew nothing about art, but they nevertheless acted as artistic jury in the selection of designs for execution. One can easily imagine the results. What they liked, of course, as did most of the public, were finished, very detailed drawings. Knowing this I used the following tactical device. For each order there were several design variants: the one I considered the best I drew up most carefully, producing a drawing that was highly finished, whereas those I considered weaker I produced less carefully. This strategy was almost always successful, by which I mean that it was my preferred design that was chosen. In striving for economy, the people in charge of the Cabinet often had recourse to devices that were not very pleasant. When they had ordered an object from us, they would then give the model to other jewellers who made duplicates and variants more cheaply, as they did not have to bear the cost of maintaining the artists. When the job was urgent or very complicated, they would

come to the firm, knowing that the results would be good and produced in time. During the last decade, receiving orders from the Cabinet became so much a matter of ingratiating oneself and beating a path to the doors of the office that Fabergé stopped visiting in person. Of course, the number of orders was reduced still further as a result, but this was compensated by the increase of other clientele and orders from abroad, and the firm was able to use its strengths in other, more interesting work.

Private Commissions
There were many orders from the Guards' regiments. These were gifts for the officers' mess from the regimental patrons and the commanders on the occasion of various jubilees. Sometimes the officers' mess presented gifts to commanding officers or officers leaving the regiment. These were usually *bratini*, goblets, vases, clocks, candelabras, sculptured groups, sometimes icons. Those giving the orders practically always wanted the main features of the regiment to be represented in the composition and these had to be shown in detail. This was extremely difficult for the artist and was often to the detriment of the work as a whole. That is why there are sometimes awkward moments in our works – *bratini* in the shape of kettledrums or overturned helmets and shakos.

When an officer with taste and some artistic understanding was in charge of the order, it was possible to come to an agreement, avoiding the features that were too unsuitable or placing them in the background; but when the authorities were in charge, or when the orders came from the officers' mess, where there were as many different opinions as there were officers, the artistic quality of the work suffered from their interventions.

When the works depicted episodes from the history of the regiment or old weaponry and uniforms, the compositions were not without artistic interest. There are two bas reliefs produced for the Moscow Regiment. The first shows an episode from the 1812 war, the second from the Turkish campaign. The sketches were done by Samokish[23] and modelled by the sculptor Stirkh[24] The designs for the frames and the electric lamp brackets to light them were mine. Almost every officers' mess in the Petrograd regiments had similar works from our firm. For the Ulan regiment a series of lamp brackets were made and candelabras in Empire style with figures of

hussars in the uniform of the regiment at the time of its founding and also of the present day. Orders from the civil establishments of various government departments were often very similar, the only difference being that the attributes were civil rather than military.

During the last decade clients from the worlds of finance and trade became very important: the kings of the Stock Exchange, sugar and oil etc. It must be said that working with them was incomparably easier and more pleasant. They were almost always gifted practically, laid no claims to any artistic initiative and did not impose their ideas or designs. They assumed, not without foundation, that artists are specialists like engineers or accountants, so instructions would only be harmful. They frequently did not even define what the object should be, if it was a present that was required. They just indicated the price limit, for whom the present was intended, and for what occasion. In these conditions the artist could create freely, which is extremely important. He thus felt that he was completely responsible for his creation, which is hardly less important.

Some clients ordered table silver, from *surtouts de table* to small objects such as spoons, forks, etc., in the same style as the dining-room. The table silver for V.K. Kelch (née Brazanova)[25] is an example, as is the nephrite writing desk set mounted in Empire style, which was made for Eliseev.[26]

E. Nobel,[27] one of the kings of oil, was so generous in his presents that at times it seemed that this was his chief occupation and delight. Orders were constantly being made for him in the workshops and from time to time he came to have a look at them. Often he only decided for whom the present should be when the work was finished. When the workshops were closed down, several of his orders remained unfinished. Of his numerous orders the large chimney clock (a reproduction in stone of the Temple of Fire Worshippers) is worth mentioning. The fires on the corner towers are flat pieces of rhodonite in the form of flames, lit from inside by electric bulbs. The temple rests on a cliff at the foot of which are relief allegorical figures of Trade and Industry. The clock was made to the design of the artist E. Iakobson.[28] The large rhodonite vase with supporting figures of *stolniki* in costumes of the time of Aleksei Mikhailovich, and the round nephrite table with silver caryatids in Empire style[29] are also worth mentioning.

Nobel was a great lover of gold works and was particularly fond of enamels: some very decorative enamel works on gold were made for him in a special size. There was also an interesting series of small jewellery works in rock crystal set with small diamonds in the shape of frost patterns.

We should not omit the most profitable clientele. As anyone can guess, this was the *demimonde* – from ballet dancers down to gypsies and lower. Precious stones were the chief element. Women were, are, and always will be the chief consumers. How many inheritances and estates have been converted into pearls and diamonds! In family households, precious objects are passed from group to group within the family and many people avoid even having them refashioned. The opposite is true of our world which lives only for today, with no roots in the past and no future. With a few exceptions the gifts do not evoke good memories (perhaps even the opposite). After a period of time stones are taken out of their setting and used for new objects, larger and more fashionable. A pearl presented by an enraptured admirer rests peacefully beside the diamonds from an old protector. Just as the vague memories of one or other close friend blur in the memory of these women, all their images merge in the radiance of the stones of their jewellery. The world of the theatre is also not without its interesting characters, such as the singer F . . .,[30] who used to come into the shop before his benefit performances and pick out the presents toward which the shop assistants would direct his admirers the next day. In all fairness, it must be said that he always bargained desperately, protecting the interests of his admirers.

K. Fabergé was extremely witty and had no time for fops whom he detested. Once, soon after New Year, one of these, Prince G . . ov,[31] who was very proud of ribbons and decorations, came into the shop. The Prince started talking about the New Year Honours so he could boast of having received the White Eagle, adding negligently, 'Just imagine, I don't even know what I got it for'. He was expecting Fabergé to cover him with congratulations and praise, but Fabergé only smiled and said, 'It's true, Your Excellency, I don't know either'. In making witty remarks he spared neither himself nor others. Once the king of sugar K . . .[32] was complaining, 'Every year there are losses'. 'Yes, yes', said Fabergé, 'losses every year, but it's strange how these losses make us richer'.

In the year of the birth of the Heir to the throne, we were discussing the next Easter egg, planning how to use this event. Someone observed that from the moment of his birth, the Heir had been appointed Chief of the Infantry Units and that this could surely be used in the composition. 'Yes', agreed Fabergé, 'but we shall have to show dirty nappies, as that is the only result of his shooting so far'.

When Fabergé was taking an order he was always in a hurry and often forgot the details. He would ask all round his employees, looking for anyone who had been standing near him at the time. He was always amazed that anyone standing near could not remember anything. Among the employees there was a saying that the person responsible for the order was not the one who took it, but the one who was standing nearby.

This haste sometimes had strange consequences. He occasionally handed over not the finished drawings but the rough sketches where, to save time, he had shown one half of one design and the other half of another. Sometimes the craftsman actually made the object in this way.

On the back of one of the icons the 'Our Father' was to be engraved. When he had designed the typeface for the first words he wrote 'and so on'. The engraver engraved just exactly those words, 'Our Father and so on', instead of the complete text of the prayer. 'Our priests have not yet thought of shortening the service in this way', he observed.

If the drawing was not at hand, it was often difficult to tell them from the object itself and which of the artists had made it, such was the quality of works of art. When Fabergé saw something unsuccessful, he would summon me and amuse himself by making sarcastic remarks about the unknown artist. When I had cause to suspect that it might be his own work, I would send for the drawing and show it to him. He would then smile guiltily and say, 'That's what happens when there's no one to blame – you end up blaming yourself'.

During Gustav Fabergé's lifetime, one of the members of the Imperial Family was very interested in jewellery and wanted to learn the trade himself. To this end, he asked Fabergé to provide him with a list of the necessary instruments and what would be needed for a workshop. The old workmaster who was entrusted with this was a real original. In the list of instruments, among hammers, chisels, and chasers, he included 'a fairly thick flat strap'. This was noticed and questioned by the member of the Imperial Family. The old man said, 'Your Highness, it's the first and most important instrument. No pupil has ever learnt the jewellery trade without one'. A brief, truthful illustration of the method of training at that time.

The Grand Duchess Maria Pavlovna was, of all the members of the Imperial Family, a particular patron of foreign jewellers, and they made use of this all-powerful protection to bring their works to Petrograd every year without paying customs and assay duties. The intention was to sell them in Moscow and Petrograd. This trick was discovered and proved by several Petrograd jewellers, who saw to it that the pieces of jewellery were sequestered until the tax on them had been paid in full.

Foreign Trade

It was at the time of the World Exhibition in Paris in 1900 that trading began to be properly organised. Until that time many of our works were taken abroad, but by chance, as gifts, purchases made in Russia, or by agents. A decorative vase presented to Prince Bismarck, a large silver *bratina*, a present to the Abyssinian negus Menelik and many gifts from Russian Emperors to foreign courts and diplomats would be among those to be listed. The success of our work at the Paris *Exposition* allowed us to hope for a larger market, and as the clientele was mainly in London, it was decided to open a branch there.[33] The chief clients were King Edward VII and the Court aristocracy. An ever larger circle of people were buying our work, and this did not go unnoticed by English jewellers and goldsmiths, who wasted no time in taking steps to protect their interests. It should be said that there were no import taxes for these goods in England, and the laws on the hallmarking of gold allowed for wide interpretation. The Worshipful Company of Goldsmiths kept a close watch to see that these rules were observed. At first the English assaying associations were content to check the Russian hallmarks, subjecting objects to fresh examination. This, of course, did not embarrass us at all, especially as we had intentionally kept the standards slightly higher than required by law. But then, under pressure from the Goldsmiths, they started to require English hallmarking. This threatened our trade with such serious difficulties that the firm took advice from English lawyers and took the case to court. It should be pointed out that the apparently innocent request for the imposition of hallmarks meant that each object we were intending to sell in England had to make the journey there twice. The hallmark is put on the work in the rough, as the blow that accompanies the imposition invariably distorts the object and this has subsequently to be adjusted. In enamel works (and most of our works were of this type) when the blow is struck, the enamel always separates from the metal. Thus, each object had to be sent to England in the rough, returned to Russia for finishing, and then sent again to be sold. And even that was not all, as it was not possible to predict what would sell in London so all our work had to be subjected to this procedure to make sure of having a large enough selection. The court case took more than a year and the decision, predictably enough, was not in our favour.[34] The demands of the English assaying charter remained in force. The firm tried to continue its activities in London, but soon realised that this could only lead to losses. The European war finished the matter and hastened the closing of the London branch.

The London shop not only served English clients – it was the centre of our trade with France, America, and the Far East. Representatives of the London branch went to these countries, taking our goods and bringing back orders which were then sent on to Petersburg. Our gold, enamel works, and large silver works were particularly successful. This can be explained by the high technical standard of perfection of our handwork. Attempts to reduce costs had meant that foreign jewellers had long since substituted machine work for handwork, whether suitable or not, and this was to the detriment of both the durability and the thoroughness of the finish. Foreign specialists could not but notice the qualities of our handwork where the attentive eye had left nothing undone and there are none of the marks so typical of the gradual process of machine work. An interesting situation arose: while Russia was swamped with cheap foreign jewellery and silver work, we were marketing abroad work that was more expensive, but also more up to date.

We could have had the same success with jewellery if we had obtained precious stones from source and in large enough quantities, as the French and English jewellers did. But for this we would have needed more capital funds, and changes in the way things were done would also have been necessary. We should have had to follow the market and fashions more closely. Works destined for England were of a different artistic character: greater simplicity of form and more restrained ornamentation, with special attention being paid to the technical finish.

Twice a year the firm's representatives went to the Far East, mainly to India and Siam. The Siamese Royal Family and Court were very important clients. Our works were first taken to Siam by Prince Chulalonghorn, who had spent a fairly long time in Petersburg, where he had been educated at the Corps des Pages. Soon after he returned to Siam, various orders were received from the Royal Couple.[35] Carved nephrite and miniature portraits on enamel of the King and Queen, set in diamonds, had a special place in these orders.

When we discovered from people who had visited Siam that rings with precious stones were the most common article of jewellery, as soon as we could we sent a large selection of rings. Unfortunately, it did not occur to anyone that European sizes might not be suitable and, indeed, they were so large that for the next trip we had to make rings in children's sizes to fit the miniature fingers of Siamese ladies.

In Siam they have the custom of the traditional gift, like our Easter egg, but at the time of the New Year. Each year has the name of an animal, corresponding to the new year. In 1913 the Siamese Court ordered a whole series of objects and charm bracelets with the image of a pig.

Much of the work done for Siam is European in character, but there were also objects in the Siamese style. In these cases we used samples, drawings, and photographs which were brought to us from Siam. The Siamese style has traces of Hindu and Chinese influence, but it is an unusual interest and has not been much studied to date. The ornamentation is very rich and distinguished by a fine, detailed finish. The influence of Chinese colouring is very noticeable.

The Fabergé Firm's stone carvings

Stone carving was of secondary interest in the work of the firm up to 1908. Objects of semi-precious Siberian and other kinds of stone were used as subjects for settings, as background for gold, silver, and *plique à jour* work. Small objects predominate: snuff-boxes, walking-stick handles, seals, frames, etc. Sometimes larger objects were mounted, such as decorative vases, clocks, ink-stands, or lamps. Almost all stone works of this period were made to the designs and models of the firm at the Woerffel works in Petersburg and the Stern works in Oberstein (Germany). Sometimes stone articles were acquired from the Ekaterinburg artisans and passed on to us so the faults could be corrected and the polish improved at the works I have mentioned. It is interesting to note that the cost of these improvements for the most part exceeded the original purchase price. The craftsmen of the Peterhof lapidary works also supplied work that they had made at home in their free time. The ever-increasing use of stone in jewellery and gold- and silverwork, the artistic shortcomings, and the fact that some orders had to be carried out at other works without the necessary supervision compelled the firm to open its own workshop. There work could be directly supervised and the cutting of the stone could be coordinated with the subsequent jewellery and gold-chasing work.

As stones became part of the firm's production, their qualities and beauty encouraged artists to accord them first place. This meant that the significance of the settings was often purely complementary and technical: paper-clips, hinges, and locks.

Nephrite was used most often for its qualities and its appearance.

NEPHRITE came from the River Onot in boulders or natural blocks, according to Woerffel's orders.[36] It is both firm and malleable, free of the cracks that make cutting other stones so difficult, and it gives the possibility of a very high finish. Further, as we shall see, the basic green grass colour comes in many shades. When it is a boulder or a block, it is difficult to determine the colour and the quality. Often a boulder with a very promising crust is disappointing when cut, whereas a rotten crust (the soft, whitish places that crumble easily and cannot be polished are called rotten places) often conceal a marvellous core.

Nephrite can be divided into six types: 1. dark-green translucent, 2. green with gray translucent, 3. light-green translucent, 4. black-green opaque, 5. mottled, 6. fissured.

It is obvious that all these kinds could be used by someone with a conscientious attitude to his work. The dark green nephrite, when cut into thin sheets, becomes translucent and acquires a wonderful dense green colour. If left a particular thickness it appears black. Green with a grey streak is the best kind for sculpture, which demands a high degree of finish; it is very durable, firmer than other kinds and therefore polishes beautifully. The light green nephrite was used in objects of a certain thickness so as not to lose the colouring. The mottled and fissured were used in sculpturing leaves and give a very varied colour. As well as those already mentioned, there are other kinds of nephrite but they are rare: grey, white, yellowish, and even light-blue violet nephrites. Grey nephrite, known as Murgabski, is the hardest of all, but it is so rare that we used it little. The New Zealand nephrite, which was brought from England, was also worked, but it was dry (brittle) and had a thin colour, so we preferred Siberian nephrite.

Second place in our production was occupied by ORLETZ (RHODONITE). Its cracks and marks meant that it was not very suitable for sculptures, but it produced wonderful results in sheets and in larger bodies, and the bright pink clusters were marvellous material for small works of jewellery, such as walking-stick handles, umbrella handles, seals, etc. The brightness of these clusters often approach ruby. My observations of rhodonite have led me to conclude that the bright pink clusters, which are always so valued, are very close to the black layers of iron-stone. For this reason, a piece of orletz covered with a thick black crust promises more than one covered with a milky pink crust. Rhodonite's main defect is the significant numbers of fissures that are often discovered only in the course of work and prevent completion of the job.

The numerous types of JASPER are a very reliable and varied material. ORSKAIA is especially deserving of our attention. Its basic warm tone is enriched by brown and green patterns of every possible hue. Thickets of trees, cliffs, valleys, trees, and the most varied and unexpected motifs unfold before one's astonished eyes. Orskaia jasper was used mainly in thin sheets. When a large block was cut into slabs, they were carefully examined by the artist, who chose the most interesting motifs and decided how the stone should be cut further.

The sheets that were obtained in this way were used as panels, lids of snuff-boxes, boxes, and brooches, depending on their size. Of other jaspers GREY NIKOLAEVSKI was most often used in larger works, such as tables, vases, inkpots, and candelabras. The even grey tone of KALKAN jasper combined very well with gilded settings and enamelled works. Without listing all the kinds of jasper that were used in production, I say only that jaspers with a large pattern were used mainly for larger objects. Various kinds of BELORETZ QUARTZ played a large part, especially the pink and white fissured (scar − 9). The fissures complicated the work, but the results always compensated for failures and breakages. This quartz, which is completely transparent in places and covered in others with a beautiful white pattern like frost patterns on glass, was the most effective in vases and thin sheets, the thickness of which had been reduced to the minimum. SERPENTINES were not widely used, as they are soft and pervious to fatty substances. The exception is the so-called jadeite, whose marvellous green grape colour partly makes up for its defects.

BUKHARA AZURITE (LAPIS LAZULI) was widely used in small objects, especially in Renaissance and French XVII-century style settings. Siberian azurite is more often found in large pieces and was set in silver.

ROCK CRYSTAL was used in very varied work with carving and engraving. Its settings were richly decorated with enamel and precious stones. Its friability demanded of the craftsman a particular skill, and its setting was entrusted only to the most experienced workmaster. It could not tolerate the slightest heat, and the settings were never soldered, even with tin, but were assembled with clips and in other ways.

As well as these kinds of stones, many others were used, even pebbles from the beach and simple stones, if the colouring patterns were of particular artistic interest.

The firm's stone carvings can be divided into two categories: those destined to be set and those that do not require setting. The first category comprises vases, tables, candelabras, clocks, snuff-boxes, and countless other objects, both large and small, and objects of fantasy. These objects had settings of outstanding chased and engraved enamels, precious stones, and precious metals. In the second category were mainly sculptured works, figures of people and animals, flowers,

fruit, and mosaics.

The rich finish of these settings emphasised the value of the stone being set. In the list of the firm's outstanding work, to which I have dedicated a special chapter, I give some examples of this kind. In the category of sculptures, there are numerous animals and people, portrayed in a realistic, humorous, or stylised manner. These miniature sculptures were very successful with clients until very recently. They are amusing, and as they are not made of a precious material, they are very good presents when it is important that the cost of the present should not be obvious. Their distribution was also facilitated by a mania for collecting. Many highly placed people collected these figures, and others knew that additions to the collection would be favourably received. These miniature sculptures were often portraits of favourite dogs, cats, or parrots. For example, the famous French bulldog belonging to the actress Balletta,[37] commissioned by Grand Duke Aleksei Aleksandrovich, or the beloved doves of the English king Edward and many other animals — these were all made of one kind of stone, but, when possible, the stone was selected in the same tone and markings as the original. Jaspers from the Urals and the Altai were specially used, as were breccia and porphyry. From selecting the stones to look natural it was but one step to mosaic sculpture, where various stones, glued and scattered, could be combined to achieve the effects of colouring. When these mosaics were not too close to nature, the artistic impression was preserved, but the bad taste of the customer, in search of a novelty, often demanded a slavish imitation of nature and forced the artist to portray nature too closely, thus destroying the artistic effect.

The origin of these sculptures can without doubt be found in Chinese and Japanese stone carvings, and it was our acquaintance with them that first stimulated us to produce work of this kind. The manufacture of stone flowers, which has recently occupied a leading place in our work, has the same origin. We first noticed this branch of Chinese art when a bouquet of chrysanthemums was brought in for repair. It had been taken from the Court of the Chinese Emperor when it was occupied by a European landing force.

The chrysanthemums were made of corals, white nephrite, and other stones; the leaves were of grey nephrite, and the stems were made of

2. Dandelion 'seedclock', height 18.5 cm, made for Mme Yznaga, sister of the Duchess of Manchester.

square bunches of wire covered with green silk. Each petal was imperceptibly strengthened with wire attached to the cup of the flower. The skilled range of tones and the translucence of some of the stones created a marvellous impression.

But, as in the story of the steel flea, who was cunningly shoed so she stopped jumping and lost her chief point of interest, they had managed to make the stems of stone. The fragility of these flowers was increased, and they became curiosities of the stone-carver's skill rather than works of art.

Before we had seen the Chinese flowers, the firm had made enamel flowers with nephrite leaves. The dandelions were particularly successful: their fluff was natural and fixed on a golden thread with a small, uncut diamond (fig. 2). The shining points of the diamond among the white fluff were marvellously successful and prevented this artificial flower from being too close a reproduction of nature. When enamel flowers were first displayed at the Paris *Exposition* in 1900, they were immediately copied by German and Austrian factories and appeared on the market in cheap versions. The enamel was replaced by varnish, and the little vases of rock crystal by glass.

Narcissi, jasmine, branches of white lilac, and hyacinths were made in white quartz; sweet peas and other flowers in rhodonite, quartz, carnelian, and agate. The leaves are mainly nephrite, sometimes green jasper or quartz. Sometimes the flowers stood in a little glass of rock crystal, half hollow, so that the flower appeared to be standing in water, sometimes in a little pot of ... jasper or .... There was a specially successful series of dwarf cactuses in flower. Most of these were bought by Grand Duchess Maria Pavlovna or presented to her by her entourage. Individual items were safely delivered to London, in spite of their fragility, and sold there. The cost of manufacturing these flowers was considerable, and depending on the complexity of the flowers, was sometimes as much as several thousand roubles. As the stone-carving business was a separate part of the firm, I shall list the outstanding works in which the settings play a main role, and also some of the artists and craftsmen who worked in this field.

1. Nephrite wreath, placed on the grave of the Swedish King Gustav. The branches of laurel and oak are fixed to a black marble board.

2. Nephrite figure of Buddha and a lamp of the same stone, made for the Court Temple in Siam. The base of the figure is of embossed, enamelled gold. The model for Buddha was brought from Siam; the lamp was composed in Siamese style by the artist Iakobson, based on materials specially sent to him for this purpose from Siam. A series of nephrite boxes with fine engraved ornamentation was also made for the Siamese Court.

3. Of the animal figures the caricature elephants were particularly successful. They are of various stones in the form of 'bibelots', obsidian seals, and walruses. The effect of wet fur is achieved by the play of colours. The bases are blocks of ice made of rock crystal, and white bears of white quartz with a yellow streak stand on similar ice blocks. The obsidian figure of a hippopotamus with an open maw was also successful. The inside of the mouth was rhodonite of a suitable colour. It is impossible to list all the animals that were used as themes for these figures, but it should be said that the pose was always as compact as possible, as dictated by the technique of the material.

The most successful human figures were: a humorous figure of a priest in a fur coat and hat, and a painter with a bucket and brushes on his back (fig. 3). The extremely comic effect is achieved by the successful rendering of the proportions of the body. The painter's clothes, daubed with paint and lime, are of speckled Siberian azurite and Orskaia jasper. The models for these figures were made by the sculptor Fredman Klyuzel.[38]

For a Tatar street pedlar, his skull cap and tight fitting coat are made of dark grey nephrite, and the piles of scarves, socks, handkerchiefs, and lace thrown over his skull cap, shoulder, and hands enliven the figure with their colourful markings (fig. 4). The impression is rounded off by the typical face.

A boy selling lemonade is dressed in a dirty apron and carries on his head a pitcher, which is out of proportion, and a mug behind it. The upper part of the pitcher is made of rock crystal, the lower part of gold topaz, so the pitcher seems to be half full of lemonade.

3. Figure of a painter.

4. Figure of a street pedlar.

The reserve soldier of 1914 is an interesting figure, dressed in khaki and lighting a cigar. The type, the pose, and the facial expression are marvellously portrayed. His field dress, of green jasper of various shades, is also very successful.

An ice carrier. A little horse drawing blocks of ice and the boy-driver, wearing a typical hat with ear flaps, stand on a base of dirty quartz, which is the sleigh road. The blocks are made of quartz of varying degrees of transparency, and this conveys the inner cracks of the ice. The horse is brown jasper with a darker mane. The whole group [now in the Fersman Mineralogical Museum, Moscow] is treated naturally, and the sense of movement and the typicality of the figures and their details are very successful. These last figures were modelled by Georgi Savitski[39] and are evidence of his characteristic tact and powers of observation. In the numerous figures of peasants and folk types, the sheepskin coats are very well made of Beloretsk quartz: the various shades of quartz meant that old worn coats could be depicted as well as new ones.

To end this chapter on the stone carvings I must say a few words about the organisation of the business and the workmasters. When the artistic shortcomings of the work produced by Woerffel and Oberstein prompted the firm to open its own workshop, the person invited to manage the workshop was P.M. Kremlyov,[40] who had graduated from Ekaterinburg Art School and specialised in stone carving. Under his management, the artistic level of the work improved immediately. The stereotyped dryness that had characterised the work of Woerffel and Oberstein was the first thing to disappear. Many of the works were made by Kremlyov himself. It is true that the work was much more expensive than at Oberstein, but this can be ascribed mainly to the lack of technical equipment and bad management. In 1912–1914, at a time of heightened activity, there were twenty craftsmen working in the workshop, but they still did not manage to finish the necessary amount of work, and simple jobs were ordered from the Ekaterinburg workshops. In our own workshop the urgent jobs were not transferred, but we had no supply of skilled workmasters.

The workshop existed until 1917, when it had to be closed, for lack of both materials and those workmasters who had been called up at various times.

A particularly talented and original personality, Derbyshev[41] from Ekaterinburg, deserves special mention. I got to know him in 1908 when he came to Petersburg looking for work. He actually walked most of the way, working in various places as a loader or a gardener, to keep body and soul together. He arrived in Petersburg very ragged and in bast shoes. We immediately recognised a businessman and a talented worker, and the firm made haste to provide him with clothes and shoes. As the workshop was only planned at that time, he was sent to the Woerffel factory, where he worked for a year and made some money. With a recommendation from us he went to Oberstein and from there he soon went to Paris, where he worked with the artist and engraver Lalique, who was delighted with his work and wanted to make him his successor by marrying him to his daughter. But fate decided otherwise. Homesickness and perhaps fear of marriage forced him to return to Russia at the beginning of 1914. He was called up in the first months of the war and died at the taking of Lvov. The firm entrusted him with equipping and running the new workshop. It is no exaggeration to say that in him, Russian stone carving lost its best and perhaps its only craftsman with an artistic education.

The relations of the firm with the Ural factories before 1914 were fortuitous: from time to time they brought us some of their work, but it was largely unsatisfactory from all points of view. It was painful to see the beautiful stones ruined by untrained cutting. The firm would acquire these works for the sake of the stones and break them up, saving individual parts or, when possible, correcting the defects of design and workmanship. I felt impelled by this to visit Ekaterinburg to see for myself the stone and the means of production. The production was dying, many craftsmen had been called up, many of the workshops were shut or working with a third of the staff. I visited the workshops of Lipin, Lazarev, and others and had long talks with their owners, who greeted my proposals with alacrity. When I had selected in their warehouses a large number of bars, pieces, and boulders of stone, I decided on the spot how they should be used and drew up outline designs for the objects that were to be made. At the same time, I indicated the faults in the workmanship that were imperative to correct. I realised that the question of the

artistry had to be discussed somewhere else and went to the Art College. The director was on holiday, so I went to see his deputy, the artist and lecturer G. Almazov. He very readily told me about stone carving in the college and showed me the studios and the students' work. During the course of our two long talks we sorted out the reasons for the backwardness of production. This was because firstly, the college was totally isolated from the factory; secondly, it did not have enough money; and thirdly, the low level of wages at the factory deterred students from specialising in stone carving. It became clear that a whole series of government measures would be essential to guarantee the normal development of artistic production. When I was leaving I suggested that the college could send every year its most able students from the stone-carving studios to our Petersburg workshop. They would be subsidised by the firm of Fabergé and the college.

The Ekaterinburg lapidary factory was closed, their premises occupied by military billets, and many of the machines had been dismantled. As I had permission from His Majesty's Cabinet Office to acquire stones, I bought several blocks, bars, etc. for our works.

On the subject of the firm's relations with the Siberian market, I should also mention the acquisition of a whole series of small objects from the Kolyvan factory. To do them justice, they were technically very well made. Judging by the designs, they had been made some time ago and had lain for a long time in the warehouse. It was from here that we ordered a collection of samples of jasper and other stones – more than one hundred pieces and several bars of jasper and quartz.

When I was in Ekaterinburg I was able to make the acquaintance of Kalugin, a very pleasant and interesting person. On the basis of stone (may I be forgiven for such a pun), we became close friends and planned a joint trip to the Ural deposits for the next summer. He was a great specialist . . . and told me. . . .

[Birbaum's manuscript breaks off here.]

Notes

1. Archive of Russian Academy of Sciences. F. 544 inv. 7 p. 63.
2. This must be a misprint. The firm was founded in 1842.
3. See Lopato, 'New Insights into Fabergé from Russian Documents'.
4. Birbaum probably means M. Perkhin, enameller N. Petrov, and J. Rappoport.
5. The magazine *Yuvelir* was published in St. Petersburg in 1912–1913. In 1914 it was renamed *Russki Yuvelir*. The Russian Society of Art and Industry was founded in 1903 and existed until 1914.
6. The date of 1919 is not clear since Fabergé left Russia in 1918 and the firm was closed the same year. His brother Agathon Fabergé died in 1895.
7. 1908 Peacock egg, Heirs of the late Maurice Sandoz, Switzerland.
8. The Trans-Siberian Railway egg was presented to Alexandra Feodorovna in 1900. State Museum of the Moscow Kremlin.
9. The Colonnade egg, presented to Alexandra Feodorovna in 1910, is now in the collection of Her Majesty Queen Elizabeth II (cat. 20).
10. The Peter the Great egg was presented to Alexandra Feodorovna in 1903. Lillian Thomas Pratt Collection, Virginia Museum of Fine Art.
11. The Romanov Tercentenary egg was presented to Alexandra Feodorovna in 1913. State Museum of the Moscow Kremlin.
12. This might be either the Love Trophy egg or the 1907 Rose Trellis egg. See Lopato, 'A Few Remarks Concerning Imperial Easter Eggs'.
13. The Steel Military egg, presented to Alexandra Feodorovna in 1913, rests on four, not three, artillery shells, as Birbaum writes. State Museum of the Moscow Kremlin.
14. The Red Cross egg with Resurrection Triptych was presented to Alexandra Feodorovna in 1916 (cat. 129). The Cleveland Museum of Art. India Early Minshall Collection, Cleveland, Ohio.
15. Founded in 1794, Bolin was a famous jewellers firm in St. Petersburg noted for making expensive jewellery with large gemstones.
16. See Lopato, 'New Insights into Fabergé from Russian Documents'.

17. Foelkersam indicates that the clock (cat. 4) was in the Blue Study Room of Anichkov Palace and was exhibited at the Fabergé exhibition held at the von Dervise House in 1902.
18. The State Hermitage Collection, cat. 111.
19. Matilda Geddings Gray Foundation Collection, New Orleans, Louisiana. The workmaster was A. Holmström.
20. Grand Duke Aleksei Aleksandrovich (1850–1908), Emperor Alexander II's son, was General Adjutant, General Admiral, and Principal Head of the Navy and of the Navy Ministry (cat. 67).
21. The collection was purchased by the Hermitage in 1908 for 500,000 roubles. Agathon Fabergé appraised the objects.
22. His Imperial Majesty's Cabinet managed the Imperial Family's property, all the jewellery, including the diamonds of the crown, the fur trade, and three cutting factories.
23. Nikolai Semenovich Samokish (1860–1944), a well-known painter of battle scenes, was a professor at the Academy of Arts.
24. Leiser Girshevich (Lazar Grigorievich) Stirkh, a draughtsman and engraver, graduated from the Baron Stieglitz Central School of Technical Drawing in 1904 and began working for Fabergé as an engraver in 1909.
25. For further information on Varvara (Barbara) Kelch, a daughter and wife of gold entrepreneurs, whose father and husband obtained their wealth from the Lena gold mines, see Christie's, New York, 19 April 1990.
26. It is not clear about which of the Eliseev brothers Birbaum is speaking. Brothers Aleksandr Grigorievich and Grigori Grigorievich Eliseev were board members of many companies in St. Petersburg.
27. Emanuel Ludvigovich Nobel (1859–1932), nephew of Alfred Nobel, headed all the Nobel family businesses in Russia from 1888 until the Revolution.
28. Artist Evgeni Eduardovich Iakobson (1877–1940) graduated from the Baron Stieglitz School in 1898. Since the 1900s he was one of Fabergé's leading designers.
29. Birbaum must be referring to a nephrite gueridon, published in Habsburg/Solodkoff 1979, ill. p. 95.
30. Birbaum must mean Nikolai Nikolaievich Figner (1857–1918), a well-known Russian tenor who performed with the Imperial

Russian Opera since 1887. In 1895 he was awarded the title of His Imperial Majesty's Soloist.
31. Unfortunately, it is not known about whom the author is speaking.
32. Leopold Konig owned a sugar factory.
33. For detailed information on Fabergé's London branch, see Habsburg, 'The London Branch'.
34. The lawsuit between the Fabergé firm and the Goldsmiths Company in London took place in 1909–1910.
35. Chulalongkorn (Rama V), King of Siam, visited Russia in 1897. A year later his son, Prince Chakrabongse, was invited by Nicholas II to study at the Page Corps in Russia. For many years members of the Thai Royal Family received Fabergé objects as gifts, and they also bought directly from Fabergé.
36. Karl Feodorovich Werfel (Woerffel) was the owner of a bronze and hardstone factory. 'The factory was founded in 1842. Its yearly turnover was between 100,000 and 150,000 roubles. About 100 men worked at the factory. The stones were supplied from Siberia, the Caucasus, Altai, Kiev and other regions. After cutting and carving they were sold in Russia, America, England, France and Germany'. Werfel worked with Fabergé.
37. Eliza Ivanovna Balletta was a prima donna of the French company of the Imperial Mikhailov Theatre, where she worked for fourteen years. By the end of 1905 she left the company and moved to France.
38. Boris Oscarovich Froedman-Cluzel, a sculptor, graduated from the Academy of Arts in Stockholm. In addition to producing portraits of many theatre actors, he also sculpted numerous birds and animals from the Royal Zoo in Sandringham upon order of King Edward VII.
39. Georgi Konstantinovich Savitski (1887–1947), a well-known artist, was a graduate of the Academy of Arts.
40. Petr Mikhailovich Kremlyev, a stonecutter and sculptor, studied in Ekaterinburg with T. Grunberg-Zalkaln, who had worked with Fabergé in his time. One of the firm's most remarkable stone carvers, Kremlyev headed Fabergé's sculpting workshops since 1915.
41. Derbyshev also studied with T. Grunberg-Zalkaln at the Ekaterinburg Art School.

Select Bibliography

BOOKS AND ARTICLES

Andolenko 1966
Andolenko, S. *Chest Medals of the Russian Army* (in Russian). Paris, 1966.

Armand-Caillat 1903
Armand-Caillat, Theodore Joseph. *L'Orfèvrerie a l'Exposition Universelle de 1900. Extrait du rapport du Jury classe 94.* Paris, 1903.

Bäcksbacka 1951
Bäcksbacka, L. *St. Petersburgs Juvelare Guld och Silversmeder, 1714–1870.* Helsingfors, Sweden. 1951.

Bainbridge 1933
Bainbridge, H. C. *Twice Seven.* London, 1933.

Bainbridge 1934
Bainbridge, H. C. 'Russian Imperial Gifts: The Work of Carl Fabergé'. *Connoisseur*, May/June 1934, pp. 299–348.

Bainbridge 1935
Bainbridge, H. C. 'The Workmasters of Fabergé'. *Connoisseur*, August 1935, p. 85 ff.

Bainbridge 1949
Bainbridge, H. C. *Peter Carl Fabergé.* 1949 (with revised editions in 1966, 1974).

Bainbridge 1966
Bainbridge, H. C. *Peter Carl Fabergé.* 1966 (2d ed.)

Bandini 1980
Bandini, L. 'Fabergé.' *Netsuke Collectors Journal*, September 1980, pp. 27–32.

Berniakovich 1977
Berniakovich, Z. A. *Russian Fine Silver from the Seventeenth to the Beginning of the Twentieth Century in the Collection of the State Hermitage.* Leningrad, 1977.

Booth 1990
Booth, John. *The Art of Fabergé.* Secaucus, New Jersey, 1990.

Cerwinske 1990
Cerwinske, Laura. *Russian Imperial Style.* New York, 1990.

Champier 1902
Champier, Victor. *Les industries d'art a l'Exposition Universelle de 1900.* Paris, 1902.

Chanteclair 1900
Chanteclair, R. 'La Bijouterie Etrangère à l'Exposition de 1900'. *Revue de la Bijouterie, Joaillerie et Orfèverie*, October 1900, p. 61 ff.

Donova 1973
Donova, Kira V. 'Works of the Artist M. E. Perkhin'. *Material and Research* (in Russian), Moscow, 1973.

Fagaly 1972
Fagaly, W. A., and S. Grady. *Treasures by Peter Carl Fabergé and other Master Jewelers.* The Matilda Geddings Gray Foundation Collection, New Orleans, Louisiana, 1972.

Foelkersam 1907
Foelkersam, A. von. *Description of the Silver Objects at the Court of His Imperial Majesty* (in Russian). St. Petersburg, 1907.

Forbes 1979
  Forbes, Christopher. 'Fabergé Imperial Easter Eggs in American Collections'. *Antiques*, June 1979, pp. 1228–42.
Forbes 1980
  Forbes, Christopher. *Fabergé Eggs, Imperial Russian Fantasies*. New York, 1980.
Forbes 1986
  Forbes, Christopher. 'Imperial Treasures'. *Art & Antiques*, April 1986, pp. 52–57, 86.
Forbes 1987
  Forbes, Christopher. 'A Letter on Collecting Fabergé'. *Burlington Magazine*, September 1987, pp. 10–16.
Goldberg 1961
  Goldberg, T., F. Mishukov, N. Platonova, and M. Postnikova-Loseva. *Russian Gold- and Silversmithwork XV-XX. Century* (in Russian). Moscow, 1961.
Habsburg 1977
  Habsburg-Lothringen, G. von. 'Carl Fabergé, Die glanzvolle Welt eines königlichen Juweliers'. *DU Europäische Kunstzeitschrift*, December 1977, p. 51 ff.
Habsburg 1981
  Habsburg-Lothringen, G. von. 'Die Uhren des Peter Carl Fabergé'. *Alte Uhren*, January 1981, p. 23 ff.
Habsburg 1987
  Habsburg, Géza von. *Fabergé* (English book edition of Munich 1986/87 catalogue). Geneva, 1987.
Habsburg 1987 (K&A)
  Habsburg-Lothringen, G. von. 'Carl Fabergé – Ein Plagiator?' *Kunst und Antiquitäten* II, 1987, pp. 72–79.
Habsburg/Solodkoff 1979
  Habsburg-Lothringen, G. von, and A. von Solodkoff. *Fabergé, Court Jeweler to the Tsars*. Fribourg, 1979 (new ed. 1984; German ed., Wasmuth, 1979).
Hawley 1967
  Hawley, H. *Fabergé and his Contemporaries. The India Minshall Collection of the Cleveland Museum of Art*. Cleveland, Ohio, 1967.
Hill 1989
  Hill, Gerard. *Fabergé and the Russian Master Goldsmiths*. New York, 1989.
Houillon 1900
  Houillon, L. 'Les Émaux à l'Éxposition de 1900'. *Revue de la Bijouterie, Joaillerie et Orfèvrerie*, November 1900, p. 98 ff.
Kelly 1982/83
  Kelly, Margaret. 'Frames by Fabergé in the FORBES Magazine Collection'. *Arts in Virginia*, 1982/83, pp. 2–13.
Kelly 1985
  Kelly, Margaret. *Highlights from the FORBES Magazine Galleries*. New York, 1985.
Kirichenko 1991
  Kirichenko, Evgenia. *Russian Design and the Fine Arts: 1870–1917*. New York, 1991.

Kovarskaia 1984
  Kovarskaia, S. Ia., I. D. Kostina and E. V. Shakurova. *Russian Silver from the Sixteenth to the Beginning of the Twentieth Century from the Holdings of the State Museums of the Moscow Kremlin* (in Russian). Moscow, 1984.
Kovarskaia 1987
  Kovarskaia, S. Ia. *Russian Gold of the Fourteenth to the Beginning of the Twentieth Century from the Holdings of the State Museums of the Moscow Kremlin* (in Russian). Moscow, 1987.
Krairiksh
  Krairiksh, ed. *Fabergé in the Royal Collection*. Thailand, n.d. [1984].
Kremlin 1992
  Muntian, T.N., V.M. Nikitina, and I.I. Goncharova. *The World of Fabergé: The 150th Anniversary of the Russian Jewellery Company* (in Russian). Moscow-Vienna, 1992.
Kuchumov 1981
  Kuchumov, A. M. *Russian Decorative and Applied Arts in the Collection of the Pavlovsk Palace Museum* (in Russian). Leningrad, 1981.
Kunst um 1900
  Kunst um 1900 aus dem Sammlungen der Schlossmuseen und Parke Petrodworez. Schloßer und Garten Potsdam – Sanssousi, 1985.
Kunstkatte fra Zarernes Hof 1990
  Kunstkatte fra Zarernes Hof 1860–1917. Gaesper Aarhus Kunstmuseum, Denmark, 1990.
Leningrad 1974
  Prikladnoie Iskusstvo Kontsa XIX – nachala XX veka (Applied Art of the Late Nineteenth and Early Twentieth Century). Leningrad, 1974.
Leningrad 1984
  Pamiatniki Kultury i Iskusstva Priobretennyiie Ermitazhem v 1983–1984 gg. (Culture and Art Objects Purchased by the Hermitage in 1983–1984). Leningrad, 1984.
Leningrad 1985
  Kunst um 1900. Leningrad, 1985.
Leningrad 1987
  Russian Enamels from the Twelfth to the Beginning of the Twentieth Century in the Collection of the Hermitage (in Russian), Leningrad, 1987.
Leningrad 1991
  Pamiatniki Kultury i Iskusstva Priobretennyiie Ermitazhem v 1988–1990 gg. (Culture and Art Objects purchased by the Hermitage in 1988–1990). Leningrad, 1991.
Lesley 1976
  Lesley, P. *Fabergé, a Catalog of the Lillian Thomas Pratt Collection of Russian Imperial Jewels*. Richmond, Virginia, 1976.
Lopato 1984
  Lopato, Marina. 'New Light on Fabergé'. *Apollo* 1984, pp. 43–49.

Lopato 1991
Lopato, Marina. 'Fabergé Eggs. Re-dating from new evidence'. *Apollo*, February 1991, pp. 91–94.

McNab Dennis
McNab Dennis, J. 'Fabergé's Objects of Fantasy'. *Metropolitan Museum of Art Bulletin* (New York), n.s. 23, March 1965, p. 229 ff.

NYCC 1973
Fabergé from the FORBES Magazine Collection. New York Cultural Center, New York. April 1973.

Pfeffer 1990
Pfeffer, Susanna. *Fabergé Eggs: Masterpieces from Czarist Russia.* New York, 1990.

Postnikova 1985
Postnikova-Loseva, M., N. Platonova, B.L. Ulyanova, and G. Smorodinova. *Historic Museum, Moscow* (in Russian). Leningrad, 1985.

Rodimtseva 1971
Rodimtseva, I. A. *Fabergé's Goldsmith's Work* (in Russian). Armoury Museum, The Kremlin, Moscow, 1971.

Ross 1952
Ross, M. C. *Fabergé.* Walters Art Gallery, Baltimore, Maryland, 1952.

Ross 1965
Ross, M. C. *The Art of Carl Fabergé and his Contemporaries (The Collection of Marjorie Merriweather Post, Hillwood, Washington, D.C.).* Norman, Oklahoma, 1965.

Shkabelnikov 1902
Shkabelnikov, G. Z., and P. I. Petrov. *Medals of Philanthropic Societies and the Principles of Decorations for Rendering Assistance by Charitable Acts* (in Russian). St Petersburg, 1902.

Snowman 1953
Snowman, A. K. *The Art of Fabergé.* London, 1953.

Snowman 1955
Snowman, A. K. 'The Works of Carl Fabergé: The English Royal Collection at Sandringham House'. *Connoisseur*, June 1955, p. 3 ff.

Snowman 1962, 1964, 1968
Revised and enlarged editions of Snowman 1953.

Snowman 1962 (*Conn.*)
Snowman, A. K. 'A Group of Virtuoso Pieces by Carl Fabergé and an Easter Egg in the Collection of H. M. the Queen'. *Connoisseur*, June 1962, p. 96 ff.

Snowman 1963
Snowman, A. K. *New York Objects of Art by Fabergé in Private Collections.* New York, 1963.

Snowman 1977
Snowman, A. K. 'Carl Fabergé in London'. *Nineteenth Century*, Summer 1977, pp. 50–55.

Snowman 1979
Snowman, A. K. *Carl Fabergé, Goldsmith to the Imperial Court of Russia.* London, 1979.

Snowman 1983
Snowman, A. K. 'Fabergé in Great Britain in New York'. *Antiques*, April 1983, pp. 812–19.

Solodkoff 1982
Solodkoff, Alexander von. 'Fabergé's London Branch'. *Connoisseur*, February 1982, pp. 102–105.

Solodkoff 1983
Solodkoff, Alexander von. 'Ostereier von Fabergé'. *Kunst und Antiquitäten*, April/May 1983, pp. 61–67.

Solodkoff 1984
Solodkoff, Alexander von. *Masterpieces from the House of Fabergé.* New York, 1984 (reprint 1989).

Solodkoff 1986
Solodkoff, Alexander von. *Fabergé Clocks.* London, 1986.

Solodkoff 1988
Solodkoff, Alexander von. *Fabergé.* London, 1988.

Stolitsa i Usadba 1914
'Something about Fabergé' (in Russian). *Stolitsa i Usadba*, no. 2, January 1914, p. 13 ff.

Stolitsa i Usadba 1916
'The gifts of Tsarina Alexandra Feodorovna' (in Russian). *Stolitsa i Usadba*, no. 55, April 1916, p. 3 ff.

Swezey 1983
Swezey, Marilyn Pfeifer. 'Fabergé and the Coronation of Nicholas and Alexandra'. *Antiques*, June 1983, pp. 1210–13.

Taylor 1983
Taylor, Katrina V. H. *Fabergé at Hillwood.* Washington, D.C., 1983.

Taylor 1988
Taylor, Katrina V. H. *Russian Art at Hillwood.* Washington, D.C., 1988.

Thyssen 1984
Somers-Cocks, A., and C. Truman. *Renaissance Jewels, Gold Boxes and Objets de vertu in the Thyssen-Bornemisza Collection.* London, 1984.

Truman 1977
Truman, C. 'The Master of the Easter Egg'. *Apollo*, July 1977, p. 73.

Ulyanova
Ulyanova, B. L. *Fabergé Jewellery* (in Russian). Historic Museum, Moscow, n.d.

Vever 1906
Vever, Henri. *La Bijouterie Française au XIXᵉ Siècle.* Vol. I. Paris 1906.

Waterfield/Forbes 1978
Waterfield, H., and C. Forbes. *C. Fabergé: Imperial Easter Eggs and Other Fantasies.* New York, 1978 (London, 1979).

Willumsen Krog 1986
Willumsen Krog, L. 'Fabergé and the Danish Royal House'. *Apollo*, July 1986, pp. 46 ff.

EXHIBITIONS

ALVR 1949
Peter Carl Fabergé: An Exhibition of his Works. A La Vieille Russie,
New York, 1949.

ALVR 1961
The Art of Peter Carl Fabergé. A La Vieille Russie, New York, 1961.

ALVR 1968
The Art of the Goldsmith and the Jeweler. A La Vieille Russie, New
York, 1968.

ALVR 1983
Fabergé, A Loan Exhibition. A La Vieille Russie, New York, 1983.

Amersfoort 1972
Les Années '25'. Amersfoort, The Netherlands, 1972.

Baltimore 1983/84
Fabergé, The FORBES Magazine Collection. Baltimore Museum of Art,
Baltimore, Maryland, 1983/84.

Boston 1979
Imperial Easter Eggs from the House of Fabergé. Museum of Fine Arts,
Boston, Massachusetts, 1979.

Cooper-Hewitt 1983
*Fabergé, Jeweler to Royalty, From the Collection of Her Majesty Queen
Elizabeth II and other British Lenders.* Cooper-Hewitt Museum, New
York, 1983.

Corcoran 1961
*Easter Eggs and Other Precious Objects by Carl Fabergé (The Lansdell
Christie Collection).* Corcoran Gallery of Art, Washington, D.C., 1961.

Detroit 1984
Fabergé, The FORBES Magazine Collection. Detroit Institute of Arts,
Detroit, Michigan, 1984.

Edinburgh & Aberdeen 1987
Fabergé and the Edwardians. Fine Arts Society, Edinburgh, and
Aberdeen Art Gallery and Museum, Aberdeen, Scotland, 1987.

Elagin Palace 1989
The Great Fabergé. Catalogue of the First Exhibition in the USSR (in
Russian). Elagin Palace-Museum, Leningrad, 1989 (Helsinki 1990).

Fort Worth 1983
Fabergé, The FORBES Magazine Collection. Kimbell Art Museum, Fort
Worth, Texas, 1983.

Genoa 1992
Fabergé e l'Art Orafa alla Courte degli Zar. Genova, 1990.

Hammer 1937
Fabergé: His Works. Hammer Galleries, New York, 1937.

Hammer 1939
Presentation of Imperial Russian Easter Gifts by Carl Fabergé. Hammer
Galleries, New York, 1939.

Hammer 1951
A Loan Exhibition of the Art of Peter Carl Fabergé. Hammer Galleries,
New York, 1951.

Hanau 1985/86
*Imperial Gold and Silver. Treasures of the Hohenzollern Dynasty at
Doorn Palace* (in German). German Goldsmiths' Museum, Hanau,
1985/86.

Helsinki 1980
Carl Fabergé and His Contemporaries (in English and Finnish).
Museum of Arts and Crafts, Helsinki, 1980.

Helsinki 1988
Keisarilliset lahjat (Imperial Gifts). A. Tillander, Helsinki, 1988.

Helsinki 1989
Tsaarinajan aarteet (Treasures of the Tsarist Era). Museum of Arts and
Crafts, Helsinki, 1989.

Helsinki 1991
Dialogi – hopeaarteita Baltiasta, Pietarista ja Suomesta (Dialogue –
Silver from Balticum, St. Petersburg and Finland). Museum of Arts and
Crafts, Helsinki, 1991.

Kunstkatte fra Zarernes Hof 1990
Kunstkatte fra Zarernes Hof, 1860–1917 (in Danish). Hermitage,
Leningrad, and Gaesper Aarhus Kunstmuseum, Denmark, 1990.

LACMA 1979
Treasures by Peter Carl Fabergé. Los Angeles County Museum of Art,
Los Angeles, California, 1979.

Leningrad 1974
Applied Arts of the Late Nineteenth and Early Twentieth Century (in
Russian). State Hermitage Museum, Leningrad, 1974.

Leningrad 1975
*Lighting Appliances from the Seventeenth Century to the Beginning of
the Twentieth Century in Russia* (in Russian). State Hermitage
Museum, Leningrad, 1975.

Leningrad 1981a
*Artistic Metalwork in Russia from the Seventeenth to the Beginning of
the Twentieth Century* (in Russian). State Hermitage Museum,
Leningrad, 1981.

Leningrad 1981b
*Miniatures in Russia from the Eighteenth to the Beginning of the
Twentieth Century* (in Russian). State Hermitage Museum, Leningrad,
1981.

Leningrad 1984
Monuments of Culture and Art Acquired by the Hermitage in 1983–1984
(in Russian). State Hermitage Museum, Leningrad, 1984.

London 1935
Catalogue of the Exhibition of Russian Art. Belgrave Square, London,
1935.

London 1991
Fabergé Silver from the FORBES Magazine Collection. A Loan Exhibition.
Sotheby's, London, 1991.

Lugano 1986
Ori e Argenti dall'Ermitage. Villa Favorita, Castagnola, 1986.

Lugano 1987
Fabergé Fantasies. The FORBES Magazine Collection. Collection Thyssen-
Bornemisza, Villa Favorita, Lugano-Castagnola, 1987.

MAD 1961/62
Le tabac dans l'art, l'histoire et la vie. Musée des Arts Décoratifs, Paris,
1961/62.

MAD 1966
Brunhammer, Yvonne. *Les Années '25'. Collection du Musée des Arts Décoratifs.* Musée des Arts Décoratifs, Paris, 1966.

Memphis/Los Angeles/Dallas 1992
Catherine the Great: Treasures of Imperial Russia from the State Hermitage Museum, Leningrad. City of Memphis, Tennessee, 1991. Travelled to Los Angeles, California, and Dallas, Texas, 1991–1992.

Mikimoto 1991
K. Fabergé and the Golden Age of Russian Jewellery. The State Historical Museum Collection (in Japanese). Mikimoto, Tokyo, 1991.

Munich 1986/87
Fabergé, Juwelier der Zaren. Kunsthalle der Hypokulturstiftung, Munich, 1986/87.

NYCC 1973
Waterfield, H. *Fabergé from The FORBES Magazine Collection.* New York Cultural Center, New York, 1973.

Paris 1987
Fabergé, Orfevre a la Cour des Tsars. The FORBES Magazine Collection. Musée Jacquemart-André, Paris, 1987.

The Queen's Gallery 1985/86
Fabergé from the Royal Collection. The Queen's Gallery, Buckingham Palace, London, 1985/86.

San Francisco 1964
Fabergé, Catalog of an exhibition at the M. H. de Young Memorial Museum. San Francisco, California, 1964.

San Diego/Kremlin 1989/90
Fabergé, The Imperial Eggs (in English and Russian). San Diego Museum of Art, San Diego, California, and Armoury Museum, State Museums of the Moscow Kremlin, Moscow, 1989/90.

Sofia 1984
Russian Decorative and Applied Arts from the Seventeenth to the Beginning of the Twentieth Century (in Russian). Sofia, Bulgaria, 1984.

St. Petersburg 1902
Exhibition of Objets d'Art and Miniatures (in Russian). Niva, 1902.

Tokyo 1975
1900–1925: Image des Années Insouciantes. Grand Magazin Isetan, Tokyo, 1975.

V&A 1977
Fabergé, 1846–1920. (Held on the occasion of the Queen's Silver Jubilee). Victoria and Albert Museum, London, 1977.

Vienna 1991
Treasures from Fabergé (in German). Naturhistorisches Museum, Vienna, Austria, 1991.

Virginia/Minneapolis/Chicago 1983
Fabergé, Selections from The FORBES Magazine Collection. Virginia Museum of Fine Arts, Richmond, Virginia, 1983.

Wadsworth Atheneum 1963
Russian Imperial Treasures and Jewels. Wadsworth Atheneum, Hartford, Connecticut, 1963.

Wartski 1949
A Loan Exhibition of the Works of Carl Fabergé. Wartski, London, 1949.

Wartski 1953
Carl Fabergé, Wartski Coronation Exhibition. Wartski, London, 1953.

Wartski 1971
A Thousand Years of Enamel. Wartski, London, 1971.

Wartski 1973
Fabergé at Wartski: The Famous Group of Ten Russian Figures. Wartski, London, 1973.

Wartski 1992
Fabergé from Private Collections. An Exhibition in Aid of The Samaritans. Wartski, London, 1992.

Washington 1985/86
Treasure Houses of Britain. National Gallery of Art, Washington, D.C., 1985/86.

Zurich 1989
Carl Fabergé. Kostbarkeiten Russischer Goldschmiedekunst der Jahrhundertwende. Museum Bellerive, Zurich, 1989.

Index

Numbers in italics refer to figure captions on that page.

Index II

Types of works by Fabergé

(Numbers refer to catalogue entries, pages 169–425)

Index III

Workmasters

(Numbers refer to catalogue entries, pages 169–425)

Index IV

Collections

(Numbers refer to catalogue entries, pages 169–437)

Photo acknowledgments

Christie's, London: Page 111
Fabergé Archive, Geneva: Page 38
Géza von Habsburg: Pages 21–28, 38, 125, 128, 438–42, 445, 459
K.E. Hahn: Pages 46, 47
Library of Congress, Washington, D.C.: Page 57
Musée des Arts Décoratifs, Paris: Pages 119, 120
Anne Odom: Page 117
Hugo Oeberg: Page 21
Yuri Shelaev, Historical-Archival Humanist Centre, St. Petersburg: Pages 40–43, 45, 48–52, 63, 64, 67–69, 72, 75, 437
Sotheby's, Geneva: Page 95 (right)
Sotheby's, London: Pages 107, 157 (top)
State Historical Museum, Moscow: Pages 143, 144, 146
A. Tillander: Pages 88, 90–93, 94 (bottom), 95 (left), 96–101, 139
Vladimir S. Terebenin: Pages 30, 32–35; Cat. 4, 6–8, 16, 26, 31–58, 64, 66–69, 71, 74, 95, 103, 111, 113, 116, 121, 123–25, 130–134, 139, 140, 141, 153–55, 171, 172, 183, 184, 189, 191, 196–201, 205–208, 210–12, 221, 222, 225–30, 236–44, 255, 256, 265, 266, 269, 272, 274–76, 297–368

Kristina Bowman: Cover, cat. 113
A.C. Cooper Ltd: Cat. 108
Prudence Cummings Associates Ltd: Cat. 223, 252
H. Peter Curran: Cat. 10, 23, 28, 61, 72, 98, 146, 173, 262
Helga Photo Studio: Cat. 15, 101, 102, 112, 120, 127, 142, 155, 166, 167, 175, 194, 203, 219–222, 247, 263, 270
Arvo Kuva: Cat. 143
Erik Landsberg: Cat. 77
Annu Männynoksa: Cat. 179–82
Peter McDonald: Cat. 110
Edward Owen: Cat. 4, 9, 12, 13, 59, 60, 70, 76, 128, 141, 190, 202, 213
Oy Foto-Hasse Ab: Cat. 253
Royal Collection, St James's Palace © Her Majesty the Queen: Cat. 11, 18, 20, 29, 81, 83–91, 94, 148, 149, 165, 168, 185
Reproduced by gracious permission of Her Majesty Queen Elizabeth The Queen Mother: Cat. 106, 150
Larry Stein: Cat. 1, 19, 21, 23, 24, 30, 62, 63, 75, 78, 96, 105, 109, 115, 126, 135, 144, 145, 176, 178, 192, 195, 231, 232, 261
Kit Weiss: Cat. 79, 80
Robert Wharton: Cat. 82, 273